Bazaars and Fair Ladies

Bazaars and Fair Ladies

The History of the American Fundraising Fair

Beverly Gordon

The University of Tennessee Press • Knoxville

Library of Congress Cataloging-in-Publication Data

Gordon, Beverly.
    Bazaars and fair ladies : the history of the American
fundraising fair / Beverly Gordon. — 1st ed.
        p. cm.
Includes bibliographical references and index.
ISBN 1-57233-014-7 (cloth: alk. paper)
    1. Bazaars (Charities)—United States—History.
    2. Women in charitable work—United States—
        History.
    I. Title.
    HV544.G67 1998
    361.7'0973–dc21   97-45425

Ladies: I was asked . . . to tell of the early history and struggles of the Ladies' Hebrew Benevolent Society [of Anniston, Alabama in 1890].

In order to achieve our aim, to build a temple, we had to have funds, and . . . it was decided a bazaar should be held. As you can imagine . . . we worked faithfully. We gave of our time and of our substance. We met at the homes of the members weekly at half past two in the afternoon. Light refreshments were served for which a small sum, ten cents, was required. That money . . . was used as a needle work fund. I believe our [synagogal] windows were bought with that money. . . .

Suffice it to say, our little band accomplished much. Some really beautiful pieces of embroidery and fancy articles were made. We were enthused and wanted to accomplish our exalted purpose. After a winter of work and really pleasant meetings, we decided the time had come to hold our bazaar. Our vice-president thought it would be a good move to enlist the outside support of our husbands and other members of the congregation in our work. So we asked them to write to the firms they had "biz" dealings with for aid in our cause. Nearly all responded generously. We actually received merchandise and money amounting to over a thousand dollars. That was a busy time for a small number of willing workers, for not alone did we rely on the fancy articles we had to sell, but we served dinner and supper for three days to the public, besides replacing the articles we saw there was a demand for. Of course there was raffling, and other means of chance were resorted to. After three days of arduous labor our bazaar was closed. We had the means on hand wherewith to build a sanctuary.

—Mrs. Leon Ullman, at a meeting
of the Sisterhood, February 1917

Contents

Illustrations

Tables

Acknowledgments

I have been at work on this project for a great many years and have been helped by numerous individuals and organizations. I wish to thank the University of Wisconsin–Madison Graduate School for providing financial support, and my colleagues in the departments of Environment, Textiles and Design and Women's Studies for their emotional and intellectual support. When I was first ready to tackle the huge task of revising and streamlining the text, the Blue Mountain Center provided me with a residency in a dream-come-true environment in the Adirondacks. I am grateful both to the staff and my fellow residents.

Two wonderful students, Diana Hobart Dicus and Dawn Danz-Hale, helped with archival research. Archivists were also very helpful. Ruth Wilbur of the Northampton Historical Society and Elise Feeley of the Forbes Library were more than accommodating, as was the entire staff of the Sophia Smith Collection at Smith College. Craig Cramer provided a reassuring, friendly presence through my countless hours in the microforms room of the State Historical Society of Wisconsin. Russell Lewis of the Chicago Historical Society was also extremely encouraging, and I am in his debt for many wonderful illustrations. May Katz earned her "spurs" as a researcher in looking through historical papers for me, and Kathryn Kish Sklar, Jane Przybysz, and Barbara Kirshenblatt-Gimblett kindly sent me their works in progress. Martin Perdue kept sending helpful references, almost as soon as they appeared in print. I thank Meg Barden Cline for providing a home for me during my initial field research and Dorothea Britton and Dorothy Miller for their thoughtful contributions and overwhelming enthusiasm. I appreciate the insightful comments on the manuscript from Karal Ann Marling,

Judith Strasser, Susan Cook, and Barbara Kirshenblatt-Gimblett, and I appreciate Mike Topp's help in manuscript preparation. I also am very grateful for the time and consideration offered by the many women who were willing to speak with me about their experiences; I hope they realize what an important dimension they have added to the book. Finally, Steven Vedro has been enormously supportive and served as a top-notch reader.

Introduction

"How did you ever get involved with a project like that?" people would ask me when I explained I was working on a historical study of bazaars and church or charity fairs. "Why would you want to spend so much time on that?" Sometimes individuals didn't say anything, but their body language implied they considered it an unimportant, almost embarrassing subject. I understood their discomfort. I too carry a slightly condescending mental image of the bazaar. I imagine a church basement filled with somewhat dowdy, matronly women presiding over tables laden with plastic-wrapped paper plates of cookies and cupcakes. Also on the tables are sale objects like crocheted baby booties or, more pointedly, cloying, "cute" items like pink toilet paper covers shaped like ladies (their skirts are large enough to envelop the offensive rolls). The uneasiness these images evoke for me does not come from my own experience. On the contrary, my childhood memories of bazaars are not particularly negative and do not include overly precious sale goods. I can see myself at about the age of eight, going back and forth along the rows of tables at a fair where my mother was working. While she sat drinking coffee and chatting with customers and her fellow workers, I carefully studied the array of small items like potholders, paring knives, and stationery, solemnly deciding how to spend my bit of money. The memory seems pleasant enough. It seems to be about shopping and an amiable community endeavor.

Where then does the discomfort come from? The scene I just described is very ordinary and has been repeated over and over again in communities of varying sizes throughout the nation. Bazaars are ubiquitous and taken for granted; they are part of the social landscape, like a summer picnic or winter skating party. They have supported churches and synagogues; schools and colleges; temperance and suffrage organizations; civic buildings and historic monuments; and hospitals and homes for the poor, aged, and orphaned. They have also benefited mutual aid and fraternal societies, human relief and animal welfare societies, and social or political groups and clubs. Even if we do not know the full range of causes they have been called into service for, we know they are useful—we have heard aphorisms like "bazaars put the roof on the church and the cushions on the pews." We know too that they are women's events, based on volunteer labor and donated goods, and that it is through activities like bake sales and bazaars that women have been able to raise money for their pet projects. We might even have seen the bumper sticker that reads "I'M WAITING FOR THE DAY WHEN THE MILITARY HAS TO HOLD BAKE SALES TO BUILD ITS BOMBS!" Shouldn't such a laudable, straightforward activity be appreciated and applauded? Instead, many of us—as indicated, I have been prone to this myself—react to the idea of a bazaar with embarrassment, condescension, even distaste. It seems a silly, perhaps wasteful endeavor.

The bumper sticker alludes to one of the sources of these feelings: those who give bazaars—those who have to resort to tedious "homey" activities like knitting or baking to raise money—are considered by our society to be disenfranchised, rather marginal individuals. They are people without power or seeming importance. The bazaar also involves the sale of seemingly throw-away products, some in questionable taste, that nobody really wants or needs, but which people feel compelled or obligated to buy. There are strong associations, then, not just with marginality, but with make-work, and tedium. In earlier periods, however, the institution created discomfort for other, very different reasons: it was associated with "danger" and exoticism. There are allusions to these feelings in the scene in *Gone with the Wind* where Scarlett O'Hara first meets Rhett Butler. The setting is a bazaar, held to raise money for the Confederacy. Scarlett is supposed to be in mourning, but she ignores propriety and dances with abandon, ostensibly "for the sake of the cause." She is focused on romance and play, in other words, even in the midst of a serious, devastating war. The bazaar is associated in the scene with a frivolous person—with frivolity in general—and with incipient sexuality. Although sexual innuendo and danger is long gone from our experience of such events, these associations run deeply in our literature and rhetoric and perhaps remain somewhere in our collective memory. Bazaars or fairs were formerly highly staged, theatrical affairs that purposefully stimulated the senses and created a feeling of excitement, even when sexuality was not specifically at issue. Frivolity was emphasized in order to create a sense of well-being. All these associations contribute to the generally negative reaction to the bazaar, and the reaction is deeply ingrained. I even had many potential publishers tell me that this subject would have too limited a market—i.e., that not very many people would be interested in women's work at bazaars.

Why then *would* I spend my time with this subject? What got me "hooked," despite my own ambivalence and this unreceptive response? I hadn't been to a bazaar in decades and was not part of a network of women routinely called into service at such events. The original source of my intrigue lies in the historical record. In the course of previous research on nineteenth-century women's work, I kept coming across references in magazines like *Godey's Lady's Book* to "things to make for fancy fairs." These were lighthearted, ephemeral little objects—e.g., baskets made with sprigs of lavender, penwipers shaped like sheaves of wheat (fig. 47)—that I recognized as the "foremothers" of today's toilet paper ladies. I was even more fascinated by descriptions and tantalizing illustrations of turn-of-the-century bazaar booths—imaginative little stage sets with tall canopies or fanciful shapes, draped in swaths of fabric or crepe paper—and saleswomen dressed like flowers, Grecian maidens, or romantic gypsies. Events like "The Fair of the Good Fairies" were something quite distinct from the bazaars I was familiar with. As a historian of design, I was excited about these environments, for I recognized an unexplored genre and an undiscovered chapter in the story of evolving design ideas. I also kept thinking about the enormous amount of time and creative energy that would have gone into such endeavors. Surely the turn-of-the-century bazaars could not be cost-effective, once labor was taken into account? Why would the women *want* to expend so much effort on these events?

I kept asking more questions. Was it the theatricality and dress-up that the women loved? And, if so, why and when in the history of the fair did that get lost? What did the theatricality mean to the audience—the fairgoers? What was it like to step into an environment with salespeople dressed as marigolds, poppies, or snowflakes and to be surrounded by thousands of flowers, a profusion of color, and tables filled with thematically presented goods? Did simple objects take on new meanings in their fanciful contexts? An iced cake offered by Lady Winter (she only sold "cold" things) might seem very different from a cake in a kitchen filled with dirty dishes. And again, if a transformative environment was the key to selling everyday objects at bazaars, where are those environments now, and how is it that bazaars continue to exist without them? Where and when did bazaars or fairs originate? If indeed they put the roof on the church and were a dependable way for women to support causes they believed in, wouldn't it be important for those of us who want to understand women's lives to know more about them? Since some women's groups depended on these events for their very survival, wouldn't the story of bazaars be a significant part of the history of women's benevolent and political organizations? I had seen references to fairs held in support of abolition, temperance, suffrage, and historic preservation—very diverse causes, and very different from those bazaars support today. I marveled that a single institution could be used by people with such divergent beliefs and goals and saw that it must be highly adaptable, almost chameleon-like.

I soon realized the richness and significance of the topic. I also knew, almost in my bones, that a subject that seemed to embarrass people in this way might have something important to tell us. Previous scholars have shown us the value of looking closely at popular culture and trying to understand it from an emic, or insider's, perspective. For example, Robert Darnton's analysis of a practical joke played by printers' apprentices in eighteenth-century France demonstrates how much can be learned by entering fully into the motivations, actions, and ideas of another time and place. A prank that seems odd and tasteless to us now was brilliant in its own day, for the workers were ingenious at manipulating symbols in their own idioms. Darnton's explication of the humor provided an important interpretive key to the broader French culture of the time.[1] Closer to our own time and to the subject of women's culture is Janice Radway's study of romantic fiction. Radway insists that we cannot dismiss romance readers' own understanding of their interest in the genre; they are not passive, unsuspecting recipients of these stories, but active consumers who choose their books for particular reasons that make complete sense in their own framework.[2] Just as we cannot make condescending assumptions about their choices without asking for explanations, so too we cannot judge the bazaar without asking those most involved, both now and in the past, what its meanings are and were for them.

I knew, too, how much there is to learn from what is generally considered in our culture to be "trivial." Much of my previous professional work has focused on subjects deemed too familiar and "small" to be important: needlework and other forms of domestic textiles; the adornment of the body and the home; amusements or entertainments; and souvenirs, including beaded "whimsies" and other items sometimes classified as "kitsch." I have repeatedly come up against the quick dismissal of my subjects—against the assumption that these are unimportant things that aren't worthy of serious attention. I am certain this is not so. These topics are not about the heroic, or about the "important" work of exceptional people who are thought to have "created" history. Rather, they relate to daily, ordinary things, and to the parts of life that embody playfulness. The subjects I have been most interested in make up, in fact, what radical feminist philosopher Mary Daly calls "the background." As Kenneth Ames explains it, the background is where "the deep rhythms of life are affirmed; memory, connectedness and wholeness are valued; the depths of the self . . . find nourishment; and . . . relatedness is acknowledged and honored." In the "foreground" of conventional patriarchal culture, hierarchy, competition, fragmentation, and obsession with dominance and control are primary values. Work is defined as something that leaves a permanent mark; it must be a nonrepetitive activity that takes place in the "outside" arena rather than the inner world of the home or the ordinary. In contrast, the background is about everyday life, where work is made up of repetitive acts. As in the case of a well-cooked dinner, the background's activities may leave no traces. We may also talk about history in these terms. "Traditional" history is about the foreground—about the unusual, about power relationships, hierarchies, and heroic deeds. Background history is about ordinary events, about cooperative interactions and friendship, and about the small, intimate things that prove amusing and quietly meaningful.[3] Although they have been very public events, bazaars have been women-centered spaces, situated for the most part in this kind of background reality. They have been dismissed because they represent an alternative paradigm to that which usually informs our sense of what is important. It is time to pay more attention to that paradigm and see what we can learn from it.

I was drawn into the story of bazaars, in sum, because I was intrigued by their former elaborateness, by their paradoxes, and by the feelings they seemed to evoke. When I saw how important they were as part of women's lives and as a form and outlet for creative expression, I was drawn in still further. When I realized how many of the objects and issues I have personally been concerned with—issues concerning domesticity, costume, decoration, handwork—were incorporated into these events, and when I understood what a representative, ubiquitous, and tenacious part bazaars have played in the background history I am trying to bring to light, I knew I could not leave this subject alone.

What I have come to understand, and what I argue in this book, is that the bazaar—what I call the fundraising fair—is a major institution that has remained largely invisible in American cultural history, even though it collectively has involved millions of people and raised many millions of dollars. Historians have recently looked at closely related institutions and phenomena such as pageants, retailing outlets like department stores, amateur organizations and clubs, and other kinds of fairs (agriculture-based state and county fairs and business-based industrial trade fairs and expositions). Some of the work on world's fairs has particularly focused on the contributions of women—Jeanne Weimann's study of the Women's Building at the Columbian Exposition is a case in point—but the American fundraising fair has remained essentially absent, even in the growing discussion of women's lives.[4] This is a serious omission. The fundraising fair involved women, not just once in a lifetime or every twenty years in a few selected cities, but every year, in every community, over a much longer period of time. Women didn't have to struggle to be included in fundraising fairs as they did in expositions, because these were their events, where they had control and relative autonomy, and where they could express their own vision and priorities. They used fairs as showplaces where they demonstrated their skills, creativity, and efficiency.

I maintain that the fundraising fair was the *woman's fair*, the female manifestation of the broader fair phenomenon. Many of the trends seen in so-called "real" (male-identified) fairs were not only seen in fundraising fairs, but also were often evident there at an earlier date or in a more prominent fashion. The recent discussion of (male) fairs has demonstrated that they both reflected and impacted upon a wide range of cultural phenomena, including methods of aesthetic display and presentation, the reshaping of public entertainment, attitudes about consumption and commodities and about other cultures and ethnic groups, and perceptions and attitudes about the past.[5] It is time that women's contributions and agency in these matters, expressed primarily in their "own" institution, is fully credited and understood.

Feminist scholars investigating other topics have shown that women's activities and ideas have been excluded from the public record and that their cultural innovations have sometimes even been purposely made invisible. In *The Obstacle Race*, for example, Germaine Greer demonstrated that many highly touted women's paintings were intentionally "reassigned" to men.[6] In some cases credit for successful fundraising fairs was disproportionately given to male figureheads,[7] but I am not suggesting that history was nefariously rewritten. Rather, I feel that women's fairs have simply been conveniently forgotten or dismissed. In earlier times, their theatricality and purposefully amusing and lighthearted tone was such a successful mask, a kind of trope, that even though people acknowledged them as the single most powerful instrument for making money in the fundraising arena, they could rarely be discussed in serious or respectful terms. In addition, the fundraising fair was so identified with women (the woman *was* the fair; the fair was the woman) that it could generally not be evaluated as an accomplishment or institution at all. A man's fair was about his work, or what he had done. Because a woman's work was not really acknowledged as work, but as an extension of her self, a woman's fair seemed almost an oxymoron. The more contemporary associations with triviality and the edge of defensiveness that surrounds any discussion of fairs have blinded scholars as well as the general public to the deeper cultural meanings of the institution. This is unfortunate, for the fair presents a mirror of—and a window into—women's issues, concerns, and interests over the last 175 years. It also serves as a kind of self-contained microcosm of social, cultural, and aesthetic change, considered from a woman's point of view.

This book surveys the fundraising fair phenomenon in America. Because I was so fascinated by the elaborate turn-of-the-century fairs, I had originally thought to limit my study to that time, but found it impossible to do so. I thought it important to understand the origin of the fairs and began to work backward to their introduction in the antebellum era. I kept returning too to my impressions of—and ambivalence about—contemporary fairs. I finally realized I had to approach the story holistically, considering its entire range. This was an enormous project and a difficult one, not only because of the overwhelming amount of information and the many stages and paradoxes of the fair, but also because the subject has no clear boundaries. At many points in its history the fundraising fair has literally blended into other types of fairs, including the agricultural fair, the industrial or commercial exposition, and the art fair. It has been incorporated into or has incorporated into itself the benefit performance, the pageant, the tableaux and other types of theatrical entertainment, the party or tea, and the rummage sale, auction, and raffle. Individuals who read my manuscript in its early stages sometimes wanted even more discussion of topics like the rummage sale or the contemporary flea market, for the narrative raised many questions for them about related phenomena. My decision was to limit the primary discussion to events that met three criteria: they were based on women's voluntary labor, were held for fundraising purposes, and they included the sale of handmade items. I mention related activities in order to contextualize women's fairs, but do not dwell on them at length.[8]

I adopted the phrase "fundraising fair" as a general descriptive epithet for the sake of expediency, clarity, and historic impartiality. Over the course of their history, these events have been variously known as sales of work, ladies' sales, ladies' fairs, fancy fairs, church fairs, charity fairs, fetes, festivals, carnivals, boutiques, and church or charity bazaars. They have varied considerably in complexity and focus over time, but at least until recently their proceeds have by definition been designated for a specified cause or charity rather than for individual profit. The fundraising fair epithet has not to my knowledge been used by individuals or organizations sponsoring the events, but it is an inclusive phrase that avoids pejorative associations or associations with particular periods. Other terms are more limited. The word "bazaar" generally evokes something quite different now than it did one hundred years ago, and, depending on their past experiences, it may imply different things to different people. The word was not even in common use at all at these events until the latter half of the nineteenth century. The term "fancy fair" was popular in the early part of that century, but is generally unrecognizable today. Fundraising fair is a "generic" phrase that subsumes all variations on the theme.

The book follows the story of the fairs chronologically. I experimented with various other organizational structures and tried to develop thematic chapters that would highlight in turn different elements of the story. Given the time span of close to two centuries and the profound changes the fair has undergone, however, that proved unworkable; certain themes remain constant, but the contexts in which they occur become so transformed that I could not discuss them nonchronologically without hopelessly confusing the reader. The first chapter of the book describes the trajectory of the fairs with a brief overview of their development. It explores the themes that weave through time: the contested terrain and inherent contradictions of the fundraising fair and the shifting ways that women used fairs to play with and against their domestic and sexual roles; the overriding importance of the fair as an arena for fellowship and community, aesthetic expression, and aesthetic experience (the fair was, in many senses, an art form in itself); and the fair as a reflection of the American consumer culture. Remaining chapters present a detailed picture of the changing contours of the fairs and their reception. Description is "thick" in many instances; I have tried to give a tangible sense of what it felt like to walk into a Civil War sanitary fair, for example, or into Boston's "Atlantic City Boardwalk" (1922), where sale goods were displayed in a fanciful environment with a literal boardwalk, sand, and rolling wheelchairs. Occasionally the image of the fair is a composite, drawn from descriptions of events held in different parts of the country at approximately the same time. This is possible precisely because the institution of the fair was so pliant and adaptable; it was equally usable to women representing a range of different constituencies or causes, and whether it was held by Jewish women paying off the debt on their temple building, Danish immigrants funding a commemorative statue, or suffragists fighting for equal voting rights for women, the format and conventions of the fair remained very consistent at any given point in time.

Where possible, I have discussed the individuals who worked at fairs. Certainly, these events were created by real, specific people; the women's agency in these endeavors is a major part of the story I am trying to tell. Some players, such as Maria Weston Chapman, Mary Livermore, and Marietta Pratt, emerge clearly in the narrative. However, these women are the exceptions, for they were atypically self-conscious leaders who wrote about or kept scrapbooks of their efforts. It is important to remember that this is not their story alone—it is not the story of heroes or exceptional people as much as it is the story of the group, of those who worked together on these labor-intensive projects and now remain anonymous and largely undifferentiated to us. It is significant too that no strong individual emerges in my narrative after the 1920s, for since that time the fair has been associated not with cultural leaders or innovators, but with a more retiring, conservative part of society. Fairs have become fully a part of popular culture, moreover, with instructions and ideas spread in part through the mass media. Some of the most important actors in this saga may be the women who wrote columns in widely read magazines like *Ladies' Home Journal* and *Woman's Home Companion*. Many of these authors remained anonymous, and even when they signed their names they left no further clues about themselves. I have been unable to learn anything about women like Caroline Hart Benton, who wrote on fairs for *Good Housekeeping* and later published a book on the topic. We may extrapolate a general picture of who these people were, but can fill in few specific details.

This leads me to a discussion of the sources, methodology, and guiding principles for my work. The work of other historians was useful for developing an understanding of related institutions, such as pageants, retail outlets, and world's fairs, but there was effectively *no* secondary source material about women's fairs in America when I began this project. By the late 1980s a few scholars were looking at specific types of women's fairs—sanitary fairs, for instance, and even more recently abolitionist or Masonic fairs. I believe their work indicates an awakening interest in this topic and an acknowledgment of its importance, but no other scholar has looked at the women's fair as an overall phenomenon.[9]

To make sense of such a complex, multifaceted subject, I developed a complex, multifaceted research plan. I drew on interviews, personal (participant) observation, material culture analysis, content analysis of both prescriptive and descriptive literature, and iconographic analysis of engravings and photographs. I also examined a great variety of historical documents, including institutional records, newspaper reports and announcements (including a subset of special newspapers produced explicitly for the fairs), personal reminiscences and diaries, fiction, and poetry. Taken together, these different types of data helped me build a composite picture of the constantly changing fair. The data corroborated and expanded upon itself in a rewarding, illuminating fashion.

I followed a specific strategy in my historical search. I first made as exhaustive a study as I could of references to fairs in popular books and magazines from 1830 to the present time. The survey was limited, for the most part, to the North American press, but I found a number of useful sources from nineteenth-century England. The historical literature included prescriptive (instructional) articles, commentaries, satirical essays, fictional accounts, and poems. Here again, the boundaries of my source material were somewhat permeable, and I studied many references to related activities like church entertainments. In order to determine if this popular literature was an accurate reflection of actual events, I decided to track documented fairs held over the years. I chose two communities as sample historic sites, namely, Northampton, Massachusetts, and Madison, Wisconsin. Madison was selected because it was convenient and fit my guiding criteria. I was living there and thus had access to local records and documents, and I knew the extensive archives of the State Historical Society of Wisconsin would prove helpful. Madison was also a community that would be small enough to get a handle on, but not so small as to preclude religious, ethnic, and social diversity. As the home of a major university, the county seat, and the state capitol, it included a range of people that might not otherwise be found in a medium-sized city (almost 200,000 at present), including both a highly educated academic and professional community and a working-class population. The city was urban, but was surrounded by rural communities. My second site had to share some characteristics with Madison, but provide some contrasts. I selected Northampton because it too housed an academic institution and a number of factories, and it too was surrounded by farms. It was also a county seat, but was located in an area of the country that was already well established at the time when fairs were first held in America (i.e., it was an older community) and presented a somewhat different ethnic mix. It too had good local history resources, and two important women's history archives, the Sophia Smith Collection at Smith College and the Arthur Schlesinger Library at Radcliffe, were located in the nearby area.

I searched records of churches and other organizations in these communities and studied iconographic collections for relevant photographs. The most tedious part of my investigation was a search of newspaper reports on fairs. To cut the task to a manageable size, I scanned relevant sections of selected papers for an entire year at five-year intervals (e.g., all of 1840, 1845, etc.). Where more than one newspaper was published, I tried to determine which was most likely to report these events in detail. This sampling technique worked well generally, although it was not completely consistent. For example, it was workable for the early decades in Northampton, when the paper was published weekly, but it became very difficult after the turn of the twentieth century. Different kinds of information were reported in different periods and in different papers, and modern-era newspapers provided little substantive data. Despite these problems, I learned much about fairs in the two communities, and I cite the newspaper reports extensively.

I also discovered that for a few decades at the end of the nineteenth century, fundraising fairs were indexed in the *New York Times*. Coverage of the fairs was extremely detailed in this era, so a wealth of data emerged from this source. In order to counterbalance a possible northern bias from these northern cities, I also did spot checks of newspapers from the south and west (i.e., Richmond, Virginia; Atlanta, Georgia; Houston, Texas; Los Angeles, California) at different points in time to see if the general trends emerging in Massachusetts, New York, and Wisconsin were also seen elsewhere. I found this to be the case and that the trends also "matched" the prescriptive literature and general commentary.

Newspaper reports after 1930 were sketchy—in fact, fairs were typically ignored by the press by that time—but magazine articles, instruction books, and personal reminiscences helped fill in the missing information. I conducted open-ended, informal interviews, usually about an hour and a half in length, with thirty-five women, some of whom remembered fairs from the early years of the century, and some of whom were still actively involved. I had originally thought to interview an equal number of people from my two case sites and at first felt concerned that I might miss something important when I was unable to do so. I came to see, however, that the geographic distribution would have added little of importance, for, in the twentieth century, the culture of fairs is essentially a national one. Fairgivers read the same books and articles, and the same types of sale items appear in California, Georgia, or New Jersey. Several of the individuals I interviewed had lived in different parts of the country, and they found few substantive differences in fairs held in varying areas.

It is necessary to qualify the idea of the national fair culture in one respect and to indicate an area I unfortunately did not tackle head-on. The women I interviewed were all either white or African American; I did not meet or seek out Asian Americans or fairgivers with Hispanic backgrounds. The written documents I found also rarely referred explicitly to these communities. If I had originally realized the comprehensive scope the study would take on, I would have purposefully included an additional case site in my research design (e.g., San Francisco or a southwestern city). (My first concerns were with the early history of the fair, and I did not initially think beyond the boundaries of the first western frontier.) Without having expressly studied these groups, I am not certain how they have or have not used the institution of the fair. My educated guess is that it was more thoroughly embraced by the Hispanic population, whose Latin American heritage is European-based. (Enthusiastic participation by Latin Americans in the 1896 Cuban-American Fair supports this hypothesis.) The fair seems to be an essentially Western tradition, and I suspect that at first Asian immigrants were probably less likely to hold fairs of their own, although this may well have changed once they had partially integrated into American life. Wherever possible I have included specific information about the workings and meanings of fairs given by minority groups, but I know that ethnic variation is an area that future research should explore more thoroughly.

Whenever I could during the course of the study, I also visited fairs. I looked at the booths, the sale items, and the decor, and I watched and listened to people and their interactions. I tasted baked goods and often found myself buying a "little something" to take home. I have many vivid mental images of the mix of people, objects, and spaces, and I believe that these visits also added to my affective understanding of the fair, at least in its contemporary guise. The material elements of the fairs—the myriad sale items, the environments, and the costumes that took so much of the women's time and attention and were worked on so lovingly over the years—were sources of information for me. I documented these elements when I visited contemporary fairs and studied instruction books and photographs of "sure-fire best sellers." I compared these items to those I had seen in prescriptive literature and visual images from earlier times. I was also lucky enough to find a few actual examples of historic sale objects. My training in material culture analysis—and the work of important material culture scholars like Jules David Prown, Kenneth Ames, and Katherine Grier[10]—has convinced me that artifacts (and environments are themselves artifacts) have much to tell us about the people and cultures that make and use them; they are nonverbal messengers about other times and places. By looking at the materials, design, construction, and metaphors of the booths, costumes, and products, and by understanding the presentation and layout of the halls, we can learn more about the underlying values and ideas of the culture shared by fairgivers and fairgoers. Much of my interpretation of the experience of the fair in different eras comes from my consideration of these variables.

My analysis also draws on an aspect of the fair that relates to these material elements, but is in itself more intangible. I believe it is possible to understand and evaluate events and experiences in terms of the aesthetic—in terms of the aesthetic excitement and satisfaction they provide. This kind of analysis is completely foreign to most historians, sociologists, and other scholars, but a few individuals in diverse fields have tried to acknowledge and clarify its usefulness. As early as 1944, J. Huizinga described play as one of the "main bases of civilization"; he explained that "civilization arises *in* and *as* play, and never leaves it." Huizinga identified play with the aesthetic, but articulation of the centrality of aesthetic experience has been even more pointed in recent work. Ellen Dissanayake talks about aesthetic elaboration, or "making special," as a human need, a way of heightening reality. Yi-Fu Tuan also considers the aesthetic a basic, rather than extra, element of human life; he refers to it as the "emotional-aspirational core" of culture. Tuan demonstrates that the more we are attuned to the aesthetic (defined as a sensual awareness or feeling, not a philosophy or intellectual concept), the more we fully participate in life. Folklorist Michael Owen Jones, drawing to some extent on the work of Franz Boas, analyzes the way that aesthetic meaning is manifest in daily activities and in settings not usually thought of in aesthetic terms, such as the office. He maintains that regardless of their background, training, or philosophical bent, people are predisposed to aesthetic experience by virtue of their sensual awareness. They take in experience through their senses and react or respond to it on a sensual (emotional) level. Sometimes the response is negative (i.e., the stimuli is judged nonaesthetic), but the experience is still an aesthetic one because sensual awareness has been heightened, and the person feels more alive. (The opposite of aesthetic is *an*aesthetic, which is usually defined as a deadening of the senses, or a substance which blocks sensation.) Theologian Thomas Moore uses the word enchantment to describe much the same phenomenon of heightened experience in his recent best-seller, *The Re-Enchantment of Everyday Life*. He states unequivocally that "soul has an absolute, unforgiving need for [this]; it requires [it] like the body needs food and the mind needs thought."[11]

Like these authors, I too maintain that people have an aesthetic impulse or need. I believe this impulse is often particularly recognized and even elaborated in "background" arenas, and it is certainly an extremely important variable in the history of the fundraising fair. I have tried to locate the aesthetic experience of the fair and make it a tangible part of my narrative. To do this, I focus on the sensual input at different events—I look closely at elements like textural and aural stimulation and consider the smells and feelings of the fairs. I take the element of play seriously in my analysis and assess the gestalt of the aesthetic pleasure the fairs provide. I highlight the affective meaning of the fairs because it is at the heart of the story I am trying to tell. It is hardly accidental that in Western culture it is women who are most closely associated with the aesthetic. They are the "*sensitive* ones," the ones who seem most responsive to sensual stimuli like color and texture and are most concerned about the way things look and feel. To seriously evaluate a woman-identified, background institution, we must not only include, but intensively examine, the variable of aesthetic meaning.[12]

Consideration of aesthetic meaning returns me to a discussion of my broader theoretical framework and the previous scholarly work that has helped shape it. As indicated, my ideas are strongly influenced by the background perspective discussed by Mary Daly and Kenneth Ames. Implicitly, the alternate paradigm of the background also relates to the relational model of development posited by feminist psychological theorists like Carol Gilligan and Jean Miller. This model suggests that men and women in our culture have distinctly different experiences of the world as they are growing up; connection, empathy, and intersubjectivity are the central organizing concepts of women's lives.[13] The model certainly bolsters my understanding of a woman's institution so tied to group effort and cooperation and lends support to my argument that the fair remained meaningful, and has probably survived, because it contributed to fellowship and community building. My understanding has also been helped by scholarship on the history of American women's organizations, especially scholarship that highlights the way women have used domesticity in the public arena; the work of individuals like Barbara Epstein, Mary Ryan, Nancy Cott, Karen Blair, and Kathleen McCarthy informs much of my unfolding discussion.[14] Finally, perspectives on the late-nineteenth-century "culture of consumption" offered by Jackson Lears and William Leach have been useful in my understanding of the lure and meanings of goods.[15] In sum, my point of view is, like my research strategy, a composite. It draws on feminist theory and history and on interdisciplinary work in material culture and philosophy. I am interested in constructing a holistic portrait of a tenacious woman's institution, and understanding it on its own terms—from the inside out.

In closing, I wish to say that although there were times when I felt overwhelmed by the sheer scope of this project, I have been enormously enriched by it. It has deepened my awareness and appreciation of a myriad of interesting and complex issues. It has also brought me closer to a part of the American experience, and to a part of the lives of countless women, most of whom must remain unidentified. *Bazaars and Fair Ladies* is intended to bring them to life on these pages and to bring their fairs further into public consciousness. It tracks the development of a rich institution, including the causes it supported and the women who were involved. It also chronicles the bazaar as an experience and a site of cultural production; it considers people's reactions to fairs and the sale products and environments that fairgivers created. The study adds to the history of American women by uncovering many of the cultural innovations they pioneered and by taking one of their institutions on its own terms; i.e., by focusing on a woman-centered reality, a part of background history, with its own value system and priorities. It describes a previously unacknowledged element in the history of American entertainment, for fairs were, from their inception, centers of performance and both participatory and observational amusement. Finally, the study brings to light a formerly invisible part of the history of design and material culture, showing how the design concerns and ideas of the "public" male world were interpreted by women, and how meanings were invested in material objects. I hope I have presented this multilayered story accurately and sensitively and have opened new areas for future debate, discussion, and exploration.

CHAPTER ONE

The Many Meanings of the Fundraising Fair and an Overview of Its Development

Over the course of their history fundraising fairs have embodied many different kinds of contradiction, tension, and paradox. I begin my discussion of the fairs by trying to articulate these paradoxes, for it was in the process of trying to make sense of them that I began to comprehend the fairs' deeper meanings and associations. The unresolvability of these tensions proved to be an important key to interpretation and understanding.

Women's fairs were at times perceived to be and indeed functioned as the symbol of conservative propriety and time-honored domestic values. At other times, they were criticized as hotbeds of crass commercialism, risqué behavior, and rampant sexuality. Fairs have always had a serious intent or purpose, but were seen as the epitome of frivolity and lightheartedness. They were secular events, but often seemed almost synonymous with religious institutions. They were also adapted by or associated with seemingly opposite groups—by temperance workers and those who served liquor, for example; by people from rural hamlets and sophisticated cities; by elite, "establishment" populations and new waves of working-class immigrants. The same fair often meant one thing to women, and another, almost completely different thing to men. If we look at women's fairs on a structural level, we see that they created a confusion between the consumer and the consumed, between charity and materialism, and between work and play. They hovered on the very boundary between private and public: they brought private, domestic values into the public, commercial arena, but in so doing domesticated or privatized many of the elements of that public world. Domestic activities, artifacts, and roles become the object of public consumption at fairs; the fair was where the "stuff" or focus of daily domestic work became the focus of leisured play. Women's fairs also simultaneously venerated and undercut or mocked domesticity and simultaneously empowered women and kept them "in their place."

Stallybrass and White's discussion in *The Politics and Poetics of Transgression* of other kinds of fairs is helpful in dealing with these conundrums. They demonstrate that *all* fairs represent duality, a play between opposites, or a point of intersection between forces that usually remain separate. Even at the earliest medieval market fairs, there was a tension between opposing forces like work and play, the foreign and the familiar. The fairs constantly expressed ritual reversal, the turning upside-down of normal expectations.[1] As the woman-identified manifestation of the fair phenomenon in the industrial era, fundraising fairs predictably also functioned as a locus for inversions and dialectical balancing acts. However, many of their particular paradoxes and contradictions were unique, for they stemmed from cultural attitudes about women and from the roles women played—or were assigned—in industrial (and postindustrial) society.

Women and Sexuality: The Meanings and Associations of "Bazaar"

Many of these attitudes related to women as sensual and sexual beings. We can begin to understand this by looking closely at the word that was attached to the woman's fair: *bazaar*. In the Western (male) stereotype, a bazaar is seen as a foreign, simultaneously alluring and frightening place. It is an Oriental (Near Eastern) market, filled with luxurious, tantalizing goods and sensual pleasures. It is associated with intoxicants, with mystery and self-transformation, and with indulgence and the loss of self-control. Stereotypically, there is also an underlying belief that people as well as goods are for sale at the bazaar, and there is an underlying fear that the unguarded man might be seduced and brought to a state of helpless abandon by its irresistible, alluring women.[2]

The term was also applied in the nineteenth century to Western commercial establishments that featured nonnecessary, or luxurious, goods, which seemed to be similarly imbued with a sense of excitement and desire. Some of these establishments referred to the Eastern bazaar through visual and architectural form. In 1830, for example, Frances Trollope's Cincinnati Bazaar featured a mosquelike facade and a ballroom fashioned after the Alhambra.[3] Other so-called bazaars of the antebellum era alluded to the Oriental more obliquely, through their association with women. In the popular mind, that was enough to make them seem alluring and sensational.

The controversy surrounding what may have been the earliest Western establishment is illuminating. This institution, which opened in London's Soho Square in 1816, had a simultaneously commercial and charitable purpose. Entrepreneur John Trotter rented space to needy women who could provide "sufficient testimonies of their moral respectability" and amass sufficient amounts of handwork to maintain a permanent sales booth. The idea was that he could help the women support themselves through the "produce of their labors"; they need not become destitute if they did not have a husband or responsible male relative to rely on for financial support.[4] Despite Trotter's emphasis on morality and reputation, in the popular mind the Soho Bazaar still took on some of the seeming dangers of its imagined Eastern prototype. To some extent this had to do with the sale items, which were for the most part made up of "fancywork"—i.e., decorative needlework and related goods. Even more to the point, however, was the fact that women were engaged in selling, and they were "on display." Respectable women were not expected to work in public settings in the early nineteenth century, or to hawk goods of any kind. The women's very presence in the bazaar thus seemed to outweigh the moral and charitable purpose of the institution. Gary Dyer argues in a compelling article in *Nineteenth Century Literature* that these establishments in fact represented the Englishman's attempt to contain or control the dangers of women and unbridled consumption. Middle- and upper-class Englishmen feared the sensuousness of the bazaar and of women—both were construed as alien and essentially "other." Their version of the bazaar was meant to transform the dangerous or foreign into something identifiably moral and English; it was an attempt to tame it. "To associate the Oriental bazaar with Englishwomen—with 'sacred home,'" Dyer says, "was to [try to] assimilate, to *domesticate* that foreign presence and . . . make it chaste, respectable." Nevertheless, the men could not get over their fear that the women would be selling themselves; they felt women were inherently lustful, and their lust might rise to the surface at any time. Because domesticity also seemed inherently incompatible with consumption and alluring goods, there was always a tension between the charitable purpose of the institution and the materialism it seemed to represent.[5] In sum, it was never fully possible to eliminate the perceived threat of the bazaar. In the male mind, it remained a dangerous place.

In part because of these perceptions and in part because of its clientele, the Soho Bazaar was from its inception associated with frivolity and amusement; in 1823 an American visitor called it a "fashionable lounge" patronized by "all who have nothing to do except to see and be seen."[6] At the same time, however, it was associated with charity and good works. This was also related to the fact that, regardless of the men's concern with containment, women were involved as more than salespeople. Wealthy matrons served as patrons, helping to "place" orphans and other needy young ladies at the sale tables, and they were the bazaar's primary customers. As an 1818 children's book explained, "[Mrs. Dunford] determined to encourage the [saleswomen] by purchasing several of the prettiest articles. . . . Her daughters had been taught a variety of fancy works by their governess, but their mama felt a pleasure in purchasing these, because she trusted that she was doing good [and] assisting to support some worthy object in distress."[7]

The woman-run events that eventually also became known as bazaars emerged at approximately the same time as these commercial/charitable establishments, and the two institutions shared many elements (booths, women selling handwork, a charitable purpose). They were typically treated as a single phenomenon; even Dyer conflates the two types of bazaars in his discussion.[8] Dyer's analysis helps explain the long tradition of derogatory, attacking diatribes applied to women's fairs, for on an unconscious or structural level, the fair was also equated with danger and otherness. The fundraising bazaar was perceived as particularly threatening, furthermore, because women were in charge—i.e., there were no men to contain and control the women.

Dyer points out that nineteenth-century English literature is filled with innuendoes and derisive references to women's fairs; Scarlett O'Hara's romance was presaged by a number of earlier novels that linked bazaars, women, and sexuality. In Disraeli's *The Young Duke,* for example, an illicit affair is begun at a bazaar; in *Sketches by Boz,* Dickens disdainfully paints the bazaar as a marriage market. Thackeray's *Vanity Fair* even goes so far as to suggest that the woman's fair was a pose concealing pretense and superfluity, corruption, and greed. The "vanity fair" epithet became a familiar one with the wide circulation of this novel, and, as the term crept into the language, the concept became generally accepted on both sides of the Atlantic.[9] The concept of the vanity fair was so insidious, in fact, that even women fairgivers often made a point of trying to distinguish their "serious" events from the feared stereotype. Abolitionists, for example, would issue statements that their antislavery fairs had a more noble, political purpose and were not "mere vanity fairs." In reality, the distinction was a false one. Almost all of the women's fairs were held to raise money for some sort of external, charitable cause, and most featured very similar products and attractions. Unfortunately, the concept of the vanity fair has been taken at face value. The false distinction between different types of women's fairs was recently perpetuated in a contemporary study of antislavery fairs,[10] and today's popular image of the fundraising bazaar carries some of the same largely unwarranted associations.

An identification between the bazaar and women was evident in many nineteenth-century contexts, and sensuousness was typically a primary link. Women's magazines often made reference to the Oriental bazaar, linking it with women and "women's products" like fabric and clothing. A successful publisher who added a woman's magazine to his periodical line in 1867 even adopted the title *Harper's Bazar,* explaining in the premiere issue that a bazaar was a "repository for whatever can comfort the heart and delight the eye."[11] By implication, it was a sensual place, and sensuality, comfort, and delight were identified with women. The women's magazines spoke of these matters in a positive light, but when men spoke of bazaars and sensuality, the connotations tended to be more negative. Jackson Lears's discussion of the Victorian identification between women and interiors is relevant in this regard, for like the bazaar, the nineteenth-century interior was sensual and exotic. Lears speaks of the "messy details of biological existence" that "embodied the iconography of female experience" and were evident in the middle-class Victorian home. He refers to a profusion of flowered wallpaper and exotic bric-a-brac, for example, that symbolically referred to fecundity and sexual energy.[12] The same kind of images and items were associated with the bazaar, and both the bazaar and the rich interior environment tended to make men uncomfortable. The associations and the discomfort were explicitly drawn in Mary Braddon's 1887 novel *Like and Unlike*. A male character discovers that his house has been redecorated in his absence, and he is quite disturbed. It has been so filled with "mysterious, uncanny" exotic objects, like Japanese screens and Indian rugs, that he likens it to an "Oriental warehouse." "You expect me to live in a room of this kind, like a stall at a charity bazaar!" the man cries. He leaves the house in exasperation and retreats to his club, a place where women cannot penetrate.[13]

In sum, some of the negative associations of the bazaar relate to the culture's underlying assumptions or attitudes about women (they are sexual, alluring creatures) and about sensual goods or experiences (they are dangerous, frivolous, and overwhelming), which are in turn associated with them. Fairgivers found themselves in a no-win situation and were bound to be criticized no matter what they did. A fundraising fair had to stress qualities like sensuousness and good feeling; at least until the twentieth century, a fair had to be "alluring" if it was to raise money for charity. Fairgivers needed to find ways to ensure that visitors spend freely, which they would be inclined to do if they were enjoying themselves and suspending their ordinary, workday reality. By its very nature, then, a fundraising fair had to evoke something unusual or extra-ordinary. Like any other fair, it was set apart from daily life, but as a fundraising event, its very success was dependent on the creation of an environment where people would forget themselves and act with abandon. Abandon, of course, was the very thing that was so deeply or unconsciously feared. The paradoxes were inherent in the nature of the fair and could never be resolved.

Domesticity as a Fair Staple

Abandon and frivolity also seemed to be at odds with the laudable purpose of helping the poor or raising money for a good cause, with the perceived goodness of the women who work for charity, and with the nurturing qualities of the domesticity the fair celebrated. Domesticity was the given of the woman's fair, for it was what women had to work with. In one sense, it was for sale. Fairgivers offered mouth-watering meals and beautiful hand-stitched products; they transformed cooking and sewing into salable products.[14] In other words, they converted their domestic skills and expertise—their labor—into a commodity. This created another unresolvable tension. Domesticity and commercialism also seemed antithetical, for the commoditization of domesticity was a contradiction in terms.

Beyond sale products, many other elements of domesticity were integral at fairs. The fairs' festive quality and amusing tone, for example, were drawn from the domestic. The elaborate decorations and costuming that created the festive atmosphere were all part of the woman's domain—decoration and dress are so identified with women, in fact, that even today they comprise the major elements of the "women's pages" of newspapers and magazines. Almost everything that made the fairs appealing, from flowers to perfume to music, was part of what women dealt with daily. Fairgivers dramatized the elements of their everyday experience, in other words, transforming them into something with seemingly greater import and deeper meaning. It is interesting to note that a similar dynamic was evident in other women's enterprises that evolved contemporaneously; Mary Ryan argues, for example, that the women who "produced" parades in the early nineteenth century created a "stylized dramatization of their gender role."[15] In both cases, domesticity was lauded and yet gently mocked. It functioned as a symbol of moral uplift, but it was also played with, and turned into the stuff of fantasy and imagination.

The fact that these events supported the betterment of the community rather than the individual was also a clear reflection of women's roles and of the domestic ideal; women's collective identity was associated with nurturing and caring for others. Feminist historians have repeatedly demonstrated that women in the premodern era were often willing to step outside of the home or the domestic domain and engage in public activity when it would benefit someone else rather than themselves. Work for nonprofit groups and charitable or moral causes was accepted as a rightful part of women's work and an extension of women's sphere.[16] The very act of holding a fair for the benefit of the needy or for a hospital or school was then an acknowledgment and affirmation of culturally assigned gender roles.

Ironically, given the rash of criticism the woman's fair received as a dangerous (immoral, seductive, or too commercial) institution, it was also subject to constant trivialization on the basis of its *un*importance as an extension of the domestic sphere. This trivialization of women's concerns, evident long before the modern era, stemmed from structurally oppositional gender roles. As stated, women's activities were not really accepted as "work," and the vanity fair trope was a way of reducing women and their interests to superfluity and meaninglessness. It is true that the hard work of a fair was presented in a playful context, but the reason it wasn't *seen* as work was probably due more to its domestic nature than its presentation. Men often insisted on keeping women's fairs a thing apart; they tried to distance their fairs, which specifically highlighted the world of work, from the seemingly frivolous women's institution built around what was "not work" and "not serious"—i.e., around women and their domestic interests. In 1876, for example, John Sartain went out of his way to emphasize that the Art Bureau he worked with at the Philadelphia Centennial had nothing whatever to do with the woman's building; he worked for an exhibition, not a bazaar.[17] As we shall soon see, the different types of fairs were never really that distinct, but the frequent attempts to make them seem so indicated the prevalent male discomfort with things domestic.

We must remember that while women were in the aggregate "forced" (or in some observers' assessment, "reduced") by virtue of their social position or role to giving fairs to raise money for the causes they wanted to support, individual women often embraced this work with gusto. Many initiated or participated in fairs not because they *had* to, but because they found them enjoyable and rewarding. Both of these seemingly contradictory statements can be true. Women may have had few other alternatives, and some may have felt constrained and resentful, but others felt plea-sure. In order to fully understand or assess the fair, it is necessary to use a kind of double vision, considering both the attitudes and experiences of specific, identifi-able women, and the general historical situation and cultural attitudes that helped shape them.

The Advent of Gender-Identified Fairs in the Industrial Era

The fundraising fair and the agricultural fair both came into being at the begin-ning of the nineteenth century. They both "descended" from the medieval Eu-ropean fair, and both perpetuated many of its features. The European fairs had originated as religious festivals, but had evolved into commercial trading events mixed with revelry and entertainment. They were typically set up with rows of stalls or booths, forming a kind of town-within-a-town. At the old Sturbridge Fair, according to Defoe, an array of taverns, eating houses, and booths of retail and wholesale deal-ers were "placed in rows like streets." While some of the early events were specifically dubbed "pleasure fairs," all trade fairs had their share of diversions, and spectacle and commercialism effectively overshadowed religious and moral overtones by the seventeenth century. By the end of the eighteenth century, however, when increas-ing industrialization had engendered new institutions and attitudes, these market extravaganzas had been reduced to a shadow of their former selves. It was precisely at this time that the new generation of fairs emerged. Like their medieval predecessors, nineteenth-century fairs featured food, drink, goods, and varying forms of entertain-ment, but they were at least superficially less concerned with revelry and more with "serious" endeavors.[18]

The fundraising or woman's fair first appeared as a simple "sale of work" that com-bined elements of the market fair and the charitable/commercial Bazaar. The prod-ucts resembled those seen in the Bazaar, but the sales were temporary events, typically held on a predictable, seasonal schedule, and they involved no entrepreneurs. To the best of my knowledge, the first such sales were initiated in England by the same lei-sured women who patronized the commercial institution. They not only encour-aged needy women to sell handwork at outlets like the Bazaar, but through recently formed groups like the "Ladies' Society for the Education and Employment of the Female Poor" they instituted their own sales of members' fancywork. Proceeds were donated to the less fortunate. Some evidence indicates the women's sales may have actually predated the opening of the bazaar: one source claims they were already popular in the late eighteenth century, and as early as 1804 the Ladies' Society's annual report noted its members were considering how "by example or influence" they might promote the use and sale of articles that cottager's wives and daughters could make in their homes. In any case, the sales were commonplace and even fashionable by the 1810s, when the commercial Bazaar was in its heyday. Another group, the "Ladies' Royal Benevolent Society for Visiting, Relieving and Investigating the Condition of the Poor," held a sale annually from 1813 into the 1820s.[19]

The linking of fundraising and sales or fairs was not new. Fundraising had been a component of some of the oldest English events; in the twelfth and thirteenth centuries, for example, both the St. Bartholomew Fair and the Sturbridge Fair raised money for local hospitals. Church "Ales," or drinking feasts, where money collected from drinks and amusements was donated to local parishes, are even said to have been a primary source of church revenue before the Reformation.[20] Nevertheless, these nineteenth-century charity sales were considered a novel, unique phenomenon, because they were organized and operated by women and centered around women's wares. This led, as we have seen, to denigrating associations with the Near Eastern bazaar. The fact that many of the products at these early sales were made by the wealthy confounded the situation, further contributing to the idea of the nonserious, "vanity" fair. Fancywork was indeed a superfluity in the lives of these women of leisure; it was something they used to fill their time, and something they could afford to give away. Moreover, since the work was generally purchased by other well-off women, the fair functioned as something of a closed system, and the whole enterprise seemed particularly silly, vain, and unnecessary. Logic would argue that the women could just give their money to the poor and dispense with this "play-acted" transaction.

The fact that women chose to "work," to produce something that had a cash value and would be marketed, actually says much about changing cultural values and about women's roles in the emerging industrial era. Activities—and people—were increasingly judged by their market value or worth. Women, however, were consistently kept out of the market system. I believe that the emergence of women's sales reflects an acknowledgment of what was considered important in an increasingly capitalistic society, and much of the subsequent criticism of the commercialism of the woman's fair was a masked criticism of women's encroachment into territory that was "claimed" as male. I also believe that the sales and subsequent fundraising events continued not because they were commercially important, but because they filled other kinds of needs. I will argue this point shortly, but first wish to further clarify how these fundraising events functioned as part of the re-emerging fair phenomenon, specifically as a counterpoint to the male agricultural fair.

Wayne Neely maintains that the agricultural fair was a function of an increasingly commercialized and industrialized society—a society where people were no longer providing most of their needs in self-sustaining, small-scale communities, and where agriculture could itself become a commodity. It was the "gentleman farmer" who initiated the agricultural show or exhibit at the turn of the nineteenth century. (In the United States, these events are traced to Elkanah Watson, who founded the Berkshire Cattle Show in Pittsfield, Massachusetts, in 1810.) This type of man not only had some scientific education, but had the leisure to experiment with new agricultural ideas and methods because his was not a hand-to-mouth operation. Such men exhibited and shared ideas about their work at agricultural fairs and were thereby able to further consolidate and give credence to their professional identities. In a parallel fashion, women exhibited their products—food and handwork—at *their* fairs. Since we have established that women's collective identity was associated with nurturance, women were not advocating their own advancement at their fairs, but were working for charity, or the betterment of others. Despite this selfless purpose, we can intuit that the women similarly shared ideas there and found what Neely terms a "conception of their own importance." The originators of the two types of fair also shared a similar socioeconomic profile; the well-placed women who initiated sales of work were akin—might even be married to—the leisured gentleman farmers. The ladies' fair and the agricultural fair sometimes specifically intertwined. In the early nineteenth century agricultural fairs typically included the display and sale of women's handwork. The men encouraged such exhibitions because they found it a way of increasing interest and attendance at their events.[21]

Mechanics' or trade fairs (institutes), which featured industrial products and technologies and thus also served as an extension of the men's professional role, arose in the 1820s and 1830s. This was the same period in which women's fairs began to proliferate. By the second half of the nineteenth century, all categories of fairs were thriving, and much of their subsequent development remained parallel.

To a certain extent every type of fair provided opportunities for networking and an exchange of ideas and for the experience of fellowship. As a woman's institution, however, the fundraising fair had an additional, unique function: it provided a place where, working from their assigned cultural role and using their acknowledged skills, women could effect what they wanted, demonstrate their competence, and operate relatively independently of men. It was a place, in other words, where, within limits, women could achieve their desired ends on their own terms and under their own control. As we shall see, their terms included unparalleled insistence on aesthetic excitement, pleasure, and community.

The Trajectory of the Fair: An Overview of Its Development in America

In order to help readers understand the changing ways that women achieved their ends and worked with and against their expected roles, I provide a brief overview of the development of the fundraising fair at this point in my narrative. I believe this will allow the reader to contextualize subsequent discussion of the fair experience and to understand who these individuals were and how they approached and responded to their diverse situations. I hope the discussion that follows about the satisfactions and aesthetic meanings of the fair will come alive against this background portrait. The overview should also reinforce the image of the fair as a seemingly irrepressible institution. Despite its time-consuming and labor-intensive nature, despite the fact that there have always been more efficient ways of raising money, and despite a continual barrage of scathing criticism based on moral, economic, and social arguments, the fair has never really died. Rather, it has returned again and again in yet other, slightly different guises.

Nineteenth-Century Fairs

The fundraising fair came to North America by the late 1820s.[22] Although the typical American ladies fair was initially a relatively simple event, it was, like its English prototype, perceived as a rather risqué, exciting enterprise. Fairgivers soon capitalized on these sexual associations by featuring young, unmarried women as the most visible salespeople. By the 1830s, for example, fairs often included "post offices," where women stood ready to hand out playful pre-written and flirtatious letters to gentlemen who paid a small fee. Other attractions alluded to abundance and imaginative well-being. The sales soon became "fancy fairs" not just because they sold fancywork, but because of their ever more fanciful qualities.

Despite the fanciful image of the fairs, the organizers of antebellum American fairs were not quite like the leisured aristocrats who were active in England. They were generally established, educated community leaders such as the wives of judges and ministers,[23] but they were often among the progressive or forward-thinking women of their class. Many were concerned with serious social action. They not only held fairs to raise funds for local charity, but supported regional projects such as the completion of the Bunker Hill Monument (this was perceived as a woman's project) and even radical causes like abolition. Although fair leaders were typically well connected, general participation was not limited to any one religion, race, or ethnic group.

Fairs of all types were thriving in America by the middle of the century. Agricultural fairs were prevalent almost everywhere there was settlement, and mechanics' institutes and commercial expositions were becoming increasingly common. The woman's fair had become so taken for granted as a part of the cultural landscape that it was no longer a daring or radical act to sponsor one, and even those who would be considered politically conservative or temperamentally modest had begun to be involved.[24] The temperance cause, which at this early stage drew much of its constituency from the working class, was sometimes funded through fairs, and ladies from almost every church denomination began sponsoring fairs of their own. Free black women in the North held fairs to support their churches or the more general African American cause. In the 1850s satires about fairs began to appear in popular newspapers, and *Godey's Lady's Book*, the most widely read American women's magazine, ran a regular column, "Articles [To Make] for Fancy Fairs." The fair had become the assumed or accepted mechanism, in other words, by which women could "do their mite."[25]

A significant shift occurred during the Civil War, when fairs became more complex and drew a different kind of attention. Women mounted large-scale regional fairs to raise money for the Union (and, to a lesser extent, the secessionist) cause. Northerners organized a series of "sanitary fairs" (named after the U.S. Sanitary Commission, the agency to which the proceeds were channeled) that together raised over five million dollars—a sum that would be closer to about seventy-five million today. While still women-run events, these were no longer simple ladies' fairs. Men became active participants, and they brought in many of the elements of their own types of fairs, including exhibits of machinery and livestock, professionally designed horticulture displays, and a wealth of commercial sale merchandise. To house the mammoth events, they even erected grand new facilities. The sanitary fair became something of a hybrid institution, in other words—a cross between a woman's and a man's fair. As a result, fundraising fairs became even more acceptable. Organizers were so efficient at soliciting assistance and wartime feeling was running so high that huge numbers of women became involved; organizations from sewing societies to reading clubs worked with the Sanitary Commission, and most contributed to the fairs.[26]

Fair work contributed to a growing sense of accomplishment, camaraderie, and sisterhood, and the institution became fully entrenched as a result of the war. Abba Gould Woolson, a New England educator and reformer, wrote in 1873, "The great fairs held . . . during the past few years have become such a recognized and important part of our social life that any picture of woman's work, to be complete, must give them special mention."[27] The terms "fancy fair" and "ladies' fair" essentially disappeared; more typically, the events were now called bazaars or were named after the cause they supported (e.g., "Homeopathic Hospital Fair"). Nevertheless, they were still unequivocally women's endeavors, and they reflected the full spectrum of women's ideas and activities. The institution was flexible enough to encompass both an expansion of women's roles and a continuation of old, limiting forms, and women with very different social and political views were involved. Many of the period's most progressive women continued to hold fairs to support their institutions, but those with traditionalist ideals also felt fairs were rightfully part of their domain because they upheld domestic values. They typically worked to fund health and welfare organizations or educational causes.[28]

Turn-of-the-Century Elaboration

Fairs of all types were in their heyday during the last quarter of the century. Agricultural fairs became more grand, and national and international expositions proliferated (incorporating many of the features introduced and elaborated at the sanitary fairs). Department stores, which highlighted goods in a similar manner to fairs, not only proliferated but competed with one another for the most exotic and exciting goods and displays. Consequently, expectations for all kinds of sales events were raised, and fundraising fairs became more and more elaborate. Although there was still sexual innuendo at late-nineteenth-century bazaars, women's presence was not in itself sufficient to engender excitement. Instead, organizers created "fairylands" with elaborate decorations, theatrical displays and costuming, entertainments, and rich and exotic sale items.[29] Commercial products vied strongly with women's handwork at turn-of-the-century fairs; often, the woman's fair functioned as an alluring retail outlet that mimicked the excitement and character of the new "emporiums."[30]

Radical reformers were less involved with fundraising fairs by the late nineteenth and early twentieth century, although even they sometimes "resorted to" bazaars for the sake of expediency. Despite significant gains in women's education and women's inroads into the professions and public life, the very process of inclusion in the male-dominated mainstream meant, paradoxically, that the solidarity and strength of women's separate power base was eroding. Women began to hold fairs to support not just their own causes, but men's institutions such as veteran's and fraternal organizations and male choirs; "ladies' auxiliaries" raised money to build the Masonic halls and armories that would predominantly be used by men. Even when the events did not specifically fund their organizations, men were more prominently touted or given central stage at these fairs. By this time, much of the derogatory commentary about women at bazaars referred not to their sensuality (although this was by no means absent) but to their "wheedling," or coercing men to buy things they did not need. The criticism had shifted, in other words, from sexuality to economics and issues of power. Feminist reformers like Woolson knew the power games of the fairs reflected women's lack of their own funds. They critiqued the system that forced women to raise money by "reaching into masculine pockets," and turned to other methods of fundraising when they could.[31]

Although the fundraising fair had always been perceived as a social event, sociability and commercialism almost completely eclipsed its charitable function by the turn of the century. Even when they were church-related, fairs were usually built around amusing themes, and were announced in newspapers under headings like "entertainments" or "sociables."[32] This strong social emphasis reflected a more general secularization in church life and an increasing preoccupation with packaged amusement in the culture as a whole. This was the era in which amusement parks were developed and in which the serious educational function of the agricultural fairs and national expositions was largely eclipsed by their carnival-like midways and amusement sections.[33]

The new social fair was linked on one hand to youth (it touted the same Never-Never Land quality as the contemporary novel, *Peter Pan*), and, on the other, to the newly dominant society matron. The juvenile tone was reflected in themes like "A Violet in Fairyland" or "The Mystic Midgets." Booths or even entire fairs might be based on nursery rhymes or fairy tales, and dolls were not only important sales items, but sometimes constituted the very basis of the fair. A play with scale was frequently worked into the decorations, with entire booths shaped like oversize objects or salespeople dressed as enormous flowers (see illustrations in chapter 5). Although the primary actors in the drama of the fundraising fair were still adults, more and more young people were drawn in. Sometimes fairs were staged by adult-supervised youth groups or by college students. The title of one of the first full-length books that included instructions for fairs, *The American Girls' Handy Book: How to Amuse Yourself and Others* (1893), makes clear the associations between fairs, youth, and entertainment.[34] It reminds us that the girls, like the fairgiving women who functioned outside the money economy and the "serious" world of work, supported their activities by exploiting their very outsider status and creating "play" events. This volume also indicates that the "threat" of the fair was considerably reduced. The exoticism of the bazaar had so thoroughly infiltrated life in the consumer society that the actual bazaar—the fair—was in a sense reduced to child's play. The increasing number of printed instructions for fairgivers also meant that the fair could be mastered by any-one; women or girls in even the most remote hamlet could learn the latest ideas and techniques and stage their own events. This accessibility further contributed to the sense that fairs were lightweight, frivolous activities.

Frivolity was also a quality associated at the time with the social elite, and by the early 1880s fairs were reported in the *New York Times* under headlines like "The World of Society." The presence of "well-known society ladies" almost seemed to be a benediction for a successful fair, and because certain charities were identified with the upper class, it was as much a mark of prestige to be seen working at a fundraising event for one of these causes as it was to be invited to an exclusive party. There also was a charity fair "season," just as there was a lawn party or post-Lenten season. Some of the affluent women even ran fairs as a kind of professional (though still unpaid) business. In order to become a member of the Junior League, in fact, a 1901 debutante had to show that she could "present an entertainment"—run a charity benefit like a fundraising fair.[35] The American fair, in some ways, had come to resemble its ear-lier English antecedent, as the fairgivers of this Belle Epoque mimicked the lifestyle of the British aristocracy.

Some socially prominent women used their skills to support progressive causes; they worked at bazaars funding dress reform organizations, for example, or, especially in the early years of the twentieth century, funding women's suffrage. However, politics was now largely secondary to the social function of the fair, and suffrage was by this time no longer a radical idea. Most reformers had turned to direct solicitation or other fundraising activities, and these wealthy women were often the wives of in-dustrialists rather than of judges or clergymen. Fairs were not strongly identified with any one ideology at the turn of the century, probably because they were so pre-dominantly social. It is important to understand, too, that even at the most socially "significant" fairs, the general public was welcome. Unlike late-twentieth-century char-ity balls and similar events with hefty admission prices and exclusive guest lists, fundraising fairs drew an audience from a range of classes. Organizers even exploited the fact that there were many who were curious about the very rich; they highlighted their position and their association with luxury and good taste, making those qualities a part of the attraction.[36]

The grand, commercialized, and professionalized fair reached its climax during World War I and the early 1920s. Large events were typically sponsored by a consortium of groups, as when representatives of thirty war charities worked together in 1917 to stage a "Festa" in New York, but the socialites were still a dominant presence. A "troop of autos containing society women" set out in a parade to sell tickets for the Festa, and any man who made an effort to enlist at the fair was entitled to be kissed by a "society girl." Wartime fairs included gambling and midway-type games of skill, motion pictures, and dances. The attractions were spectacular, although the fairy-tale theme had largely disappeared; another fair was built around a kind of real-life theater, with moving pictures taken at the front, and a replica of the Hindenburg line trenches. After the war women's groups got together to stage events like the previously mentioned Atlantic City Boardwalk. These were "productions," with rented scenery and props, and the participation of hundreds of professional retailers. They also involved huge numbers of workers. At the 1923 Boston Boardwalk, more than twenty-five hundred women agreed to sew nightwear for just one of fifty sponsoring organizations. Contributors included immigrant and working-class women as well as professionals.[37]

Domesticity Returns in the Modern Era

By the Depression era of the 1930s, the profile of the fundraising fair changed substantially once again; in essence, it reverted back to an event that highlighted domesticity through the sale of handmade goods. Although there was a last spate of fairs with festival themes before the stock market crash, the age of the "dangerous" or elaborate fundraising fair was essentially over. With movies and other forms of mass entertainment, and with the completed transition into a consumer culture where an abundance of goods was taken for granted, the fair no longer served as an important outlet for fantasy. The juvenile tone of the fair largely dropped away, and the frivolity and excesses of the earlier times seemed out of place. The fairs that did take place were relatively straightforward sales, with little in the way of commercialism, decorations, or amusement. Sale items were dominated by useful, rather than fanciful, homemade products. These events were not associated with sensuality or society. They were rarely connected with social reform, either; at this time, they typically supported causes that were once again extensions of the so-called woman's sphere.[38] I believe it was during the 1930s, furthermore, that the fundraising fair became especially identified with the working class and with small towns; while the urban public would no longer support the excesses of its elaborate carnivals, people in small communities were still willing to help local groups or relief efforts by purchasing small, practical items. "Down-home" fairs were appreciated, moreover, because they fit well with the romanticization of grassroots American life that characterized the Depression era.[39] These same associations with tradition, work, and simplicity were reinforced during World War II. Very few fairs were held, although some of the war relief shops that sprung up throughout the country had bazaarlike features. The scarce written references to fairs appeared in magazines like *American Home,* which appealed to a conservative, generally rural audience, and the tone of these articles was somewhat condescending—the women were presented as unsure of themselves and in need of assistance.[40] The assumption that the women who organized bazaars would need reassurance was something new; fundraising fairs were now to be tackled by the unsure, less wealthy, stay-at-home housewife. As the affluent, assertive, and powerful women who had been associated with the fairs disappeared, the institution was increasingly thought of as even more trivial and unimportant.

Fairs changed again in the postwar years, although these last associations remained constant, as indeed they have ever since. Local fairs were well received in the 1950s social climate that emphasized home, family, and community life; they were perceived as community events that reinforced wholesome family values. They were still organized and run by women, but ironically women's agency became increasingly invisible. Men's contributions were prominently highlighted in fair publicity, as was a sense of bounty or plentifulness, evidence of the "normalcy" that returned with the men after the war. During the Vietnam War era of the 1960s and 1970s, the bazaar was often repackaged as a boutique or art fair, and in recent decades the focus has shifted even more decidedly to "arts and crafts." A plethora of instruction books and articles has appeared about fairs in the last twenty years, almost all of which focus on craft projects rather than on matters such as organizational structure and publicity. Titles like *Country Bazaar Crafts* and *McCall's Big Book of Bazaar Crafts* hint at the prevailing qualities that contemporary fairgivers like to promote: a sense of homeyness and a suggestion of "good old fashioned values" nostalgically associated in the popular mind with the imagined community—and the bazaars—of the past.[41]

Profit and a Change in the Meaning of Time

The realities of present-day women's lives have significantly changed, however, and fairs have begun to change with them. With the majority of women working outside the home, the number of people available for the daytime work sessions and errand running that go into a bazaar has been reduced dramatically. Even more significantly, there has been a decided shift in the perception of time and its value, and as women begin to count the value of their labor and factor that into their calculation of final profit, they are often less willing to put in the requisite long hours of fair preparation. Several results are evident. First, fairs are thriving within a new demographic niche, i.e., among senior citizen and retirement groups whose members do not have to consider their hourly value. Most often, the seniors' participation in fairs begins in age-specific organizations such as seniors' clubs or retirement homes. Second, there has been a new blurring of the boundary line between profit and not-for-profit events. Since the late 1970s many church and other nonprofit groups have allowed craftspeople who are selling their wares to rent space at fundraising events and/or to contribute a percentage of their profits. These entrepreneurs may be from outside the community of the sponsoring group, but sometimes they are even group members; they are often the very same women who previously would have donated their handmade items to fairs. For-profit craft sales that look like bazaars and feature identical merchandise have also proliferated. The public does not seem disturbed by, or even always aware of, the blurred boundaries. A related trend occurring in at least some areas of the country is that bazaars are now taking place in shopping malls, places where profit making is paramount.

In sum, the American fundraising fair has moved through many phases, and the profile of the fairgivers and the causes the institution has stood for have followed a definite trajectory. Broadly speaking, the institution was originally used by well-connected, well-educated women who were seriously interested in social change; early fairs were often held to support the most progressive or radical causes of the day. Over time, the fair became associated less with women's causes and social change than with maintaining the status quo, and its identification with commercialism, sociability, amusement, and triviality became even stronger. In the twentieth century the commercial aspect receded. Fairgivers increasingly came from less highly educated and more working-class backgrounds and from more traditionalist, conservative groups, or from the ranks of younger (teenaged) or older (retired) people. The fair became associated with old-fashioned values and with the homemade, and lost its seemingly exotic quality. What has remained constant is that the fair has been a fundraising vehicle used primarily by those who did not earn their own money; it has always been an institution dependent upon volunteer labor. The trajectory can be understood as a reflection of the shifting profile of voluntarism, of women's roles, and attitudes about domesticity. It was possible for the same institution to be associated both with conservative propriety and domestic values and with radicals and risqué behavior precisely because of those shifting ideas. When it was considered radical to bring domesticity (and women) into a public arena, it was often radicals who worked at fairs. When women's public presence was no longer questioned and when domesticity seemed an endangered value system, the women who were involved with fairs could be characterized as more traditional and retiring. It appears that the primary identification with voluntarism and domesticity is beginning to shift in our own time and that the fair is beginning to change more fundamentally than it has to date. Be that as it may, the woman's fair has proved to be a remarkably resilient institution. In the remaining part of this chapter we will look more closely at what I believe are the underlying reasons for its continued appeal.

Why Fairs Continue: Their Pleasures and Deep Satisfactions

Community Bonding, Fellowship, and Ritual Celebration

Through its many changing phases, the woman's fair provided important opportunities for social interaction, amusement, and good feeling. These are deeply felt human needs, and comments from fair participants in all eras tell us that these elements were a significant part of their experience. Ultimately, I feel the fair has persisted not just because it was an available means to an end or because women had no other choices, but because of these satisfactions.

Sentiments about a satisfying feeling of community were expressed over and over again—by abolitionist fair organizers, for example, by members of late-nineteenth-century ladies' auxiliaries, and by participants in contemporary retirement center programs. A sense of fellowship[42] or social bonding arose from working with others toward a common goal, especially because the work was directed toward a "greater" cause. Maria Weston Chapman, who spearheaded antislavery fairs in the 1840s, claimed fair work was appealing because it brought Christian fellowship and "spiritual strength and comfort." Fifty years later Mary Lowe Dickinson defended church bazaars by insisting that they afforded more opportunities for the entire membership to come together than any other church activity. Everyone was brought closer through joint effort, she said, for people had to learn to cooperate and find each other's strengths. "From loving the cause they learn to love each other," she concluded. Her position was echoed in 1924 by Mrs. James Anthony in a piece written for *Homiletic Review*. "[The bazaar] is a helpful agent in drawing the women closer together and broadening their sympathies, thereby enlarging their outlook on life. The meetings afford afternoons of friendly intercourse for many women who are tied pretty closely at home; and . . . this help[s create] happier and more satisfied living from day to day, [and] tends to quicken their minds. . . . As people work together they come to understand each other better. It has meant an increase of good fellowship."[43]

These sentiments are still expressed today. *Without exception*, every person I interviewed talked about the fellowship involved in working for a fair. The institution is still heralded for its efficacy in bringing people out of themselves and giving them a chance to interact with others. "When our church is working on a fair the feeling of community and sharing and friendship grows," stated the chair of a large bazaar. "Everyone is more in touch with everyone else—even the fellowship hours after church are longer." A member of a Catholic parish commented that one of the worst times in the history of her church community was when the priest insisted that there be no more fundraising activities like fairs and rummage sales; the parish would enforce a 5 percent tithe and its financial needs would be met. The priest was correct in his assessment of the financial situation and the parish did generate adequate funds, but because no one had to work together for a common cause, there was a serious loss of community spirit and involvement in the group. Eventually the need for fellowship became so apparent that activities like fundraising fairs were reinstated, and the community found itself once again. Dorothea Britton, who has observed bazaars in communities throughout the northeast, goes so far as to say that efforts to eliminate or "subvert" these activities *never* succeed; the need for fellowship is so strong that it eventually pushes itself through. Another woman put the feeling in very simple terms: "We loved to get together because we could *talk*," she stated. "We just talked and talked."[44]

Even beyond the obvious opportunities for fellowship, involvement in fairs helps cement a given community together by creating a sense of group loyalty or identity and contributing to a sense of group or local pride.[45] The nineteenth-century practice of "voting" at fairs for favorite pastor or school or military regiment (see chapter 3) was not only a clever way of collecting dollars, but also a way of reinforcing allegiance and belonging. Today, some of the most popular bazaar sale items are community cookbooks and calendars that serve as reminders of the group even after the fundraising event is over.[46] The local talent that was showcased at fairs in the premodern era (see below) also enabled communities to feel a sense of cohesion and identity.

Fig. 1. Henry Bergmann, an amateur photographer who documented many scenes of community life in southeastern Wisconsin, took this shot of an unidentified bazaar near Watertown in the 1890s. The many women gathered in the booth are reminders of the close cooperation and fellowship that fair work involved. Photograph WHi(B6)6467; courtesy of the State Historical Society of Wisconsin.

Fellowship and sociability are also related to the ritual and ceremony that are embedded in the fair. The Englishwomen's "sales of work" epithet wasn't satisfactory for long because it seemed too prosaic and dull; "fair" was soon substituted in order to align or associate the event with the qualities of the festival. "Fair" is derived from the Latin *feriae,* which means holiday. This word in turn implies a day that is out of the ordinary (literally, a holy day), a day associated with leisure, plentiful food, and drink, and even pageantry and entertainment. Fundraising fairs, even more than their agricultural or industrial counterparts, carried these associations. They became rituals in their own right and were typically held in conjunction with holidays, especially Thanksgiving, Christmas, Valentine's Day, or Easter.[47] Many groups held fairs so regularly on a seasonal basis, in fact, that members thought of the tradition as inviolate. "We *always* had a Christmas bazaar," I was told by several people I interviewed during the course of my research. "Our fair came every year."

The fair was deeply integrated into the yearly cycle in other ways as well. Committees were formed for the next year's event shortly after a fair ended, and they met at regularly increasing intervals. Certain preparations could only be done at certain times of the year—women who contributed jams and jellies, for example, could only make them when the fruit was ripe. A sense of predictability or ritual even pervaded work meetings, which typically followed set hours and included expected activities such as serving tea at a certain point in the gathering. Such preparatory activity in itself came to take on holiday significance and added to the sense of group cohesion and value.

Ritual also entered into both the event itself and the way people attended a fair. It could become "traditional," for example, to attend specific fairs, and even to do so with specific other individuals. I was told about two women who lived in a town about twenty miles from Madison who happened to be in the city and see signs to a nearby bazaar. They arrived in time for lunch and enjoyed themselves so much that they made a point of returning to the same bazaar together every year, eventually bringing two other friends with them. The fairs themselves usually follow a regular sequence, organized around meals, and may even begin and end with ritual ceremonies. Theorists have pointedly discussed how festivals, which are characterized by ceremony and ritual, bring communities together. It is no accident that fundraising fairs were—and are—sometimes even called festivals, and when the term is not explicitly used in the title, it sometimes is understood metaphorically. Abolitionist Mary Grew referred to antislavery fairs as "Passover Festivals" which provided "refreshment and strength" for the antislavery "tribe."[48]

Entertainment, Playfulness, and Aesthetic Elaboration

Refreshment also relates to the pleasurable aspects of the fair or festival—the type of amusement and play that occur when ordinary reality is replaced by the extra-ordinariness of the holiday. Again, the costuming, theatricality, parades, and multiple forms of entertainment that characterized the woman's fair all had their roots in the preindustrial fair tradition. Some of the entertainment was staged for the visitors. As the medieval fairs had featured puppet shows, "drolls," musicians, dancers, and processions, so too did fundraising fairs include shows of their own. Vocal groups, dancers, gymnasts, mimes, and actors were routine fair attractions before about 1930. In the days before film, radio, and television provided constant mass entertainment, fairs were clearly identified as community entertainment and performance centers.[49] As the program of entertainment staged in the art gallery of Milwaukee's Bazar of All Nations on May 13, 1896 (see the sidebar below) makes clear, the events typically highlighted local talent and gave community members opportunities to work and perform together. Fair organizers arranged different entertainments on each day, hoping to draw customers back even when they had exhausted the sale tables and other attractions. Organizers particularly recognized the value of lively, energizing music for lifting spirits and helping people relax and spend money. "Mirth, music and money-making formed a trinity of irresistible fascination," noted the *Los Angeles Examiner* in its description of a 1913 church fair (alliteration apparently even extended to journalistic reports). The music's effectiveness in raising the general excitement level was made explicit in an 1871 description of working at a fair booth. A "certain monotony" had fallen over "the industrious kiosk-dwellers" during the day, according to the worker, but in the evening "a fresh breeze of enthusiasm seems to float over the place; with the music and the crowd our spirits revive, and we not only accept our task, but rejoice in it."[50]

Much of this entertainment was participatory. For example, for more than one hundred years, fairs often doubled as community dances. The selling floor would be cleared in the evening, and couples who paid an extra fee were able to move to the sounds of a featured orchestra. During World War I, fairs incorporated Red Cross dance halls. At the turn of the century, fairs were also sometimes structured as folk dance festivals or included maypole dances and other kinds of participatory choreographed movements like those listed in the Bazar of All Nations program.[51]

Similarly, while tableaux and formal theatrical performances were given at fairs—e.g., a "Symbolic Play Festival" was a highlight of a 1908 New Jersey bazaar; a suffrage play was featured at a 1909 suffrage bazaar[52]—the most important drama was also participatory. Like the medieval fairs, this was often evident even at the outset, with processions of tellingly costumed individuals. England's Wolverhampton

Fig. 2. Music and dance were an integral part of fundraising fairs from their earliest days. The kinesthetic involvement they provided made the fairs more memorable and meaningful. Proceeds from the sale of sheet music for the "Sanitary Fair Polka" were donated to the Mississippi Valley Fair in 1864. This sheet is in the Chicago Historical Society Library. Courtesy of the Chicago Historical Society.

Fair had begun with a march of men wearing old armor, and Avingham Fair had featured an equestrian parade from one end of the town to the other led by fancifully dressed pipers.[53] Turn-of-the-century fundraising fairs were often initiated with candlelight processions of young maidens or marches of "Spanish damsels" and "Italian senoritas."

Costuming of this type was first introduced at women's fairs during the Civil War, and soon after that time it became typical for salespeople to dress up and impersonate some sort of romantic or amusing character. Fairgoers would enter a theater-like hall— complete with sets, props, and costumes—and encounter a variety of actors vying for their attention. At a turn-of-the-century fair it was a convention to peg the attractions to a specific theme. At one "Fete of the Heroines," for example, booths were based on Becky Sharp, Juliet, and Alice in Wonderland, and saleswomen would become the characters from popular literature. Even the "audience" was at times encouraged to come in costume to participate in theater games and reenactments; fairgoers could become the actors. Helen Hoover Santmeyer, reminiscing about fairs in late-nineteenth-century Ohio, recalled one event where townspeople dressed as chess pieces and, in Alice-in-Wonderland fashion, acted out a life-sized game. She remarked that everyone would go to all three nights of a fair, "not willing to miss the fun of strutting for a few hours in costume" and effectively playing at being someone else.[54] Whether or not they were dressed up in costume, fairgoers were drawn into the play of the fair. The charged atmosphere allowed them to become different characters who could leave their usual habits of thrift and caution behind. Everyone could become someone else in the transformed environment.

The participatory nature of the entertainment at nineteenth- and early-twentieth-century fairs reflects a premodern approach to amusement—i.e., it was not prepackaged or enjoyed only passively. Fairs were by no means the only available amusement centers, and the entertainments that took place there were always also found in other settings. At the turn of the century, for example, large numbers of people were also involved with music, movement, and tableaux through so-called parlor theatricals and choreographed activities like pageants and sings.[55] However, fundraising fairs have not been credited or acknowledged at all in previous studies of American entertainment, despite the countless references to them in newspapers, magazines, and contemporary narratives. Fairs provided both a forum and an excuse for participatory play and represent a major amusement outlet. Their function as entertainment centers—entertainment that highlighted "culture" and refinement, but not in a heavy-handed or exclusionary fashion—is part of their persistence and appeal. Fair entertainments added greatly to the feelings of fellowship, community, and aesthetic satisfaction.

Aesthetic satisfaction and playfulness were evident in more than dramatic entertainment and display. Like ritual, they were often extended into every element of the fairs, including preparatory activities. Work gatherings could easily turn into work parties, and even here costuming could be used to transformative effect. I attended a

An Evening's Entertainment:
The Bazar of All Nations, Milwaukee, 1896

The American [i.e., in English rather than german] entertainment will be given in the Art Gallery tonight. It has been arranged by Prof. Brosius and Mr. Edmund Gram and the programme is as follows:

Grand Symbolical Tableaux, Our Washington and Lincoln—
    Thirty-five young ladies and gentlemen.

Quartette, The Flower of Liberty—Tem-Quartette.

Grand Tableau, Our Country, with song by the Temple Quartette.

Club Swinging and Grouping, ten ladies, concluding
    with a Solo-Swing by Mr. Emil Rom.

Tenor Solo, Queen of the Earth, Pinsuti—Mr. R. Thomas.

Ballet, Trans-Reigen with Castanets—Twenty girls of the
    German and English academy, concluding with a Spanish
    dance by four ladies.

Pyramids on Chairs and Ladders—Sixteen young men.

Vocal. Creole Love Song, Smith—Mrs. S. Williams,
    Accompanied by Quartola Mandolin club.

Fencing (Foils) (a) School, (b) Assault—Messrs. Fred Vogel
    and Waldimar Kraemer.

Quartette, The Flag Without a Stain—Temple Quartette.

Grand March, National Flag—Reigen with grouping,
    by thirty-two girls. Arranged by Otto Mauthe.

In addition, the bicycle committee has arranged a bicycle carnival and parade in which a number of decorated wheels will take part.

—*Milwaukee Journal*
May 13, 1896

bazaar work session at a retirement community, for example, where individuals spontaneously decided to dress in silly hats and other costume elements. The overriding tone was one of good feeling, almost glee.[56]

Playfulness is, as I indicated in the introduction, identified with the aesthetic; in some languages, in fact, the same word is used for both. Ellen Dissanayake explains that play and art both involve an escape from the everyday and heighten reality through the process of "making special."[57] Aesthetic elaboration helped make work seem like play and brought a different kind of satisfaction to the fair experience. Fairgivers found great pleasure in the many physical details of the fair—in making sale goods and presenting them attractively, in arranging appealing environments and entertainments. Fairgoers responded to those same environments and objects. The importance of this aesthetic experience, like the importance of fellowship and community, was clearly expressed by participants. Even in the earliest account of the Soho Bazaar, we find Mrs. Dunford purchasing several of the "prettiest articles" and "feeling a pleasure" in doing so. Helen Santmeyer similarly described turn-of-the-century church carnivals in great sensual detail. Speaking of the costumes at a Japanese booth, for example, she remarked on "soft, silken kimonos" and "fascinating" hairpins with "butterflies set on tiny springs so they quivered with every motion."[58] Contemporary informants also spoke of good feelings brought to them by aesthetically pleasing details at fairs. One echoed Mrs. Dunford when she spoke of making and selling aprons that were "so pretty" that no decorations were needed to create a festive fair environment. Others recalled long-ago sensual stimuli with great satisfaction. A woman who attended pre–World War I bazaars told me she can still remember the good smells of those long-ago afternoons. Another recalled the look and feel of the bazaar-related craft classes she took over forty years before. She could still picture the sun shining on projects laying out on tables in the church yard where the classes were held. "I remember the pleasure of that," she mused. Even the language used to describe a long-past fair was laden with sensual, dramatic imagery. Maude Howe Elliot, who recalled helping her mother at Civil War fairs, spoke of "festivals of patriotism" where halls were transformed for a week into "a wonderful hive of multicolored bees, all 'workers,' all humming."[59]

At an elaborate (e.g., turn-of-the-century) fair, every detail might be planned for maximum sensual effect. Visual stimulation was provided through eye-catching decorations, typically based on drama, variety and complexity, and bright color. Each booth might be a veritable study of form; stepping into a fair could mean encountering everything from the strong, angular lines of a windmill or a soaring triangular canopy to the studied composition of a latticework flower booth or the more intimate experience of a diorama-like table-top display with irregular, picturesque outlines (figs. 8, 9, 53, 57).[60] At other times the booths, saleswomen, and sales items all "matched," with a play on both color and idea. A "daffodil booth" might feature egg dishes, custards, and angel and sponge cakes under

The Costumed Procession at the Opening of the
Bazar of All Nations, Milwaukee, 1896

When, to the rumbling of a drum corps, the shrill music of the bagpipes, the strains of Clauder's military and Hensler's juvenile bands, the twanging of Japanese guitars and the tinkling of Spanish castanets and gypsy tambourines, the long procession of booth attendants, arrayed in all conceivable costumes, wound its way about the gallery and across the lower floor, the fortunate people who had obtained seats near the gallery railing gazed upon a spectacle rarely seen in these northern climes.

Before the march was called the floor presented an animated appearance. Graceful goddesses in Grecian robes of sea-green and white flirted with rakish-looking gypsy lads, and dignified dames in colonial dress of stiff brocades with powdered hair and patches promenaded with swarthy Mexicans in white duck trousers so wide that they might pass for divided skirts. Across the floor would toddle a dear little Jap maid under the protection of a gorgeous umbrella and then would come what might have been taken for old Father Time with his robe and long beard.

A group of nurses from the Training school in striped seersucker gowns, white caps and aprons, were in striking contrast to the high-born German maidens with their picturesque puffed sleeves and tiny head dresses. Highland chiefs, in all the bravery of tartan, exchanged notes with girls in the curious peaked black hats of Wales, and the French peasants and German warriors forgot old-time feuds. From the American headquarters tent would occasionally come women in the dress of the '60's, which, in spite of many points of resemblance to the gowns of '96, were hopelessly antiquated in appearance. Spanish damsels with fascinating mantillas, and Italian senoritas, all sorts of peasants, Irish, Swedish, Norwegian, Danish and Polish, in the distinctive dress of their nationality—added to the brilliancy of the scene, the like of which was never witnessed in this city before.

Suddenly a trumpet sounded, and there was a general scurrying back to booths, from each of which presently issued a procession, walking two by two. The gypsies, Spaniards and Mexicans came heralded by castanets and tambourines, scarlet military uniforms beating toy drums and singing the Marsellaise, the colonial and American sections by a drum corps, and all gathered in the gallery where a company of National guardsmen were in waiting.

The German village, a population of ancient warriors, peasants and nobility made a striking procession by itself as headed by costumed bell ringers and led by a juvenile band it wound its way in serpentine fashion through the hall and up stairs. The procession was so large that it more than reached around the gallery and when finally it appeared on the floor below and Mrs. Ely, with her beautiful white hair, took the lead, escorted by Sculptor Conway, the hopeless tangle in which the long line soon found itself could not have been avoided. But the snarl itself was picturesque, as all gathered in a huge group in the middle of the floor and there disbanded, each section departing for its own booth, where business was speedily begun.

—*Milwaukee Journal*
May 7, 1896

a large yellow umbrella; a "White City" table, inspired by the architecture of the Columbian Exposition, might sell white aprons, gloves, collars, and rice. Even tickets and invitations to fairs might be issued in thematic hues. The element of light was also exploited, and when electric light was still a novelty, this was very exciting. Effects could range from a "pink bower," bathed in pools of pink light created by tinted lampshades, to an entire "Rainbow Bazaar" featuring a waterfall running over four hundred rainbow-hued bulbs.[61]

Aural stimulation was provided at fairs by music, conversation, the clatter of dishes, footsteps, and sounds like the calls of peddlers and auctioneers. The proximate senses—touch, taste, and smell, which Yi-Fu Tuan insists are often undervalued by adults in our culture—were also heightened. Texture was stressed in sales items and costumes, and many booths were covered with highly tactile materials. A dome-shaped booth might be covered with cotton, for example, to evoke the sensation of a huge "snowball," or a simple lath framework might be hidden under abundant thatched grass (fig. 12). There were also enticing smells, such as the aroma of fresh flowers and the spicy fragrance of evergreens. The latter was mentioned consistently in descriptions of early fairs and was still evocative enough one hundred years later to be included in the bazaar scene of *Gone With the Wind*.[62] Other fairs were permeated

Lemonade in heavy mugs is served by small girls

by the odor of perfume (the exotic associations were made explicit in booths with titles like "The Odors of Araby")[63] or by the aromas from baked goods and other foods. Taste "treats" like ice cream were indispensable at fairs, and hearty meals were sometimes important in themselves. Even the action of the breeze might be used for sensual effect. A description of a 1904 fair echoes Santmeyer's description of fluttering butterflies on a Japanese hairpin. Here, the butterflies were made of crepe paper and suspended from invisible wires above a candy booth. They too "fluttered in the vibration of the air."[64] Costumes, of course, were also sensually stimulating. They rubbed against the wearer's body (imagine the effect of a crepe paper dress) and were sometimes sufficiently risqué to titillate the fairgoers.[65]

This kind of aesthetic elaboration typically strikes the twentieth-century observer as compulsive or overdone. Although the general response was more favorable in the premodern era, it was even remarked upon in its own time; its very exuberance was one of the salient characteristics of the fairs. J. M. Barrie satirized fairgivers' tendency to "cover" or embellish everything in sight. In "Bazaars," written for a souvenir book sold at an 1890 fundraising event, he made the tongue-in-cheek statement that one of the functions of a bazaar was the encouragement of art, for everything from a cigar to a grain of rice to an ink bottle or coal scuttle would be

Figs. 4 and 5. (above) "Lady Winter" and "Lady Spring" were featured at the "Fair of the Good Fairies." Lady Winter sold only "cold" items like ice cream and iced cakes. The stars at the top of Lady Spring's booth were said to represent "fairies' candles in the sky." From *Ladies' Home Journal,* October 1916.

Fig. 6. (right) Women enjoyed experimenting with other identities by dressing up as women from seemingly exotic times or places. This booth was outfitted with standard Japanese props, including parasols, lanterns, and fans. The upright posts were draped in fabric for a particularly exotic effect. From *Ladies' Home Journal,* November 1900.

hand-painted for the occasion.[66] While it may indeed have become obsessive at times, "making special" was what made the fair memorable.[67]

Again, fair preparation could also be a sensual experience. The woman who prepared the "Seaside Booth" described in *Harper's Bazar* in 1895, for example, might have spent weeks getting it ready. Decorated with oars, net, cork floats, and shells, the booth featured thematic sale items like scallop shell lampshades.[68] The woman might have spent hours roaming the shore, observing, experiencing, and collecting materials. She might have taken the shells and other materials home, sorted and cleaned them, and eventually turned them into finished products. Preparing for the fair would have included the experience of sand beneath the feet, the ocean breeze, the smell of the sea, and the feel of the shells and stone and driftwood. It was a tactile involvement that could leave a lasting impression.

Playfulness was also evident in another type of aesthetic elaboration: poetry and word play. The very occasion of the woman-identified fair seemed to inspire men to pen verses in the early nineteenth century, and for decades poems were routinely included in the

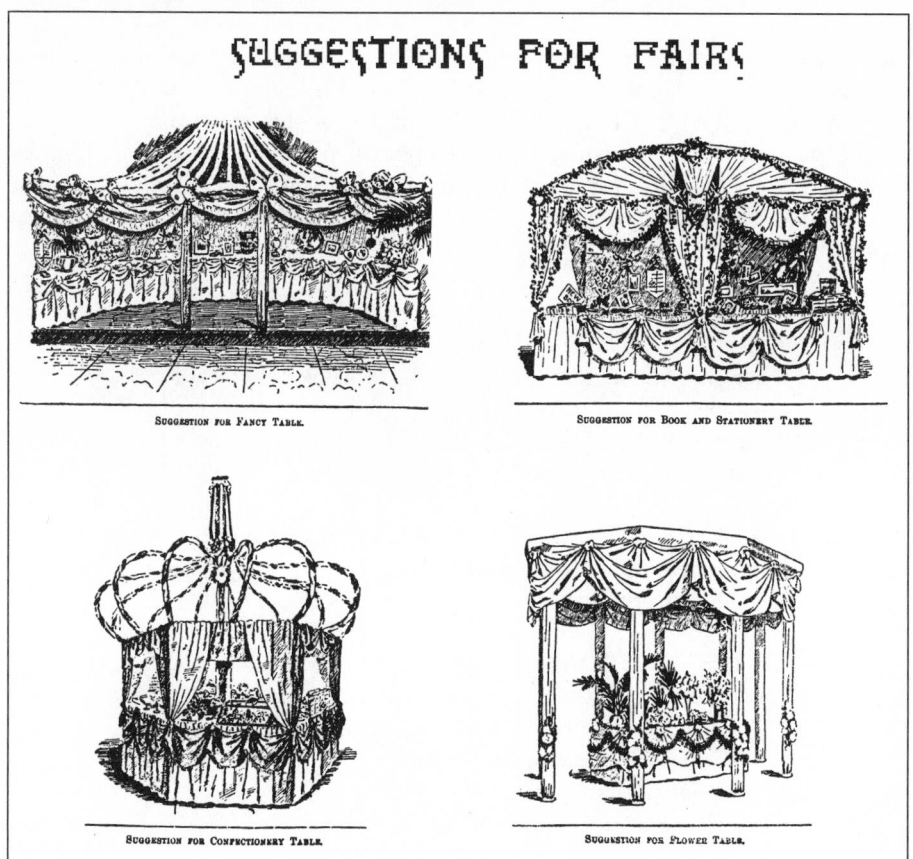

Fig. 7. Images that appeared in the February 1895 "Suggestions For Fairs" article in *The Delineator* illustrate how each booth functioned as a miniature stage-set that was complete unto itself. Many booths even included the proscenium arch that was so familiar to theater-goers.

Fig. 8. (left) A towering
structure made with
children's hoops was illustrated in *Ladies' Home
Journal* in October 1907.
The sale items (toys) are
suspended from the hoops.

Fig. 9. (right) This flower
booth, designed by
Winnifred Fales and il-
lustrated in *Ladies' Home
Journal* in November 1914,
is based on the premise
that booths should be
unique and eye catching.

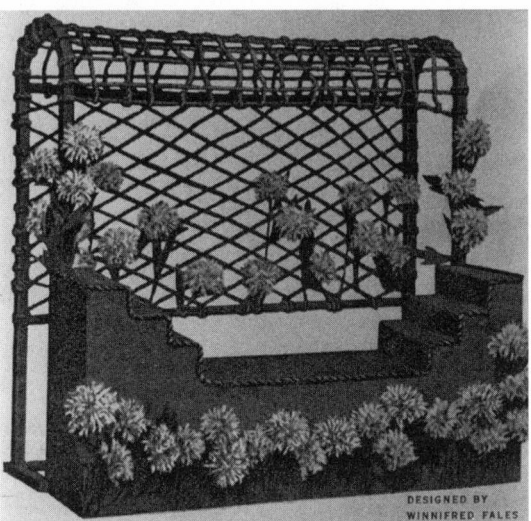

special newspapers written for many of the larger events. By the latter part of the century,
the poetry was usually humorous; rhyme was pointedly used as a play with the event and
with language. As Dissanayake points out, words taken out of their everyday context take
on a greater potency, and become the essence of ritual. Word play was used to heighten
the experience of the fair. In 1875, popular women's magazine *Godey's Lady's Book* published a poem that reinforced humorous conventions about the fair and gently satirized
fairgoers and fairgivers:

> . . . opening the entrance door, what is it meets my view?
> A host of lovely fairies, in robes of every hue.
> They gazed upon me sweetly, they had such winning ways
> That, before I understood it, my head was in a daze . . .
> I had stopped at all their tables that I might look and question,
> And gazing at their beauty got a horrid indigestion.[69]

A "poetic summons" to a bazaar work party published in a Madison newspaper in 1915
indicates how word play and its lighthearted tone was even incorporated into a routine
task like calling fellow workers together:

> Tenth ward Circle will give a shower
> Next Wednesday, the 14th, 3:00 is the hour.
> Our friend, Mrs. Coombs, a hostess most kind,
> At 1934 Monroe Street you'll find.
> Bring idea, material and pattern complete,
> For something which will with ready sale meet.[70]

Alliteration and puns have also been commonly worked into fairs from the earliest era to the present. Sale goods at the antebellum abolitionist fairs, for example, included "anti-slavery [pot]holders" (fig. 18) and "anti-Graham crackers" (this was a political pun; Graham was from a rival abolitionist group). Verbal and conceptual punning was evident at the turn of the century in Lady Winter's "iced" goods (fig. 4), the orange color scheme at a fair held in Orange, New Jersey, and "Miss Cholly Flower," who presided over a produce booth. More recently, a Madison senior citizen group's "Ap-pealing Boutique" featured a partially peeled apple on its publicity posters. Visual punning was evident in functional items made to look like something else— pincushions made as butterflies, for example, or as fish or pieces of fruit (figs. 45–46).[71] There were also mock art galleries featuring commonplace objects with humorous, pun-based labels. A broken piece of toast, for example, would be labeled "The Parting Toast," and attributed to Childe. A pile of hay might be labeled "The Horse Fair, after Rosa Bonheur." Even restaurant menus were filled with double entendres. The oyster course at the 1900 Masonic Fair in Atlanta was announced with the line "A Slippery Treat"; the ice cream with the line "Farewell Heat and Welcome Frost." Sometimes there were even puns on the very concept of the fair. "There are many kinds of fairs," the gathering was told at the opening speech of a New York event. "After you get into a fair you see 'the fair' and 'the fair' go around and show you the af-fair, and sometimes they treat you fairly and sometimes you fare badly."[72]

Advisors about successful fairs often included reminders about this kind of playful treatment. The authors of a 1924 instruction book stated pointedly that humorous placards should be used in profusion at fairs. Fifty years later, Dorothea Britton expressly recommended in her 1970s workshops on bazaar organizing that fairgivers play with language to loosen up their creative process and create a happy atmosphere at their events. She suggested looking at popular trends and free associating. The "kitchen witch," a product currently on the market, could, for example, be taken to "kitchen bitch," "kitchen snitch," and even "closet queen." The point was to make something that would "make everyone smile."[73]

Fig. 10. This page from *The American Girl's Handy Book* (1893) illustrates two of the thematic ideas in vogue at the turn of the century. The booth in the background is topped by flags that proclaim the month of May; May baskets and other springtime objects are for sale. The insert illustrates a "Seeing" booth at a Fair of the Five Senses. Mirrors, lamps, lanterns, and stereopticon views are among the sale items.

Fig. 11. (left) Turn-of-the-century fairgoers were fascinated by effects created by electric light, especially as filtered through colored lampshades. The fact that lamps and lampshades were themselves the focus of this candy booth illustrates their novelty and appeal. From *Ladies' Home Journal,* July 1917.

Fig. 12. (right) A highly textural "grass hut" was one of several designs featuring thatch and straw illustrated in *Ladies' Home Journal* just after the turn of the century. This example was ostensibly Hawaiian, but it is similar to the "native hut" at the Cuban American Fair of 1896. From *Ladies' Home Journal,* November 1900.

Exhibition and Aesthetic Training Centers

Fairs also had aesthetic meaning in that they served as exhibition centers for women's creative work. Well-made items found a receptive audience at a fair, and the best products were always the first to be sold. Handmade items were subjected to aesthetic scrutiny by a community of peers, in other words, and were acknowledged and credited by that community. This kind of aesthetic outlet was extremely important because much of the women's work took forms that fell outside the standard definition of art posited by the society at large—needlework, for example, was judged to be a merely decorative or "minor" art. It was only in a woman's space like a fair that such work was able to take center stage and be understood, appreciated, and critically evaluated.[74] Other scholars have previously pointed out the importance of exhibitions of women's work at agricultural fairs and women's exhibits at international expositions.[75] The fundraising fair provided the same kind of reinforcement, but it also allowed room for more playful or fanciful work, and as we have seen, helped transform that work into something more than evidence of domestic labor and accomplishment. Fundraising fairs still function as showplaces for women's art today.

During the nineteenth and early twentieth centuries, fundraising fairs also functioned as temporary galleries for work done by prominent artists (male and female) in more prestigious media. Until about 1870, expositions and fairs were often *the* most likely place individuals could go to see exhibitions of so-called fine art, for public art museums were not common until the end of the century. Paintings were displayed at fundraising fairs at least as early as 1842. Large art galleries featuring well-known artists such as Frederick Church were among the most successful features of the Civil War sanitary fairs, and it was there that many people of varying backgrounds had their first exposure to both collections of art and important individual artworks. Since the galleries showcased American artists in particular, they also helped

Confederate Memorial Bazaar.

RESTAURANT.

•••• ARMORY HALL. ••••

Mock-Turtle Soup	10c.	Maccaroni	5c.
Cold Ham	10c.	Irish Potatoes	5c.
Beef Tongue	10c.	Asparagus	
Deviled Crabs	10c.	Tea, Bread and Butter	15c.
Croquettes, each	5c.	Coffee, Bread and Butter	15c.
Chicken Salad	25c.	Chocolate, Bread and Butter	15c.
Fried Oysters, 3 for	10c.	Bouillon	10c.
Stewed Oysters	10c.	Salted Almonds	10c.
Half Spring Chicken		Fruit Snow Balls	15c.
Sweet Breads	30c.	Plain Cake	10c.
Sweet Breads with Green Peas	50c.	Jelly Cake	10c.
Stuffed Eggs	10c.	Sponge Cake	5c.
Roast Beef	10c.	Ice Cream	15c.
Beef Steak	25c.	Strawberries	
Veal Cutlets	10c.		
Lamb Chops	10c.		
Baked Tomatoes	5c.		
Spinach	5c.		

☞ Parties are respectfully requested to vacate the Tables as soon as they have finished eating.

Fig. 13. A variety of hearty foods was served at the restaurant at the Confederate Memorial Bazaar in Richmond, Virginia, in 1893. Oysters, which were featured in two dishes here, were popular at fair restaurants throughout the nineteenth century. Courtesy of the Museum of the Confederacy, Richmond, Virginia.

strengthen the perception that there was significant indigenous culture on the western side of the Atlantic. Painting exhibits continued to be routinely included in fairs until about World War I and resurfaced again after World War II.

A final point about the aesthetic meaning of the fairs is that they served as training centers or laboratories in which women could learn about aesthetic issues—about painting and sculpture, but even more significantly, about effective or good design and aesthetic quality. We have seen how, in order to stage a successful fair, the women would have to consider the effects of color, light, texture, scale, and other design principles. They might pick this up informally from a particularly skilled individual who took the lead and made suggestions or offered critiques, but instruction and guidance was also offered in the popular press. At first,

Fig. 14. The "Oriental Water Carrier" must have been strongly aware of her costume at all times as she served lemonade, for her dress was made of paper. The caption that accompanied this illustration stated that "the importance of unique dressing cannot be overemphasized." From *Ladies' Home Journal,* July 1919.

Oriental Water Carrier

IN SOFT flowing crêpe-paper robes of the East, she serves you lemonade in to-day's sanitary style: from a porcelain container, in paper cups.

instruction focused exclusively on sale objects, but by the time of the Civil War every feature of the fair environments might be described in great detail, even in newspapers like the *New York Times.* After about 1875, the proliferating books and articles offered pointed and practical design instruction. In her 1895 "Suggestions for Fairs," for example, Margaret Nourse clarified what happens to individual colors when they are seen under different lighting conditions.[76] This training helped many women develop a design vocabulary and greater artistic competence.

The idea that fairs served as centers for aesthetic training is also evident in the close identification between the fairs and the era's artistic movements. At the turn of the century, art organizations and magazines that identified themselves with the Aesthetic and Arts and Crafts movements (e.g., *Ladies' Home Journal, House Beautiful*) all aligned themselves with the woman's fair. *Art Amateur,* a periodical geared to the artistic woman, even critically reviewed fair products in the 1870s. Instructions for fairgivers often discussed imagery of well-known artists and designers such as Walter Crane, and fair sale objects sometimes came from noted Arts and Crafts workshops.[77]

Pleasure in "Good Work"

The lighthearted tone of the fundraising fair always masked an enormous amount of effort or hard work on the part of the fairgivers. As references and previous descriptions of work parties make clear, however, the work was often experienced as— even transformed into—something that was in itself pleasurable. Even when there was no particular sensual stimulus like gathering materials at the seashore or putting on a transformative costume, the feeling that came from working together with others proved energizing. The busy-bee imagery used by the 1871 bazaar worker quoted earlier was echoed in a 1952 report of a temple bazaar: "Since the announcement [of the bazaar] the phones didn't stop buzzing, the sewing machines kept up a steady hum, the knitting needles flew, paints and brushes were taken out, lunch and dinner menus were dreamed up, your torn nylons were literally peeled off your legs. . . . It was a most gratifying experience to watch this day take form."[78]

The tedium of the work was certainly acknowledged; the 1871 commentary, in fact, began with references to the monotony and routine felt by those who worked at fair booths. All of this was softened, however, by the circumstances of the fair. "The excitement of successful traffic, the pleasant interviews with friends, and accidental encounters with unexpected acquaintances . . . above all, the growing consciousness of the success of our good cause, make light the even tenor of our way."[79]

The commentary also indicates the fairgivers' awareness of the make-work quality of their enterprise and the interpersonal games that were involved. "Well they know where lurks the pincushion, which must be sold, because Mrs. —— sent it; often have their tongues faltered as they mentioned the price of ——."[80] Even these irritations fell away in the end, though, and were outweighed by positive feelings. For every complaint about having to resort to a bazaar, there was an explanation that it was worth the effort because it served a higher good and brought people together in the process. These words were repeated again and again, and clearly reflected deeply-held feelings. We must not dismiss this kind of explanation as an excuse or compensatory remark; we must accept that doing "good work" was in itself often a source of pleasure and reward.

Rhetoric about moral goodness was at its peak in the antebellum era, but so was the rhetoric about bewitching young women who stole men's hearts and emptied their pocketbooks. In the next chapter we will take a detailed look at fairs that drew crowds of curious and excited individuals to a new kind of social outing. We will see how crusaders like Maria Weston Chapman marshaled the enthusiasm and energies of women on both sides of the Atlantic to work on fairs as a kind of holy cause, and how curiosity-seekers were drawn into the company of reformers with a radical message. We will examine the true "ladies fair," and look more closely at the kind of domestic and sexual power plays that imprinted themselves so deeply on the American consciousness.

CHAPTER TWO

The Tensions of the Antebellum Fair: Moral Crusades and "Bewitching" Ladies

---

We have vainly endeavored to quiet our excited nerves and compose ourselves to write, with truth and soberness, an account of the Ladies Fair [held] last Wednesday. . . . Having mended our goose quill (which, by the way we purchased at the Fair of one of the prettiest and most irresistible of all Salesmen) [we can begin.]

> —comment on a fair held by the Young Ladies Benevolent Society for the American Bible Society, *Northampton Courier,* Nov. 3, 1830

We have been accused of the sin of partiality to the ladies, but at the expense of our reputation we recommend all to attend the Ladies Fair, if for no other benevolent motive than that of seeing the fair *ladies.* Let [a man] purchase largely and pay liberally in behalf of her gratuitous and generous efforts; . . . the heart of woman expands with benevolence, and she delights in witnessing its influence and operation upon "sterner stuff."

The ladies are irresistible creatures, and unless one goes clad in an armour of cold selfishness and callous heartedness . . . he is sure to come away with his hat and his pockets filled with comical merchandise, and perhaps the loss of his [heart].

> —comment on a fair held in aid of the American Education Society, *Northampton Courier,* Oct. 26, 1831

The Earliest Fairs: Excitement
and a Play between the Sexes

In the 1830s, American newspapers were filled with dramatic rhetoric and pointed witticisms about ladies' fairs.[1] These comments indicate both how prevalent the woman's fair was becoming at this early date, and the kind of excitement and contradictory feelings it was engendering. It was something of a convention to pay tribute to female generosity and goodness, but the women's efforts were poked fun at, and it was sexual allure that was emphasized in these writings. The idea that women were selling themselves as well as their wares—that they were the real merchandise at the fair, as discussed in the previous chapter—was clearly implicit. In the men's own words, they could seemingly not resist a female salesperson, and they warned each other to "guard [their] hearts." An 1836 poem called *The Ladies Fair*, written in conjunction with a Long Island, New York, event, expressed it succinctly: "Who, then, can well refuse to buy, when they/Such lovely beings at each stand survey?" A commentator on a Weymouth, Massachusetts, fair asked, "Are all these nymphs bewitch'd for trade?" "Not quite bewitched their goods to sell," he replied, "But *witching*, if you note them well." The *Northampton Courier* remarked that single gentlemen could "supply themselves" at an upcoming (1835) fair with "some of the most beautiful products of *nature* as well as art;" "he who stays away will do well, but he who attends the sale . . . will do much better."[2]

The antebellum ladies' fair clearly dramatized the play between the sexes and their accepted domains. Women used the fairs to promote and support "good" causes like Bible societies and educational institutions, which were seen as extensions of their proper domestic sphere and fell within the realm of their supposedly natural interests and proclivities. As these quotations indicate, men paid lip service to the women's benevolence and the virtuosity of their causes, but did not seem to take them—or by extension, the domestic values they represented—seriously. According to the ideology that became entrenched with industrial capitalism, the woman's domestic domain was contrasted with the male's public, "worldly" sphere of commerce and industry. Men could operate in the marketplace because they were believed to be by nature more aggressive, pecuniary, and susceptible to lower passions than women. Women's altruistic, self-sacrificing, and moral qualities belonged more naturally in the home or in church.[3] The idea that women would engage in public commerce went against this separate sphere ideology, therefore, and represented a challenge to accepted norms. The men's condescension toward the fairs, including their dismissal of the women's "comical merchandise," stemmed from discomfort with these blurred boundaries; their distanced, slightly superior stance helped reinforce their own sense of authority and place.

The women were not victimized in this situation. They played up the men's discomfort, effectively using it for their own ends. They exploited the general belief in their moral superiority and authority, highlighting the domestic nature of their work and using its positive associations to garner support and sympathy. Many took full advantage of capitalistic attitudes and business practices, even while aligning themselves with altruistic causes and good works. They also played with their sexuality and the idea that they could bewitch men into buying goods they did not want. They recognized the fair as an efficacious way to raise money, in other words, and learned to manipulate it effectively. At the same time, they used it to enjoy themselves. The fair remained a social event, and even while women used it for serious purposes, they, like the men, still experienced it as an entertainment—a place to play.[4] In the antebellum period perhaps more than any other time, the fundraising fair represented something of a game—a playing field—where both sexes dramatized their roles and amused themselves with each other. It is not difficult to understand its popularity, or why it became a significant part of the social landscape in this country soon after it appeared in England.

The first reference I have found for an American fair dates to 1827, when a Baltimore group raised sixteen hundred dollars to support needy children victimized by the Greek War of Independence. Within a few years fair sponsorship was already considered an effective way for women to raise money. In 1831, when Sarah Josepha Hale (editor of the Boston-based *Ladies Magazine* and later the influential *Godey's Lady's Book*) campaigned for the completion of the monument at Bunker Hill memorializing the battles and fallen of the Revolution, she implored her readers to hold fairs to raise the necessary funds. By 1833 the *Northampton Courier* noted that such "interesting and useful exhibitions, got up and superintended by the ladies" were "becoming very fashionable." In the Northampton area alone, four different ladies' fairs were held in as many months. The earliest fairs were well publicized and stirred considerable interest; the public seems to have been hungry for information about them. The 1833 Boston "Grand Ladies' Fair" held in support of the blind was described in great detail in the Northampton newspaper, though the town was approximately one hundred miles west and outside the range of easy travel. The original reports focused on the general setup of the fair, but even two weeks later there were itemized lists of the articles on display.[5] Another hint of the prevalence and perceived importance of fairs was indicated in 1834 in a printed rebuttal to businessmen who had made a hostile "address to the citizens of Philadelphia on the subject of fancy fairs." The anonymous author of this counterattack—judging from the context, probably a woman—chided the men about their unwarranted concern with unfair competition for the city's businesses and the poor women who had to make their living with their needles. The arguments were refuted in great detail. It is likely that fewer fairs were given in the South in this period. I have found fewer references in southern newspapers, and certainly nothing quite so forward as the Philadelphia rebuttal has emerged from any southern city. Nevertheless, the events were by no means a northern phenomenon. Organizations like the Richmond (Virginia) Female Humane Association were among the earliest documented fair sponsors.[6]

Fairgivers and Their Causes

The Richmond group represented a new kind of voluntary society that was proliferating in tandem with women's fairs. Such societies ranged from maternal associations, in which women strove to perfect themselves in order to become exemplary mothers and thus raise the character of succeeding generations, to groups dedicated to reforming the moral character of others or providing for those in poorer circumstances than themselves. All of these societies were predicated on a belief in woman's role as the compassionate, moral guardian of society, and through them women reaffirmed the values of their sphere. Many of the groups were relatively unstructured and informal, focusing loosely on reform rather than holding to a specific agenda, but others were more pointed. Some had grown out of pre-existing church or sewing circles and combined good works with evangelism. The most radical end of the spectrum included the women's societies dedicated to a highly political moral cause—the abolition of slavery.

Whatever their orientation, almost all of these voluntary groups included sewing and needlework among their activities. At "cent" and "Dorcas" societies, for example, gatherings were usually devoted to sewing for the poor. (The cent society took its name from the custom of donating a penny to the group at each meeting; Dorcas societies were named after a Biblical character—a pious, generous woman who sewed clothes for the needy [Acts 9:36–43].) In "fragment" and "scrap" societies, members joined together small scraps to form a usable fabric that might keep someone warm.[7] The sales of needlework that evolved into fairs represented a variation on the theme of charitable sewing and, based as they were on the women's primary marketable skill, were a logical way for the groups to raise money. Society members even presented sewing as a kind of moral force. An 1834 notice in *The Liberator,* the publication of the Boston Anti-Slavery Society, implored the "philanthropic ladies of New England" to use their needles for the "cause of bleeding humanity." In 1835 the abolitionists stated, "We have not forgotten that the needle may be used in the cause of the oppressed in our own land, as well as for suffering Greece, and the benighted millions of India."[8]

The antislavery fairs were highly focused, but like some of the voluntary organizations that sponsored them, other early fairs were rather general in their intent; enthusiasm for the idea of a fair seems to have been stronger at times in the 1830s than dedication to a particular cause. Fairs were often announced without indication of a specific purpose: they were simply "to aid the cause of charity." Decisions sometimes had to be made almost after the fact about where the money earned at a fair would go. Individual charitable societies also changed their focus over time. An Andover, Massachusetts, group came together in 1831 as a "Reading Association," for example, and the $120 it earned at its first fair presumably went to a related cause. In 1832 proceeds were donated to the Seaman's Friend Society, and in 1838 the group reconstituted itself as a mission society, with fair proceeds going to church work.[9]

Who were the members of these benevolent organizations? Scholars who have studied the phenomenon agree that the groups were very widespread and were di-

Excerpt, *"The Ladies' Fair," A Poem in Aid of the Ladies' Scrap Society,* 1836

The ladies, foremost in each noble cause,
Command our admiration and applause!

. . . Such a society whose efforts shew,
What good, if but disposed, we all might do;
And whose benevolence, and fervent aim,
Our high regard, and admiration claim.

Joined in a band of union, and good will
Each member strives her portion to fulfill,
The scraps are saved, which once were thrown
     away,
And thus a lesson to us all convey,—
Never to waste, not e'en the smallest thing,
Which, into use, hereafter, we may bring;
Since, hence are furnished what around we see,
Wrought with much taste, and ingenuity.

The articles prepared throughout the year
Are annually disposed of at a Fair,—
"The Ladies Fair"—'tis called, for well they
     claim
The credit, who thus put our sex to shame.

Now all attend, and something here they buy
For friendship's sake, or that of charity;
As best may please the fancy or the eye—
A little basket, purse, or needle-case,—
Or pocket-book, in which the Ladies place
Their work, and thimble, scissors, bodkin too,—
Or yet perchance a lover's billet-doux,—
And all the implements wherewith they sew;
Thread, silk and cotton, tape, and pins beside,
Which every housewife should at once provide.

. . . But, should some fragments still remain on
     hand,
The Ladies some kind of gentleman command,
To hold at night an auction, or vendue,
Thus to dispose of all the residue;
Whom purchasers, en masse, encircle round,
Whilst bidders for each lot are quickly found;
Hence competition heightens every sale,
And mirth and fun throughout the room prevail.

—for the fair at Christ Church,
North Hemsptead, New York, 1836

verse enough so that many different kinds of women might participate.[10] The groups most likely to sponsor fairs in the 1830s and 1840s typically had fairly educated members, many of whom were wives or daughters of professional men. Frances Trollope's rather sarcastic 1832 treatise on *The Domestic Manners of the Americans* includes a description of a Philadelphia Dorcas Society meeting attended by wives of senators and lawyers of "the highest repute." (The ladies worked together producing objects like pincushions, penwipers, and watchcases, talking "of priests and missions, the profits of their last sale, and their hopes from the next.")[11] Northampton fair organizers were also often married to judges, ministers, or doctors, and many of the abolitionist fairgivers were similarly well connected. While some of these individuals were in fact wealthy, they were not aristocratic or "leisured" in the same sense as their English counterparts. Whatever their income, they were likely to see themselves as middle class.[12]

If there seems to be a disjuncture between this portrait of established matrons and the alluring young ladies indicated in the reporters' romantic prose, it is easily explained. The majority of the women in charge of the fairs were married and probably past the stage of rearing young children, but they made sure that it was their younger helpers who were most visible. Records from 1840s fairs indicate that the majority (e.g., twelve of fourteen) of the managers and women in charge of individual tables were married, while the majority (twenty-nine of thirty-three) of the salespeople were not. A reminiscence about the antislavery fairs similarly indicated that large numbers of young people came to help out, but they reported to Mrs. Chapman and other matrons.[13] The presence of the young women was heavily touted for its effect, in other words, but they did not generally have the organizing ability, the social position, or the experience to see the fairs through from beginning to end.

For most of the antebellum period, the great majority of fairgivers were white Protestants of Anglo-Saxon descent, although small numbers of women of other groups were also involved. As indicated in chapter 1, I have not determined if there were fairs in Hispanic communities in Florida or what became the American Southwest, but in what was then the United States, Catholics and Jews held fairs by the 1850s.[14] A few black women participated in antislavery fairs as contributors and saleswomen as early as 1834, but by mid-century, they too were organizing and producing their own events. Some of their fairs funded Methodist Episcopal churches, while others targeted racial equality or African American relief. In Rochester, New York, the Union Anti-Slavery Society held fairs to raise money for Frederick Douglass and joined with radical white abolitionists to manage the large annual fair held in Corinthian Hall. In 1849 in that city, one hundred people of "all classes and colors sat down to eat together."[15] The Women's Association of Philadelphia was another African American group formed in support of Frederick Douglass (specifically, in support of his weekly paper *The North Star*). Fairgiving was even mentioned in the constitution of this group: the object of the association was "to hold Fairs or Bazaars for the support of the Press and Public Lecturers, devoted to the Elevation of the Colored People of the United States." A different North Star Association, formed in New York City, raised over a thousand dollars for the Colored Orphan Asylum at an 1860 fair. Contributions came in to this fair from other communities, some as far away as Troy, Ohio.[16]

Perhaps because the American fair did not carry the same quality of *noblesse oblige* as its English prototype, it was not a monolithic institution; as indicated, it was adapted by individuals with a range of ethical and political beliefs. Some of the contradictions and tensions that surrounded antebellum fairs were exacerbated by the fact that different groups tried to shape them as they respectively saw fit. When moral reform groups were the sponsors, for example, they often downplayed the commercial and made a point of highlighting the domestic. From descriptions of the fairs, the differences seem at times to have been more symbolic than substantive, but they still seemed to matter a great deal.

The idea that the fair might function as contested territory is well illustrated by the story of the struggle for control of the Boston Female Anti-Slavery Fair. The abolitionist community had split into two factions in the 1830s—a radical group linked with William Lloyd Garrison and an evangelical group linked with Amos Phelps. The factions represented what Nancy Hewitt characterized as political versus moral "suasionists."[17] Moral suasionists advocated individual conversion as the primary means of social change and criticized the church's collaboration with slaveholders. They hoped to bring the antislavery message to a wide audience. They effectively embraced the values identified with the domestic sphere, in other words, and used them to achieve their goals. In contrast, the political suasionists were actively involved with male-identified activities and institutions. They were not concerned with religion; rather, they pressed for legislative change through the political arena. (Ironically, their own associations were separatist, for they believed women could best influence the movement from their own gender-based groups.)[18] There was also a class difference between the factions, as Debra Hansen argues in *Strained Sisterhood: Gender and Class in the Boston Female Anti-Slavery Society*. She characterizes the political group as wealthier and socially well connected, even referring to leader Maria Weston Chapman as a "socialite-turned-radical." Hansen dem-

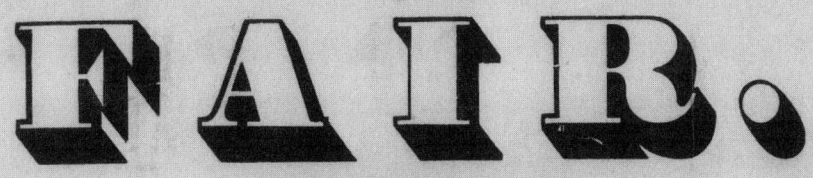

FAIR.

The Ladies (of color) of the town of Frankfort propose giving a **FAIR**, at the house of Mrs. **RILLA HARRIS**, (*alias*, Simpson,) on Thursday evening next, for benevolent purposes, under the superintendence of Mrs. **Rilla Harris**.

All the delicacies of the season will be served up in the most palatable style----such as *Ice Creams, Cakes, Lemonades, Jellies, Fruits, Nuts, &c. &c.*

It is hoped, as the proceeds are to be applied to benevolent purposes, that the citizens generally will turn out and aid in the enterprise.

JULY 6, 1847.

Fig. 15. This handbill, announcing a fair given by a group of African Americans in Kentucky in 1847, was typical of the type of publicity fair organizers used in the antebellum era. Note that the "benevolent purposes" the fair is supporting are not specified. Courtesy of the William L. Clements Library, University of Michigan.

onstrates that Chapman worked to attract the upper class to the fairs she organized and to associate the whole enterprise with the "local aristocracy." The evangelicals were more solidly middle class and did not have ties to the elite.[19]

The "battle of the fairs" began in 1839, when the evangelicals wrested control of the Boston Female Anti-Slavery Society by taking over its annual fundraising event. Chapman and her friends had instituted the fair five years before, and it had become such a significant source of income and publicity that this was a major coup. The radical women were furious. They disassociated themselves from the "bogus" event and sent protest letters to abolitionists throughout New England. They mounted their own "Fair of Individuals," assuring the public that it was the "true" antislavery fair. The rent in the organization was so deep that the group broke apart in 1840, splitting into the Massachusetts Female Anti-Slavery Society (Chapman's radical wing) and the Massachusetts Abolition Society (the evangelical wing). The latter group soon stopped holding fairs, but for several years there were competing events in the same city. As might be expected, the evangelical or moral suasion group emphasized the domestic at their fair. They called it a sale and expressly favored handmade products like aprons and workbags. Their decorations consisted of evergreens and other natural elements; decorations that were too fancy were considered unsuitable. Chapman's group was happy to proclaim its event a fair, to stress the material, and to generally create a treat for the senses. Its 1840 fair was even dubbed a "soiree," with decorations such as porcelain, silver candelabras, and reproduction Italian paintings. Women's products were certainly prominent among the sale goods, but exotic commercial items like English china were also included—so much so that eventually there were complaints about the antislavery fair's undercutting local business.[20] In the case of these two groups, then, there were indeed tangible differences in their fairs. Nevertheless, in the popular mind they tended to blend together—they were both antislavery fairs. It becomes easier to understand how, given the different approaches to fairs and their varying characters, the institution itself could be heralded both as a showplace of domesticity and of commercialism and crass behavior.

An Atmosphere of Abundance, Pleasure, and Romance

Most antebellum fairs seem to have fallen between the extremes represented by the evangelical and radical abolitionists' events, but since fairs *were* entertainments, fairgivers were effectively pressured to highlight the pleasurable. Typically, they strove for a lighthearted tone, a sense of abundance, and a quality of prettiness. Spaces—whether rooms in private homes or public or community halls (fairs were not held in churches before mid-century)[21]—were always transformed in some manner. The greenery used by the evangelical antislavery women was an almost expected kind of treatment. Not only were the tables dressed with evergreens and flowers at an 1833 Northampton fair, but the walls were "almost concealed" by foliage and shrubbery. A Boston fair of the same year featured such a profusion of these elements (including an evergreen arch framing one end of the room) and of artificial fruits and singing birds, that one observer was reminded of a "new Paradise." Abundant lamps and candles typically also made the rooms seem especially bright and cheerful.[22]

By the 1840s some fair organizers were struggling to come up with fresh ideas to transform the space even more dramatically and bring yet more people into the fairs. Maria Weston Chapman seems to have had a particular gift for these innovations, and the 1840 soiree was only one of her many dramatic environments. She was also responsible for the Christmas tree mentioned in the first chapter. Unquestionably, it had great sensual (aesthetic) appeal: "[It was covered with] gilded apples, glittering strings of nuts, tissue paper purses filled with glittering egg baskets and crystals of many colored sugar, with every possible needlebook, pincushion, bag, basket, cornucopia, penwiper and doll that could be afforded for ninepence. [It was illuminated by] wax candles and colored lamps."[23]

Most objects at antebellum fairs were displayed on tables placed in the center of the room or against the walls. These were arranged to give the impression of plenty: tables were inevitably said to be "filled," covered with a "profusion" of objects, or "heaped with goods." (A *Boston Advocate* reporter even calculated the number of goods available at an 1833 fair. He counted 7,280 separate articles, most of which were "handmade by the ladies.")[24] The image of abundance in fact extended to the whole gestalt of the fair; even the hall was typically reported as "filled," "thronged," or "bustling." Historian Harvey Green has pointed out that images of abundance were common symbols in the antebellum era, and we can see how they helped contribute to the sense of well-being and moral righteousness of the fairs.[25] At the same time, phrases like "heaped with goods" echoed contemporary descriptions of the Oriental bazaar. The imagery must have reinforced the sense of the exotic and tantalizing nature of the ladies' fair.

Crowding was, however, more than a rhetorical device. Fairs were such attractions that large numbers did attend (fig. 16). The night the tree was unveiled at the 1842 Massachusetts Anti-Slavery Fair, the crowds were so great that many could not get in. Seemingly "the whole city" of Boston came to a hall which had a capacity of eight hundred, creating an enormous "crunch" and "press" of people. "My wife and children are upstairs," one man who was refused entry said sarcastically, "and I hope to see them again by tomorrow morning." The crowd was so large that the organizers could not follow their original plan to distribute the prizes on the tree.[26] Similar problems were reported in diverse locations. The Northampton papers typically mentioned "throngs" of fairgoers. In England, the doors to Covent Garden had be closed repeatedly to the capacity crowds trying to get into a large bazaar, even though the Garden could accommodate nine thousand. People waited on the sidewalk through a heavy rainstorm, but even when they could get in, they were pushed or "rolled" along. Eventually, organizers raised the admission price in an effort to help reduce the crowds. At a festival held by the Buffalo Benevolent Association in 1859, over two thousand people were admitted, but hundreds more were left waiting outside. In Charleston, South Carolina, an 1850 fair was "overwhelmed" with people. "The Hall is too small and the atmosphere too oppressive for anything like comfort," the *Daily Courier* complained.[27]

When they did get in, as we have seen, there were many features that helped fairgoers feel pleasure. With the sound of cheerful music in the background, they might feast on an abundance of "treats"—varieties of cakes and pastry, custard, ice creams, jellies and fruits, wine and lemonade. Most were tempted by the wealth of attractive sale goods. Even when the fair was a modest one that stressed handmade, nonluxury sale goods, fairgivers tried to make them as appealing as possible, even advertising them as items to "please the eye, gratify the taste, and tickle the fancy." Sale items could seem "fancier" if they were made with unusual materials or presented in an imaginative manner, and thus we find references to baskets made with fragile-looking, ephemeral materials like pieces of wheat or sprigs of lavender, and references to costumed dolls arranged in vignettes or tableaux. The 1842 Massachusetts Anti-Slavery Fair included a doll dressed as an Irish nurse, a peasant doll shown "driving pigs," and a bridal doll displayed in an evergreen bower. Some conservative groups were concerned about the trend toward increasing fancifulness (members of a Rochester society, for example, expressed concern by 1849 that local farm families would find the sale items "too ornamental"), but even they seem to have continued to make them that way.[28]

The lighthearted tone of the prototypical antebellum fair was even carried into print through special fair newspapers (the regular press referred to their prose as "sprightly and amusing"). Typically, these were published daily for the duration of a given fair. They included descriptions of the fair, stories, poems, humorous anecdotes, and observations on uncontroversial topics. They had something of the feeling of a gossip sheet, but were mild and inoffensive. The newspapers helped make the fairs into *events* that warranted press coverage; in today's terms, we would say they were a part of the dramatic performance. They heightened the excitement level and furthered a sense of (temporary) community, and they could be taken home as mementos of the fair experience. Other fair elements functioned similarly. Often, the whole event was often capped off with an auction of unsold goods, which served as a kind of finale and engendered good-natured competition and community feeling (see the sidebar from *The Ladies Fair* above).[29]

The newspapers, auctions, admission fees, and proceeds from attractions like fortune-telling booths all added to the net profits, and despite their frivolous tone the fairs raised considerable sums of money. In the earliest days (the 1830s) in Northampton, profits were typically in the $300–$350 range. Springfield, Massachusetts, fairs yielded about $600 in the same period, and a Salem fair earned over $3,000.[30] In other words, profits depended at least in part on the size of the community and the relative wealth of its citizens. It is impossible, however, to arrive at any dependable figure of the total amount raised at fairs in any one location. Some small-

scale fairs were never reported in the press, and when they were, profits were not always indicated. Causes that were funded by fairs also received contributions from cent and mission societies and from direct appeals in churches. The system was so informal that no central records were kept. In 1835 the *Northampton Courier* reported the ladies of the town raised $1,100 through their "various little societies," but the societies were not delineated. This money went to aid equally unspecified "religious, moral and charitable associations in the state."[31]

Although one 1834 Massachusetts fair was said to be "closed to gentlemen," this was unusual, and may have in itself been a pose designed to tease out interest. On the contrary, many of the amusements of the antebellum fair explicitly played on sexual tension. Women were as likely as men to adopt a teasing, flirtatious manner and to play up the idea that the "fair ladies" were indeed irresistible. Flirtatious poems appearing in fair newspapers like *The Weal-Reaf* ("How many a young gallant, alas!/ Who having tried his best/Returns with an aching heart/A (pen)wiper in his breast") may well have been penned by the women themselves.[32] Some of the women's activi-

Fig. 16. The unidentified artist who sketched this comical portrait of a "bazaar and fancy fair" portrayed the same sort of densely packed crowd described in most written descriptions of antebellum fairs. The well-dressed, busy shoppers are accompanied by the music of a brass band, visible at the top of the image. The illustration appeared in Britain's *Cornhill Magazine*, September 1861.

ties specifically functioned as sexual games. By 1836 they had instituted post office booths, for example, where male customers could always find eager young ladies ready to hand them "personal" mail for a small fee. One such booth was described in the 1836 poem written "in aid of the Ladies Scrap Society:"

> . . . we see from younder office fly
> Letters dispatched by post to standersby;
> Who their contents quite eagerly peruse,
> As if they'd just received important news,—
> And so delighted seem with what they say
> That they inquire for more throughout the day;
> Certain to find them ready to command,
> Delivered out by some young fairy hand.[33]

The women also dressed up as "fate ladies" (fortune tellers) and gave amusing or slightly risqué readings. At the 1842 Massachusetts Anti-Slavery Fair where readings were offered for four and a half cents, for example, one visitor was told that her husband was deceiving her. Sometimes too the women provided an unexplained attraction called "The Gentleman's Horror." "Those who [have] explored this mysterious stall," noted the *Boston Transcript* in 1840, "keep an impenetrable silence."[34]

Contemporary newspaper reporters, like fiction writers, offered images of the fair as a sexual meeting ground. The *Northampton Democrat* described one event as follows: "young farmers and mechanics might be seen in every direction in *tete-a-tete* with their sweethearts, while old bachelors were attempting to look love and whisper soft sawder [*sic*] in the ears of their never-to-be-obtained lady loves."[35] It is difficult to determine how accurate this kind of characterization was: did the fundraising fair really function as a liminal space where sexual mores were somewhat loosened, or was it all a grand rhetorical pose? My guess is that the truth lay between the two extremes. The fair environment allowed the participants to play up their sexuality, but it remained a romantic game, or a piece of theater, fully contained within the stage of that environment. This was actually a safe way to play with these roles, and the games need not be carried into "real life." It is certainly the case that I have not encountered a single substantiated reference to actual immorality at a fair. While the women no doubt enjoyed dressing up and acting wanton and uninhibited, they *were* acting; they were playful and rather innocent. If they were selling themselves, it was in a metaphoric rather than a literal sense. It is interesting to note, too, that when women talked about the fairs, they rarely focused on the game playing or sexual poses. Their letters and commentary were usually concerned with the work involved in the fair and with its ultimate purpose. They sometimes referred to the good feelings the fair engendered, but these came from the kind of fellowship and aesthetic satisfaction discussed in the previous chapter, not from sexual activity.[36]

The Work of the Fair: Networking, Organization, and Preparation

Despite any helpless poses or rhetoric about women's unsuitability for the work of the marketplace, antebellum fairgivers actually demonstrated an impressive amount of organizational savvy and sophistication about running a complex community event. From decisions about when and where to hold a fair to planning details regarding features like fortune-telling booths, they made good use of their resources and indicated keen awareness about the world they were operating in. Their ability to work with whatever would be most efficacious in any given situation is testimony to their agency and innovativeness.

Antebellum fairgivers used their distinct "women's culture" to good advantage. They repeatedly emphasized the separate, *female* nature of the fundraising fair. For example, the organizers of the 1840 Bunker Hill Monument fair (a consortium of "patriotic New England women") called women to band together and be counted as a group. By acting together, the organizers said, the women would accomplish what men had not (i.e., the completion of the monument) and would build a sense of solidarity and connection. Many other appeals to women reminded them that they were "excluded from direct interference in political matters," but by contributing to the fair in question, they might directly and noticeably affect social conditions. Some made specific or pointed references to "injured sisters" and distressed families.[37]

Existing women's networks were used to great advantage for various aspects of the fairs. At events like the Monument Fair, organizers operated a central office in Charlestown that handled publicity and physical arrangements, but many of the contributions came from local organizations (e.g., from ladies' church circles and voluntary associations) in communities across the region. Each group was responsible for a table at the fair, which was identified by a scroll or banner, and, not surprisingly, the groups vied with one another for the best displays. The good-natured competition stimulated quality work and creative presentation, but it in no way reduced the sense of sisterhood the women from the different communities felt with one another. When the monument was at last completed, Massachusetts women held a special celebration. Fifteen hundred ladies who had worked for the fair came from all over the state for the festivities in 1843.[38]

In the case of the antislavery fairs, there was even a transatlantic dimension to the women's networking. Chapman's organization was able to count on contributions from British sympathizers who had themselves organized antislavery societies. They followed American events through *The Anti-Slavery Reporter* and various missionary publications, and regularly sent fancywork and other goods to Boston. Just as important, perhaps, they also sent statements of support. In 1848 forty thousand Scottish women signed such a document. When an "endless line" of signatures was festooned around the walls at the Massachusetts fair, there was still not enough room for all of them.[39]

Did the women function in a truly gender segregated world—were men involved in any aspects of fair organization? In most cases in the early years men's presence was nominal, although once the efficacy of the institution was apparent and it was clear the fairs were not a passing fad, there was a certain amount of male encroachment.[40] Most typically, men were recruited to carry out tasks that their business connections made possible, such as drawing up contracts or soliciting contributions from merchants. Sometimes they spoke "for" the women (the seemliness of women's public speaking was still in question), but they were actually mouthing what the women wanted them to say. Tellingly, the men who were most involved in these activities were often married to fair organizers.[41] This kind of legalistic fiction also prevailed in other arenas in the nineteenth century; as Rook and Schnell put it in describing the organization of orphan's homes, the ladies "watched as men drew up documents."[42]

Many details of fair operations show how thoughtful and farsighted the organizers were. When they appealed for contributions, for example, they gave supporters plenty of time, encouragement, and even guidance or alternative options about fair items. Appeals for donations went out several months before a fair; antislavery activists, as a case in point, were always asked in October for items for a Christmas event. Potential donors to Chapman's fair were assured that even the most unpretentious item was welcome—"whatever it is, do not think it trivial," stated the 1841 appeal letter. Pieces of fabric were requested, even if they were quite small, for they could be printed with antislavery devices or mottoes and attached to sale articles. A donor might also have a motto embroidered for her for a slight fee, or if she preferred, she could ask to have the fabric printed and then returned to her so she could embroider it herself. Patterns for fancywork, cabinetwork, and children's clothing were also sent on request. (Separate, customized requests for goods also went out to manufacturers and merchants.) When these donations came in from far-flung locales, workers in the central organizational office grouped them together and priced them. Organizers of the Bunker Hill Monument Fair even thought in advance about souvenirs: they prepared certificates of participation, complete with a view of the battle of Bunker Hill, for fairgoers to purchase and bring home.[43]

Antebellum fairgivers were equally thoughtful about scheduling. In western Massachusetts, for example, they made sure their fairs coincided with agricultural exhibitions so as to draw from an unusually large audience. The Bunker Hill Monument Fair organizers planned their event to take place at the same time as a Whig convention that brought thousands of nonresidents to Boston. Planners also scheduled fairs on or near holidays such as Independence Day, Supreme Court Day, or, most important given the hunger at the time for gift items, Christmas. In 1831 the Massachusetts Female Anti-Slavery Society applied to the managers of the Boston armory to rent rooms for their fair,[44] but was told the space was already rented to the ladies of Grace Church, who were planning a fair of their own. The abolitionists felt the armory managers were using this as an excuse, but whether or not this was so, the story indicates that even at this early date the Christmas season was becoming a popular time for fundraising fairs.[45]

By the 1850s, organizers in western Massachusetts had devised ways to increase fair attendance by providing transportation for out-of-towners. They specifically invited citizens of neighboring towns to come to their events, explaining in area newspapers that special trains would be added to bring individuals back and forth. When Northampton's Baptist women held a fair in 1860, for example, a reduced-fare train ran from Springfield, about twenty miles away. The train stopped to pick up passengers at several towns along the route, but the only drop-off point was Northampton. According to the newspaper report, 150 people used the special train. When the Methodist women held a fair a few weeks later, they arranged a similar train and even included the fair admission with the purchase of a round-trip ticket. At this same time, fairs in the Northampton area were often jointly sponsored by women of different denominations. Episcopalians and Unitarians worked together in 1850, for example, as did Congregationalists and Unitarians. (While most church fairs took place by this time in church facilities, these jointly sponsored events were held in Town Hall or similar nonsectarian spaces.)[46] I have not seen documentation of similar transportation schemes or multidenominational endeavors in other communities, but fairgiving innovations spread rapidly, and it is unlikely that this practice was exclusive to any one region.

Effective planning for maximum attendance and impact at a fair—a kind of macrolevel thinking—was matched by effective strategies for the completion of everyday, microlevel tasks. Organizers of the Philadelphia Anti-Slavery Fair, for example, met weekly in one another's homes from early fall through December to prepare sale articles. The meetings followed the same pattern as women's church circle get-togethers, in that an afternoon was spent sewing, and a pot-luck type meal was shared during the course of the day. Occasionally, the men of the community were invited in for a social evening when the work was complete.[47] The gatherings were sometimes quite large. In the 1850s, over sixty women who worked together at Lucretia Mott's house were later joined by a sizable number of men.[48] The image of these get-togethers reminds us of the important role of the fair in promoting fellowship and community, but it should also reiterate the idea that women put in many, many hours of work for their fairs and that they were good at finding ways to make that work seem enjoyable.

The Mid-Century Proliferation of Fairs and New Kinds of Criticism

By the middle of the nineteenth century, the fundraising fair was generally perceived as an expected women's activity, and as the most obvious means for them to raise money. The fact that the women of Grace Episcopal Church of Madison held a fair in 1846 illustrates this point. Madison was a new community with a total population of 625 at this time, and a small group of Episcopalians, including eleven women organized as a benevolent society, had just founded a church in March. The women decided to hold a fair to raise funds in December. They realized $155, which they used to purchase land for a permanent building. (Fairs were held regularly in this church for years to come.) A similar story comes from Philadelphia. Rebecca Gratz wrote to a relative in 1857 that the hard economic times had made it difficult for her women's group to support their benevolent project, the Jewish Foster Home. They determined to hold a fair.[49] The great proliferation of fairs was also demonstrated by the appearance of stories about fairs in contemporary magazines and the first published instructions for salable fair items.[50]

There were several reasons for the explosion of fairs at this time. On one hand their novelty had worn off because they had been part of the social landscape for an entire generation; the very success of the earliest fairs had helped make the institution seem "normal," acceptable, and worthwhile. On the other hand, women were also stepping even further into the public arena and becoming involved with new kinds of causes that needed funding. At the same time, there was a marked proliferation of other types of fairs, including agricultural and industrial exhibitions (the first large-scale industrial fair, the "Crystal Palace" Exhibition, was held in London in 1851).[51] The whole idea or institution of the fair was becoming entrenched in the American psyche, in other words, and the fundraising fair was an integral part of it.

Mid-century fairs were often held for new causes. Few temperance organizations still sponsored fairs,[52] but societies working for civic improvement did. Some groups were particularly concerned with public beautification and held fairs to pay for public parks and open spaces. (In 1848 the influential Andrew Jackson Downing expressly suggested in a *Horticulturist* editorial that women organize fairs and tea parties for this purpose.)[53] Other groups funded cultural centers like the Pennsylvania Academy (women raised nine thousand dollars for this institution) or the Essex Institute, a museum and learning center in Salem, Massachusetts.[54] Church fairs were much more common by the 1850s. As we have seen, these were perceived more as social than as religious events, and some were sponsored by interdenominational groups. Even when this was not the case, they were frequented by more than the members of the sponsoring congregation.

As the fairs proliferated, organizers experimented with their form. Fairs further blended into entertainments. A "tea party" might be a purely social event, for example, but it also might be set up as a fair. One such party held in Northampton Town Hall in 1855 included refreshment and sale tables, a picture gallery, a post office, and a musical performance. Double names, such as "fair and festival," were given to other events. "Strawberry festivals" were usually seasonal parties featuring strawberry shortcake and other dishes, but they could include sale tables or tableaux as well. Even the word "supper" could be misleading. Suppers were held as part of "entertainments" and were incorporated into fairs where sale tables were the focus of attention.[55]

Fundraising fairs could also be blurred with fairs of other types, as alluded to previously. At Northampton's Cattle Show sponsored by the Hampshire, Hampden, and Franklin [County] Agricultural Society, for example, dairy and horticultural exhibits and demonstrations of new agricultural machinery were not the only attractions. Women's fancywork—the same sort seen at fancy fairs—was available for sale; in effect these were fundraising fairs *within* agricultural fairs. Harvey Kirkland, secretary of the agricultural society, specifically invited the ladies of the community to "improve" his fair with "specimens of their ingenuity, skill and industry," contributed for their "respective associations for religious and benevolent purposes." Without the women's help, Kirkland admitted, the society feared its show would not be heavily patronized.[56] Industrial fairs also featured handmade items more often thought of in relation to the women's events. The second annual South Carolina Institute Fair, held in Charleston in 1850, included a display of locally made fancy goods, including palmetto and pine baskets, embroidered fans, and worsted mats. The *Charleston Daily Courier* remarked, "[T]he samples of needlework, embroidery and millinery attest that the delicate fingers of Eve's industrious daughters have been busy in lending their cooperation."[57]

As the woman's fair became more ubiquitous and successful, popular rhetoric about it took on a somewhat different tone. By mid-century there was less of a bemused tolerance expressed in the press and more instances of biting, even hostile criticism. The arguments were no longer limited to the seductiveness of the fairgivers; typically, they also involved the theme of unfair value. The fairs were seen as commercial enterprises, and the women were seen to be engaged in a type of extortion. In "Doesticks Attends a Ladies' Fair," a satirical piece in the *Hampshire Gazette* in 1855, reference was made to "speculating females" "playing 'keep store'" at the fair. According to Doesticks, pretty girls were placed with the least attractive merchandise, which was sold at the highest price, and the girls flattered themselves that their looks made it a "fair exchange." The purposes of the feminine institution of the Ladies Fair, Doesticks concluded, were "[f]irstly, to give the ladies an opportunity to show their new clothes, and to talk with a multitude of unknown gentlemen, without any preliminary introduction. Secondly, to beg as much money as possible from the gentlemen aforesaid, under the transparent formality of bargain and sale—which sale includes the buyer, who is really the only article fairly sold in the whole collection. [Only] thirdly, to give some money to the ostentatiously poor."[58]

A similar distrust of women's fairs appeared in a story by Kate Sutherland. Written as a kind of moral allegory and published in *Peterson's Magazine* in 1848, it featured as its central character an innocent and kindhearted young man who had no idea of the "danger" he was to meet at the fair. He was immediately dazzled by the display and bewitched by a pair of bright eyes, rosy lips, a winning smile, and a low sweet voice, so much so that he parted with several of his hard-earned dollars through coerced purchases. He lost the rest of his money in a raffle, and after he had "gambled and lost all," he had nothing left for his destitute mother.[59] Many of the period complaints implied that fairgoers were tricked in the extra-ordinary atmosphere of the fair. Doesticks held that prices were exorbitant and men were connived into buying items they really had no need for. Sutherland's hero, too, found himself in possession of a doll he was actually embarrassed to be seen with.

This new type of criticism reflected a discomfort with something larger than the fundraising fair. American culture as a whole was gradually becoming more and more focused on consumer goods; the very presence of the enormous industrial fairs indicated how much mass production had changed everyday life. Accusations about unfair advertising and extortion were directed at women, but I believe they were really as much about the increasingly commercial nature of all fairs—and of society as a whole—as they were about gender. The women bore the brunt of the criticism because they were supposed to represent domesticity, the antithesis of the commercial. As the woman's fair moved further into the mainstream and became more multidimensional, it reflected the pressures of the society of which it was a part.

Potholders and Politics: More on Antislavery Fairs

I have already described the contested terrain of the antislavery fairs and have made many references in the course of this narrative to details of their operation. Recent excellent studies of the Boston fairs by Debra Hansen and Lee Chambers-Schiller explore the phenomenon in depth, and I do not feel it necessary to repeat their stories fully. However, I believe further discussion of the antislavery fairs is warranted, because they offer an excellent window of understanding on the ways that antebellum fairs functioned as community institutions. A look at the forceful personality and influence of Maria Weston Chapman, furthermore, serves as a brief case study of a fair organizer and reminds us that in the antebellum era the fundraising fair was the primary political organizing mechanism of even the most radical activist.

As indicated, the antislavery fair was Chapman's "invention." A year after she had helped found the Female Anti-Slavery Society in 1833, Chapman decided a fundraising fair would be a good way of helping the cause. She solicited the help of her sisters and friends, notably Eliza Southwick, Louisa Loring, and Lydia Maria Child, and they organized a fair the next year. This event brought in about three hundred dollars, an amount roughly comparable to the proceeds of a fair in the much smaller town of Northampton. As the 1834 *Liberator* report concluded, the "friends of this righteous cause were as yet neither numerous or wealthy."[60] (The modest returns did not discourage Chapman's counterparts in Philadelphia. When Sarah Pugh, Lucretia Mott, and others in their group learned of the event, they organized their own antislavery fair in 1835.) The Boston fair continued to grow, however, and over time became the single most visible and significant enterprise of the New England abolition movement. The same small group of women remained in control of the fair for more than two decades, and there is no doubt that Chapman was its real leader or guiding force.[61]

There was from the beginning a tension, even at Chapman's unabashedly "materialist" fairs, between the seriousness of the cause and the necessary frivolity of a fundraising fair. The organizers tried to make as many political statements as possible within the constraints of the event. They covered the walls with messages such as "The truth shall make us free," or "Let the oppressed go free, and break every yoke." They posted signs such as "Persons are requested not to handle the articles, which like slavery, are too 'delicate' to be touched." Similarly, they tagged sale items with mottoes: sugar bowls were inscribed "Sugar not made by slaves," and penwipers were inscribed "Wipe out the blot of Slavery." They turned potholders into "anti-slave holders" (fig. 8).[62] These pointed statements were controversial, and the early fairs engendered considerable comment,[63] but the controversy also

Young Wife—"Oh! my dear, there is a most lovely set—pin, ear-rings, and sleeve-buttons. Do go buy them."
Mr. Tightstring—"Yes! my dear, I mean to go by them as quick as possible!"

brought the public to come see what they were about. Attendance and proceeds both rose dramatically; by the early 1840s profits were well over two thousand dollars (equivalent to perhaps forty thousand in today's terms).

Fig. 17. Cartoons like this were common in the popular press in the mid-nineteenth century. Women were portrayed as wheedling creatures who coerced men into buying things they did not need. From *The Drumbeat* (Brooklyn and Long Island Sanitary Fair, 1864); courtesy of the Chicago Historical Society.

Other political features of Chapman's antislavery fairs included lectures and addresses about the cause (many of these were given by women—a controversial feature in itself) and the publication of *The Liberty Bell*, an annual "giftbook" or compendium of antislavery articles, stories, and poetry produced for the fair from 1843 to 1857. It was marketed as a souvenir of sorts, but was a serious collection of literature rather than a gossip sheet about the events of the fair. It featured contributions from most of the active abolitionists of the day, and from well-known intellectuals like Ralph Waldo Emerson, Margaret Fuller, and Elizabeth Barrett Browning. Although *The Liberty Bell* proclaimed itself written by "Friends of Freedom," it was Maria Chapman who started the publication and edited it annually.[64]

As stated, Chapman did not shy away from commercial items at the sale tables. She and her circle used their connections to procure merchandise, even for the earliest fairs, and they often shopped personally for sale items. (The fact that these women were likely to travel and even had the capital to purchase the articles is in itself revealing about their social status.) Swiss pictures, Parisian cut glass, and Turkish embroidered bags are examples of the articles they found. Customers came to count on the fair as a source of exotic goods, especially suitable as Christ-

Excerpt, "A Dream of the Fair," 1860

I went last night to the "Institute Fair,"
And wandered about 'midst the gorgeous show there,
Until my poor head was all in confusion;
I was ready to say 'Twas an "optic illusion."
I went home quite late and crept into bed,
Relieved on my pillow to lay down my head;
But no sooner to sleep did I close my eyes,
Than visions unwelcome did straightway arise.
For tidies and ottomans loomed up in view,
And babies and sugar plums—of elephants too,
While a huge Mariposa hung over my head,
All gorgeous in colors of yellow and red;
And a brilliant-hued Afghan enveloped me round—
Its weight almost dragging me down to the ground.

. . . . . .

There were toys without number (no time to describe),
And of babies and dolls appeared quite a tribe;
All dancing around me by magical power
Seemed gifted with life for the time and the hour.
The ice cream advancing, said: "Pray try a glass";—
The pears and the apples came trooping "en masse,"
All trying to tempt, as the evening before,
To open the purse-strings, "just one time more."

—*The Weal-Reaf,* Essex Institute
(Salem, Massachusetts) Fair
September 7, 1860

mas presents (the abolitionists were sure to advertise them as such), and sometimes even put in advance orders. There was a general protest one year when the
shipment from Paris was delayed. Chambers-Schiller argues that the growing
commercialism of the Massachusetts Anti-Slavery Fair was eventually an important factor in its demise. The women spent less and less energy on making their
own products because there was more money to be made with retail goods; "crass
profiteering" became a problem. As the fair moved away from its primary identification with women and the domestic, Chambers-Schiller implies, it lost its special quality and, in effect, its heart. Chapman decided to disband the fair in
favor of a subscription campaign in 1858. Her primary explanation was that the
fair had become too time consuming, but she also acknowledged the dilemma of
success at the price of identity.[65] As we have seen, this was not a unique situation,
but because this was such a well-documented fair, it is particularly easy to see how it
played out.

The money raised at the fairs was critical in their longevity—several accounts indicate the Female Anti-Slavery Society was dependent on the regular fair income,
and Massachusetts fairs eventually raised over sixty thousand dollars—equivalent to
about a million dollars in the 1990s[66]—but fairs were equally valued as mechanisms
for attracting the public and exposing it to the antislavery idea. Chapman stated in

Excerpt, Poem for the Weymouth, Massachusetts, Antislavery Fair, 1842

To see the Ladies' Fair I went,
And pleasantly the time was spent;
And things for sale, both rich and rare,
The labor of their hands, were there;
And smiling girls, as Chapman bland,
To traffic at their tables stand.

. . . . .

A holy calling they are in,
That must your approbation win;
And every freeman must respect
The zeal of this devoted sect.
The profits of this Fair are meant
On patriot mission to be sent,
to dig for tyranny a grave,
And burst the fetters of the slave;

To soothe the frantic mother's heart,
When forc'd from all she loves to part;
To break her exil'd offspring's chain
And give them to her arms again.
To wash away our country's shame,
And purify her spotted name;
To make her what she yet shall be,
    The dwelling only of the FREE!
To aid this cause they held their Fair
And, "Help them, Heaven!"
    is the Christian's prayer.

—F. M. Adlington,
The Liberator
January 7, 1842

Fig. 18. A clear antislavery message is evident on this potholder from the Chicago Historical Society. Museum records indicate it was purchased at the Great Northwest Sanitary Fair, but it is typical of the pointedly political sale items at the antislavery fairs of the antebellum era, and may have originated at such an event. Chicago Historical Society Decorative and Industrial Arts Collection; courtesy of the Chicago Historical Society.

1841 that the annual fair had "done more towards softening the public heart towards [the cause] than many a more imposing instrumentality." Although the workers found mounting an annual event exhausting, she said, the effort was decidedly worthwhile. The fairs helped raise the society's image in the world at large to one of respectability and prosperity. At the same time, they brought the abolitionists together with a spirit of enterprise and purpose.[67] They provided important opportunities for fellowship and internal networking. "The Fair was a social anti-slavery exchange," Chapman said. "Persons came daily to meet their friends. . . . It afforded an excellent opportunity for the abolitionists, who had long known each other by report, to become personally acquainted." Since by the late 1840s there were antislavery fairs even on the Ohio frontier, networking extended across the country as well as across the ocean. Testimonies in the abolitionist press indicate how strongly these events contributed to a sense of bonding within the community.[68]

Some of this networking was interracial; as I have indicated, black women were sometimes present at radicals' antislavery fairs. On a rhetorical level, much was made of the fairs as a meeting ground for the two races. Charlotte Forten, an African American from Philadelphia, filled most of her description of a visit to the Boston fair with remarks about the contacts she had made with "the noblest and best of women." She was particularly delighted with the experience of walking arm in arm through the hall with Maria Chapman. In 1850 Sojourner Truth made a pointed appearance at the fair, and Antoinette Brown, one of the first women to be ordained as a Christian minister, spoke eloquently about interracial contact.[69] In actuality, true racial understanding was probably rare. Chambers-Schiller claims that black women who were holding their own fairs in Salem and New Bedford were sometimes required to buy leftover merchandise from the larger, predominantly white events; socioeconomic differences were disregarded by the white crusaders.[70] In any case, the very idea of racial mixing made the fairs seem even more exotic. Many spectators came to a Rochester fair just to get a glimpse of Julia and Eliza Griffiths, Englishwomen who had lived for a time with Frederick Douglass. "Long lines of curious townspeople who wished to see what kind of . . . ladies would reside at the home of black man" formed near the women.[71]

The antislavery fair was in one sense a unique phenomenon, focused as it was on a particular political agenda, but in many ways it reflected the more prototypical ladies' fair. It was an institution that struggled to integrate a moral agenda with the realities of the marketplace and to maintain an association with domesticity despite operating in a sophisticated manner in the public arena. It was predicated on the idea that women might work together, from their own separatist, gender-based organization, with a unique approach to social change. Through the fair, women both played upon that domesticity (i.e., by selling domestic products and using domestically based expertise and dramatizing their own piety and charitableness) and played against it (i.e., by acting flirtatious and aggressively pursuing the saleswoman role). The story of the antislavery fair highlights the agency of antebellum fairgivers, pointing to their innovations in advertising, presentation, sales, and social organization. It shows us both how much a single strong-willed, powerful woman might accomplish and how strong and far-reaching women's networks were.

These same women's networks were to mobilize millions of people and raise millions of dollars during the Civil War. They were to help create a fair "mania" that swept over the northern states and involved almost every single citizen, no matter how young or remotely located. We shall look at their activities in the next chapter, and come to understand how the issues of domesticity and commercialism temporarily fell away during wartime. We shall see what an important social event the fundraising fair was during the conflict, and how the active involvement of large numbers of men changed this type of fair forever.

CHAPTER THREE

The Excitement
and Lasting Legacy
of the Civil War
Sanitary Fairs

Such a furor of benevolence had never before been known. Men, women, and children, corporations and business firms, religious societies, political organizations—all vied with one another enthusiastically . . . as to who should contribute the most. . . . As the Hebrews, in olden time, brought their free-will offerings to the altar of the Lord, so too did the people of the Northwest . . . lavish their . . . contributions on the altar of the country.

—Mary Livermore, *My Story of the War*

The story of the great fundraising fairs of the Civil War is so rich that it could easily comprise a book in itself. Indeed, the fairs were the subject of many proudly recorded, enormously detailed nineteenth-century books. The composite story is a high spirited and dramatic one, with elaborate scenery, a cast of thousands, and action rising to a crescendo over a two-and-one-half-year period. Many of the characters were leading players in many other nineteenth-century dramas—organizer Mary Livermore, for example, was a leading suffragist and lecturer—and many of the attractions and dramatic tensions reflected prominent cultural and artistic ideas. It is ironic that even with the recent spate of interest in the Civil War, the story of the sanitary fairs has not commanded much attention. The fairs have not been taken very seriously, I believe, largely because they *were* fairs; they have been dismissed, as are all fairs, as mere pastimes. Even in the new discourse about the war, in other words, women's voices are still muted. Their contributions are still judged in "male" terms, primarily in relationship to the battlefield. As we shall see in this chapter, the women's contribution was more fully acknowledged in its own time, and the fairs were the subject of great public interest and excitement. They combined elements of the ladies' fair with elements of the new, large-scale expositions, and were hugely successful because they resonated with so many public hopes and needs. They fed the general hunger for diversion from the horrors of the war and the longing for entertainment, art, and culture. At the same time they drew on the intense emotions generated by the war: a sense of charity, responsibility, and concern for the suffering soldiers; a feeling of patriotism and national (Union) pride; and regional loyalty. They generated a strong feeling of fellowship and community participation and helped people feel they were part of a "great," important undertaking.

Ladies' Aid Societies and the Sanitary Commission

When the Civil War broke out in 1861, people quickly mobilized the home front on both sides of the Mason-Dixon line. Businessmen contributed to subscription funds to help the war effort, and manufacturers donated goods—a tinware dealer equipped a military company with cups and plates, for example, or a mattress dealer donated bedding. Others donated buildings or services.[1] Women were equally active. In addition to taking over tasks formerly done by the now absent soldiers, they used their familiar skills and networks to supply those soldiers with clothing and other necessities. The response was immediate, especially in the North, where efforts were more quickly coordinated and centralized. In Bridgeport, Connecticut, a woman's aid group met on April 15, the same day Lincoln called out the troops. Chicagoans formed an aid society on April 18. By April 29, a body of New York women had already formed the Woman's Central Association of [Soldiers'] Relief, which functioned as an auxiliary to the medical and human services branch of the Union army and as a liaison to local aid associations.[2] The Relief Association was soon subsumed into the United States Sanitary Commission, the agency responsible for the "sanitary interests" of the troops (soldiers' diet, clothing, living conditions, and transport, and care of the sick and wounded). The commission served as the (northern) woman's organization of the war. Hundreds of women worked directly for the commission, usually in the Department of General Relief (these were generally unpaid positions). Hundreds of thousands of others identified strongly with the organization and regularly donated to it.[3] It was women who worked with the commission who initiated large-scale fairs to raise money for the sanitary cause.

We shall return to the story of the sanitary fairs momentarily, but because each of them was organized independently, a few words about the operations of the commission are in order. There were twelve regional branch offices and an independent branch in St. Louis. Each office put out calls for the supplies most urgently needed at a given time and then served as a central receiving point for the constant stream of donations that came in from local aid societies.[4] A wide variety of women's organizations—church circles, Dorcas societies, even reading clubs—worked with the commission by sewing, soliciting door-to-door for goods and money, or taking up collections in churches, factories, and schools. Children sometimes formed their own organizations, typically called Alert Clubs, that conducted independent subscription campaigns.[5]

Supplying the soldiers and the Sanitary Commission was a constant, ongoing endeavor that began almost as soon as the war was underway and continued at an often frenzied pace. A Northampton organization designated to work with the Sanitary Commission was formed on July 26, and by August 2, it had a box with 521 hospital garments ready for shipment. In 1862 the *Free Press* reported that women were meeting daily in a local church to prepare such garments.[6]

The Beginnings of the Sanitary Fair

During the first two years of the war, northern women held many fundraising fairs to raise money for the soldiers. Typically, they were sponsored by nonsectarian groups and conformed to long-familiar prewar traditions. Often, they were held on holidays—in Northampton, for example, a Union Festival took place on New Year's Eve—a practice that allowed people to celebrate in good conscience despite the ravages of the war. Some of the fairs were lengthy, and many followed one another in rapid succession. In Columbus, Ohio, as a case in point, the Ladies' Soldier's Aid Society gave a week-long "Grand Union Bazaar and Tableaux" in 1862, and only a few months later a committee of women from Catholic and Protestant churches sponsored a soldiers' fair. In Worcester, Massachusetts, sponsors of a "Ladies' Levee" soon participated in a countywide fair to fund a home for wounded soldiers. The women's aid organizations were universally recognized throughout the Union as the primary fundraising channel; even men's groups turned over benefit proceeds to them. In Northampton, the all-male Horticultural Club donated earnings from a festival to the aid society, and a group of Smith College professors donated profits from a benefit concert.[7]

Perhaps the first fair held specifically as a benefit for the Sanitary Commission took place in Lowell, Massachusetts, in February, 1863. This too was a joint effort on the part of diverse religious organizations of the city, and it was large enough to generate $4,850 (about $15,000 in today's dollars.)[8] However, it was still only a local (citywide) endeavor. Full-fledged sanitary fairs were regional events, usually organized through Sanitary Commission branch offices. The first was held the following fall in Chicago. This fair created a stir throughout the Union and functioned as a turning point—a kind of sea change—in the way women's fairs were perceived and operated in the nineteenth century. The story of the "Great Northwest Fair" and the women behind it offers a fascinating glimpse of mid-century gender politics and once again shows us the strength of women's networks and organizing acumen.

In *My Story of the War*, Mary Livermore, associate director of the Chicago branch of the Sanitary Commission, described the situation she and her colleagues experienced in the fall of 1863. Although women had been holding fairs and benefits in "every city, town and village" to raise funds for the commission, she reported, there was still not enough money coming in to meet expenses. Livermore and fellow director Jane C. Hoge determined that a grand-scale regional event would both replenish the treasury and boost morale. "Accordingly," said Livermore, "we consulted the gentlemen of the Commission. [They] languidly approved our plan, but laughed incredulously at our proposal to raise $25,000." (This would be closer to $400,000 in present-day dollars.) Livermore and Hoge were undaunted by this skeptical reaction; they knew what the women could do if they pooled their resources. Livermore herself had grown up in Boston and had both attended and taught at a school in Charlestown, Massachusetts, where the Monument Fair was held in 1840. She was in all likelihood well aware of the mechanics and efficacy of the regional fair. She and Hoge sought grassroots support by writing to affiliated aid societies throughout the area, and sending out newspaper notices and ten thousand circulars asking for delegates from every town to come to a regional women's planning convention. These delegates formed yet another women's network and a new kind of sisterhood. The planning convention closed with a support rally that, in Livermore's words, "kindled a flame in the hearts" of the women present, allowing them to return home with energy and enthusiasm for their project.[9]

Fair Mania

Livermore stressed repeatedly how little encouragement they got from the men when they embarked on this endeavor: "This fair . . . was an experiment, and was pre-eminently an enterprise of women, receiving no assistance from men in its early beginnings. The city of Chicago regarded it with indifference, and the gentlemen members of the commission barely tolerated it. The first did not understand it, and the latter were doubtful of its success."[10]

Livermore and Hoge were well connected, highly organized, and efficient leaders, however, and they worked to generate broad-based support.[11] They contacted every imaginable authority figure, from local teachers to area governors and federal legislators, and appealed to citizens throughout the country. On one occasion alone, Livermore claimed, seventeen bushels of mail relating to the fair were sent out from their office. They also exploited their personal connections to the fullest. Livermore turned to contacts in Boston, and Hoge traveled to old haunts in Pennsylvania where she implored "stores of friends and relatives" to solicit donations from manufacturers, artisans, and merchants. The women requested contributions of all kinds—money, salable goods, artworks, or curiosities that could be borrowed for display, pledges for musical or dramatic entertainment. Eventu-

Fig. 19. Mary Livermore and colleague Jane Hoge understood the potential of a concerted fundraising effort of women of the Northwest region. Their success in mobilizing people and resources for a large-scale fundraising fair eventually won the respect of their male co-workers. From Livermore's *My Story of the War* (1889); courtesy of the Chicago Historical Society.

ally, according to Livermore, "even men became inoculated with the fair mania." Some pledged the gross receipts of a day's labor; others donated cultivators and threshing machines, livestock, or hay and grain. In the last week before the fair opened, the men "atoned for their early lack of interest" with an "avalanche" of donations.[12]

It does seem from descriptions of this first sanitary fair that a type of mania took hold of the public. Even allowing for nineteenth-century hyperbole and romanticization, one cannot help but be impressed by accounts of the fair and sense how deeply the cause touched the lives of everyone in even the most remote location. The very personal response is evident in lists of donations to the fair. Madison women sent such handmade items as knitted socks, infant's shirts, a pair of cushions, and a doll's cape, along with three cans of peaches. There were also contributions of previously purchased, commercial items like photographs of a famous "guerilla" [*sic*], Polish boots, china ornaments, and books. Children's contributions were listed separately. One boy gave two bookmarks, while two of his friends donated beaded mats. The School Girls Soldiers' Aid Society of the Fourth Ward of Milwaukee, comprising twelve girls under the age of thirteen who did all their work on Saturday afternoons, contributed bookmarks, watchcases, and similar items.[13] These donations had great resonance at the time. The goods would be used to help the soldiers, either directly or indirectly, through cash sale. At the same time, they represented the devotion and sacrifice of the donor. In this mid-century period consumer products were highly valued as markers of the good life, and such tangible symbols held particular meaning.

Descriptions of the opening day of the fair reflect the general excitement that surrounded it. A conversation with one of the farmers who came from Lake County, Illinois, in a procession of one hundred wagons filled with donated produce and livestock (fig. 21) was reported in Livermore's book. Although he brought quantities of vegetables and poultry collected from neighbors who lived in a one-mile radius, the farmer apologized for the paucity of his load. "We didn't get notice that the wagons were going in 'till last night about eight o'clock and it was dark and raining at that," he said, "but we did the best we could."[14]

The fair mania was fueled by a sense of loyalty and charity, but Livermore, Hoge, and their helpers made certain the event was festive and exciting enough to capture everyone's attention and imagination. They saw to it that the usual affairs of the city of Chicago were suspended on opening day—post offices, courts, schools, factories, and stores were all closed—and that the opening parade, featuring marching bands, decorated horses, and waving banners, was spectacular. The fair was held in Bryan Hall, which was elaborately decorated with a central two-story pagoda and abundant festoons of red, white, and blue bunting and flags. Music played almost continually. Attractions included a curiosity shop with displays of war mementos, Indian artifacts, natural specimens, and the "biggest trophy of all"—the original copy of the Emancipation Proclamation. Livermore had written to the president to ask that he donate the document, and Lincoln complied, despite his own sentimental attachment to it. He wrote to the "ladies in charge of the fair": "I had some desire to retain the paper, but if it shall contribute to the relief or comfort of the soldiers, that will be better." The document was featured in its own special display and was auctioned to the highest bidder for three thousand dollars.[15]

Because the fair was a hybrid (i.e., part fundraising fair, part exposition), it offered something for everyone. The exhibitions of livestock, produce, and manufactured items were so extensive that they were compared to those at "a good-sized state fair." There were mili-

Fig. 20. The title page of *The Spirit of the Fair*, the Metropolitan (New York City) Fair newspaper, captures the sentimental, patriotic feeling that the sanitary fairs appealed to. Courtesy of the Chicago Historical Society.

tary drills by the Ellsworth Zouaves, said to especially attract the rural citizens who had been able to take advantage of special railroad excursion rates to Chicago. There were also separate children's concerts and a young people's dance, and a "grand ball" for the Germans. Thousands of visitors were drawn to the Art Gallery or to the lectures by the young orator Anna Dickinson, who had broken ten previous engagements when she realized the Northwest fair was a woman's rallying cause. Chicago businessmen flocked to the large restaurant that served dinners in sequential sittings. Up to fifteen hundred men were fed daily; some days, hundreds were turned away.

Fig. 21. This engraving, which appeared in Frank Goodrich's *The Tribute Book. A Record of the Munificence, Self-Sacrifice and Patriotism of the American People During the War for the Union* (1865), illustrates the procession of Lake County, Illinois, farmers in the opening-day parade of the 1863 Northwest Fair. The farmers are donating produce to be used at the fair restaurants. Courtesy of the Chicago Historical Society.

The restaurant was *the* place to eat for the two weeks of the fair, for many of the women who worked there were among the social leaders of the city.[16]

A dramatic, high-spirited, and symbolic finale that took place on the last day of the fair indicates that both men and women acknowledged the fair as a woman's achievement. Six hundred soldiers from Camp Douglas and local hospitals were treated to a free dinner, and according to the *History of the North-Western Soldiers' Fair*, two hundred businessmen came in after the first seating and asked that the women allow them to serve the troops. The women returned later "to find the gentlemen grotesquely attired in their serving-gear, the uniform of white aprons and caps." All was in disarray ("the motley condition of the tables gave evidence of the handwork of men") but finally "the masculine attendants gave up in utter [good-natured] despair, declaring themselves 'completely tuckered out.'" The businessmen's gesture was slightly satirical, but it was nevertheless a tribute to the women's expertise in this kind of endeavor. The women also acknowledged their own effort. After the men departed, the managerial committee held an informal meeting to thank Livermore, Hoge, and others. They proclaimed the fair an "unparalleled suc-

THE CHICAGO FAIR DINING HALL.

Fig. 22. During the course of the Northwest Fair, hundreds of businessmen ate their noon meal in the fair dining room. Waitresses were local volunteers. Illustration from *The Tribute Book* (1865); courtesy of the Chicago Historical Society.

cess—not merely in a pecuniary point of view, but as a great uprising of the women of the Northwest."[17] When the final receipts of the fair came to nearly eighty thousand dollars, more than three times Livermore's original projection and equivalent to more than a million dollars today, it was a woman's triumph.

Other regions of the country were impressed with the results of the Chicago fair and caught the sanitary mania. They followed in rapid succession with their own even more spectacular fairs (see table 1). Almost all subsequent sanitary fairs had the support of men and active male participation from the very beginning, however, and although they were still women's fairs in the sense that the vast majority of the work was done by women, they were never again so clearly identified as women's projects.[18] The Chicago event was officially referred to as the "Northwest Ladies Fair," but subsequent sanitary fairs did not carry this epithet. Condescending male rhetoric toward fundraising fairs generally disappeared at this time and did not reappear after the war. As Virginia Gunn, who wrote about Ohio fairs, noted, the women's "war efforts helped shatter the stereotype of nineteenth century women as emotional, helpless ornaments incapable of sustaining long term efforts or understanding big ideas."[19]

Table 1

Features of the Major Civil War Sanitary Fairs

PLACE and NAME	DATE	AMOUNT RAISED	SPONSOR, PURPOSE	NEWSPAPER	RESTAURANTS	FLORAL HALL (OR DISPLAY)
Lowell, MA	Feb. 1863	$4,850	said to be girls' idea			yes
Chicago, IL Great Northwest Fair	Oct. 1863	$78,682	proposed by women Sanitary Commission workers; men had to be convinced	*The Volunteer*	large restaurant served 3,000 at a time	
Portland, ME	Oct. 1863			*The Commissioner*		
Boston, MA Boston Sanitary Fair	Dec. 1863	$146,000	New England Women's Auxiliary of Sanitary Commission	*The Knapsack*	large dining room	
Rochester, NY	Dec. 1863	$10,319	Ladies Hospital Association; men had to be convinced	*Bazaar Bulletin*		"Fairyland" flower exhibit
Cincinnati, OH Great Western Fair	Dec. 1863	$279,647	first propsed by men, but 2,000 women work through 119 existing women's organizations to carry it out Kentucky women help	*Ladies' Knapsack*		yes— "Floricultural" exhibit
Brooklyn, NY Brooklyn and Long Island Fair	Feb. 1864	$403,000	Woman's Relief Association of Brooklyn	*The Drumbeat*	75 tables in Knickerbocker Hall; facilities for private parties	

AGRICULTURAL AND COMMERCIAL BOOTHS	INTERNATIONAL AND COLONIAL THEME BOOTHS	CURIOSITY OR TROPHY DEPARTMENT	OTHER TYPES OF BOOTHS	ART GALLERY	REMARKS, SPECIAL FEATURES	INFORMATION SOURCES
					minor, but can be considered first real sanitary fair	Goodrich
yes					fair exceeds expectations fair extended 2 weeks involves individuals from the east also	Goodrich Livermore *History of the Northwestern Fair* Schnell
no donations solicited from manufacturers			24 booths, one for each contributing town		so crowded that prices raised on second day to lower attendance archery range	Goodrich Reynolds
	yes				pioneered tableaux-like booths includes "living wax works" tableaux Albany women come to take lessons fair extended	Goodrich *Report of the Christmas Bazaar*
yes		yes			includes lectures, concerts, gymnastics ends with a ball (dance) 2 buildings constructed	Goodrich Boynton
yes	yes historic reenactments in New England Kitchen: "living history" with donation party, quilting party, etc.	yes		yes	buildings constructed for fair, then auctioned for lumber helps "put Brooklyn on the map"	Goodrich *History of the Brooklyn and Long Island Fair*

Table 1 *(continued)*

PLACE and NAME	DATE	AMOUNT RAISED	SPONSOR, PURPOSE	NEWSPAPER	RESTAURANTS	FLORAL HALL (OR DISPLAY)
Albany, NY Army Relief Bazaar	Feb. 1864	$83,000	Executive Committee comprised only of men	*The Canteen*		yes
Cleveland, OH Northern Ohio Sanitary Fair	Feb. 1864	$79,000	organizing committee had formerly run the "Union Bazaar"	*Sanitary Fair Gazette*	large dining room serves 1,000	yes; major focus of attention
Poughkeepsie, NY	Mar. 1864	$16,262	"young ladies" idea	*Report of the Dutchess County Fair*		
New York, NY Metropolitan Fair	April 1864	$2,000,000 (estimates vary)	separate committees of men and women Sanitary Commission president involved	*Spirit of the Fair*		yes Floral Temple
Washington, DC National Sanitary Fair	April 1864	$50,000				
Baltimore, MD Institue Fair (also called Maryland State Fair)	April 1864	$80,000 (split between Sanitary and Christian Commission)	U.S. Christian Commission (for spiritual and temporal welfare of soldiers)	*The New Era*		yes
St. Louis, MO Mississippi Valley Fair	May 1864	$554,000 (highest per capita profit)	Western Sanitary Commission	*Daily Countersign*		yes
Pittsburgh, PA	June 1864	$319,217	men and women both involved			yes Floral Hall is major feature

AGRICULTURAL AND COMMERCIAL BOOTHS	INTERNATIONAL AND COLONIAL THEME BOOTHS	CURIOSITY OR TROPHY DEPARTMENT	OTHER TYPES OF BOOTHS	ART GALLERY	REMARKS, SPECIAL FEATURES	INFORMATION SOURCES
	yes	yes		yes	building constructed for the fair	Goodrich
yes	yes Continental Tea Party	yes—pegged as "museum"	Ohio county booths	yes	buildings constructed for the fair concerts, plays, tableaux	Goodrich Brayton
	yes Dutchess County Homestead "gypsies"			yes	held at Vassar College small scale	Goodrich
yes	yes Knickerbocker Kitchen with reenactments	yes		yes private collectors open home galleries	billed as larger than a fair—"a national exposition" some European contributions schools participate "voting" instituted	Goodrich *Record of the Metropolitan Fair* *Arthur's Home Magazine* *Tribute to the Fair*
					no information available	*Frank Leslie's Newspaper* June 25, 1864
yes	yes New England Kitchen	yes	nursery theme tables such as Cinderella and Old Woman in a Shoe	yes	could place orders for commercial products	Goodrich
	yes New England and Holland Kitchen	yes			buildings constructed for the fair	Goodrich
yes "Mechanical" department		yes			mock battle of the Monitor and the Merrimack buildings constructed for the fair some $ to Christian Commission	Goodrich

Table 1 *(continued)*

PLACE and NAME	DATE	AMOUNT RAISED	SPONSOR, PURPOSE	NEWSPAPER	RESTAURANTS	FLORAL HALL (OR DISPLAY)
Philadelphia, PA Great Central Fair	June 1864	$1, 035, 398	help from Dela- ware, NJ and from the Sanitary Commission branch office	*Our Daily Fare*	9,000 fed daily in restaurant	yes
Dubuque, IA	June 1864	$76, 494	Ladies Aid Society —most $ goes to Chicago branch of San. Commission; some to build local soldiers' home			
Boston, MA National Sailors' Fair	Nov. 1864	$247,056	to fund sailors' home (not strictly a sanitary fair)	*Boatswain's Whistle* (edited by Julia Ward Howe)		
Springfield, MA Springfield	Dec. 1864	$19,000	to fund soldiers' home	*Springfield Musket*		
St. Paul, MN Minnesota Soldiers' Fair	Jan. 1865	$9,559	Sanitary Commission officers propose "if women agree"			
Chicago, IL Northwest Soldiers' Home Fair	May 1965	$325,000	to fund soldier's home and Sani- tary Commission debts	*Voice of the Fair*	several smaller, professionally-run restaurants	yes—"a miniature Central Park"
Milwaukee, WI Soldiers' Home Fair (also called State Fair)	June-July 1865	$80,000	to fund state- supported solders' home	*Home Fair Journal*	dining room seats 1,500	yes

AGRICULTURAL AND COMMERCIAL BOOTHS	INTERNATIONAL AND COLONIAL THEME BOOTHS	CURIOSITY OR TROPHY DEPARTMENT	OTHER TYPES OF BOOTHS	ART GALLERY	REMARKS, SPECIAL FEATURES	INFORMATION SOURCES
yes	yes Pennsylvania Kitchen "Turkish" dept. smoking booth	yes	"model homes" booths children's department	yes largest of any fair	huge building constructed— 20,000 sq. ft. enclosed gaslight displays "voting mania"	Goodrich Stille
				yes	premiums given for large donations, even for items like butter	Goodrich
commercial "novelties"		yes	nursery theme booths some tables still organized by town literary magazines under Whittier, Holmes		New England primary held there Monitor and Merrimac tent wounded sailors give "testimony"	Goodrich Reynolds
	New England Kitchen					Reynolds
					"giant pig" exhibited	Goodrich
yes	yes New England Farm House	yes		yes	building constructed, follows Philadelphia model	Goodrich Henshaw
yes	Holland Kitchen	Wis. Science Dept. shows specimens glass blower's booth	"Lincoln's House" booth		building constructed features shooting gallery includes July 4 celebration	Goodrich Hurn

Costumed Characters and Theatrical Presentation

Several more sanitary fairs were held before Christmas in 1863. The Boston fair was a popular New England event that brought in nearly twice the amount of its Chicago predecessor, but it had been in the planning stages at the same time as the Northwest fair and was less significant on a national level. However, the sponsors of the Rochester Christmas Bazaar pioneered a new type of setup, marketing, and theatrical presentation that soon became standard at fairs of all types. Organizers arranged a series of tableaux-like booths, each of which featured costumed salespeople set against appropriate backdrops and thematically related sale goods. When fairgoers first entered the hall, they encountered the Russian booth, "topped by a lofty, snow-capped dome" and surrounded by "icicle-covered northern pines." Five characters, "leaning on hangings of thick furs," sold skates, sleds, and items made of worsted or Russian leather. Visitors passed on to other booths representing in turn Turkey, Italy, Ireland, and China, and at the far end of the hall they found a section devoted to the United States. There they found a Yankee booth with a satirical family (Mr. and Mrs. Jonathan Slick and their children Sophronia, Jerusha, and Jonathan) selling cider, doughnuts, and comic "Yankee notions"; and a National booth with patriotic characters like the Goddess of Liberty, General and Mrs. Washington, and a corps of salesgirls in military-style red, white, and blue outfits.[20] Finally, fairgivers could visit "Fairyland," an area designed by a professional horticulturalist, where pendant evergreen wreaths and flowers hung over a fountain, rock garden, and trees filled with exotic birds. Flowers, fruit, and perfume were sold in Fairyland by day, but picturesque tableaux featuring young children in costume were also presented in this romantic setting in the evenings.[21]

Costumed characters and thematic tableauxlike booths were incorporated into all subsequent sanitary fairs. Albany women who had come to Rochester to "take lessons" brought many of the characters to the fair they held two months later; Brother Jonathan and his wife prevailed at another Yankee booth (figs. 25–26), and the same fur-clad individuals gathered under the icicles in a Russian stall. The Albanians embellished the dramatic tradition, however, by adding a Japanese booth and a regionally appropriate Saratoga Springs stall.[22]

The fairgivers were innovative in their combination of humorous theatrical presentation and marketing. They were among the first—perhaps *the* first—to bring these elements together.[23] They were building on what they knew; tableaux vivants and

Fig. 23. The layout of Corinthian Hall, the site of the Rochester, New York, Christmas Bazaar, was illustrated in the book-length *Report* published by the Ladies' Relief Association in 1864. Distinct thematic booths were initiated at this event.

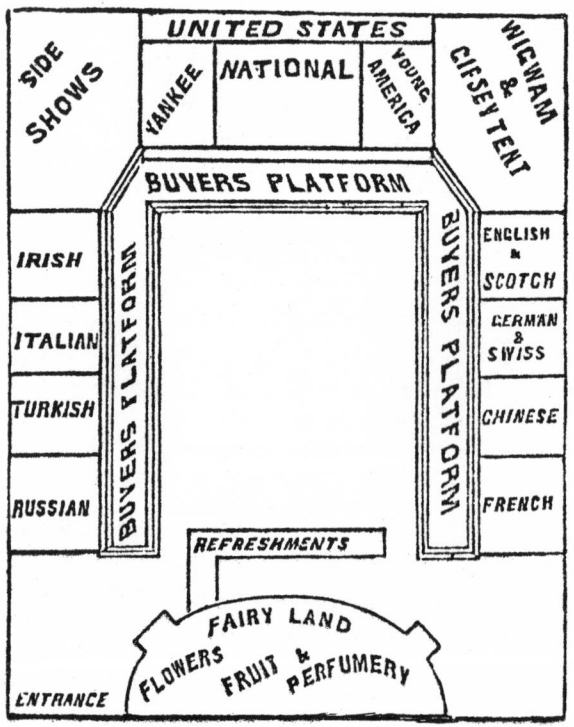

other types of costumed enactments were popular at the time in other contexts. In *Confidence Men and Painted Women,* Karen Halttunen discusses the rise of "disguises, masks and parlor theatricals" in American culture in the 1850s and 1860s, arguing that they reflected a new acceptance of the theatricality of social relationships. Guides like *Hudson's Private Theatricals for Home Performances* were "pour[ing] off the American press," providing instruction on props, costumes, characters, and constructing stage sets. Tableaux were also popular—almost *de rigueur*—in the professional theater. Staged as feature events, as afterpieces, or as part of actual plays, they were offered as three-dimensional, "living" works of art or scenes of literature or history.[24] The women took a form of expression that was familiar to them, in other words, and turned it into a playful but sophisticated strategy for earning money. Their international theme booths were undoubtedly influenced by the country-by-country arrangement at recent international expositions (the *Rochester Democrat* even commented that "an inventory of [the Bazaar's] effects would do no discredit to a world's fair"), but they played against the seriousness of those expositions, simultaneously honoring and mocking them. Such lighthearted play was characteristic of the ladies' fair and seemed very "feminine," but it was also effective. The novel combination of tableauxlike theme booths and marketing brought together by the sanitary fair organizers remains an uncredited innovation. Historians have explored the tension of actual international theme booths and amusement areas at later expositions and have looked at similar ploys in late-nineteenth-century retailing establishments, but none have realized that many of these features were actually pioneered at Civil War sanitary fairs.

The proportionate size of the booths at the Rochester Christmas Bazaar—the area devoted to the United States was about one-third of the whole, and the National booth was double the size of any other—reflected the relative importance given to patriotic themes. The images were further brought to life in a series of historic theater games or enactments. At Albany's "Holland Booth," for example, "descendants of the old stock" dressed in eighteenth-century garments and "revived the glorious customs of the past" by re-enacting a quilting bee, "chatting as of old," and offering the visitor "a puff on a friendly pipe." At the Brooklyn and Long Island Fair, members of the local Sanitary Aid Society set up what in contemporary terms could be likened to a living history museum: they turned a forty-by-one-hundred-foot room into the "New England Kitchen," a restaurant and exhibition area designed to present a faithful picture of New England farmhouse life in the period just before the American Revolution. The overriding idea behind the kitchen was the promotion of a revived revolutionary spirit. "We shall try to reproduce the manners, customs, dress, and if possible, the idiom of the time," explained the circular issued by the committee in charge. Actual antiques were used in the room, and the central feature of the display was a huge fireplace with swinging pots. Despite this seemingly noble purpose, the kitchen was an amusing place that generated good feeling. Costumed "dames" spun before the fire and knitted in the corner of the room. An "Indian," "hideous in horns and paint," periodically stalked the crowd. Long tables were laden with pork and beans, cider, brown bread, and other New England specialties, and diners were served by "damsels with curious names and quaint attire." The most talked-about features of the New England Kitchen were specific, staged entertainments: a series of "old folks concerts," featuring century-old musical numbers;[25] a "donation visit," which re-created the colonial practice of contributing goods to the local minister; a quilting party, which concluded with a young people's festival; an apple paring (bee), which included storytelling and riddles (figs. 27–28); and, as a finale, a staged wedding, where an already married couple humorously reenacted their nuptial ceremony in colonial attire in front of the 250 people who had purchased tickets. The actors in these kitchen dramas came together for the duration of the fair in a spirit of play and theatricality. They took on assumed identities, with stage names and exaggerated dialects and speech patterns. One participant stated afterwards that she "never enjoyed anything more than [her] five days' work in the New England Kitchen."[26]

The New England Kitchen was an unmitigated success—the *History of the Brooklyn Fair* noted its kitchen was always crowded and would have made more money if it had been held in a larger space—and was emulated at fairs that took place later. Not to be outdone, Poughkeepsie, New York, women featured a one-hundred-year-old Dutch farmstead at their March fair. Manhattan women followed with a Knickerbocker (Dutch) Kitchen in April; and at the Mississippi Valley Fair in May, fairgivers included both a New England and a Holland Kitchen. Other kitchens appeared at the Maryland Institute Fair,[27] the Great Central Fair in Philadelphia, and the second Chicago fair. In Chicago, fairgivers repeated the reenacted colonial wedding, but improved on the Brooklyn version by requiring that all wedding "guests" also appear in costume. They choreographed participatory games such as blindman's buff and thread-the-needle to follow the ceremony.[28]

The kitchen exhibits presented, in effect, a distaff view of the colonial past, as they reproduced female-identified domestic environments. They were a natural embodiment of the separate sphere ideology and echoed the sentiments and ideas of contemporary "environmentalists" like Catharine Beecher and Harriet Beecher Stowe, who believed in the moral influence of the home. There was even a strong precedent for gender-identified history based on home-based activities.

Fig. 24. The plan of the main building of the Metropolitan Fair indicates how the sanitary fair came to blend features of trade expositions and ladies' fairs. Industrial exhibits ringed the hall, but the Floral Temple sat at the center, and booths representing the four seasons and the Alhambra were clustered near the Art Gallery. The Knickerbocker Kitchen and International Hall were in a separate location. From *Record of the Metropolitan Fair* (1867).

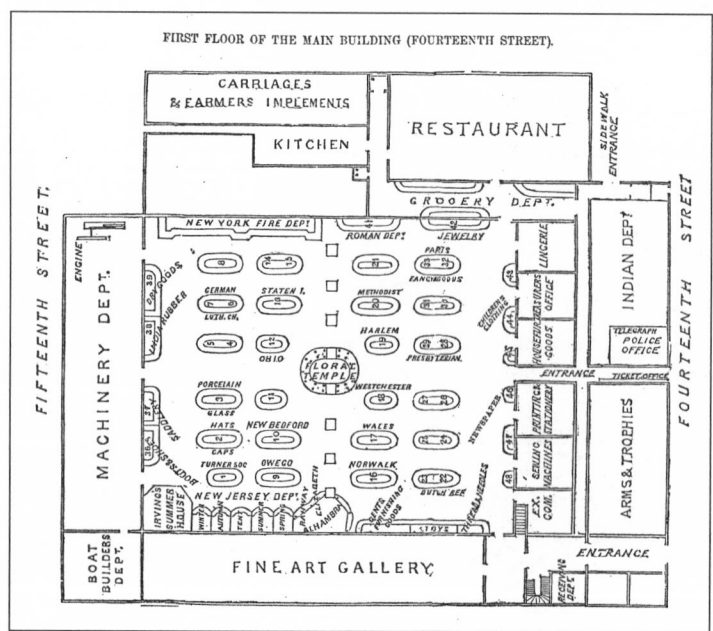

Figs. 25 and 26. Costumed salespeople from the Albany Army Relief Bazaar (1864) posed with props from their booths. These images come from an album labeled "Photographs of the Bazaar," now housed in the Manuscript and Special Collections Division, New York State Library, Albany, New York. Pictured here are individuals from the Yankee Booth. Photograph by the author; used by permission.

Figs. 27 and 28. Apple paring and quilting parties were staged in the New England Kitchen of the Brooklyn and Long Island Fair. Fairgoers were much taken with the costumed "colonialists" and the quaint surroundings. These illustrations appeared in *The Tribute Book* (1865). Courtesy of the Chicago Historical Society.

Elizabeth Ellett's 1851 work, *Domestic History of the American Revolution,* for example, focused on everyday endeavors such as making stockings and boycotting tea. Rodris Roth argues that the kitchen dramas were probably based on Stowe's 1859 novel, *The Minister's Wooing,* which devoted whole chapters to "The Kitchen," "Miss Prissy," and "The Quilting." Stowe celebrated what Jane Przybysz calls a "secular religion of everyday life" and presented the domestic setting as a place where women carried out almost heroic deeds.[29] The kitchen exhibit organizers took this seriously, but at the same time they used the domestic as a pose; they not only venerated the kitchen, but made light of it. Their attitude to the past was similarly double-edged; it too was simultaneously venerated and gently mocked.

These playful, carnivalesque reenactments allowed individuals to identify with the people and places of the earlier time, but remain distant from them. The kitchen environments were among the earliest manifestations of the colonial "period room" (erroneously, this distinction is often credited to the New England Kitchen at the Centennial Exposition),[30] but they did not represent the same kind of sanctimonious Colonial Revival sentiment that was to take hold later in the century. They did not evince an antimodernist yearning for an earlier, golden era; on the contrary, they reflected a somewhat self-satisfied attitude, a stance of superiority toward the past. Mid-century Americans believed in progress, and, by turning the colonial kitchen into a comic kind of place, they were able to reinforce their sense that, notwithstanding the war, they were living in a more advanced era.[31]

Almost as a counterbalance to these domestic dramas, some sanitary fairs included miniaturized, staged reenactments of the battle of the *Monitor* and *Merrimac.* The warships were presented at one-twenty-fourth actual size, as the mock battle took place in an eighty-five-foot pond. The drama, complete with powder, smoke, and sound effects, was performed three times a day.[32] The contrast between these two types of amusements epitomizes the gendered differences in approach. The battle reenactments were staged by men. They honored militarism and power, were based on a technological tour de force, and included no human characters. The women's reenactments honored the domestic. They were based on human interaction and relationships, and involved food, drink, and comfort.

Sanitary Fairs as a National Exposition

The same miniaturized warships were apparently taken from one sanitary fair to the next, much like the carnival equipment at today's state fairs. This is just one example of the cooperation that existed among fair organizers and the speed with which ideas and attractions moved across the North. In some ways, in fact, we can even see that, largely due to the well-networked aid groups, the fairs functioned as a single Union-wide phenomenon. The Albany women who attended the Rochester fair were typical; at every sanitary fair there were visiting representatives from other regions who came to observe, confer, and return home with ideas. Mary Clark Brayton, a member of the organizing committee of the Northern Ohio Sanitary Fair, reported that her branch of the Sanitary Commission sent its president, vice president, and treasurer to Chicago, and they came back with a much-expanded sense of what they might accomplish. Artworks, novelties, and mementos featured in the trophy or curiosity departments or raffled off to the highest bidder were also routinely taken from one fair to another, and in some cases they were able to generate higher and higher sums in each location. For example, a huge ox dubbed "General Grant" made its way from New York's Metropolitan Fair, where visitors paid ten cents to see it, to the Boston Sailors' Fair and then to the second Northwest Fair, where it was viewed for a dollar. A piece of black bread that had been purchased at Gettysburg for five cents was sold at the Philadelphia fair for $100, redonated, and resold there for $290. It then appeared yet again in Chicago in 1865.[33] There are also indications that horticultural displays were transplanted from one location to another, although I have found no explicit acknowledgments to that effect. Many of the features of the Floral Hall from the Cleveland fair (discussed in detail below) were later evident at subsequent sanitary fairs; they were

Fig. 29. From the evidence in this photograph taken at New York's Metropolitan Fair, it appears that women of different ages volunteered to work in the Knickerbocker Kitchen. Although purporting to be citizens of the eighteenth century, these individuals are wearing fashionable 1860s hairstyles and undergarments. From *Record of the Metropolitan Fair*, 1867.

Fig. 30. The Knickerbocker Kitchen was outfitted with colonial antiques donated by local residents. These formed a convincing backdrop for historic entertainments. Photograph by Matthew Brady; courtesy of the Still Picture Branch, National Archives.

probably built with much of the same scenery and may have been put together by the same designers.[34]

Notable personalities were asked to contribute to one fair after another. Painter Frederick Edwin Church was so deluged with these requests that he declined to donate work to the second Chicago fair, claiming, "You cannot have the slightest conception of how much Artists have been taxed to contribute to hundreds of fairs . . . held all over the Union. If I had acceded to all the demands I would have done nothing else for two years." Many artists dealt with this dilemma by exhibiting the same pieces at a series of fairs. This was a common enough situation to warrant a boastful announcement on the part of the Northern Iowa Fair organizers that none of the art or other articles on display at their event had previously been seen elsewhere.[35]

There was in fact an almost siblinglike rivalry among the different sanitary fair groups; it became a matter of local pride to have sponsored the biggest and best sanitary fair possible, and each region was spurred on to its best effort by the good-natured competition. This was symbolized by a huge broom that was prominently displayed at the Brooklyn fair. The outsized artifact had been sent by the Cincinnati committee with the message, "We have swept up $240,000; Brooklyn, beat this if you can." A proud Long Islander added to the sign, "Brooklyn *sees* the $240,000 and

MAIN BUILDING OF
THE GREAT NORTH WESTERN SANITARY FAIR
CHICAGO.
OPENED MAY 30 th 1865

goes $150,000 *better.*"[36] As these descriptions indicate, the fairs created a Union-wide showcase of objects and ideas that functioned in the aggregate as a kind of national exposition. In the long run, I believe, they also helped encourage the evolution of a national museum.

As would befit a national exposition, sanitary fair organizers shifted from using existing facilities to building new facilities expressly for the fairs. Early in 1863 an Albany newspaper was already commenting on the crowding in Rochester, saying, "What discomfort! Is a new building impracticable?" Organizers quickly realized that high profits were dependent on adequate space, and by December, new facilities were constructed for the Great Western Fair in Cincinnati. Two structures, which together provided 50,000 square feet of exhibition space, were added to already existent, adjacent buildings. From then on, new structures were the general rule (New York City's Metropolitan Fair, housed in a large armory and in other satellite buildings, was the one notable exception). Clevelanders "took a deep breath" when their building committee proposed building a 64,000-square-

Fig. 31. Once it was clear that sanitary fairs were profitable endeavors, fair managers began to erect special structures for the events. This large building, which enclosed much of Chicago's Dearborn Park, provided sufficient exhibition space for a "monster fair." Courtesy of the Chicago Historical Society.

INTERIOR VIEW OF THE UNION HALL, NORTH-WESTERN SANITARY FAIR BUILDING, CHICAGO, ILL.—From a Sketch by Mr. L. Hurd.

Fig. 32. An interior view of Union Hall of the 1865 Chicago Fair gives a feel for the enormous scale of the buildings at major sanitary fairs. From *Frank Leslie's Illustrated Newspaper*, courtesy of the Chicago Historical Society.

foot, Greek cross-shaped structure that would cost about $10,000 to build; no charitable enterprise in the city had yet even grossed that amount of money. The final cost of the building was actually lower, however, as lumber, hardware, and labor were donated by local businessmen, and the effect was, in any case, sensational. The building was sold for $8,500 at the end of the fair to the building committee of the Pittsburgh Sanitary Fair, furthermore, and was put to use once again in another location.

Philadelphia's Great Central Fair, held concurrently with the Pittsburgh event, featured an innovative building plan. All of Logan Square, an area of 200,000 square feet, was enclosed, and the entire length of the street that framed it was sheltered by Gothic-style vaulting. Other buildings were attached as wings or ribs positioned on both sides of a central spine. A similar arrangement was effected in Chicago's Dearborn Park at the second Northwest fair (figs. 31–32).[37] The women of Chicago had so well proven their point about the efficacy of fundraising fairs—they were borne out not only by their own 1863 success but by the chain of even more successful fairs that followed—that there was no hesitation the second time about spending sizable sums of money on a physical structure.

The grand buildings would not have been possible without the active participation of the business community. The men had not only been won over, but had in some respects taken over; facilities committees at the later fairs, for example, were all dominated by men. The increasingly exposition-like quality of the fairs was a clear reflection of male intervention. At the same time, it is interesting to note that the two features of the sanitary fairs that may have had the strongest impact on the public and on future cultural institutions and facilities—i.e., the art galleries and horticultural environments—related to areas generally associated with women—i.e., art and gardens. "Womanly" qualities like culture and beauty remained an irrepressibly important part of the legacy of the fairs.

The Rarified Atmosphere of the Sanitary Fair Art Gallery

The picture gallery included in the first Chicago fair was such a successful feature that it was emulated at the majority of subsequent events (see table 1). These galleries were among the most highly praised features of the fairs; they were consistently described in the press with epithets like the "crowning achievement," the "rarest attraction," and "the one thing that should not be missed." They stood as symbols of cultural achievement and were associated with wealth and the "best" people (see below). Fairgoers took the rhetorical hyperbole to heart and made it their business to visit the galleries. At the Chicago fair, public interest was so great that the gallery was kept open an additional two weeks after the fair closed; 1,850 tickets were sold on a single day, and 25,000 people attended in all.[38] The response was similar elsewhere; in Brooklyn, 2,000 people were attracted to a preview gallery "reception and promenade" before the fair even opened. The displays were always crowded. A tongue-in-cheek description of the Metropolitan Fair gallery included the statement that "were the air here half as good as the pictures, we would willingly stay 'till morning." The crowding is particularly noteworthy because the spaces were typically quite large. In Philadelphia, where over 1,000 works were shown, the 15,000-square-foot gallery ran the whole length of Logan Square.[39]

Planners paid considerable attention to state-

Fig. 33. A close-up view of a display at the Metropolitan Fair shows how dominant flags and bunting were when the environment was experienced from a human scale. Individuals are visible in the foreground. Photograph taken from *The Spirit of the Fair* (1864).

Fig. 34. Individuals pose at "Burden's Booth" at the Second Northwest Fair. Burden, from Troy, New York, had recently patented a machine that manufactured horseshoes. He traveled to several different sanitary fairs to sell miniature versions as good luck charms. Courtesy of the Chicago Historical Society.

of-the-art lighting and display. In Rochester, they dimmed the light in the Athenaeum library so that "day was turned into night . . . after the most approved plan of lighting an Art Gallery." In Milwaukee, they painted the walls a warm drab color and draped them with maroon cloth. The light was filtered through screens which were moved to different positions as the day wore on and the sun changed its position. The general feeling was subdued, in other words, and contemplative. A description of the second Chicago Fair gallery captured the quality when it referred to a "dim religious light from above." Paintings were placed close together, following the contemporary ideal; juxtaposition of this sort enabled the viewer to determine which works were truly superior (fig. 36). The effectiveness of the displays was discussed by publicists, reporters, and even members of the gallery-going public. Maria Lydig Daly, a judge's wife, saw fit to discuss the Metropolitan Fair art exhibit in her personal diary. "The gallery is very beautifully proportioned," she noted approvingly; "the pictures are well hung and well lighted."[40]

The peaceful atmosphere was repeatedly emphasized in promotional literature and internal fair newspapers. "The turmoil and hurry of the crowd at the great building, the feverish clatter of plates at the New England Kitchen [and other noisy distractions] are all absent at the Gallery," stated Chicago's *Voice of the Fair.* "After the Babel of the Grand Bazaar . . . the quiet study of so much beauty will be remembered," echoed an Albany newspaper. The Milwaukee *Home Fair Journal* noted, "[T]he Gallery is the quiet[est] place in the building and a most pleasant retreat." The insistence on this rarified atmosphere was inseparably tied to a prevailing belief in the uplifting, beneficial nature of art. In Milwaukee, where the gallery at the Soldiers Home Fair was the first public art exhibit in the state, the newspaper lamented the fact that it might be a long while before the local populace might have "another opportunity of improving their taste and giving encouragement to one of the most elevating influences of society." In an art gallery, noted an *Arthur's Home Magazine* correspondent, "each man 'stands confessed,' and reveals at once his true nature."[41]

To guide gallery-goers through the experience, catalogues listed each work with the artist's name (e.g., Jacob Bierstadt) and title (e.g., "Scene in the Rocky Mountains") and described its pictorial content. Other than a listing of the painting school with which a given painter was associated, there was little in the way of interpretation. The same model was followed by commentators who wrote for the local press or the fair newspapers. A feature in *Our Daily Fare* on June 20, 1864, for example, which purported to "dwell at some length upon the magnificent Art Gallery for the sake of all those, including posterity, who were not able to come to the Great Central Fair,"

Figs. 35 and 36 *(below).* Two views of the Art Gallery at the 1864 Metropolitan Fair in New York, photographed by Matthew Brady. Although the massing of artworks looks crowded to the contemporary eye, this was state-of-the-art display in the Civil War period. Courtesy of the Still Picture Branch, National Archives.

discussed "Rocky Mountains" almost entirely in descriptive terms: "The artist has given us a glorious picture of green sward, water fall, mountains and sky, with the eternal hills piled up in the back ground, and melting away in dreamy distance, while in the foreground savage life is illustrated with wonderful fidelity to detail."[42]

The art seen at sanitary fair galleries was a mix of old masters—occasionally seen in actuality, but usually in the form of copies—and original work by both local and nationally known American artists. Women's work was represented to some extent. The types of art most in demand were landscapes, portraits, and historical paintings.[43] Because some paintings were shown repeatedly in different cities—Church's "The Heart of the Andes" was exhibited in both Philadelphia and New York, for example—the exposure of this body of indigenous work had a national impact. The paintings were discussed in the local press and in national publications like *Arthur's Magazine* and *Frank Leslie's Illustrated Newspaper*. Charles Boynton remarked that if these fairs were studied in Europe, the general European impression that Americans lacked culture would be rectified.[44]

The galleries carried strong class associations. Many of the artworks were themselves connected with the rich and famous. In Brooklyn, for example, some of the most popular paintings had been loaned by such well-known citizens as H. E. Pierrepont and Henry Ward Beecher. In New York, citizens had the opportunity to visit the homes of the wealthy in order to see their private collections (admission fees were donated to the Art Gallery). The gallery committees themselves were comprised of the kind of well-situated women who would feel comfortable soliciting these wealthy collectors or artists for loans, and these same women presided over the galleries when the fairs were open. In Chicago, several of the "most cultivated ladies of the Northwest" volunteered to interpret the artworks to the uninitiated. The exhibitions were also frequented by the elite. Maria Daly wrote in her diary about meeting the "most agreeable" and fashionable people at the Metropolitan Fair gallery, including noted generals such as Burnside and Frémont. Some of the artists, including Bierstadt himself, were also present.[45]

Many people may have been attracted to the art galleries because of their elitist associations, but the fact remains that the galleries had a strong impact precisely because they were so widely attended. This was an opportunity for people of all social classes to see art, and since there were as yet few public art museums, it was an unusual opportunity. Maria Daly noted that she sent her three women servants to the New York fair and encouraged them to visit the important attractions, and given the press coverage and popular attention paid to the gallery (the fifteen-thousand-dollar sale price of "The Heart of the Andes" had created a stir), it is likely they went to see what it was all about. The idea that country bumpkins or "rubes" went to see the sights was satirized in more than one fair newspaper. "Sally Popcorn" wrote letters to her sister in "Pumpkinsville" from the Metropolitan Fair, for example, describing her adventures. Her letter about the art gallery was lengthy and, to a person knowledgeable about the artworks (i.e., everyone who read the *Spirit of the Fair*), humorous. In her description of the Bierstadt painting, she spoke of the mountain stream as a splendid spot for Nephew Jehial to fish for catfish. In her description of "a Church painting," she complained she "could see no church—only two tall rocks with sunshine behind them—and no congregation other than three or four deer who had come to the pond for a drink."[46]

The sanitary fair galleries were highly profitable; $85,000 was realized from the sale of artworks alone at the Metropolitan Fair. Monies also came in from admission fees (often as high as a dollar), from sales of catalogues and donated work, and from the raffling of composite albums. In Brooklyn one of these albums included 120 sketches made by "major" artists. "Shares" cost $10 apiece. Shares in another album containing sketches by "amateurs" cost $5.[47]

The art galleries clearly made a strong impression on the people of a war-torn nation, and their impact was lasting. Many observers expressed the wish that the galleries remain open ("Would that it might be permanent! was on the lips and heart of almost everyone").[48] Their importance can be inferred, also, by the regularity with which they were emulated after the war. Art galleries were featured at fundraising fairs almost as soon as the war was over (in Northampton they were included at even

Fig. 37. At several sanitary fairs, albums containing artists' sketches were raffled off to the highest bidder or given to door-prize winners. Illustrated is a scene at the Brooklyn and Long Island Fair, taken from *The Drumbeat* (1864). Courtesy of the Chicago Historical Society.

relatively small fairs in 1866 and 1867) and they were almost ubiquitous in the 1870s and 1880s. It is significant that the movement for the establishment of public art museums, which had been slow in America compared to Europe before the war, grew rapidly during this time. Many of the same wealthy individuals who had worked at the fair galleries were instrumental in founding the Metropolitan Museum of Art in New York and the Museum of Fine Arts in Boston in the 1870s, and the Philadelphia Museum of Art and the Art Institute of Chicago in the 1880s.[49] In sum, the sanitary fair galleries brought the concept and experience of the art gallery further into public consciousness and helped make the institution a public priority. There was a gallery at the Centennial Exhibition and its presence accelerated this process, but the first art museums were already in existence by 1876, and the Centennial Exhibition only added momentum to a movement that was already underway.

Picturesque Horticultural Environments

Although plants had been incorporated into fairs for over thirty years and every sanitary fair had a separate area for appealing floral displays, special halls were installed in five instances. These spaces were expanded versions of Rochester's Fairyland: they featured a potpourri of picturesque attractions such as lichen-filled grottoes, "sylvan glades" with rustic bridges and fish-filled streams, groves of exotic palms, and formal French gardens. The halls were large, designed interior landscapes and, like the art galleries, were in keeping with progressive contemporary design ideas. Like the art galleries, they too were highly appreciated and instrumental in furthering public artistic consciousness.

The first Floral Hall made up the central area—it was the centerpiece—of the specially erected building at the Northern Ohio Fair in Cleveland in 1864. The area was octagonal, with a seventy-five-foot diameter and a sixty-five-foot rotunda. The general design, if I have correctly interpreted Mary Clark Brayton's description, was based on a formal plan but was so broken up by changes in elevation, winding paths, and varying vistas that it appeared informal and picturesque (fig. 38). Light from the dome bounced off "evergreen thatched" walls, and columns and archways were twined with laurel and hemlock to simulate forest trees. A peak or hillside broken into distinct mini-environments dominated the middle of the room. Visitors walked around different vignettes: "wild mountain growth struggling out between huge boulders," a "forest nook" with a cascade that widened into an "alligator-infested sedgy pool," or a Rhineland scene with a castle, cottage, and grazing livestock by a waterwheel. The visitors were surrounded by leaf-covered walls and encountered "cunningly hidden" features like bird's nests, rabbits, and other animals (fig. 39). Around the perimeter of the room they could visit "summer houses" and pagodas to buy items like Indian beadwork or picture frames made of pine cones and sticks, or they could stop at the "Wayside Inn" for refreshments. "Gypsy" fortune tellers lingered nearby. Still other attractions included a chapel made of pebbles and glass and a Garden of Eden area where life-sized stuffed animals mingled with marble statues. The hall was heated by underground steam vents and was filled with the hot, humid air of a summer day.[50]

Pittsburgh's Floral Hall was similar, with the same sort of central hillside and rustic sales booths around the outside. Local variation was seen in a hillside vignette designated an "iron and coal mountain." The Horticultural Department of the Philadelphia fair was more original and much more grand; its central rotunda had a diameter of 190 feet. It was still dominated by a plant-covered summit, but this was constituted as a pyramid of exotic plants set on an island. The pyramid functioned as a fountain, with sheets of water cascading from each side and hundreds of water jets shooting up around the perimeter. The jets were in turn surrounded by a ring of flame. *Our Daily Fare* enthused about this extraordinary feature: "The effect . . . is indescribable. The thousand fantastic colors sent forth must be seen, and when seen will never be forgotten. Every drop of water becomes a jewel."[51] Other Philadelphia features included an aquarium "containing earth, air, fire and water" (this was not described more fully) and two adjacent rooms with diorama-like displays, respectively representing the Arctic Circle and the Torrid Zone. The Horticultural Department of the second Chicago fair included the expected central summit (dubbed "Point Lookout" after one of the sites of Union victory) which in this case could be climbed by means of a staircase winding amid splashing waterfalls. It also included a variety of live animals—fawns, swans, a crane, and even an eagle—who were "free to wander about" and interact with passersby, and a formal garden likened by the *Chicago Tribune* to Versailles.[52]

These horticultural environments involved an enormous amount of coordination, advance planning, and mobilization of resources. Designers had to prepare water conduits, bring in rocks and boulders, and plant vast amounts of grass. (Chicago's Floral Hall did not come into its full glory until it had been open for more than a week, as the grass was not fully grown when the fair opened.) Thousands of plants and hundreds of gardeners were needed to make the landscapes come alive. In Milwaukee, with a relatively small horticultural exhibit, nine florists provided much of the material, but the public was also encouraged to send contributions of potted flowers by train. Each city called on its citizens in a similar manner, not only for plants, but for equipment of all kinds. In Chicago, individuals loaned statues, wrought-iron garden structures, and fountains for the duration of the fair.[53]

Although women were instrumental in planning most of the details of the sanitary fairs, they were likely not involved in the basic design of these interior landscapes.[54] The similar features of the environments imply that local horticultural professionals worked from a basic prototype which conformed to the current American Romantic style. This was the time when New York's Central Park was being constructed, and a description in the *Voice of the Fair* made a point of connecting Chicago's hall with that notable environment. "Imagine Central Park epitomized and intensified, and you have the Hall," boasted the author.[55]

Central Park was designed by Olmsted and Calvert Vaux, who firmly believed that the public park or landscape would be uplifting enough to raise the level of popular aesthetic taste. The fair landscapes were seen at the time in much the same way. In "The Influence of Exhibits in Improving the State of the People" that appeared in Chicago's *Voice of the Fair,* the author argued the importance of such firsthand experience as a way of elevating public taste. A later piece in the same paper also addressed the positive impact of Horticultural Hall: "We cannot but feel certain this vision of beauty will not merely linger in the imagination of those who have enjoyed it, but will incite some of our wealthy citizens—if the city authorities will not take the hint—to give us something like this on a larger scale. . . . [If this were the case, people could] resort to [such a landscape] to cultivate their taste for the beautiful."[56] The horticultural halls, like the art galleries, were referred to in quasi-religious terms: they also had a special light

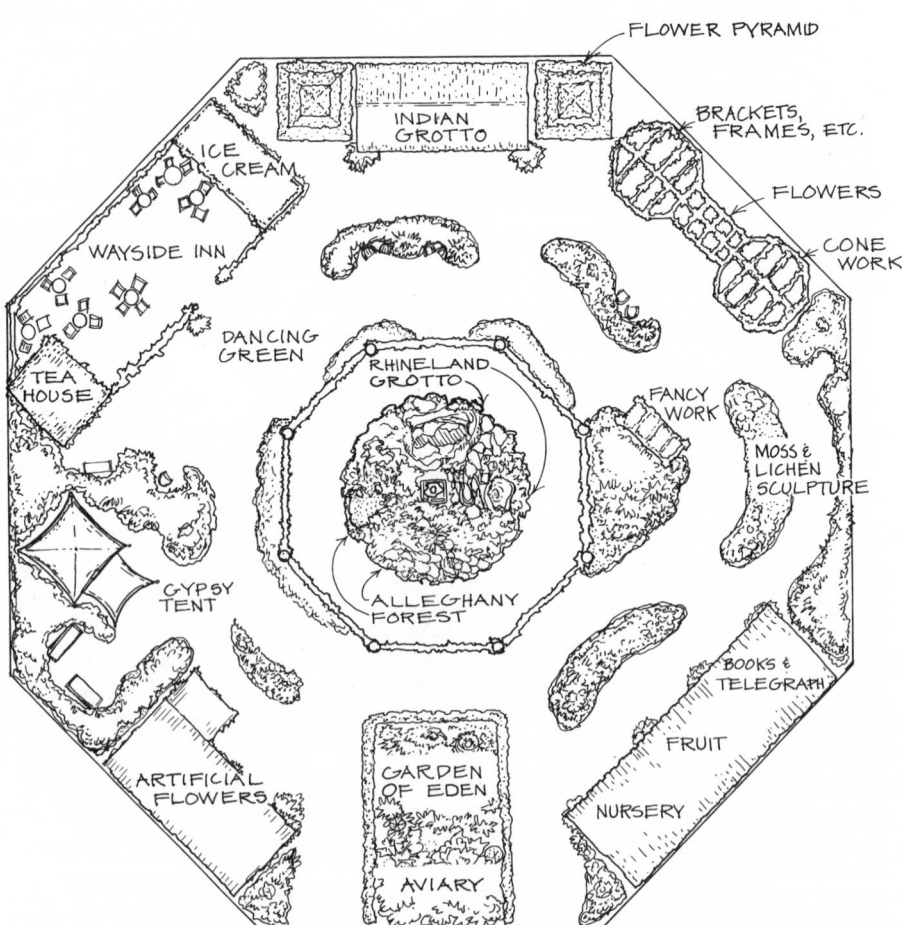

Fig. 38. This plan represents the author's conception, based on written descriptions, of the overall layout of Floral Hall at the Northern Ohio Fair (Cleveland, 1864). Illustration by Julie Shaull.

(it was filtered through cloth, stained glass, and masses of foliage) and were acknowledged as quiet places of respite and retreat from the din of the fair. They too had separate admission fees in some locations (this was the case in Philadelphia, where even before the fair closed horticultural admissions amounted to eighteen thousand dollars), but were nevertheless crowded at all times.[57]

Again like the art galleries, the landscaped halls were visited by hundreds of thousands of people in an era when public parks, conservatories, and botanical gardens were still more of an incipient idea than an established reality. They not only provided perhaps the majority of Americans with their first experience of such environments, but also did so in a context that gave great import to the experience. A spate of park building followed shortly after the war. Many major American cities, including Philadelphia, Chicago, Baltimore, Albany, Pittsburgh, Cincinnati, and St. Louis, all of which had hosted sanitary fairs, were in the process of planning parks by 1868.[58] It is not unreasonable to conclude that the impetus to the parks had been reinforced and perhaps hastened by the experience of the fairs. The late-nineteenth-century penchant for conservatories has been credited to the Horticultural Hall built in Phila-

Fig. 39. This illustration of Floral Hall appeared as an engraving in *The Tribute Book* (1865). It is rendered after a work by George L. Clough, a Cleveland artist who was commissioned to paint scenes of the fair. The original painting is in the History Collection of the Western Reserve Historical Society.

delphia for the Centennial Exhibition, but it too may have been stimulated by sanitary fairs. Philadelphia itself had experienced an equally impressive and far more imaginative Horticultural Hall eleven years earlier at the Great Central Fair.[59]

The Evolution, Efficacy, and Legacy of the Sanitary Fairs

The last great sanitary fair, also held in Chicago (Ann Hosmer, who worked on the organizing committee of both Chicago events, called the city the "alpha and omega" of the sanitary fair phenomenon)[60] incorporated almost every feature that the collective experience of the sanitary fair committees had found successful. In addition to the attractions Chicago itself had pioneered (the art gallery, trophy/curiosity collection, and commercial exposition) and previously mentioned attractions like the New England Kitchen, the fair also generated money and excitement through the mechanism of "voting." This was a lucrative fundraising scheme, first instituted at the Metropolitan Fair, which consisted of awarding a predetermined prize to the person who received the greatest number of paid "votes." In Chicago there were hotly contested races, with running totals of the tallies reported daily in both the in-house fair organ and the city newspaper. "Elections" were for favorites like the most popular general (awarded a set of prize pistols) or the prettiest girl in the city (awarded an English dressing case valued at one thousand dollars). The latter contest stirred up great feeling. "The young beaux are extremely anxious" about the outcome of the vote, reported the *Voice of the Fair*; "the girls are all in a flutter." Anna Wilson won, but barely so; 1,073 votes had been cast for her, 1,068 for runner-up Mattie Hill, and 1,022 for Amelia Carley. A description of an election at a different fair indicated that each vote cost one dollar, and people took "especial pleasure in neutralizing their predecessor's vote." There was no limit on the number of votes an individual could cast. These contests reflected the increasingly pecuniary quality of the sanitary fairs; they involved expensive prizes and turned a popularity contest into a commercial enterprise. The whole thrust of the sanitary fair evolution was in the direction of professionalization and commercialization, and as we have seen this often mirrored the stronger male presence.[61]

Many of the unique elements of the 1865 Chicago fair also reflected the same trend. For example, large numbers of children were "enlisted" by a Mr. Alfred Sewell into the "Army of the American Eagle." The sole purpose of this organization was to sell pictures of Old Abe, the bird who had been carried throughout the war by the Eighth Wisconsin Division and had become an emotional symbol of the Union cause. Children could become "officers" if they sold sufficient pictures: the sale of ten earned a child the rank of corporal; twenty pictures earned a sergeant's badge, one hundred a captain's, and so on.[62] This "army" raised fifteen thousand dollars before the fair opened. Hierarchical and militaristic, it was a far cry from the small-scale Alert Clubs that had formed in 1861.

Dining arrangements at the two Chicago events also contrasted sharply. At the first fair, as we have seen, the women organized and staffed one large restaurant. In 1865 there were a number of smaller, more picturesque eating establishments, at least some of which were professionally run. John Wright, a Clark Street confectioner who oversaw a restaurant overlooking the formal garden in Horticultural Hall, had a staff of "colored helps" assisted by young volunteers.[63] Even the physical environment of the second Chicago fair followed a well-planned, centrally coordinated design rather than a haphazard effect. The enclosed avenue created by the long Union Hall structure (figs. 31–32) made the event seem more like a trade show than a ladies' fair and reflected the more structured organization and male participation that had become standard at sanitary fairs.

Mary Livermore and Jane Hoge were again in charge of the second Chicago fair. They had at first been reluctant to take on the task because they knew how much work was involved and they were discouraged by what they had learned about the limits of their legal authority.[64] Livermore was shocked to find in the course of her arrangements for the 1863 fair that her signature was not sufficient on a contract in Illinois; even if she earned her own money, she was told, she could not spend it without the written consent of her husband. "We two women were able to enlist the whole Northwest in a great philanthropic, moneymaking enterprise and had the executive ability to carry it forward," she wrote in her reminiscence of the war. "[Despite this], our names were not worth the paper on which they were written." Livermore was greatly radicalized by the lessons of the sanitary fair and vowed to take up the cause of women's rights as soon as the war was over. (She did so with alacrity, as she organized a woman's suffrage convention in 1868.) For the duration of the war, however, she continued to work within her assigned role. She was the actual director of the second fair, but acceded to working under an all-male executive committee and to moving within and around the necessary legal restrictions.[65]

Large regional events like the sanitary fairs were decidedly good for Union morale; as Livermore's story of the first Chicago fair makes clear, people found it easy and gratifying to rise to the occasion of a fair and to help out with a particular event. Numerous other descriptions reinforce the appeal and force of community feeling and the impact on the public imagination. In Rochester, workers commented on the "vortex of interest" that became perceptible as the "whole community was drawn into its whirling current"; they claimed that the pronoun "we" became the operative one in the city as the bazaar became the "transcendent theme." Similarly, New Yorker Maria Daly noted in her diary that the fair was so much the focus of attention for several weeks running that it swallowed other concerns.[66] Individuals felt great pride in their local groups and solidarity with other people of their region, as well as with the Union as a whole.

From the point of view of the Sanitary Commission, the success of the fairs was less clear-cut. After four or five fairs had taken place, the commissioners reported they actually felt more in need of assistance than they had earlier. The general population

Fig. 40. The black ribbon on this badge, worn by a worker at the Curiosity Department of the Second Northwest Fair, was a sign of mourning. President Lincoln had been recently shot, and there was some feeling that the fair shouldn't take place, but plans were too far advanced to make cancellation feasible. Chicago Historical Society Decorative and Industrial Arts Collection; courtesy of the Chicago Historical Society.

was well aware of the large sums that had been raised at the fairs and felt more complacent about the sanitary cause. The needs of the commission were not fully met, however, as the primary contributions before the fairs had been in the form of supplies rather than money, and once the fairs were underway, supplies were harder to come by. Sewing societies turned from making shirts to making dolls, and women who had contributed foodstuffs directly to the soldiers contributed them to fairs instead. This meant that though the treasuries were full, clothing, bedding, and food still had to be procured, and there was lag time before it reached the troops. Another problem was that monies from the fairs went to branch offices of the commission, leaving the central treasury depleted. The branches were able to buy supplies and ship them to the central distribution points, but the central office could not afford to distribute them. This situation was ameliorated somewhat by the fact that the proceeds of the Metropolitan Fair were funneled into the central treasury, but subsequent fairs were still regional, and there remained a significant difference between public assumptions about the Sanitary Commission coffers and its actual condition.[67]

The sanitary fairs served as a turning point in the history of the fundraising fair. After their stunning success, women's fundraising activities were definitely taken more seriously. There was little more condescension about women selling merchandise, and even the rhetoric about women selling themselves died down considerably.[68] Paradoxically, however, the women lost some of their autonomy and control, and the events were no longer so unequivocally "theirs." Whereas once they had effectively negotiated the whole infrastructure of society—rerouting trains and streetcars, closing post offices, arranging for donations from gas companies and other commercial enterprises—and had worked jointly with men, their fairs became more dominated by "professionals" and incorporated more activities outside the women's control. Even the sales items changed at fairs, as machine-made consumer products were increasingly evident, competing with women's handmade goods. The sanitary fairs had many lasting effects, but the general appreciation of the women's agency in these endeavors was undercut.

The leaders of the regional northern fairs—those who shaped their cultural and social agendas—were educated, erudite (the excellent quality of their prose is striking in many of their reports), urban, Protestant, and generally upper middle class; they represented the power structure of mid-nineteenth-century America.[69] However, a relatively broad cross section of the population did become involved in fair activity. Catholics and Jews worked on fair committees (in Rochester, the Jewish women specifically stated that they did not want to be isolated in their own organization, but to work "as Americans" throughout the bazaar), and even those isolated on the frontier were able to contribute, either as constituency groups, like the Germans of the Northwest, or as individuals. A few blacks were also involved. The women of St. Thomas Episcopal Church in Philadelphia worked for the Sanitary Commission and seem to have been welcome at the fair, although their presence was compromised by the fact that they couldn't ride on the city railways, and they eventually decided to hold their own fair for the commission in December. (The more common scenario may have been that African Americans worked, as at the restaurants, in servant roles.) Even prostitutes were said to have donated the proceeds of a day's labor to the Philadelphia fair.[70] The contributions of these less-enfranchised groups and individuals must be remembered in any assessment of the sanitary fairs, for they formed the backbone of the labor force that made the fairs possible.

Many of those who worked in leadership positions at sanitary fairs subsequently went on to other organizing and reform work. Some, like Livermore, campaigned actively for women's rights. Sanitary fairs provided unprecedented opportunities for networking on a national scale, and women's experiences there strongly contributed to their sense of what they could do when they worked together. Sanitary fair networking undoubtedly hastened the eventual development of the many women's clubs and organizations that flourished at the end of the century, and should be considered a predecessor or contributing factor in future studies of the turn-of-the-century women's movement.

We have chronicled many types of cultural innovation the women effected at these fairs and seen how they influenced the development of art and history museums, public parks and conservatories, and phenomena like the Colonial Revival. We have seen how the fairs provided strong opportunities for fellowship and aesthetic elaboration, often in this case through playacting in complicated theatrical environments. We have seen too how the inherent paradoxes of women's fairs were demonstrated at these events, and how the women played with and against their assigned roles at them (highlighting the domestic and yet making light of it, highlighting their sexual attractiveness and yet working in the most efficient, businesslike manner). In the succeeding chapters we shall see how in ensuing decades many elements of the sanitary fairs became standard and even exaggerated at other fundraising fairs and how the tensions of the fairs grew ever stronger.

CHAPTER FOUR

Other Fairs of
the Civil War and
Reconstruction Periods

She had worked twice as hard as any girl in town, getting things ready for
the bazaar. She had knitted socks and baby caps and afghans and mufflers
and tatted yards of lace and painted china hair receivers and mustache cups
. . . embroidered half a dozen sofa-pillow cases. . . . [Now] she was actually
at . . . the biggest party Atlanta had ever seen. . . . She . . . looked up and
down the long hall which until this afternoon had been a bare and ugly
drill room. How the ladies must have worked today to bring it to its
present beauty. It looked lovely. Every candle and candlestick in Atlanta
must be in this hall tonight. . . . In the center . . . the huge ugly lamp,
hanging from the ceiling by rusty chains, was completely transformed by
twining ivy and wild grapevines. . . . The walls were banked with pine
branches that gave out a spicy smell, making the corners of the room into
pretty bowers where the chaperons and old ladies would sit. Long graceful
ropes of ivy and grapevine and smilax were hung everywhere . . . [around]
the brightly colored cheesecloth booths. And everywhere amid the
greenery, on flags and bunting, blazed the bright stars of the Confederacy
on their background of red and blue.

—Margaret Mitchell, *Gone With the Wind*

The sanitary fairs were the most important and influential fundraising fairs of the Civil
War era, and they certainly warrant a chapter of their own, but they were by no means
the only fairs that took place. Even while sanitary fair mania was sweeping the North,
there was never a dearth there of independent events for the Union or nonwar, related
causes. Confederate women also put great energy into fairgiving. We will explore other

wartime fairs in this chapter and will look at the way the fair developed in the following fifteen years. We will examine how fairs were used for women's causes—how the same kind of networking and activism evidenced in the antislavery and sanitary fairs was now extended to fairs for suffrage and related causes—and at the ways the feminist community was itself plagued by the fairs' contradictions. We will also look at the increasing tension between commercialism and domesticity, and the ways it was reflected in organizational structure, environmental presentation, and sale goods at fairs during the Reconstruction era.

Non-Sanitary Fairs in the North

Fair mania was so strong in 1863 and 1864 that, in addition to participating in regional sanitary fairs, some women initiated other fundraising events for the war effort.[1] Some local fairs were relatively large and involved; women in Columbus, Ohio, for example, held a separate week-long "Grand Bazaar" in December 1863 while the Great Western Sanitary Fair was taking place in Cincinnati.[2] Other events were small and relatively spontaneous: toward the end of the war, as a case in point, the women of North Hadley, Massachusetts, sponsored an almost impromptu fair "for the soldiers" that generated only $28.23. Many of the small fairs funded locally identified projects. For example, women in Worcester and Springfield, Massachusetts, held fairs to support area soldiers' hostels that were stopover points for troops heading south from New England.[3]

Although they were considerably reduced in number during the heyday of the sanitary fair, there were also women's fairs for "civilian" causes. In the Northampton area, for example, several bazaars raised money for church buildings and activities. The women of the Baptist Church raised five hundred dollars to repair interior damages caused by a fire, and a newly formed congregation in nearby Easthampton held a fair for its facility. African Americans gave a festival for the benefit of the Methodist Episcopal Church in 1865 (the *Free Press* bemoaned the fact that too few people of other denominations were present). Like this festival, most nonwar-oriented fairs took place toward the end of the conflict. As Robert Bremner points out in a study of philanthropy and welfare in the Civil War era, the war at first brought a period of unprecedented economic prosperity to the North, meaning that destitution was temporarily reduced. At the same time, the strong awareness of difficulties engendered by the war led to increased voluntary contributions to all kinds of charitable societies, and the receipts of such organizations were at new highs. However, by 1865 there were new needy groups, including war widows and orphans, disabled veterans, and refugees from the South, and fairs were held to ease their plight. Church groups also began to hold fairs again because maintenance that had been allowed to slide for several years could no longer be put off.[4]

Like the sanitary fairs, local fairs provided legitimate opportunities for pleasure and festivity in what was predominantly a dark and difficult period; Reynolds even states that most wartime social life revolved around benefit programs and charitable activities. It is hardly surprising that the fairs were often scheduled on holidays, when "permission" for merrymaking was implicit. When two Northampton area fairs were scheduled on Valentine's Day in 1865, the *Northampton Free Press* intoned that it expected "all the young folks of marriageable age to choose their mates . . . and go their way rejoicing."[5]

Confederate Fairs

The importance of the social dimension of the wartime fair is particularly striking in the case of the major events organized by women of the Confederacy. Like their northern counterparts they had immediately formed soldiers' relief organizations, but these were never united into anything as centralized as the Sanitary Commission.[6] The South was more rurally based and far more devastated economically and materially by the war, and with most of women's energies directed to basic survival, it was hard for them to coordinate fundraising efforts. There were local fairs, raffles, and entertainments, but only one event involved the cooperation of a whole region, and it took place toward the very end of the war. Without the extensive networking and intercity cooperation that was possible in the North, southern fairs essentially followed the antebellum model; they remained ladies' fairs. Nevertheless, they were emotionally and symbolically significant, and the excitement of the well-documented events is still palpable.

In 1862 "Ladies Gunboat" campaigns were launched by women in Charleston, Savannah, New Orleans, Richmond, and other communities. Because one of the strategies of the Union government was to set up a naval blockade around the southern states, thereby cutting off imports to and exports from the Confederacy, the construction and presence of blockade-fighting gunboats were critical to the economic survival of the South. Southern women threw themselves wholeheartedly into fundraising drives for these vessels. The Charleston Ladies Gunboat Fair and Raffle was held to support the construction and outfitting of the *Palmetto State,* a South Carolina flagship. Fairgivers stocked the tables with the usual variety of handmade items (appropriately, a great many were made of local palmetto) and goods donated from local manufacturers; dolls dressed as daughters of the Confederacy were among the offerings. They decked the hall with large state and confederate flags and served ample "creature comforts" like ham, chicken salad, crab, and coffee.[7]

Based on the rather scanty reports of the fair (there were no long, self-congratulatory treatises comparable to those written in the victorious North), it appears the southern women had to contend with an even greater male skepticism and protectionism than their Union counterparts. According to the *Daily Courier,* gentlemen were "detailed for superintendence" of the Gunboat Fair.[8] The newspaper report was particularly insistent about the morality and goodness of the fairgivers; entire columns were devoted to women's "holy object" of charity, and more was made of the propriety and industry of the ladies than had been common in the North for two decades. The rather defensive tone may have had something to do with the centrality of raffling, which some saw as a questionable activity. The raffle was an event-within-an-event, advertised long before opening day, with a separate twenty-five-cent admission. Each chance cost a dollar, and raffle items, ranging from silver spoons and china plates to sofa cushions and saddle cloths, were on display at all times. The Gunboat Fair raised approximately ten thousand dollars.[9]

Three years later, South Carolina hosted a much larger fair that involved most of the South and raised more than thirty times as much money as the Gunboat Fair.[10] Women in the capital city of Columbia announced plans for a Great Bazaar in May of 1864 and secured the cooperation of groups from other Confederate states. I have found no information on the networking channels that were established and do not know if assistance came from existing soldiers' aid groups or from more personal social contacts, but the general impression is of a less efficient organization. Nine months passed before the event actually took place (four months was a more typical lead time in the North), and there seems to have been no single coordinating repository. The fair was held in the statehouse, and contemporary descriptions of the decor bring to mind antebellum antislavery fairs rather than environments effected by professional designers. On reaching the structure, visitors found the massive columns twined in smilax and strung with a banner proclaiming in gold letters that the fair was "A Tribute to Our Sick and Wounded Soldiers." Inside, the visitors were directed to the Senate Room and Hall of Representatives, where, against a backdrop of thick red curtains, they found sale tables representing the different states of the Confederacy. These were dramatically draped with red and white cloth to look like camp tents, and the room was embellished with the usual evergreens, mottoes, and flags. On the last night, one hundred candles were lit on a huge Christmas tree. Post office and fortune-telling booths also added to the festive atmosphere, and trophies such as Union flags captured during battle were scattered among the displays.

This event seems to have been one of most significant social occasions of the war for the besieged people of the South. The Columbia *South Carolinian* remarked that the bazaar had "for some weeks been the topic of the parlor, drawing room, and street," and crowds flocked to see it. Although the capacity of the two statehouse rooms was said to be fifteen hundred, thirty-eight hundred tickets were sold the first day. "Such a jam!" exclaimed Emma Le Conte, a seventeen-year-old Columbia resident who worked at the South Carolina table and described the event in her personal diary. Even the sale items were festive and suggested a sense of plenty as a counterpoint to the deprivations of daily wartime life. The Soldiers' Relief Association specifically requested fancy items for the fair, rather than plain or strictly practical contributions; straw and palmetto bonnets, crochet, and tatting were given as examples. Commercially produced sale items, many of which were from England, had also been brought through the blockade.

The fact that there was an abundance of goods that had not been available for years helped create a "high carnival spirit," and people spent great sums of money. Le Conte

Fig. 41. This well-dressed doll came with a trunk full of fashionable dresses and accessories and was raffled to the highest bidder at the Second Northwest Fair. It was later donated to the Chicago Historical Society. (A similar doll and wardrobe from the Brooklyn and Long Island Fair are found in the Brooklyn Museum). Dolls were also raffled at Confederate fairs, and brought in staggeringly high sums. Courtesy of the Chicago Historical Society.

noted that one imported wax doll raffled for two thousand dollars, a sum her uncle remarked could "buy a live Negro baby." "How can people afford to buy toys at such a time as this!" she wondered. The answer was hinted at by Grace Elmore, who wrote a fictionalized historic account of "The Last Bazar" for *South Carolina Women of the Confederacy*. In Elmore's story, Pvt. Frank Elden and his cousin Nell were wandering through the fair when they came on such a doll. "Where did this come from?" asked Frank. "All the finery of the country seems collected on this child." Nell replied that the doll was wonderful, and she would be envious of its silk and lace if not so grateful for its safe arrival. "It braved the whole United States fleet, and the swamp angel besides, to be present at the bazaar," she exclaimed. Le Conte also answered her own question when she remarked that it was hard to believe that there was a war going on when one went into the bazaar; it was the very contrast with the hardships and destitution of the war that made people so extravagant.

Impressive repasts were also offered at this fair. There were restaurants at several of the state booths. The Louisiana menu followed a French theme, including such specialties as *blanc mange,* mock turtle soup, and eggs *à la Creole.* The Texas restaurant countered with (true) turtle soup, alligator steak, venison, and wild turkey. Food, like everything else, was expensive. A small slice of cake cost two dollars, and a spoonful of Charlotte Russe cost five.

As in Civil War fairs of the North, there was also a strong personal or sentimental component to the Great Bazaar. Women were said to have donated wedding rings to the sale (this act was immortalized in Margaret Mitchell's *Gone With the Wind* bazaar scene), or silver cups that had belonged to their soldier-sons when they were babies. Elmore's fictional soldier recognized a remnant of his sweetheart's silk gown sewn into a tobacco bag spotted on a sale table.

There was one feature of this Great Bazaar that had no equivalent in previous events or in any northern fair. News from the front was more and more ominous as January wore on, and spirits began to flag after a few days. Although the fair was originally intended to run for two weeks, it was closed early because of the proximity of General Sherman's forces. One of Elmore's characters remarked that the gaiety of the bazaar was ill timed; it was like "Nero fiddling while Rome burned." Le Conte expressed a similar sentiment. "I had expected to take great interest in the Soldiers' Bazaar," wrote this young lady, "but I cannot. It seems like the dance of death, and who can tell that Sherman may not get the money that was made instead of our sick soldiers." What became of the money from the Great Bazaar is not clear, but Sherman did march into Columbia on February 17, and the city was destroyed by fire. It was only a matter of weeks until the devastation of the South was so complete and irreversible that Lee surrendered at Appomattox. The irony of the timing of the single regional fair of the Confederacy is poignant, especially because the tragedy that followed was in such strong contrast to the high-spirited gaiety of the fair. Later accounts of the fair all stress this dramatic contrast, and to southern women the fair stands as a symbol of the optimism, dignity, and tragedy of their foremothers.

Juvenile Fairs

At the same time that women were honing their fairgiving skills and men were becoming increasingly involved in women's fairs, there was also an increased interest on the part of children. As indicated, young people enthusiastically contributed to the sanitary fairs and were part of the general northern fair mania.[11] The attraction was strong enough, however, that children wanted fairs of their own. Livermore describes a juvenile fair mania that swept through Chicago in the summer of 1863—notably, several months before the first sanitary fair in that city. She explains that children from ages nine to sixteen planned and staffed fairs that they held at home. Some contemporary commentators called these events "doorstep fairs," since they so typically took place on front lawns or porches—in the liminal area between the public and private space of the home (see fig. 42). Other names for children's fairs were "mimic bazaars" or (especially after the war) "doll's fairs."[12]

Livermore's description of one Chicago doorstep fair gives a feeling for what transpired and communicates the kind of benevolent amusement adult patrons seem to have felt toward these events. The bemused attitude toward children as salespeople is, tellingly enough, a kind of exaggerated version of the attitude men first had toward saleswomen at earlier ladies' fairs. Livermore's description also shows us how children perceived the fundraising fair as a central part of adult life and played "fair" much as they would play "house" or "school"; it was part of their rehearsal for adulthood.

> A boy of eleven stood at the gate as custodian, gravely exacting and receiving the five cents admission fee. Another little chap, of ten, perambulated the sidewalks for a block or two, carrying a banner inscribed, "SANITARY FAIR FOR THE SOLDIERS!" and drumming up customers for his sisters under the trees. . . . The fair tables were [covered] with an assortment of toilet-mats, cushions, needle-books, penwipers, patriotic bookmarks, dolls, and confectionery. The national colors floated over the little saleswomen, some of the very smallest sit-

Figs. 42 and 43. Children held fundraising fairs of their own in the Civil War era. Many were set up on porches of private homes. Both illustrations are taken from *The Tribute Book* (1865); courtesy of the Chicago Historical Society.

ting in high dinner-chairs, and all conducting their business with a dignity that provoked laughter. . . . Big brothers and sisters stood behind them, ostensibly to assist in making change, but in reality because they enjoyed the affair.[13]

Children (primarily girls) held fundraising fairs for more than the Sanitary Commission—they held them for the same gamut of causes that their mothers did. For example, in Flushing, New York, three girls organized a fair for the Patriot Orphan Home, an institution their mothers had recently established for children who had been made homeless or destitute because of the war. The girls met weekly to make sale items, and, like their mothers, they fully exploited family connections. One, according to Goodrich, "importuned" her influential father to rent Flushing Town Hall for the event; another "worked on" her father until he collected $500 from his fellow workers on the stock exchange. Adult women relatives also contributed their time and effort, and the fair raised $1,300 for the orphans.[14]

This story reinforces the theme that those with no power or resources of their own resort to a kind of indirect influence. At the same time it reminds us of the complexity of power. These girls were children with no seeming authority, but they did have power, for they were able to effect just what they wanted. The story also reminds us again of the privileged social position of many of the fair organizers. It is important to reiterate, however, that not all of the children's fairs were so profitable, and not all of the children who put them on were equally wealthy. In all, the 1863 Chicago children's fairs yielded about $300, and some of the individual events were so small that they netted only about $5. The scale of children's auxiliary sanitary fairs in other cities also varied. Ten Brooklyn girls organized a fair that raised $164; an unspecified number of Boston children raised $300.[15] Since children incurred no expenses (they were effectively subsidized by their parents and did not have to pay rent, hire bands, etc.) the whole of their profits could go to their respective causes.

Fairs and Women's Causes: Feminist Ambivalence

It might seem that after the pecuniary and social success of the sanitary fairs, activist women would throw themselves even more wholeheartedly into fairgiving after the war. The reality was more equivocal. On one hand, many organizers had grown increasingly impatient with the subsidiary role that forced them to resort to the kind of indirect influence described above—the radicalization that Livermore experienced during her work for the Sanitary Commission is a case in point—and they were sensitive to the continued criticism of fairs that re-emerged after the war. Nevertheless, even those in the forefront of the feminist community sponsored fundraising fairs during this time, and many radical women's institutions depended on them for financial support. Fairs were more ubiquitous than ever; women across the social and political spectrum began to use them to fund a growing variety of causes. Concomitantly, there was a range of attitudes about the institution of the fair. Some individuals threw themselves into fair work, but others were less enthusiastic and found them a kind of necessary evil.

Criticism of the fairs came from many sources, but much of it stemmed from a renewed disdain for women's "wheedling." Even a sympathetic description of a typical fair scene indicates how, given the ideology of domesticity and the fact that respectable middle-class women were still not expected to work outside the home, they usually had little money of their own and, like children, generally still had to rely on their husbands or male acquaintances to raise funds. The following appeared in the newspaper published for Boston's Congregation House Fair in 1872: "[Husband and wife are sitting at a table at the cafe.] If you look close . . . you will see a telegraphic sign pass between [them]. Presently as he takes out his purse to pay the dinner check, he tosses out a few 'greenbacks' to the partner of his joys and sorrows, and you may be sure, if you go to their church next Sunday, that their little boy or girl has a new . . . article of clothing."[16]

The women were not doing anything unseemly, but their behavior was nevertheless often treated condescendingly. Sometimes the criticism even came from other women. Reformer Abba Gould Woolson accused her sisters of wheedling when she wrote about fairs in *Woman in American Society* in 1873. "Their own individual supplies are procured in this manner," she stated, "and it is not strange that they make it the basis of that extemporized shopkeeping which they call a fair." She sarcastically complained that the "elaborate nothings" sold at fairs were appropriate, as these were events where buying and selling were only pretexts for the "real" work of coaxing and compelling. The sale items did not meet any actual needs, for the articles were not made to suit the customers—the customers were "procured to suit the articles." This latter complaint had almost become a leitmotif in the Reconstruction era. In "My Experience at the Fair," a poem in *Godey's Lady's Book* in 1875, for example, a gentleman who had come to a charity bazaar upon the importuning of a young lady described how he had been taken in. He "purchased right and left" until he spent all his money, but then realized he had no use for the items he bought: he didn't smoke, but had purchased cigarettes, pipes, and smoking caps; he had no wife or children, but found himself with toilet cases, aprons, baby blankets, and dolls.[17] If fairgivers did wheedle—and this is a matter of interpretation—it was because it was their only choice; they were using the only "tools" they had at their disposal. What should have been criticized were the limited roles that women were allowed to play. This is no doubt what Woolson meant to do, but her critique still put the women at fault.

Even women who were aware of these contradictions worked at fairs; Woolson herself ran a table at the Woman's Suffrage Bazaar in Boston in 1871. Let us look briefly at that event and at the fairs held for the New England Hospital for Women and Children. We shall see how integral fairs were to the woman's community, and how feminists built on networks, ideas, and features from fairs of the past.

The Woman's Suffrage Association (also called the Equal Woman Suffrage Association) was founded shortly after the war by Mary Livermore, Lucy Stone, and Henry Ward Beecher (Livermore moved to Boston in 1869 to serve as vice president and to edit the group's newspaper, *The Woman's Journal*). The 1871 bazaar was only the second fair sponsored by this group, but it was already a very sophisticated operation. It was run much like a sanitary fair, with separate chapters contributing goods and proceeds going to a central association treasury.[18] Organizers made special ticket arrangements with the railroads to bring people into the city and arranged for lodging for out-of-town helpers. They also elicited the cooperation of other groups, such as the Good Templars, and engaged a Mr. Vogel as a "chief marshall" who took care of miscellaneous business arrangements. Vogel bought supplies in bulk, negotiated with florists to supply plants and help decorate the hall, and secured "sideshow" attractions—a miniature skating rink and a glass-blowing demonstration— from the sponsors of another, recently completed fair. The suffragists demonstrated great familiarity with profitable attractions and effective organizing tactics and ideas. They mounted an art gallery, held a raffle and an end-of-fair auction, and provided entertainment and lectures about the cause. They paid a local newspaper, the *Charlestown Chronicle,* to publish twenty thousand copies of their *Bazaar Gazette.* Although the *Gazette* was given away, it was still a profitable endeavor, because a committee of thirty women had worked soliciting advertisements before the fair. Soliciting was also recommended on a very intimate scale: according to the records kept by the bazaar secretary, "each lady connected with the Bazaar should beg a can of cream from her milkman" for a "suffrage cake."[19]

I cannot tell from the fair records how many of these arrangements Livermore herself was involved in, but she did preside over several of the organizational meetings. In any case she was the unequivocal iconic heroine of the association and the fair. A card-sized photograph of Livermore and Hoge was a popular sale item, and the company that produced these also offered a "life size crayon head of Mrs. Livermore." The suffragists evidenced a strong sense of solidarity with the woman's community and proudly honored their leaders and their nascent cause. (Note that Livermore continued to work with the suffrage fair for many years. As late as 1886, when she served as president of the bazaar, she was said to be very concerned when she was called out of town and could not supervise the day-to-day fair preparations.)[20]

The feminists of Boston also supported the New England Hospital for Women and Children (hereafter abbreviated NEHWC), which was located in neighboring Roxbury. This was a radical institution, founded and staffed by women. While women had made some inroads in the field of medicine before the war was over (many had worked in hospitals, and a few went through nurses' training), they were still not really accepted in the profession. Elizabeth Blackwell, who had served on the Sanitary Commission board and had earned the first medical degree granted to an American woman, could not find a position as a physician in an established hospital. She decided to open an alternative institution, the New York Infirmary for Women, which would both employ women and serve a female clientele. The NEHWC was set up at approximately the same time as a sister institution by one of Blackwell's protégées, Marie Zakrzewska. It served as the nation's primary training center for female nurses and doctors for the rest of the century, and when African American men were refused entry into regular nursing programs, they too were accepted there for on-the-job training. From its inception, the NEHWC was an integral part of the local feminist community. Lucy Stone (who was Blackwell's sister-in-law) was an ardent supporter. After she took over the editorship of *The Woman's Journal* in 1872, in fact, Stone regularly ran long reports about the hospital. Ednah Cheney, founder of the New England Women's Club and the New England Women's Association, served on the hospital board for forty-eight years.[21]

In 1864 the hospital board and local supporters decided to defray expenses with a fair, although they were concerned that it might be difficult to garner support because of the war.[22] Their fears were allayed when they raised $547, and they subsequently repeated the fair annually. For many years, it provided a good proportion of the institution's operating funds. In 1866, for example, the treasurer reported two sources of income for the hospital: proceeds from benefit activities (an unspecified entertainment, a tableaux performance, and a fair), and a grant from the state. The fair brought in $2,700, more than half as much as the operating grant of $5,000. In 1869 the state only contributed $1,000, but a fair brought in over $4,000.

NEHWC fairs were held in private homes until 1868, when space was rented, first in Warren St. Chapel and later in Horticultural Hall. They were consistently successful; even in 1874, when the board almost canceled the event because of a horse disease epidemic and an extensive citywide fire, receipts totaled $5,300. The figure was nearly tripled five years later. The fairs came to symbolize the hospital and, by extension, the feminist community. Women rallied around the events to show their solidarity and support—even former patients pointedly contributed goods and came to help out. The hospital secretary referred to the 1876 fair, in fact, as a "social reunion." The staff found the fairs time consuming and exhausting, but, in keeping with the pattern we have already become familiar with, recognized their continued importance as community builders. The 1878 *Annual Report* of the hospital included the following: "We hope, when times are brighter, to be spared this arduous way of making both ends meet, yet feel that the necessity for our sales is not wholly to be deprecated. They have won an enviable reputation as pleasant and well conducted, and they bring about social relations between the Directors and friends of the cause."

Children also organized fairs for the hospital. There were several children's events in the 1860s (Ednah Cheney turned her house over to her children for one of these), and they were even more prevalent in the 1870s. Proceeds ranged from $7 to $110.

Other Women's Causes: Domesticity Enlarged

Northern women, as we have seen, had gained considerable experience in organizing and networking during the war years, and social reformers in both North and South found women increasingly willing to work in the public arena after the war. Nevertheless, because most women's groups were still predicated on the ideology of domesticity, most postwar fairs still supported activities that were perceived as extensions of the woman's domain. Large numbers of women worked tirelessly to raise money for (non-feminist-identified) hospitals. In New York, for example, the Ladies' Aid Society joined forces with the Ladies' Homeopathic Hospital Association in 1875 to stage a huge fair (the first of many) that ran for several weeks. It represented a great community effort, much like the previous decade's sanitary fair.[23] Later that year New Yorkers of many denominations also flocked to the Hebrew Charity Fair, held to aid Mt. Sinai Hospital. The institution itself was nonsectarian, serving "the poor and unfortunate of all creeds and nationalities." The *New York Times* called it the largest charity fair since the war; attendance reached about five thousand on each of the first two nights. The fair was "opened" by the governor. Chicago women ran a similar grand event in 1873 to support the Hahnemann Hospital Attending League.[24]

Education was also seen as an appropriately domestic cause, and women organized fairs for education-related causes—especially in small communities—for public schools. Support for vocational training for needy women was also forthcoming. The Women's Educational and Industrial Society, for example, sponsored an 1875 fair in New York for free training and cooking schools. Committee chairs included prominent wealthy women such as Mrs. J. J. [Cornelia] Roosevelt and Mrs. W. H. [Louisa] Van Buren.[25]

Changes in church demographics and emphasis also contributed to a proliferation of church fairs after the war, and because religion was also perceived to be

in the woman's bailiwick in the nineteenth century, these too were embraced enthusiastically as women's causes. In Protestant congregations there was at this time an increased secularization or focus on community or social life, resulting in a call for new
church facilities such as kitchens and social halls. Fairs helped pay for these spaces. There
were also more active church members and shifts in the leading denominational groups.
Ann Douglas notes that twice as many Americans belonged to churches in 1850 as in
1800, and due to an influx of new immigrant populations, the leading denominations
by 1855 were Catholics, Methodists, and Baptists. Catholics, who did not carry a Puri-
tanical legacy, embraced the idea and the institution of the fundraising fair especially
enthusiastically. In the 1870s they organized huge and popular "cathedral fairs" in
many cities. One, held in the South End of Boston in 1871, created enough interest to
warrant discussion in the newspapers in the western part of the state. Another, representing a joint effort on the part of many New York parishes, was open for nearly a
month and generated over $160,000 (perhaps now worth about ten times that
much). Many non-Catholics attended cathedral fairs (New York's mayor addressed
the Grand Bazaar of the Church of the Holy Trinity in 1877, although he was
not Catholic himself), and the events were generally treated respectfully by the
press. Cathedral fairs followed the usual patterns of other bazaars of the time,
although unique activities such as the staging of a two-act drama, "Ireland and
America" (in Northampton in 1874, for example) were occasionally included. Fairs
were also held for Catholic charities and Catholic monks; a fair benefiting New
York's Paulist Fathers lasted for two weeks in 1877. Jews similarly embraced
fundraising fairs. The Shaare Rachim Fair was another two-week event, held to aid
the Norfolk Street (New York) Synagogue in 1878. This was so well publicized in
the Jewish community that it was announced in a Cleveland newspaper.[26]

Support for church work and educational and medical projects sometimes came
together after the war in the form of fairs for parochial schools and foreign
missions. These too were frequently large-scale events; for example, the New
York Branch of the Women's Foreign Mission Society held a week-long bazaar to
fund medical work in India and China in 1875. Many of the women on the organizing
committee of this event were physician's wives, presumably well positioned in New
York society.[27] Although most were probably politically more conservative than the
suffragists or supporters of the NEHWC, it is important to note that one of Jane
Hoge's activities after the war was to head the Presbyterian Board of Foreign
Missions in the Northwest. The boundaries between different women's causes
or political positions were far less rigid than they are today.[28] Like the abolitionists
and the feminists supporting the hospital, leaders of the mission movement argued in
1876 that the sociability of bazaars would help attract new members for their cause.
They particularly noted that the bazaar gave women who had no money an opportunity to contribute what they did have, i.e., their labor.[29]

The emphasis on relief that had been so salient during the war also led to increased attention to both foreign and domestic relief during the Reconstruction

era. Fairs were again the preferred fundraising mechanism.[30] Boston-area women assisted Cretan refugees (fleeing from the Turks) in 1867 and victims of the Franco-Prussian War in 1871. Eight years later French Bostonians sponsored a table at the fair for the Swiss Benevolent Society as a "token of gratitude" for help the Swiss had offered French soldiers during that war. Some of the domestic relief activity—and fairs—continued to focus on local charity (the 1874 financial report of New York's Association for Befriending Children and Young Girls indicated that nearly half its total income of $13,660 was raised through fairs), but other relief centered on new groups of needy. For example, destitute southern blacks were helped by Freedmen's Aid Societies in New York, Boston, Chicago, and other northern cities. Struggling white survivors of the war were also assisted by people who lived in more prosperous regions. St. Louis residents held a fair for southern widows and orphans in 1866, raising approximately $150,000, and Baltimore women raised about the same amount at their April 1866 "Fair for the Destitute South." In North Carolina, if not throughout the South, the funds were distributed almost equally between black and white recipients.[31]

The Reconstruction era charitable impulse extended in many directions. It was evident even in relation to creatures of other species; in 1871 the Massachusetts Society for the Prevention of Cruelty to Animals held a "Dumb Animal Fair" in Boston that was supervised by a committee of one thousand ladies representing nearly every town in the state.[32] More significant, this impulse was expressed in the explosion of mutual relief or benevolent societies associated with veterans or other social, political, and ethnic cohorts. The auxiliaries of these organizations—i.e., the women's groups associated with them—began to hold fairs by the late 1870s. Because veterans' and fraternal groups were at their peak at the turn of the century, they will be discussed in greater detail in the next chapter.[33]

In sum, women's fairs of the Reconstruction period supported a spate of new and newly defined causes, most of which were tied to a domestically defined identity. This observation echoes the point made by several historians that causes taken up by women after the Civil War used and reinforced domestic values but pushed them in new directions. Ruth Bordin's study of the Woman's Temperance Crusade of 1873 and 1874, for example, concludes that women were drawn to participate because the crusade corroborated domestic values and the idea that women's place was in the home, but it gave them a public forum in which they could express those values and impact upon a wide audience. Karen Blair's study of women's clubs, the first of which were founded just after the war, makes a similar point, as does Lee Ann Whites's study of charitable activity in postwar Augusta, Georgia, and Mary Ryan's treatment of postwar activity in western New York.[34] Part of the tension of these late-nineteenth-century fairs, as we shall see, is that they did not seem very domestic. There was an apparent mismatch between their domestically based causes and ideologies and their ever more frivolous character.

The Reconstruction Era Fair: Choreographed, Fairyland Environments with Amusing Attractions

Following the spectacular events of the Civil War, fairgivers had a new standard of excitement to live up to; simple ladies' fairs would no longer generate much interest. Consequently, postwar fairs tended to be elaborate and packed with amusing attractions. The very environments of the fairs were affected. Rather than the more casual arrangement of the antebellum hall that reflected an alliance of participating groups, rooms in the 1870s were typically set up as coordinated, dramatic wholes, with a central focal point often defined by a floral display. For example, the 22nd Armory was transformed into a "wilderness of beauty" for the 1875 Homeopathic Hospital Fair in New York. Under a canopy of azure gauze sprinkled with golden stars, the center of the room was dominated by a circular, rustic-style Floral Temple. Visitors were led to the temple by means of "avenues" defined by silver-leafed palm trees alternating with huge vases of flowers. The booths around the periphery were also decorated with simulated tropical vegetation, and there were flags and streamers, highlighted with colored light (beams from calcium lamps filtered through tinted glass).[35] Even when there was no floral bower, the center of the salesroom was typically emphasized. At a fair at the Metropolitan Opera House, for example, evergreen and holly were suspended from the dome and looped onto the theater boxes at regular intervals.[36]

These more "choreographed" environments were influenced by the displays the professional horticulturists had prepared for the sanitary fairs; the public remembered the sensuous appeal and transformative feeling of the Floral Halls and looked for something comparable. Comments about the decoration of the halls and the artistic quality of the fairs were common in newspapers of this period, and the press routinely used adjectives like "brilliant," "attractive," "picturesque," and "rich" to describe fair installations. In describing the Homeopathic Hospital Fair, the *New York Times* mentioned repeatedly that women had been working for months to create its magical environment and pronounced the embellishments so superb that a "view of them would alone repay a visit." Given the importance of these environments, the decorating committee became an ever more important variable in fair planning; an overarching vision could help make an event stand out. The committees were primarily composed of volunteers, but florists supplied the materials, and as the Woman's Suffrage Bazaar records make clear, the committees sometimes hired professional firms to create special effects. Sophisticated, designed environments further blurred the boundaries between expositions and charitable fairs, as the same "look" might be found at each.[37]

As indicated, the ideal image of the environments—the image that began to dominate the press and the popular imagination by the later 1870s—was "fairyland." In 1878 the *New York Times* raved about the environment at the Hahnemann Hospital fair, where it "looked as if a thousand fairies had been at work." (The actual decorating committee was made up of women, who effected the transformation in forty-eight hours. Men worked in the capacity of "assistants," primarily carpenters.)[38] Fairyland imagery was a convention, by no means limited to women's fairs, but it was especially strong there and persistent enough to remain a fair trope until World War I. We shall revisit the subject later, but it is important to note at this time that the origin of the theme may indeed possibly be traced to the floral displays of the Civil War. The first reference to fairyland that I have seen was the environment at the 1863 Rochester Christmas Bazaar described in chapter 3. This was a flower and perfume booth, the site of an evening performance called "Undine's Vision in Fairyland." Tellingly, the tableau represented a dream in which the heroine was introduced to the attractions of the earth (flowers, fruits, and groves) by a group of fairies, played by children two to six years of age. From the beginning, then, fairyland was linked to a dream state, to a woman, to the senses, and to theatricality; it coincided perfectly with the characteristics of the bazaar.[39]

Many postwar fair environments drew their picturesque quality from something else pioneered in Rochester: fanciful international imagery. A Swiss Benevolent Society fair featured a "chalet set against a background of the alps," for example, and a fair held for French relief was set up as a French boulevard, with Parisian-style newspaper kiosks and cafes. Oriental settings, often intentionally evoking the Eastern bazaar, became popular at events of all kinds. This was an undifferentiated Orient, a generalized, romanticized East. At a single fair there might be booths fashioned as mosques, temples, and pagodas, and publicity referred to the portrayal of "all manner of Oriental customs." Notably, Japanese tables and tea houses were attractions at fundraising fairs well before 1876, when Japanese themes captured the public imagination at the Centennial Exhibition.[40]

Given the patriotic thrust of the Centennial, it is hardly surprising that colonial settings and dramatizations, some based quite closely on the New England Kitchen prototype, were also ubiquitous in the 1870s. Even the French Relief fair included a "Mt. Vernon Street," and the event was ushered in with "calico parties." The Homeopathic Hospital fair included "Lady Washington's Cottage," and the Women's Foreign Missionary Society included both a Centennial Tea Party and a display of colonial relics at its 1875 fair. These themes were not limited to the Northeast; in Madison, women of the Congregational church planned a New England dinner and a Quaker booth at their 1870 fair. The colonial theme was certainly also stimulated by the Centennial Exhibition, but, once again, it had been anticipated at earlier fundraising fairs.[41]

Other features of the sanitary fairs continued, or were elaborated, after the war. For example, post office booths, which had been particularly popular at sanitary fairs— wartime fair post offices sometimes handled legitimate as well as playful mail[42]—continued to flourish. A description of the way one woman prepared letters for the post office at an 1877 Boston fair indicates how involved or even obsessive women's fair activity might be. This individual apparently wrote over one thousand letters during the three weeks preceding the fair. "[They were written] in a style so versatile that even intimate friends of the author could not guess the writer. . . . They came from distant classic spots, from dwellers beneath the sea, [and] from every conceivable spot in and around Boston, and in many cases just enough mystery was mingled with every-day coincidence to bewitch the readers."[43]

There were also "Old Woman in the Shoe" doll booths (the "too many children" were of the miniature variety and could be sold off; see fig. 44); magic skating ponds (miniature skaters, mimicking those on the relatively new Central Park rink, danced back and forth unassisted, presumably propelled by hidden magnets); Punch and Judy shows; and mealtime band concerts. Lemonade stands took the form of "Rebecca's Well," where costumed Rebeccas and other biblical characters "slaked the thirst of modern Jacobs." Tableaux performances were frequent, and curiosity exhibits were still popular (in peacetime no overriding theme was necessary; eight-hundred-year-old parchments coexisted with colonial relics).[44]

Voting contests were such a favorite and expected feature that the Methodist Church ladies society assured would-be visitors to its 1875 Madison fair they would not be annoyed at being called upon to vote "anything to anybody." However, most people did seem to enjoy these highly profitable races. One-third of the fifteen-hundred-dollar proceeds of an 1871 Madison fair came from voting contests where each vote cost only ten cents. There were contests for most popular minister (priest, rabbi), most popular physician, and most popular general, but the favorite races were for "favorite gentleman" or prettiest girl. At New York's St. Francis Xavier Church fair, three contestants for the latter title were nearly tied for several days. In the last three minutes of the race, supporters of two of the contenders vied so hard for their candidates that they brought in hundreds of twenty-five-cent votes at a time. At one Denver fair the proceeds from a single voting contest came to more than the fair had earned in an entire day earlier that week. In smaller towns, the contests seem to have often had a particularly humorous tone. At an 1866 temperance fair in Northampton, for example, a pair of silver-mounted skates was awarded to the girl voted the prettiest, while a large mirror was awarded to the homeliest man. At St. Raphael's fair in Madison in 1871, town notables—the mayor, postmaster, sheriff, and hotel keeper—vied with one another for a goldheaded cane. At the Methodist church fair in Madison that year, the pastor's wife competed with another church figure for a set of chromolithographs. There were also contests for favorite high school and favorite parish.[45]

As indicated, the art galleries that had been so well received at the sanitary fairs were particularly popular in the postwar years. They were included in fairs held for causes of all kinds, ranging from hospitals and churches to monuments or kindergartens, and they stimulated the same kind of discussion as they had during the war. The fair newspaper for the 1879 Seventh Regiment Armory Fair in New York, for example, discussed gallery lighting and what was or was not an appropriate picture frame. The sanitary fair galleries were explicitly credited as the models for this exhibit.[46]

Finally, we might reiterate the idea that women were in themselves a part of the

Fig. 44. Doll "booths" that played upon the nursery rhyme "The Old Woman Who Lived in a Shoe" were popular in the nineteenth century. Displays of this type combined the kind of costuming seen in the New England Kitchens with playful themes that appealed to both children and adults. Illustration from *The Tribute Book* (1865); courtesy of the Chicago Historical Society.

spectacle of the postwar fair; like the halls, they too were increasingly "dressed" in costume to become an integral part of fairyland.[47] Because this tendency became even more salient in the latter part of the century, we will discuss it in more detail in the following chapter.

Sale Goods: Elaboration and Meaning

The emphasis on spectacle could also be seen in the goods sold in these elaborate postwar fair environments; sale items reflected the trajectory of the fairs and mirrored their current tensions. Handmade goods still seemed to define women's fairs, but they were overwhelmed in many respects by the commercial products. First, women felt pressured to make items that seemed fanciful and less homemade or plain. By mid-century convention, handwork could be characterized as useful or ornamental, or it could be both useful *and* ornamental, which was considered the ideal. Ornamentation was appreciated—if an item was plain it was unremarkable, but once embellished, it became more elegant, beautiful, and good. Beautiful objects could by their very presence have beneficial influence, but they were most highly valued when they did have a purpose.[48] It was in this context that pincushions were made to look like fish or apples, and penwipers were made to look like parasols and sheaves of wheat (figs. 45–48). The objects were useful,

"The Model Post-Office"

There is nothing more unjust than the favoritism that is usually exercised at Post-offices. In despotic countries it may do very well to make arbitrary distinctions among individuals, but it is certainly intolerable in a republic, that one man should receive a letter when he asks for it, and another should be refused. Post-offices are supported out of the common funds, for the common benefit, and yet it is within the experience of every one, that some persons are turned off without the scratch of a pen, while they want. It seems not to arise from prejudice against individuals, but to be the result of mere caprice. We, ourselves, have often been told there were no letters for us, when we were really anxious to receive one, and at other times, oftenest on the first days of January and July, we have received quantities of wretched epistles in those horrid yellow envelopes, which we felt not the slightest desire for.

In the Fair Post-office these evils have been remedied. The Executive Committee, with that wise discretion that regulates all their proceedings, have requested that all their visitors should be treated alike, and that everyone who asks for a letter should receive one. This request has been strictly complied with, and will be enforced until therefore, it is only necessary to pay for it. We trust that this great reform will meet, as it deserves, the favor of every one, and that they will show their appreciation of it by buying early and often.

—*Our Daily Fare*, Philadelphia
June 13, 1864

but like the environments and the women, they were dressed up, and their playful, fanciful quality added to the overall feeling of the fair.

The handmade fair sales items were all objects of the domestic sphere. Other than children's toys, three main categories emerge, each of which can be further classified as accessories or embellishments: there were personal accessories (usually for women and children; men's accessories were limited to items used in the home, such as slippers); household accessories or embellishments; and sewing or writing accessories, which were themselves embellished. There was generally a blurred distinction between personal and household items; objects like pincushions and bookmarks were both used by individuals and displayed in the home. The profile of these items, in other words, reflects the close identification (blurred distinction) made at the time between women and the home.[49]

Some women tried to find alternative things to make for fairs, but they met with limited success. Subscriber Abby Shaw wrote to the *Ladies Floral Cabinet and Pictorial Home Companion* in December 1875, indicating that she and others like her had become tired of making pincushions, needlebooks, tidies, and mats for fairs, but

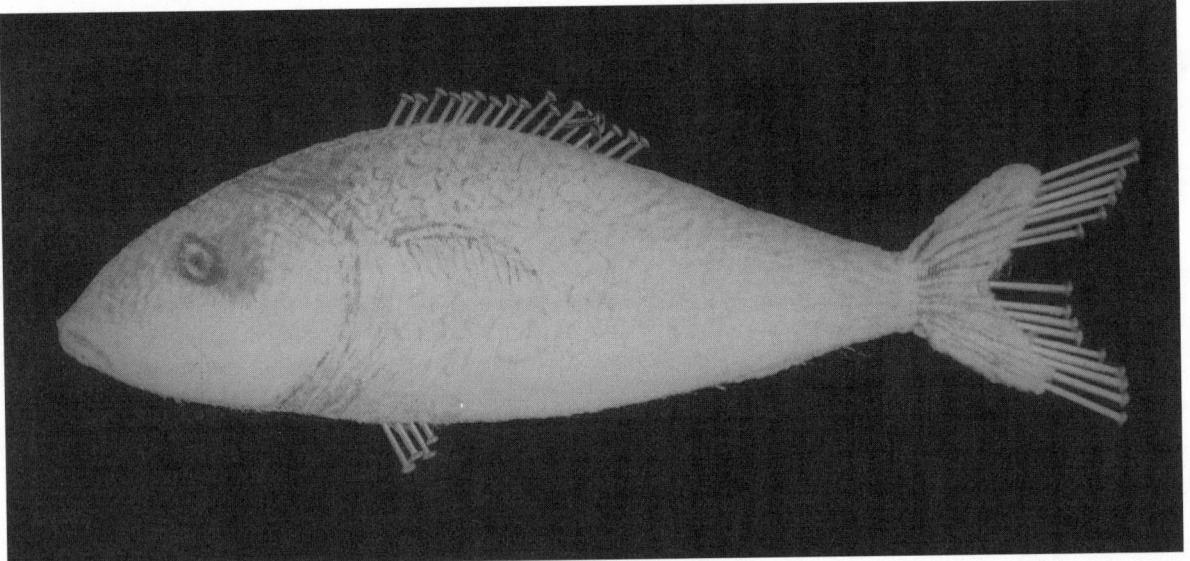

Fig. 45. A pattern for a pin-cushion in the shape of a fish appeared in *Godey's Lady's Book* in November 1868. This cushion, which was purchased at a Connecticut fair about 1870, is very similar to the printed prototype. It is made of gray silk, hand-painted in pinks and purples, and is tightly stuffed, possibly with sawdust or sand. The pins on the edge have not been moved, indicating that the cushion has not been used. Photograph courtesy of Dorothea Britton, author of *The Complete Book of Bazaars*, Coward-McCann & Geoghegan.

were perplexed about what else they might produce. She described her original solu-tion—a diorama of a quilting party, featuring six walnut-headed quilters (it sold for two dollars)—but admitted hers was an involved and tedious project that was not likely to become typical. Other attempts to break the standard pattern were often similarly thwarted. Even in 1888, when Laura Holloway admonished *Hearthstone* read-ers to make fancy articles sufficiently "shoppy in appearance" to compete with com-mercially supplied goods, the suggested items were simply variations on old themes. Holloway complained that penwipers were met with ad nauseam at bazaars, but she offered yet another penwiper pattern, this time in the form of a pensioner's hat. She also denounced pincushions as a "perfect mania," but included a pincushion design nevertheless. The new designs were lighter in feel by the time that Holloway wrote (they were in keeping with the latest Aesthetic style that caught on after the Cen-tennial Exhibition), but even she still included "masquerading" items, such as a sewing receptacle in the form of wheelbarrow (fig. 48) and a card case in the form of an easel. It was this kind of "elaborate nothing" that Woolson criticized in her 1873 commentary on the fair; these were objects that nobody really needed.[50]

The idea that sale items should be "necessary" actually misses the point of the fairs. It was the very fancifulness of these things that made them suitable for an entertain-ing occasion, and it was their elaboration that helped bring aesthetic pleasure and satisfaction. In all fairness, furthermore, the critique should have been directed even more forcefully at the commercially made goods that began to dominate the fairs. Commercial products were so much more common by about 1880 that many fairs be-gan to function as temporary retail stores. Manufactured goods had been sold at

American fairs for decades—think of the products that Maria Chapman brought to the antislavery fairs—but retailing at postwar fairs was on a different scale and involved a different kind of intentionality. In many cases fairgivers acted as entrepreneurs, soliciting products from local merchants or buying through wholesalers. An 1879 feature in *Harper's Bazar* described the latest innovation in English bazaars: fairgivers purchased products such as glass, pottery, and Japanese, Turkish, or Algerian goods from wholesale houses and then sold them at higher prices at their thematic booths. Sometimes they bought cases of fancy articles sight unseen at commercial loading docks, taking a chance on the contents; they knew that even if some pieces were broken, the low price of the bulk purchase was sufficient to offset any losses. Other women made arrangements to buy items at reduced prices from local shops, with the understanding that they could return unsold merchandise when the fair was over.[51]

Whether or not American fairgivers directly emulated these practices, they did sell great quantities of commercial merchandise and stepped well beyond the role of purveying small trifles. Organizers of the 1878 Fair for the Home for Infirm Members of the Methodist Church of New York stressed that their event provided a wonderful opportunity for Christmas shopping—a housewife could buy "everything almost, as long as her money holds out." Goods ranged from "bric-a-brac for lovers" to books, clothes, and even pianos. Both fair advertisements and newspaper announcements (perhaps taken from the fairgivers' press releases) stressed the extent of the merchandise and commonly stated their market value. Laces listed at $500 were specified for the Hahnemann Hospital fair, for example, as was a $3,000 diamond necklace. Total retail values were also cited; a fair might be listed as having goods totaling $30,000 or $100,000. The fundraising bazaar had indeed become a place where luxurious goods were heaped in profusion.[52]

These practices were in keeping with the rapid transformation into a consumer society that the United States was undergoing, based on the great availability of mass-produced goods and commercial services. The new commercialization of the fairs arose in tandem with the kind of professionalization I have argued was introduced at the sanitary fairs, and it represented a fundamental cultural shift which was also evident in other institutions. For example, Susan Davis argues that parades and ceremonies had functioned in the antebellum period as noncommercial, communicative events, but soon after the Civil War these became more commercially oriented and were tied to new patterns of consumption and advertising. The changes in fairs particularly reflected changes in other kinds of selling establishments—indeed, fairs and retail stores had long followed a parallel course. The earliest novelty stores had emerged in this country in the 1830s, the same time as the first women's fairs. The first department stores opened in the middle of the century, roughly the same time as the very large fundraising fairs. By the 1870s the department stores were turning into sensuous "grand emporiums" that helped create a new excitement about goods, much as the fair environments were being fashioned into transformative fairylands. The en-

Fig. 46. This painted silk pin-cushion that imitates an apple is worked in accordance with instructions in Adelaide Heron's 1894 book, *Dainty Work for Pleasure and Profit.* It is in the collection of Rosalind and Edwin Miller; photograph courtesy of the Allentown Art Museum.

vironments of the stores and the postwar fairs had much in common. The emporiums were typically built around a central courtyard under a high, dramatic dome, much as the fairs were designed around a central focal display. Both environments strongly stimulated the senses, and, as we shall explore in the next chapter, helped imbue the goods with meaning—they seemed to embody the excitement and positive feeling of their surroundings. The environments came to represent what William Leach refers to as a sense of transformative possibility; through them, individuals could reimagine themselves in new and pleasurable contexts. Understanding this, we can see how fair publicity that stressed the overall value of the sale items was, like the fair environment, meant to excite the public. It helped to create a kind of longing or desire for the imagined positive self and reflected how fully the fairgivers had begun to embrace commercialism.[53]

Ironically, it was not the expensive commercial product that was likely to hold the most meaning for its purchaser, but the less valuable handmade item. Despite the many humorous treatments of unwanted pincushions and similar products at the fairs, individual examples could take on personal significance. The fish pincushion illustrated in fig. 45 is a case in point. It is not an inherently valuable item, but the woman who owned it and showed it to Dorothea Britton in 1970 would not give it up because it had been purchased at a bazaar about one hundred years before, and she considered it a family heirloom. It had never been used, but was kept for its personal association and sentimental value. The same associational power was evident in the story described in the last chapter where a sale item made from a sweetheart's dress was used to symbolize the poignancy of sacrifice and loss. Handmade items are likely to be invested with time and personal attention, and, as Csikszentmihalyi and Rochberg-Halton explain in *The Meaning of Things,* objects invested in this way become "charged" with psychic energy. They come to symbolize or stand for parts of people's lives; they take on emotional and symbolic qualities as they hold memories and evoke particular times, places, and people. Mass-produced objects can also take on a psychic charge through emotional associations, but because they do not embody a maker's unique energy, they are less likely to do so.[54]

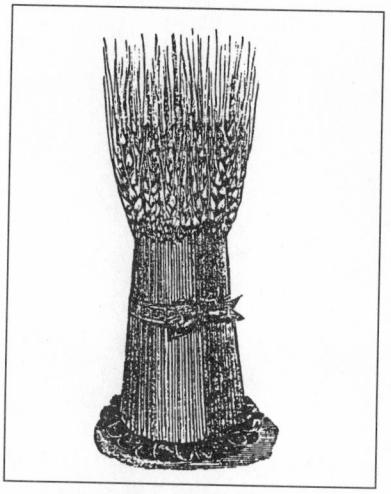

Sometimes small, seemingly throwaway items also function as social signs that take on political, religious, or other identity-group meaning. When antislavery activists purchased inscribed handkerchiefs or potholders at antislavery fairs, for example, they were buying symbols of their beliefs and way of life; even a trivial everyday item could serve as public evidence of total commitment.[55] An item purchased at a sanitary fair or the Confederacy's Great Bazaar could similarly come to stand for patriotism, perseverance, or bravery and evoke the travails of the soldiers on the battlefield. Even food or craft items associated with particular churches, ethnic associations, or other groups came to stand for these groups or communities and served almost as badges of identity for community members. Just as it is easy to dismiss the fundraising fair because of its seemingly trivial nature, then, so too it is easy to dismiss the small objects that were sold there. This brings us back to the idea of looking closely at the seemingly trivial for deeper meaning. Because pincushions and other "trifles" have, in many ways, proved as irrepressible as the fairs themselves, we must remember that objects too can hold meaning, even when they are ostensibly unremarkable.

Fanciful pincushions, suffrage cakes, sideshow attractions, and sensually pleasing aesthetic environments were to characterize the woman's fair more than ever at the turn of the twentieth century. We will see in the following chapter how these dramatic events served as an important aesthetic stimulus and outlet and, as always, afforded women opportunities for humor, creativity, social networking, and a honing of their organizing and managerial skills. We will see too the ever more materialistic face of the fairs, and the ways they reinforced prevailing social hierarchies and agendas, even while standing and working for reform.

Fig. 47. *(left)* Penwipers were also made "in the form of" other kinds of items. This suggestion for a penwiper as a sheaf of wheat appeared in *Godey's Lady's Book,* February 1870.

Fig. 48. *(right)* This fanciful accessory was made in the shape of a wheelbarrow. It was designed to compete with commercial goods at fairs, but was still special because it was handmade. From *The Hearthstone: Or Life at Home* (1888).

CHAPTER FIVE

The Heyday of the Fundraising Fair: "Anything to Attract" at the Turn of the Century

It is the end of January, in the depths of a long and bitterly cold winter. You hurry through the crunching snow on the frozen isthmus, heading for the crowd milling around the school building of the Church of the Holy Redeemer. There is a palpable excitement this evening, a promise of a grand entertainment; this is the "greatest bazaar ever held in Madison!" and hundreds are crowding into the auditorium. A facsimile of Minnehaha Falls with water running over a rainbow made from hundreds of colored electric lights! This should be something—almost like a bit of the world's fair, right here at home. . . . Will you get a place at the dinner table? The mayor and the governor were there last night; maybe you will be seated near someone like that. The colors! Every booth is a different color of the rainbow, your friend told you, and the girls are decked out to match. . . . And all those bright flowers in January, and gypsy fortune tellers, and a Goddess of Beauty tableau. . . . Maybe you'll win a prize— surely it's worth a ten cent ticket, because they're awarding whole sets of furniture, even a coach! There's ice cream too, . . . festive, like easy days of summer. . . .

—From descriptions of the "Rainbow Bazaar," *Wisconsin State Journal,* Jan. 21–24, 1895

All fairies live in woods where everything is very fanciful and very beautiful. . . . They live close to good old Mother Nature, who gives them . . . decorations of flowers and leaf and moss. . . . So at our Fairy Fairs we must have nothing tawdry or gaudy, but everything must be pretty. . . . The fairies are always doing something nice for somebody, and this is the motive that prompts us to arrange for one of these fetes so that the money obtained may be used to help some good cause. Many of the books of fairy tales, . . . poems and stories for children will give us suggestions for [our] booths. . . .

Lady Winter's palace is made of ice and snow. Jack Frost left little curious designs on the paraffin paper sides of her booth and hung his icicles from the roof. She always has very cold things to give to those who come to visit her. We call them cakes covered with icing, ice-cream cones and ice-cold fruit punch.

—From Theresa Wolcott, "The Fair of the Good Fairies," *Ladies' Home Journal,* Oct. 1916

The Commodity Aesthetic, Weightlessness, and the Search for Fairyland

Turn-of-the-century America, as several scholars have explained, was increasingly characterized by a search for sensual fulfillment. Vast quantities of goods were on display, not only at fairs and expositions, but in mail-order catalogues and in the newly ubiquitous, luxurious-looking department stores. As indicated in the previous chapter, these displays were made to be tempting; a recent innovation, in fact, was the glass show window, which allowed products to be foregrounded in an environment of color and light. Even the most casual passerby was drawn into the seeming magic, for the goods offered a vision of plenty and unlimited possibility. The appeal was a sensual one, with a part of the promise being an almost bodily pleasure and feeling of happiness. William Leach goes so far as to state that while Europeans tended to channel their aesthetic desire into art, Americans focused it on commercial products. Jean-Christophe Agnew coined the "commodity aesthetic" epithet to describe this turn-of-the-century phenomenon—a sensibility based on seeing the world and oneself within or through commodities or goods.[1]

The commodity aesthetic created a kind of "weightlessness" because it offered little to anchor the individual in any fixed place or value system. The constant supply of new and tempting goods was always whetting the appetite for more. One was in a constant state of desire, but the desire could never be realized, for there would always be another, even more exciting product, another identity that might be tried on. In speaking of the Bon Marche, the first Parisian department store, as a "permanent fair," Michael Miller concluded that the store was so dazzling, sensuous, and irresistible that it stirred unrealized appetites and provoked overpowering urges.[2]

The unfocused desire and restless search for personal pleasure and fulfillment also led to a new hunger for entertainment, particularly for spectacle, packaged amusement, or play that offered more and more sensation. It is hardly surprising that the most popular features of turn-of-the-century international expositions and agricultural fairs were their carnival-like areas (midways), or that the roller coasters, sideshows, and boardwalk games at the new resorts and amusement parks like Coney Island and Atlantic City were drawing thousands of thrill-seekers a day. Even department stores provided amusement in the form of parades and spectacular festivals. Owners knew that while a market might be entertaining in itself, its allure was multiplied when goods were presented theatrically. In this way, they further heightened the promise of the imagined other worlds.[3]

Because the kind of sensuality and search for pleasure that characterized the commodity aesthetic had long been associated with the bazaar, it would stand to reason that the fundraising fair would come into its own in the turn-of-the-century period. This was true, but the feeling of restlessness and the pervasive commercialism of the era also further affected the fair. Not only were the sale products in this era more likely to be manufactured rather than handmade, but also spectacular effects like the colored waterfall at Madison's Rainbow Bazaar seemed more and more necessary as a way of making the events "weighty" or meaningful. The fairs also became characterized by a kind of studied humor. Everything was increasingly packaged as an entertainment; even those features that had formerly been taken seriously, such as the art gallery, were turned into tongue-in-cheek amusements. Once revered items were reduced to trinkets. The type of battlefield cast-offs that had been displayed as relics at the sanitary fairs were now available for purchase; at the 1893 Confederate Bazaar that honored southern veterans, for example, nails from the battleship *Merrimac* were sold as souvenirs. Intensity of feeling was coming to seem like a product that could be consumed like any other.

The weightlessness also fed directly into the Never-Never Land quality of the fairs. As we have seen, the unsullied fairyland they presented was dreamy—a world with no dark side. Fairyland was actually an important leitmotif throughout popular culture. The title of a 1912 pageant held in Central Park, "Around the World in Search of Fairyland," captured the general longing. Advertisers routinely pictured images of "fairy figures," and commercial illustrators like Maxfield Parrish and store window dressers like Frank Baum (better known as the author of the *Wizard of Oz* books) consistently portrayed an innocent, ideal world. Many best-selling books pictured charming, almost otherworldly children—Kate Greenaway's characters wore old-fashioned sunbonnets, for example, and Walter Crane's characters in works like "Flora's Feast" and the *Baby's Opera* were tiny creatures who lived among the flowers. All of these figures, like the hero of *Peter Pan* (published in 1904), refused to grow up. Lears further notes that the image of the sickly sweet child pervaded novels, plays, and poems at the end of the nineteenth century, and he claims that this image's allure was related to a decreasing trust in Victorian definitions of selfhood and maturity. Other scholars concur. In chronicling a prolongation of female adolescence that took place in the last quarter of the century, Joan Brumberg claims that society idealized girlhood, so much so that girls were at the center of most popular period novels. Leach describes children as an important new consumer market. The strong contemporary interest in fairy tales and in seemingly primitive people also reflected the fascination with the innocent child and pervaded even the most sophisticated level of academic thought. Much of the initial attention of two fields established at the turn of the century, folklore and anthropology, was directed to what was thought of as the childlike stage of human development, the "childhood of the race." Finally, even the increasing identification of the fair with young people may have been a part of this longing for the innocent. Youth was still full of promise and possibility, and these qualities were an important part of what might be sold in these magical environments.[4]

Turn-of-the-Century Fairgivers and Causes

There were more fairs than ever at the turn of the century, in part because there were more women's organizations than ever. This was the period when the dominant interpretation of women's special mission was, as Frances Willard put it, "to make the whole world homelike"—i.e., to bring the positive values of the home ever more forcefully into the public arena. For the most part, women still chose to work with others of their sex rather than to participate in or initiate ventures with men, and huge numbers of women joined together in new mutual interest groups.[5] These ranged from clubs, primarily oriented to social bonding and self-improvement (the Federation of Women's Clubs counted approximately one hundred thousand members by 1896, six years after its founding, and nearly a million by 1912),[6] to associations that in some ways paralleled men's burgeoning fraternal and professional societies. These included the National Association of Colored Women, the Jewish Women's Congress, the Nurses Group, the Daughters of the American Revolution, the Colonial Dames of America, and the United Daughters of the Confederacy. Still other associations were devoted to effecting social change. These ranged from foreign missionary societies to the National Consumer League and the Women's Trade Union League.[7]

Given this explosion of groups, the majority of which supported their activities at one time or another with fundraising fairs, it is ironic that women often took a more defensive stance toward the fair in this era. In part this was due to the identification of the fair with amusements—"serious" groups did not want to be associated with something smacking so strongly of spectacle, fairyland, and frivolity. The defensiveness was also related to an erosion of women's separate power base, which was paradoxically tied to their very inroads into the public sphere. Despite the enthusiasm with which women embraced Willard's idea, domestic values—or more properly put, the (male) valuing of domesticity—lost ground; women no longer seemed to hold any "rights" by virtue of their superior morality or goodness. Many activities which had been left to women because they were seen as naturally part of the woman's sphere were becoming professionalized and put under male control.[8] For example, although women were still associated with charity and benevolence, this arena was no longer an exclusively female bailiwick. A new profession, "social *work*" (italics mine), was in place about 1900; by this time, benevolent institutions were often under the jurisdiction of "trained," "expert" (paid) managers. Women became "amateurs" who worked on a voluntary basis. They were reduced to auxiliary, "helping" positions.[9] Once put under male leadership, in turn, many of these benevolent organizations turned to more standard "male" ways of fundraising. The New England Hospital for Women and Children, for example, had grown to the point where it had a business manager and a portfolio of investments that yielded an annual income, and it placed greater emphasis on mail solicitation, corporate donations, and state and city contributions. The organization no longer sponsored any fairs after 1901.[10] In some ways the fundraising fair came to be associated with an earlier, less "advanced" stage in institutional development. Once fairs were given by organizations perceived as auxiliaries, fairs too were perceived as auxiliary events that were not worthy of serious consideration.

The Role of Women's Clubs and Fairgiving Associations

Women's groups typically also became more focused or cause-specific at this time and were less likely to embrace the kind of generic fair seen in earlier eras. Some groups were reluctant to be thought of as fairgivers. When I began this research I expected to find women's clubs to be major fair sponsors, for example, but learned this was not the case. Turn-of-the-century clubwomen were usually anxious to distinguish their organizations from those that did benevolent work or followed a particular political ideology. Mary Mumford of Philadelphia's Century Club, who lectured on "The Place of Benevolence in Club Work" in 1890, explained that clubwomen were already busy with such activity in other organizations:

> If there was ever a time in our history when clubs might wisely have gone into philanthropic work, that hour has passed, for . . . the [woman] who is not harried with some pet scheme of world saving is a wonder to us all. If she is not running a hospital or a nursery school . . . or a home for the indigent (or indignant) old ladies, she is at least carrying the burden of a parish church, with strivings and scrapings and putting a new bell on the tower or new cushions in the pews. . . . The Club need not add anything to this endeavor . . . I consider that the club has a special function as a refuge for those who are already too much [involved.][11]

This sentiment was frequently echoed elsewhere. Lorraine Bucklin of the Rhode Island Women's Club stated: "We have existed from the start as a club, as distinct from a society or association. While a large majority of our members are actively involved in philanthropic, educational and reformatory work, there has always been a hearty desire to retain the club spirit intact, and no friction owing to opposing interests or convictions has ever been manifested in the spirit of the club."[12]

The groups most likely to be raising money and holding fairs, then, were associations or societies. Records of the Women's Club of Los Angeles indicate how strong the impulse to keep the clubs separate must have been and the way this related to fair sponsorship. The Work Committee initiated a grand Flower Festival in 1885 to fund a boarding house for working women. The event was repeated annually for seven years, but by 1886 the sponsoring group was a separate "Flower Festival Society" rather than a club committee.[13]

Clubwomen's reluctance to hold fairs may also have had to do with the image of the club as an "elevating" institution and its alignment with upper middle-class values; if a club held a fair it would indicate its members were themselves less than prosperous. Blair profiles club members as mature women from the upper end of the socioeconomic ladder. Peiss claims that working-class women did in fact belong to clubs, although she concurs they did not generally hold leadership positions. She states that "club leaders initially sought to prevent their groups from holding fairs and entertainments to raise money, viewing them as forms of philanthropy, but they later acquiesced, acknowledging that most members couldn't pay the [the necessary dues.]" Records of individual groups indicate that, indeed, club members generally preferred to pay dues rather than to raise funds, and they must have done this when they were able. (It is significant that there was no equivocation about fairs at girls' clubs; fairgiving was an expected mechanism for club support because the girls were not assumed to have money of their own.)[14]

Rhetoric aside, club fairs were far from uncommon. They were given by groups from Boston to Pasadena, usually to support club activities or facilities. Interestingly, when the New England Women's Club held a fair in 1906, participants included many of the individuals who had worked at fairs for the New England Hospital for Women and Children, which had by that time resorted to other fundraising mechanisms.[15]

Many fairgiving associations had specified social agendas. Groups identified with reform movements or oriented to defined ideologies were particularly active. Suffragists continued to hold fairs until about 1913, conceding that they were still the "surest way of raising money to carry on the work," although enthusiasm was much stronger before the turn of the century than after, and they too sought other fundraising mechanisms when they could.[16] The political purpose of their events was certainly evident. Banners with inspiring mottoes were in abundance, and at a 1901 event one could enter a "house" made of "newspaper clippings on the suffrage question" to sign a petition. At the 1886 Boston fair, Mary Livermore was ceremonially presented with a cushion stitched from pieces of dresses that had belonged to distinguished suffragists like Susan B. Anthony. At a fair held in New York's Madison Square Garden in 1900, similarly, individual tables were dedicated to specific women's rights leaders. Sale items included handwork that Anthony and Lucretia Mott had made as children, and the featured souvenir pamphlet, a reprint from the *Woman's Journal*, profiled Lucy Stone. Nevertheless, the message was couched in the guise of "womanliness." As Elaine Hedges pointed out, suffragists pointedly used needlework at their fairs as a symbol of their domesticity and femininity. This point is illustrated by an 1886 *Woman's Journal* description of a slogan-bedecked banner made to represent the Quincy League at the Equal Woman Suffrage Association's annual fair. The banner had been made at the last minute by two league members who stepped in when original plans fell through, and the *Journal* was quick to point up their domestic prowess: "The result showed conclusively that some woman suffrage women can sew and embroider, not only with skill but with speed." The association also published a cookbook that was prominently featured at the event.[17] It is easy to see why some of those interested in changing the political status quo might have felt somewhat equivocal about supporting an institution that reified traditional domesticity.

The fact that more radical reformers struggled with an appropriate image of domesticity makes sense in the turn-of-the-century social context. Many, if not most, women's reform associations identified with or were influenced by the ideals and philosophy of the so-called Progressive movement. Progressivism was characterized by a belief in perfectibility and self-improvement, and a vision of the future where the disenfranchised might be "elevated" to a better life in an industrious, smoothly running society. With this belief, women banded together in groups like the National Congress of Mothers (a forerunner of the Parent Teacher Association) to work for progress in education, or established settlement houses, cooking schools, and classes in domestic economy to help immigrants and the urban poor. For the most part, the better life the reformers envisioned for their charges was like their own; it was based in other words on the prevailing white middle-class norm and affirmed existing social and gender hierarchies.[18] Because most associations helped perpetuate the hegemonic norm, we can further understand why radicals sometimes felt reluctant to be identified with an institution (the bazaar) so strongly identified with it. Because these were subtle and complex issues, it is also clear why women's clubs would have tried to avoid the controversies altogether.

Under the general reform umbrella, women not only used fairs to fund hospitals, schools, and charity homes, but also supported a new range of institutions and activities that would benefit other women. Fairs helped raise vacation or retirement funds for working women, for example, and supported kindergartens, day nurseries, and industrial training schools that female workers might attend in the evenings. (One event even funded the Little Mothers Aid Society, which offered excursions for girls obliged to care for younger brothers and sisters.) Many of the foreign mission societies expressly funded female missionaries concerned with the status of other members of their own sex.[19]

While it is arguable whether or not they could be counted as Progressives, it is also important to point out that relatively well-off African Americans also worked to help their less fortunate compatriots. In those black churches that had well-educated and fairly affluent populations, fundraising fairs were very common in this period, both for the churches and for charity purposes. Unfortunately, I have been unable to learn much specific detail about these events.[20]

In addition to working within the context of ongoing clubs and societies, turn-of-the-century women still formed ad hoc groups to complete short-term projects. They continued to use fairs to pay for libraries, for example, or, in a resurgence of activity, to build public monuments. The 1896 Milwaukee Bazar of All Nations was held to raise funds for a downtown monument honoring the Union soldiers; the Confederate Bazaars held in Richmond, Virginia, in 1893 and 1903 (fig. 60) raised funds for a monument honoring the Confederate soldiers and the refurbishing of the former home of Jefferson Davis as the Museum of the Confederacy. In 1895 the German American population of New York raised twelve thousand dollars for a monument to the German poet Heine, and Danish Americans raised funds for a Danish sculptor to complete a statue that would first be exhibited at the world's fair and later set up permanently in Central Park.[21]

Auxiliaries and Fairs for Fraternal and Benefit Organizations

Ethnic groups turned to fairs for a variety of purposes, in fact, and used them as opportunities to bring their communities together. "All the Danes in New York" were said to have attended the Danish fair, and its parochial nature was indicated by the fact that the prize voted to the most popular woman was a Danish flag. Bazaar programs and other written materials were prepared in the native language. There were also numerous German American fairs.[22] In New York, a German hospital was built with proceeds from fairs where elements of the homeland were prominent. In 1888 the hall was designed to represent a Viennese garden, for example, and the souvenir folio of poetry and art was entirely in German. Cuban, Czech, Irish, and Jewish immigrants all held large and successful events in New York in the 1890s. The Great Hebrew Fair was a "mammoth bazaar" held to support a sectarian educational institute in the same city. It is said to have raised approximately $225,000 over the course of three weeks in 1895. In the much smaller frontier city of Denver, the Temple Emanuel Fair had been a rallying cause for the Jewish community a few years before. As Barbara Kirshenblatt-Gimblett points out, the event combined the best of German Jewish and Anglo-American traditions. "Good old-fashioned German-style cooking" included rich dishes that might be offered at a Sabbath meal, for example, but these were supplemented by American favorites like corn bread and okra gumbo.[23] Most often, the women organizing these ethnic fairs belonged to groups with a nominally secondary status. For example, Turnverein (gymnastic) and Mannerchoir (male chorus) societies, which were popular wherever there were German communities, were typically run by auxiliary groups like the "Turnverein Wives and Daughters."

Auxiliaries were also the ones that raised significant amounts of money for other fraternal organizations, for veteran's groups, and for associations of male professionals like postal or railroad workers. It would seem a particularly selfless act for women to put so much energy into organizations from which they were excluded, but the reality was much more complex. In an article exploring women's roles in Masonic fairs in New York state, William Moore concluded that women were happy to put their energies into building Masonic temples despite the fact that they would not be allowed entry because the values and principles of Freemasonry—morality, ethical behavior, and charity—were congruent with their own.[24] I believe this helps explain women's enthusiastic participation in most of these events. The Knights of Columbus and Knights of Pythias, for example, held values similar to those of the Masons, and, like them, they were providing member benefits. Most of the other proliferating men's professional and recreational groups were also functioning as charitable organizations or benefit societies; they were, in Peiss's words, "adaptions to an industrial society with few social welfare provisions."[25] The Northampton chapter of the Brotherhood of Railroad Trainmen held a bazaar for sick members and their families in 1895, only three years after the organization was founded. New York City teachers established a pension fund for themselves through an 1890 fair where attendance figures topped 20,000.[26] Even veterans' organizations were largely concerned with mutual aid and assistance, because as the century wore on they had become responsible for more and more needy veterans, widows, and orphans. Armories, like Masonic temples, thus functioned as both physical and symbolic spaces for charitable work. It is understandable that women would want to help fund their construction.

These groups produced very large, elaborate fairs—the largest, in the aggregate, in the turn-of-the-century period. Over 25,000 tickets were sold at New York's Eleventh Armory fair in 1880, and though 5,000 people were packed in on opening night at a similar event in Schenectady, others had to be turned away. Even in the small city of Northampton, attendance was over 2,500 at a six-day GAR (Grand Army of the Republic, the Union veterans' group) fair which the press called the great attraction of 1885. The fairs also involved huge amounts of money. Moore reports a net profit of $28,000 at a 1903 Masonic fair in Brooklyn, and, while the specific net earnings of the 1900 fair given for the Atlanta Masons are unclear, the *Atlanta Constitution* indicated that it expected the fair to raise the majority of the $75,000 needed for the downtown temple. In today's terms, that figure would be well over $1,000,000.[27]

The fairs of the mutual aid and fraternal societies represented an interesting mix of male and female-identified values and activities; they seem to have been experienced as both men's and women's events. Militaristic, male-bonding–type activities included processions, drills, and promenades. At Atlanta's 1900 Masonic Fair, different lodges and fraternal groups paraded nightly (see the sidebar below), sometimes with great fanfare. Costumed Shriners marched through town to the accompaniment of a local drum and bugle corps, for example, and ended their procession with a series of "college yells in Arabic." Dramatizations of military conflict were also common. Northampton's 1885 GAR fair featured tents and posters memorializing battle sites, and, at one event held during the Cuban-American war, soldiers marched across the floor with drawn machetes and carbines slung across their backs.[28] Athletic activities included shooting galleries—there were special "sharpshooter's days," and sometimes tennis and other "sports on the lawn." Fairs also served as rallying places for other kinds of men's groups. The central event at the Northampton Railroad Trainmen's fair, in fact, was a contest between six conductors on the railroads that led into town. As the sidebar indicates, it was common for these societies to participate in each others' fairs. Constituency groups were often drawn to the events on special "dedicated" days: "Postal Night" was dedicated to mail carriers, for example, and "Wheelman's Night" was dedicated to bicyclists. At Milwaukee's Bazar of All Nations, the wheelmen of the city agreed to attend "in a body."[29]

Women sometimes participated in these "masculine" activities—for example, a rifle tournament for young ladies was announced at a New York fair in 1876—but there were other ways in which they were clearly operating in their "own" realm. At a Madison Turnverein fair, for example, there were voting contests for best housewife (she won an easy chair) and nicest little girl, and women served as judges and police officers at a mock court. Invariably, no matter how seemingly male the overall theme of the fair, there were typical bazaar-type booths. At an 1882 "Historical Encampment" in St. Louis that raised funds for a National Guard Armory, for example, the women set up tents that had little to do with the battlefield—they were instead familiar Persian, Russian, Irish, and "Hiawatha" tableaux. In other instances, women specifically played against the male-identified values and activities by introducing a lighthearted female counterpoint and making fun of what the men were doing. At the St. Louis Armory fair, they playfully mocked the military idea with a "broom brigade," where they marched with brooms and mops in place of guns, chanting lyrics like, "Our peace-loving weapons we only would wield. . . . We would brush away suff'ring and sorrow and care. . . . And everything hurtful that darkens your life." The commercialism of the era, as well as the complexity of turn-of-the-century gender role play, is evident in the fact that this mockery was in turn used by men for a very different purpose. Colonel Donan, an independent entrepreneur, was so taken with the tour de force that he brought seventeen of the marching girls to Minneapolis to perform in a promotion for the railroad. The broom brigade was subsequently featured in still other promotions along the Mississippi, sometimes drawing thousands to the small-town railroad depots, and it caught on briefly in other parts of the country. At the same time, it was also used repeatedly as an amusement at women's fundraising fairs.[30]

Men's participation in fraternal-type fairs was greater than it had been in earlier women's events. Typically, each company of veterans or lodge of Masons would sponsor its own booth (interestingly, these were often set up in a ring surrounding a booth for the overarching organization; this was the classic arrangement of the antebellum women's fair, but contemporary women's fairs rarely used this layout). There were also often hired male managers; at least two individuals actually built a career running fraternal society fairs (see below). However, there is no question that the events would not have functioned at all without women's hard work. Even when there was a professional manager, women still handled the details of planning and executing the fairs—they solicited local businesses for their help, arranged for space rental, ticket sales, labor, and publicity (most committee chairs, as well as workers, were women), and were the primary salespeople. The *Atlanta Constitution* named approximately 400 women who helped make the 1900 Masonic fair a success, and the *Eagle Daily Compass*, published for the Brooklyn Masonic Fair, listed 800 female participants. An 1885 Confederate [Veterans] Relief Bazaar held in Maryland listed 350 women on the Board of Managers. These individuals were generally wives and daughters of lodge members. The *Eagle Daily Compass* even made a special note about one worker "who had no immediate connection with any Masonic lodge . . . in the east," but participated because she was related to Masons in Wisconsin.[31]

Fraternal fairs were also perceived in their own time as a variety of women's fair. Condescending or tongue-in-cheek rhetoric, for one thing, was no different from that surrounding any other fundraising fair. The reporter for the *Brooklyn Times* who covered the 1903 Masonic event wrote, "The question on every lip was: 'Where did all the girls with strenuous ways come from?' They seemed to know at once if a man had any surplus. If it's left to them, as it will be largely, Brooklyn will have a temple second to

Constituency Nights At the Masonic Fair, Atlanta, 1900

Monday	Dec. 3	Atlanta Lodge
Tuesday	Dec. 4	Fulton Lodge
Wednesday	Dec. 5	Georgia Lodge
Thursday	Dec. 6	Gate City Lodge
Friday	Dec. 7	Mt. Zion Chapter
Saturday	Dec. 8	Knights of Pythias
Monday	Dec. 10	Atlanta Commandery, Odd Fellows
Tuesday	Dec. 11	Yaarab Temple
Wednesday	Dec. 12	Military Night
Thursday	Dec. 13	Fireman's Night
Friday	Dec. 14	Couer de Leon Red Men
Saturday	Dec. 15	Ladies' Night

Brotherhood of Locomotive Engineers,
Order of Railway Conductors

—*Atlanta Constitution*
December 3, 1900

none."[32] Masonic and similar fairs were called bazaars, and they were not distinguished from other "female" events. This is an important point, because contemporary scholars have considered fraternal fairs only in the context of (male) trade fairs and expositions; Moore specifically called them "miniature local versions" of international fairs. Once again, the pervasiveness and import of the women's fair tradition has remained invisible.

Professional Managers

Professional managers were hired to coordinate some of the most elaborate turn-of-the-century fairs. In 1889 when the *New York Times* reported on the three-week-long Centennial Festival for the Hahnemann Hospital, it noted this was the fifteenth fair Mr. De Freece had managed since 1871. The *Atlanta Constitution* similarly reported in 1900 that Noble Martin, who was coming to work on the upcoming Masonic Fair, made a "study and profession of arranging" these events and would probably return the following year to conduct a fair for the military organizations of the city. Elsewhere, Martin was described as managing fairs in such far-flung states as Nebraska, Georgia, and Washington. His main competitor appears to have been James Hanrahan, who advertised his managerial services in the weekly national Masonic newspaper. It is difficult to conclude just how common paid fair managers were, but because they were not involved in many large events such as the Bazar of All Nations in Milwaukee and the Hebrew Charity Fair in New York, I am convinced they were the exception rather than the rule at fundraising events. Although an 1894 *New York Times* column explicitly commented that wintertime fairs were "usually put in charge of a paid manager, who secures effects and plans results as a stage manager arranges his material" (summer fairs were said to be smaller), they appear to have been most frequently hired by fraternal organizations and other men's groups. The kinds of tasks they carried out—they arranged performances, props, and sets and took charge of arrangements such as contracting with carpenters and electricians—were also done by volunteers at women's fairs. It may be that men were comfortable with professional managers because they were used to hiring them for related events like civic "trade carnivals" and theatrical spectacles at department stores or fairs of other types (the Minnesota State Fair featured reenactments of the Civil War (1887) and the burning of Manila (1899)). It is possible too that the same individuals may have managed different types of events, not caring if their ultimate purpose was profit or benevolence. This confusion serves as a further example of the blurred boundaries between the various kinds of fairs, and it reminds us that premodern bazaars were fully part of the entertainment milieu.[33]

The professional manager fell into disrepute in the early part of the twentieth century, as unsavory business practices caused a certain amount of scandal. In 1905 the *Hampshire Gazette* ran an article on the numerous charities that were hiring managers to run benefits for them and finding that more profit went to the organizer than the cause. During World War I, a major New York event called the Army and Navy Bazaar showed a net return of only about $700 after a $70,000 gross. Managers working on a commission basis were eventually indicted by a grand jury.[34]

The Juvenilization of the Fair and the Role of the Socialite

I have introduced the idea that the highly packaged and entertaining turn-of-the-century fair was increasingly linked to both youth and the social elite. The childlike tone of fairyland was appealing to young people, and there were more and more child-oriented features, such as special booths (one advice-giver included the reminder that tables with attractions for children should be built low enough for them to see) and "doll fairs" (see below). Even beyond the features of the fair, however, was the fact that fairgivers were themselves often younger. There was an occasional "children's sale," reminiscent of the Civil War events where the very young acted as salespeople (instructions for one such fair specified that the children should be dressed in Kate Greenaway costumes). Listings of attractions at fairs like Milwaukee's Bazar of All Nations also indicate that children still contributed through the public schools. It was teenage girls, however, who were most often connected with these events. Many of the "Minister's Social Helper" columns in *Ladies' Home Journal* presumed an audience made up at least in part of young women, and fundraising ideas discussed in this and other popular literature were explicitly presented as suitable youth activities.[35] Young women had certainly been part of the attraction of fairs in the antebellum era, but those events had still been perceived as grown-up affairs, run by fully competent and serious women. This was a new turn of events, reflecting the era's fascination with youth and the further blending of business and amusement.

There is ample evidence that significant numbers of young people participated in fundraising events at this time. As mentioned, bazaars were increasingly a part of girls' club programming, and there was a new spate of fairs sponsored by groups like the "Busy Bee Missionary Girls" (Madison) and the "Merrie Makers" (New York). Careful reading of fair announcements indicates that "misses" (what the *New York Times* called "the sweetest young American beauties") were increasingly in charge of the booths even at nominally adult fairs. The *Hampshire Gazette* pointedly remarked that there was "nothing like having young folks for a committee."[36] Tellingly, many of the new participants were college students. These young women were poised between childhood and adulthood, but, even more important, they were typically urban and upper middle class; they would grow up to be the very society matrons who would later run fairs in a professional manner. When the girls gave fairs, in other words, they were in a sense in training for their future work. Some of the college fairs were organized for their own societies (e.g., Smith students worked at a bazaar for the college building fund), but most were for charitable causes, many of which involved children. Students at New York Normal College sponsored a fair for a free kindergarten in 1892, for example, and in 1900, students from St. Mary's College held a bazaar for a local Dallas orphanage. It was also common for the students to target their fair work to younger children. In 1909, the Smith Nu Gamma Chi sorority "afforded much merriment for the little folks" with its Mother Goose booth. A few years later, the girls who lived in University of Wisconsin dormitories encouraged children to come to their University YWCA Christmas Bazaar. It is notable that college boys also used the mechanism of the fair to raise funds for their activities, but like their relatives in fraternal organizations, they turned to their female friends for help. Juniors at the Columbia College School of Mines held a fair to alleviate their class debt and raise funds for a boat club in 1889, but they did not staff the booths themselves. The male college fairs also resembled the fraternal fairs in that constituent groups came to one another's events with seemingly good-natured rivalry. The Columbia fair included a tug-of-war contest between Yale, Princeton, and Columbia students.[37]

Collegians were also visible participants in adult fairs. There was a varsity booth at the Homeopathic Hospital fair in 1888, for example, where a boat was awarded to the college that earned the most votes. Harvard students were listed as one of the main attractions of the opening night social at an 1886 suffrage fair. Even when the students were not present, college-related themes were popular, particularly if they related to Ivy League schools. Frequently touted products included "Vassar fudges" and picture frames in "Harvard Green" and "Princeton Red." In 1894, the *New York Times* noted that students from Vassar, Wellesley, Bryn Mawr, and Barnard, who were "likely to be found in any summer resort community," would be able to suggest specialties for booths representing their colleges. While this statement might imply that fairgivers seeking advice were well-off (i.e., they could frequent a resort), this was often not the case. The kind of college fair suggested in *Entertainment for All Seasons,* where each table represented a different school, used the imagery of the elite institutions but was likely to be staged by a local group with no connections to the Ivy League. The college theme was a fantasy like any other. Such instruction indicates once again that fair imagery and conventions were dominated by privileged individuals, but were available to and indeed adopted by a broader audience.[38]

Wealthy girls who did not personally attend Vassar or Bryn Mawr were still likely to participate in fairs when they were young since the events were fully integrated into the social season; a prominent appearance at a sales booth was one way of displaying a marriageable debutante. Later, as wives of well-off corporate leaders, these individuals would be in an excellent position to manage fairs. They could devote considerable amounts of time to charitable endeavors, for they had servants to run their households and were not burdened with domestic responsibilities. They also had the connections to assure publicity and interest in their causes. By virtue of their social position, for example, they were often able to arrange new attractions and locations for fairs. Although most large, end-of-the-century bazaars were still held in church facilities or rented public halls (including the armories that were themselves built with the help of fundraising bazaars), trend-setting events took place in clubrooms, restaurants, hotels, and art galleries. In New York, Sherry's and Delmonico's restaurant banquet rooms were among the most frequently cited fair locations (Sherry's had three such events in a three-week period in 1892), and the Brunswick, Waldorf, and Manhattan hotels were mentioned as well. In Boston, fairs were given at the Copley Plaza and the Narragansett Hotels, and in outlying areas of the city they took place in casinos. Again, these settings added to the public appeal of the fair and brought in audiences who hoped to participate in some way in elite culture. Middle-class individuals delighted in going to elegant hotels and restaurants they might not otherwise be able to patronize, or to art galleries where fancywork and flowers mingled with costly paintings. The arrangements in these spaces benefited both parties: gallery and restaurant owners were pleased with the exposure and the potential of new customers, and fairgivers were pleased to add panache to their events.[39]

It is important to note that the American society women who adapted fairgiving and other charitable entertainments as a kind of career were, in contrast to some of their English counterparts, often quite dedicated to their work. These were not titular figureheads or patrons; they stayed for the duration of the fairs and did much of the actual labor. In England, charity benefits were one of the unavoidable elements of the social calendar. There was a constant pressure there for titled persons, in particular, to open fairs or run specific booths. They often did not work very hard on any one event.[40]

Figs. 49 and 50. "Fairy Girl" and "Butterfly Boy" were illustrated in *Ladies' Home Journal* in November 1919. A focus on children was characteristic of the turn-of-the-century fundraising fair, and young people were increasingly active participants.

Playing with Presentation: A Profile of the Fairyland Fair

Imaginative Themes and Dress-Up

The practice first seen after the Civil War of organizing a fundraising fair around a central organizing theme not only continued at the turn of the century, but grew to almost obsessive proportions. The themes were sometimes suggested by the cause that was being supported—the Cuban Patriot Fair, for example, highlighted "picturesque" Cuban life and warfare, meaning that fairgivers could sell products at "native huts" (see fig. 12)—but they were more often based on seasonal, topical, or purely imaginative abstract ideas. In the 1890s, for example, a "Napoleonic craze" spawned a rash of Directoire Bazaars, Empire Fairs, and Napoleonic Teas that were no different whether they were benefiting churches, hospitals, or statues. Everything that seemed connected with the period was worked into these events, from the display of Empire furniture to foodstuffs like French bon-bons and Napoleon pastries. Other fairs were based on classical Greece. When the Church of the Archangel held a fair to cover its mortgage, each of the booths was set up as a "little temple," and one hundred young ladies in white and golden Greek gowns paraded among them.[41] Historic themes were turned into opportunities for play, in other words, much as they had been in the New England Kitchens of the preceding era. In a time when history was regularly being turned into spectacle (in addition to the Minnesota reenactments, the Fall of Pompeii and the Great Chicago Fire were seen daily in Coney Island), women's fairs naturally grew more theatrical. It is important to point out, however, that their theatricality remained based on domesticity. "Nothing was tawdry" and action wasn't the point; even if the backgrounds grew more picturesque, what was highlighted was still food and household products.

Internationally based themes were also at the peak of their popularity at turn-of-the-century fairs; Italian "peasants" and wholesome "Dutch girls" could probably be found at church bazaars in any community in the country. The few scholarly treatments of these fairs discuss international themes as a reflection of what was going on at world's fairs, but we have seen that women had played with such presentation even before international expositions proliferated. In reality there was still a close relationship and interpenetration among fairs of different types. When funds were needed for the Woman's Building of the 1893 Columbian Exposition, as indicated earlier, manager Bertha Palmer held a fundraising event with the title "Bazaar of All Nations" at her home.[42] There was also a carryover of personnel and goods between fundraising and international fairs. Some of the people who had been active in the sanitary fair movement, for example, later worked for the Woman's Centennial Committee and then for the Woman's Building at the Columbian Exposition. Similarly, objects displayed at world's fairs were later seen at fundraising fairs. This was the case at an 1894 fair for the Little Mother's Aid Society: some of the sale items featured at the Italian, French, and Dutch booths had been at the Columbian Exposition the year before.[43]

As at the international expositions, the image of the rest of the world presented at a fundraising fair was in many senses self-serving; it reiterated—however play-fully—an imperialistic vision of progress, white supremacy, and social Darwinism. Nonwhites were either ignored, represented as the childlike, primitive, or savage "other," or reduced to "humorous" stereotypes. The only booths that ever represented Africa, for example, had Moorish or Egyptian themes; white Americans could not imagine themselves as blacks and would not look seriously at black African culture. As earlier descriptions indicate, African Americans were portrayed, but always as servants. American Indian themes, which had been included in some of the sanitary fair tableaux, were relatively rare at this time. Oriental images remained popular, almost emblematic, but again these images amounted to a vague Orient, and if explicit, often referred to the Near East, where people looked more like Europeans. The only parts of the Far East that were specifically represented were China and Japan. Robert Rydell explains this dynamic in relation to world's fairs; he claims that Asians were presented according to their "perceived usefulness as a market," and, because the Japanese seemed most "educable" (i.e., open to Westernization), they were especially favorably received.⁴⁴ Perhaps also because the Japanese had come to be associated in the American mind with "the aesthetic," Japanese themes were tremendously popular; some turn of the century fundraising fairs were even specifically designated as "Kwankobas" or Japanese bazaars.⁴⁵ Other popular booths and theme fairs were based on a romanticized, old-fashioned Europe, in keeping with the contemporary fascination with the simple and "primitive" past.⁴⁶ No matter how up-to-date their sale goods, saleswomen at Russian, Dutch, or similar country-based booths invariably impersonated picturesque peasants in nostalgic costume. The sidebar below demonstrates how international themes were used at one fairly representative event. When Detroit's charitable organizations mounted thematic booths, eighteen represented Euro-American themes with vaguely historic subjects like Greek temples and log cabins. Three booths represented Near Eastern themes, and one represented Japan.

A related type of fundraising scheme that swept the country at the end of the century was the kirmess (also spelled kirmesse, kermiss, kyrmiss, etc.).⁴⁷ Typically, this functioned as a combination fair and folk dance festival, with international peasant dances and representative food or sale articles from different countries. Variously attributed to Holland and Germany, the kirmess was said to represent the spring festival in which peasants flocked to public squares and indulged in holiday festivity. The American version included practiced performances with costumed dancers. (A different kind of professional manager sometimes organized the kirmess. In 1900, for example, Prof. H. E. Speedy came to Madison from Detroit to teach dances to some 150 children and 50 young adults, and, according to the *Wisconsin State Journal,* he had previously managed similar activities in fourteen other states.) Variations on the kirmess theme were endless: in Richmond, Virginia, it included tableaux performances and ballroom dancing as well as folk dances and culminated in the crowning of a king and queen. In his study of historical pageantry, David Glassberg discusses the importance of folk dance festivals and civic pageants that recreation workers offered as part of their participatory educational programs shortly before World War I. I suggest that these civic festivals may have grown out of the fundraising events, which were popular a decade earlier. (Pageants will be discussed briefly in chapter 6.)[48]

Costume or "dress-up" was perhaps the key element in these international and historical theme fairs. It helped fairgivers appropriate the other—when one dressed as a Spanish peasant, Spain was in effect reduced to a play, or turned into an amusement. However, this was not what fairgivers were consciously thinking about; rather, they were caught up in the pleasure of the experience, and were interested in the creative ways they could effect the right look. Interestingly, the fact that the costumes portrayed stereotypes that were neither ethnographically nor historically accurate did not preclude support from individuals or organizations from represented countries; German immigrants would be as likely as others to wear "Bavarian dress." The costumes heightened the excitement of the fair, both for the women who put on the clothes and those who came to see them.

Such self-conscious presentation certainly invited attention; the women in these sensually appealing outfits begged to be looked at. The press quickly picked up on this. When the *New York Times* described the young saleswomen at the 1887 Manhattan Hospital "Gypsy Encampment," it discussed their shiny jewelry and their bright garments of such startling colors as "crushed cantelope" [*sic*], "pickled olive," and "fried shrimp." The chief object of this fair, according to the *Times*, was to be photographed.[49] Newspapers constantly referred to the pleasure of seeing the "fair women at the fairs." "It is worth many times the price of admission to enjoy the bare privilege of viewing

Fig. 51. Classical and neoclassical themes—which in the popular mind were also vaguely "colonial"—were common in the 1890s. In this booth the effect of fluted columns was cleverly achieved with paper. The inset at the upper right of the illustration shows how the paper should be gathered for the proper effect. From *Ladies' Home Journal*, November 1904.

Fig. 52. Scantily clad young women were part of the aesthetic appeal of the turn-of-the-century fair. Classical dress was not used for allegorical purposes as it was in other contexts; here it was just part of the theatrical play. This illustration appeared in *Ladies' Home Journal* in April 1908.

for an evening such an assemblage of all the styles of pretty undergraduates and handsome Alumnae," commented the *New York Times* about a fair held to benefit the New York Normal College library. The same paper described attendants at another event as "bevies of pretty Jewish maidens attired in the daintiest and costliest garments, their faces flushed with excitement." The reporters who made these comments were probably men, but both sexes used rhetoric of this type. A placard with the words "Fair/Fairer/Fairest/of/Fairs" displayed by the women running the 1899 New England Hospital for Women and Children bazaar played quite intentionally upon the associations made between women, beauty, and aesthetic sensitivity.[50]

Costuming was keyed to the environments, and beginning about 1880 fair designers began to achieve their overall effects so as to consciously integrate these elements. Instead of relying on a central visual focal point or dramatic floor plan, they used coordination and "matching" to create a more conceptual cohesion. Each booth might be distinct, but it fit with the overall theme of the fair, and its costumed attendants came to look like it. According to *Harper's Bazar*, the effect was particularly striking when both were draped in a matching fabric. The hall and the individuals were dressed together, in other words, and literally became more a part of one another.[51]

Satire, Puns, and Doll Fairs

Imaginative costuming and matching were also worked into fairs based on more abstract thematic ideas. Calendar Fairs (also called Festivals of the Year), for example, included booths for each of the months. At an 1887 New York fair, "January girls" wore white dresses and sold "snowballs" filled with candy. "May girls" wore calico and caps; "June misses" sold flowers; "July maidens" sold firecrackers and fans (see fig. 4 and fig. 5). Another group used a similar theme a few years later, but reduced the settings to the four seasons, represented by a maypole, a latticed piazza, a harvest booth, and a Christmas booth. One of the most successful fairs of the Congregational church of Hatfield, Massachusetts, even carried the seasonal theme into the

supper room, where the dishes were made
out of pumpkins and squash, and attendants dressed in orange. Other variations
on the seasonal theme fair focused on
the phases of life (e.g., Old Age and
Youth), the days of the week, or particular holidays which could be imagi-
natively interpreted. The women of
Northampton's Unitarian church included
clothespins, brushes, dustpans, and similar
items at their Labor Day booth, for example, and paper pumpkin pies at the
booth representing April Fool's Day.[52] Authors' carnivals, where booths and costumed characters dramatized scenes from
popular novels or plays, have been described. Related nursery rhyme or wonderland fairs provided opportunities for
women to dress up as characters like "Marigold" and "Chrysanthemum" (fig. 55 and
fig. 56), who resembled the previously
mentioned Walter Crane illustrations.

THE brown sheathing paper used by
builders covers the rough frame construction of this windmill. A young girl
in Dutch costume serves hot cocoa and has
flower bulbs for sale.

Fig. 53. The costumed
"Dutch" girl is meant to be
seen in relationship to the
dramatic windmill. The
building dwarfs the bulbs
and cocoa products sold
inside. From *Ladies' Home
Journal,* November 1904.

At the 1885 New York Skin and Cancer Hospital Kirmess, social leaders like Mrs.
Elliott Roosevelt and Mrs. William (Lucy) Jay appeared as life-sized roses, lilacs, tulips, and poppies.[53] This kind of impersonation was also evident in other turn-of-
the-century spectacles; at an 1895 street pageant called "The Triumph of Epicuru,"
for example, eighty-five individuals dressed as the elements of a seven-course banquet. Similarly, life-sized bon-bons danced at the "Grand Ballet of Confections"
on the New York stage. Nevertheless, the fundraising fair was the perfect outlet for
such play because women were already so strongly associated with dress-up and
fairy tale themes.[54]

The visual and conceptual punning evident in the Labor Day booth and the sale
goods like the iced cakes at Lady Winter's Palace represented both a sophisticated play with ideas and the tendency to caricature or make light of everything
that was set in the fairyland environment. The mockery could be somewhat pointed—
an 1895 Northampton temperance fair included an entertainment called "An Imitation of the New Woman" (it was put on by the ladies' society)—but it was generally
mild, and by definition remained good-natured. Even the so-called New Women were
willing to play with dress-up and puns at such events. Those who convened an 1894
Congress of Women for Improved Dress supplemented their proselytizing speeches and
fashion displays with a fair, complete with amusing attractions like "Flora and Her
Maidens."[55]

Descriptions of the mock art galleries that flourished at the end of the century indi-

International Theme Booths at the
Floral and Musical Charity Festival, Detroit, 1890

SPONSORING ORGANIZATION	BOOTH THEME AND SPECIAL FEATURES
Benton St. Kindergarten	Blarney Castle Keep Tower (gypsy encampment)
Bethel Congregation (runs charity home)	Grecian Temple
Casino Tabernacle (visits poor and sick)	Maltese Fort
Children's Free Hospital	Windmill Booth (sells tulips)
Day Nursery and Kindergarten	Log Cabin
Grace Hospital	Ice Palace ("ice maidens" serve food)
Hebrew Widows and Orphans	Swiss Chalet
Helping Hand (helps women and children)	Japanese Shrine with tea room
Home for Boys	Italian Piazza (boys sing Italian songs)
Home of the Friendless	Alhambra (Spanish booth)
Home of Industry (works in prisons)	English Cottage with thatched roof (sells goods made by prisoners; dairymaids serve food)
House of the Good Sheperd	Attica Temple (sells linen from "Penelope's Web")
Industrial School	Arabian Booth (sells perfumes, dates, miniature horses)
Open Door Society (runs orphan home)	Ephesius Temple of Diana
Protestant Orphan Asylum	Eiffel Tower (40 feet high)
St. Luke's Hospital	Russian Booth
St. Vincent's Orphan Asylum	Egyptian Booth (sells goods made by orphans)
Women's Christian Association	Scottish Cottage
Women's Hospital and Foundlings Home	Scandinavian Cottage
Young Woman's Home (for working women)	Sicilian Booth
Zoar Orphan Asylum	German Farmhouse with thatched roof (German spinning room)

cate the cleverness of the fairyland caricatures and the kind of amusements they afforded. When individuals looked at "art," such as "Sweet Seventeen," attributed to S. Cane and represented by seventeen lumps of sugar, or "Drawn From Life," represented by a tooth, they could not take themselves seriously. An 1884 gallery "shrouded in mystery" was reported in the *New York Times*. "Each visitor was provided with an elaborate catalogue," explained the paper, "and however boldly he ventured behind the screen he came forth again looking a trifle foolish, as if he had been played upon." It is interesting to note that the set-up of the art gallery "catalogues" matched the format of tableaux programs (a typical tableau listing would read, "Springtime, by Cott"). Tableaux themselves had edged into the burlesque; "Chips that Pass in the Night," for example, showed women smoking and playing poker. Since tableaux had been originally based on paintings, these were plays-on-plays, reflecting a complex, self-conscious, self-mockery.[56]

This kind of satirical play was not limited to the women's fair. Scripts for such mock exhibitions and tableaux were published in books of suggested entertainments, and as the story of the broom brigade makes clear, nearly identical caricatured amusements could be used for varied purposes by both men and women. Like the brigades, there were other popular comical reenactments in this era that inverted serious rituals by playing against expected roles. At the "Tom Thumb Wedding," for example, the usually sacred ceremony was portrayed on a miniature scale, with children playing the adult roles. Susan Stewart explores these rituals in *On Longing* and concludes that

Fig. 54. The Bazar of All Nations was the social event of the year in Milwaukee in 1896. Women were themselves treated as aesthetic presences at the fair, as the front page of the May 16 *Milwaukee Journal* implies.

they were model weddings which, in their perfection of detail, expressed the very essence of the rite, but in a "cute," desexualized manner. All the danger of the wedding was thus removed. She further claims that the Tom Thumb wedding would "seem to have arisen from the Victorian cult of the child."[57]

While I have not found references to a Tom Thumb wedding at women's fairs, it is certainly closely related to other popular fair attractions, including the mock marriage ceremonies at the sanitary fairs. Caricature, desexualization, and entertainment arising from interest in the child were also evident at the so-called doll fairs, which were popular especially between 1885 and 1910. There, the usual fair themes and costumes could become even more amusing because they too were "perfectly" expressed on a miniaturized scale. At one such fair held for the New York Cooking School in 1886, for example, visitors saw a tiny "peasant booth" featuring dolls dressed in Spanish, Swiss, Italian, and other ethnic costumes. Nearby, Mary and her lamb, Little Boy Blue, and other miniature nursery characters lounged in the Mother Goose booth, and dolls dressed as a mother and her four debutante daughters presided over the society booth. Dolls were not only given complete wardrobes for these events, but were made to represent every human attitude and activity. The women of Atlanta's Sacred Heart Church included a range of characters at their 1900 fair, from "lady dolls with tailor made gowns . . . to rag and 'coon' dolls." Dolls in hygienic outfits were featured at the International Dress Congress fair, and a hospital fair included dressed "patients" at a miniature hospital ward. There may even have been times when dolls "did" what women would be hesitant to. Hale and White described a doll version of the Old Woman and the Shoe booth and suggested that identically dressed doll babies brazenly "beg" for charity. There were also doll weddings and Knickerbocker Kitchens with dolls in colonial clothing. Announcements and descriptions of doll fairs invariably played on their theatricality (dolls were "holding public receptions" or were "revelling") or mocked their nonhuman quality ("the little effigies seemed to realize their importance and annihilated all rude curiosity by well bred stares"; "their hearts were composed entirely of sawdust [and] they were very reserved"). "Character" dolls, who represented celebrities like Mrs. Grover (Frances) Cleveland, were sometimes raffled off, and well-known individuals sometimes loaned collections of rare specimens for exhibit, much as they loaned fine paintings. In other cases, publicity for the fairs stressed the individuals who had dressed the dolls; actresses, socialites, and college girls were all variously specified.[58]

These fairs reflected what has been referred to as a "doll craze" that took hold of the public at the turn of the century, and it is important to remember that while many of the fairs were clearly meant for children, they also appealed to adults. After 1900 adult women were even likely to participate in "doll shows" (still called doll's fairs in some instances) where sales personnel not only sold and dressed dolls, but dressed *as* dolls (fig. 58). At one such fair discussed in *Harper's Bazar* in 1905, it was suggested that each (full-sized) booth represent a different room in a doll's house. In the kitchen booth, the "presiding genius" would be a woman dressed as "Black Dinah, in plantation costume." Her charges would be black-faced dolls.[59]

Houses, Domesticated Spaces, and Tamed Environments

Much of the enormous physical and psychic energy that went into the theatrical fairy-land environments of the turn-of-the-century fair was focused on the design and construction of booths. We have established that booths were fanciful, elaborate, and dressed in relation to the salespeople, and we can see how they functioned as stage sets that framed the little dramas of the fairs. A closer examination of turn-of-the-century booths is revealing in other ways as well, however, and relates again to the subject of domesticity and the home sphere.

Detailed instructions for dramatic booth structures were common by about 1880. The ideal booth was unique and eye catching, and it evoked a particular feeling or

"Chrysanthemum" **"Marigold"**

Figs. 55 and 56. Women frequently dressed as flowers in the Fairyland environment of the turn-of-the-century fair. "Chrysanthemum" and "Marigold" represent an artist's conception of suitable costumes for an Eastertime bazaar. From *Ladies' Home Journal*, April 1904.

Fig. 57. This handkerchief booth, which illustrates the nursery rhyme in which the "maid was in the garden hanging out the clothes," was set up as a doll tableaux or vignette. Handkerchiefs could be removed from the line when they were purchased. From *Ladies' Home Journal*, November 1904.

told a particular story. At a single 1889 fair, for example, there was a flower stall that looked like a free-standing house with a thatched roof; a fortune-telling booth outfitted as a gypsy tent; and an enclosed area designated "the House that Jack Built." With its costumed saleswomen, each booth formed its own tableau.[60] Despite the diversity of design, however, there were consistencies among the booths. Many instructions stressed height and interesting shapes; a tall, canopied design, according to advice-givers Lina and Adelia Beard, would preclude the "flat, blank appearance" sometimes seen at "unimaginative" fairs.[61] Soaring, dramatic settings helped elevate or give importance to the sale items (fig. 7 and fig. 8). The underlying reference of the booths, however, was not a matter of scale. Rather, booths alluded to enclosure—to safe, protected, and cozy spaces. They were typically covered (they had "roofs over their heads"), sometimes, as in the case of thatch, with a thick, protective layer. Even the wide-spreading umbrella canopy that was popular after the turn of the century (fig. 59) can be seen both as a literal roof and a symbolic covering. In essence, the booths were like houses within houses, an effect that Susan Stewart argues fosters a sense of interiority and constraint. In short, the booths made references to the domestic and to home.[62]

Tents, which were especially popular in the 1890s, were one manifestation of this cozy space. The idea was fully exploited at the Confederate Bazaar held in 1893 in Richmond, Virginia, where each state was represented by a draped booth meant to evoke a Civil War tent (fig. 60). Gypsy "encampments" were another variation of the tent idea, and draped canopies were also worked into a variety of other thematic contexts (fig. 61). These forms were both visually and conceptually related to the heavily draped "cozy corner" that was at its peak in house decoration at this same time, and even to the woman's dressing table whose swathed fabric provided a private corner in the bedroom. Such "nooks" were meant to be both restful and exotic and performed a similar function in the home: they were places for dreams and fantasies.[63]

More literal houses were also devised and were incorporated into various thematic presentations. At a nursery-theme fair described in *The Ladies World*, each character was represented by a distinctive house setting: Little Red Riding Hood's booth was fashioned as a tiny cottage with "ferocious gingerbread wolves tied to the roof," and Sleeping Beauty was found under a lattice bower. In "Pudding Lane Market," held in the town of Beverly, Massachusetts, in 1906, each booth similarly represented a different nursery character and flanked a central lane (fig. 62). A related convention was to set up rows of houses into "streets": vaguely Oriental structures could be designated for the "streets of Japan," for example, or Tudor house fronts could be worked into "Old English" streets.[64] It is worth noting that the eclectic appearance of many of these fair streets reflected the eclectic nature of late-nineteenth-century domestic architecture; on any given actual street in the 1890s, houses might be built in many different styles.

As the illustrations indicate, some house booths were elaborate structures with four walls and a roof, but many merely created a houselike impression with a facade. A board might be cut with a triangular peak to represent a roof, for example, and a hole cut in the center to represent a window. The saleswoman could lean out of this opening (fitted with cozy-looking curtains) to sell her wares in a "neighborly" way.[65]

Porches and porticoes, especially those with colonnades, were another variation on the house theme. "The porch is the thing!" exclaimed Theresa Wolcott in a 1905 article on fair decorations. The house itself could be simply suggested on paper, she claimed, but a three-dimensional patio that could function as a serving area was essential. Supporting porch columns could be simply made from lath strips covered with cardboard or white muslin (fig. 51), or they could be constructed in a solid fashion. An elaborate verandah modeled after the one at Mount Vernon was created in 1896 for the "Colonial House" at Milwaukee's Bazar of All Nations (fig. 64). The *Milwaukee Journal* pronounced the house even prettier than the original, with "colored young waitresses" serving tea while "pickaninnies tumbled about in play."[66]

Houses and porches were not only part of the woman's domain—in nineteenth-century terms, they actually defined it.[67] By the turn of the century the majority of women were finding ways to get out of the house and operate in a larger, public

Fig. 58. The unnatural poses of the individuals in this photograph can be explained by the fact that they are impersonating life-sized dolls. The occasion was a doll show at Edwards Church, Northampton, Massachusetts, March 1893. From the archives of Edwards Church; used by permission.

context, but they self-consciously used the domestic imagery for their own ends. By collectively representing themselves with these familiar and accepted symbols, they were "safely" maneuvering themselves into a powerful position and simultaneously having a good time. When they transformed their sale environments into small-scale, self-contained houses, they were turning them into something they could indisputably claim, control, and even play with. They were literally representing the tropes and metaphors of domesticity in the public world—both highlighting and venerating them, but gently mocking them as well by reducing them to obvious stage sets. In these homelike environments they acted as hostesses, much as they did in their own homes, but since the houses were fanciful and lighthearted, they were only playacting, and thus transforming their ordinary tasks into something that was not ordinary at all.

The playacting metaphor was occasionally quite overt, for booths sometimes functioned almost as dollhouses or playhouses. This relationship was alluded to by *Woman's Home Companion,* which suggested in 1913 that the "household booth," a three-dimensional lath frame house covered with builder's paper and embellished with curtains and window boxes, be sold as a playhouse at the end of the fair. "Any little girl would love to have [it]," stated author Gabrielle Rosier.[68]

Other variables contributed to the sense of control the turn-of-the-century fairgivers must have felt in these environments. Not only were they focusing on their "own" domain and thus reenacting the accepted arena of women's power, but also in their play they were manipulating reality and scale, and projecting a perfect, idealized, and happy world. Idealized houses, in particular, evoked a kind of human longing, or what philosopher Gaston Bachelard refers to as a primal dream of shelter, rest, and refuge; in our unconscious, Bachelard believes, houses are happy spaces that cradle us with a sense of security. Moreover, the houses, like the dressed dolls, were diminutive, or miniaturized, and this made them all the more controllable. In Bachelard's words, "the cleverer I am at miniaturizing the world, the better I possess it." Miniaturization by definition also "makes its context remarkable"; everything becomes transformed with the play of scale, so that even an ordinary acorn can be recast as a cradle, and thus take on a new significance. These environments thus brought a sense of mastery and authority to those who made them come to life, and made what they were doing seem charged with meaning.[69]

If miniaturization is one way of manipulating scale, enlargement is another. While this was less common in turn-of-the-century booth design, it was sometimes used with amusing and startling effect when combined with images of domestic products. Playful booth structures were fashioned as oversized, literal representations of whatever was to be offered for sale: cakes were sold from booths built like enormous cakes or cake pans; candy was dispensed from a large candy basket or a booth with candy-stick posts (figs. 65–66). A preserve booth had two huge "Mason jars" flanking the framework (fig. 69). Once again the play with scale offered not only a sense of control and intimacy, but a heightened perspective or relationship with objects of everyday life.[70]

In addition to booths, other elements of the fair environments were also "tamed" or domesticated. The mock art galleries were not only amusing, but were small and easily managed. Even natural environments and materials were self-consciously manipulated and controlled. Fairgivers brought items from the outside world into the interior space of the fair and used them, not as realistic imitations of nature, as in the Civil War floral halls, but as accents and areas of textural interest in artificial, staged settings. Thatch, shells, evergreen branches, cattails, wisteria, and sometimes even whole trees were used to further conceptual themes. In 1903, when the *Ladies' Home Journal* ran a contest for the best fair ideas sent in by readers, the prize-winning entry was a suggestion for an "orange grove" fair. The grove was to be made of small ev-

Fig. 59. A huge Oriental parasol "sheltered" the flowers on this booth. The table was also well protected with a full "skirt." From *Ladies' Home Journal,* November 1906.

ergreen trees placed about the hall and hung with trinkets wrapped in orange tissue paper balls; real oranges might be sold, but the grove itself would have no hint of realism. Similar "gift trees" were popular at other fairs, especially at Christmas and at Easter. Alternately, whole fairs could be built around trees decorated with sale goods. A Calendar Tree at one fair was loaded with calendars and diaries (its salesperson was dressed as Father Time), and at a Sylvan Festival, tree "booths" functioned as puns: the ash tree featured smoker's supplies, the beech tree was hung with toy buckets and shovels, and a plane tree featured mirrors and beauty creams.[71]

Artificial materials completely replaced natural elements in many cases. As Emma Hewitt explained when she was suggesting using one material to substitute for another in her 1889 book *Queen of the Home,* "This is a day of well-regulated shams, and as they are openly practiced and thoroughly understood by all concerned, no one is deceived, and practically they are *not* shams." Miles Orvell refers to this late-nineteenth-century love of artifice as "the aesthetic of imitation." He goes so far as to proclaim imitation the "foundation" of the era's middle-class culture.[72]

Floral decorations were often made out of cardboard and paper (at a Wisteria Fair "graceful clusters" of paper flowers "drooped so naturally that one could almost inhale their fragrance"). Crepe paper was introduced in the 1890s, and was immediately popular with fair decorators. Other kinds of paper—tissue, wrapping, sheathing, gilt, and stenciled—were also put to use. When large quantities were involved (a whole "cave booth"—a clear example of primal refuge—was covered with crumpled paper), advice-givers suggested ordering from a newspaper office for maximum efficiency and minimum cost. In 1912 there was even a "Paper Crafters Booth," which sold paper supplies and items such as stationery, doilies, tablecloths, and canning labels. Paper, which could be cut, folded, twisted, and ultimately thrown away, was the ultimate controllable material.[73]

This Bassinet Booth is offered as a suggestion for the filling of a too-noticeably empty corner. It is a remarkably fresh and attractive arrangement. Your Swiss bedroom curtains may be borrowed for the canopy, and dainty garments for the baby and toys for his amusement are on sale. Special attention is called to the other "corner" booths on this page.

Fig. 60. *(top left)* The importance of texture and sheltering imagery in turn-of-the-century booth design was clearly evident at the 1893 Confederate Bazaar held in Richmond, Virginia. Most booths were fashioned as heavily draped tents. The Louisiana booth pictured here was covered in netting, Spanish moss, and palmetto and fronted by a sign reading "Down the Bayou." Courtesy of the Museum of the Confederacy, Richmond, Virginia.

Fig. 61. *(top right)* Heavy draping and safe spaces are illustrated by this design for a "booth" that could fill an empty corner. The bassinet was the epitome of the cozy, protected environment. From *Ladies' Home Journal*, October 1907.

Fig. 62. *(bottom right)* Tudor-style house facades were among those featured at "Pudding Lane Market" in Beverly, Massachusetts. From *Ladies' Home Journal*, November 1906.

A "PUDDING LANE MARKET" in Beverly, Massachusetts. Before each shop was an illustrated sign with a verse from "Mother Goose," who lived in Pudding Lane: "I saw a ship a-sailing," before the "Pretty Things" booth, and so on. A town cryer called the wares.

Fig. 63. *(top)* Although the fancywork booth is still filled with merchandise at this unidentified Christmas season fair, some of the booths appear quite empty. Earlier in the day, people probably thronged around the "Voting Contest" area at the far left. The trellis-like detailing and solid areas at the bottom of the booths are made of paper. Photograph WHi(x3)43632; courtesy of the State Historical Society of Wisconsin.

Fig. 64. *(bottom)* This elaborate structure was created for Milwaukee's Bazar of All Nations in 1896. A "reproduction of Mount Vernon," it represented the local chapter of the Daughters of the American Revolution. Tea was served on the portico. Photograph WHi(x3)43631; courtesy of the State Historical Society of Wisconsin.

One last point that relates to the sense of control is the effect of the intensive instruction about the "latest" ideas and "most attractive" environments. Periodical articles suggesting fair themes and ideas appeared first in 1879 and most frequently between 1899 and 1917, and instruction books proliferated in the same period. Turn-of-the-century women generally believed that taste and artistic sensibility could be cultivated and improved and studying this advice must have added to their sense of aesthetic competence.[74] The prescriptive literature reached a wide audience (nearly 20 percent of the homes in Muncie, Indiana, subscribed to magazines like *Ladies' Home Journal* and *Woman's Home Companion*) and was taken quite seriously. Once suggestions were in print in national magazines, ideas spread rapidly. This was indicated in the 1897 record book of the women's guild of Madison's Pilgrim Congregational Church. The secretary described how the group had been considering different fundraising plans and had enthusiastically embraced the suggestion that they mount the Art Gallery Fair described in *Ladies' Home Journal* a short time before. The plan had to be dropped when it was discovered that another Madison group had already taken steps to do the same thing.[75]

Celebrities, Commercialism, and Changing Handmade Gifts

There were some attractions at the turn-of-the-century fair that did not relate directly to fair themes but were enticing enough to draw in even the most restless excitement seeker. Sometimes this was due to the presence of celebrities. Highlighting the participation of famous people was not new; the anticipated highlight of the second Northwest Sanitary Fair was to have been a visit by Abraham Lincoln, and although he was tragically shot before the event took place, his substitute, General Grant, drew huge crowds. In this later era, the crowds not only turned out for political figures, but also for stage performers. Grace Dodge, the wife of the Russian consul general, was a popular figure at New York fairs of the 1890s, as was Frances (Mrs. Grover) Cleveland, who made a special point of appearing at these benefits when her husband was president. When she arrived at a fair for Our Lady of the Rosary Mission in New York in 1890, she spent a few hours at the floral booth selling roses, which went for ten to twenty-five dollars apiece. Lily Langtry sold posies in a similar manner at the German Hospital Fair in 1889. The almost manic quality of the late-nineteenth-century fair is illustrated by the fact that early in the evening her flowers cost three dollars, but they were subsequently raised to five, ten, and finally twenty-five dollars. Fellow actress Etelka Gerster signed autographs when patrons purchased her bouquets.[76] Tenor Italo Camanini also drew people to the St. Francis Xavier fair, but he did not sell anything. The description of his visit indicates that he stopped at different booths, purchased bouquets, admired artworks, and was invited into a private room of the restaurant. Even in the case of visiting celebrities, in other words, it was women who were the salespeople at fundraising fairs. This pattern was still evident in 1910, when there was an "Actors' Fund Fair," designed to raise money for the charitable work of the thespian's organization. "The handsomest actresses will become saleswomen, waitresses and auctioneers," explained the general manager of the fair. Male actors participated in a comedic country store and worked at the fair playhouse (which featured a moving picture), but they did not venture out of their professional role.[77]

Excitement could also be generated by using the fair as a more informal kind of public theater. At the 1896 Cuba Libre fair, the crowds poured in to witness the wedding ceremony of a doctor and nurse who were departing for Cuba to lend their services to the cause. The nurse had had to fight emigration officials for permission to go, and the story received great public attention. The wedding march ran right through the center of the fair in Madison Square Garden.[78]

Commercial products were still also highlighted in such a way as to add to the excitement. Sometimes the very theme of the fair was built around manufactured goods. Chinese curios were the center of attention at a fair supporting a missionary's boarding school in Shanghai, for example, and warm furs were the highlight of a "Prazdnix," or Russian Fete. New commercial products—everything from Edison's revolutionary telephone and telegraph to cleaning fluids or even dishrags—were demonstrated and sold where feasible. In commenting on the 1903 Brooklyn Masonic fair, the *Brooklyn Times* commented that the display of household products ranged from "an automobile and double kitchen stoves to . . . boxes of hayo, the new breakfast cereal." The 1903 doll fair that was dubbed the "Doll's Department Store" can be seen to symbolize the increasing identification of the fair as a temporary retail establishment. The sale products were all miniature versions of products the women sold at full-scale booths. In the drug department, for example, dolls would find tiny hand mirrors, boxes of powder, or hot water bags; in the house furnishing corner, they could buy small cookstoves and carpet sweepers.[79]

Even prosaic items like soap, spools of thread, or flour were included on sale tables at these fairs, and "grocery," "housekeeping," "country store," and even "utility" booths proliferated. On occasion these goods doubled as door prizes.[80] Raffling was at a peak—three thousand separate items were individually raffled at the Brooklyn Masonic Fair—and household products were loudly touted with a running patter about their interest and novelty. It was because of the transformative atmosphere of the fair that kitchen items could be made to seem exciting and packaged breakfast cereals could be included in the same list of sale products as a cookstove and an expensive car. Each item, no matter how ordinary, was seemingly charged with a sense of pleasure, prosperity, and well-being.[81]

By the beginning of the twentieth century, saleswomen even became literal peddlers at their fairs. They walked around hawking their wares, which they sometimes sold from voluminous costumes (fig. 70 and fig. 71) but more typically from baskets or carts. Whole bazaars (peddlers' fairs) were even based on this model. At a Push-cart Fair described in 1905, peddlers were to dress as Italians, Irish, and other immigrants, and to call out their wares with the "peculiar cries of the street vendor, the shriller the better." Late in the evening the carts were to be drawn to one side of the

Figs. 65–68. These cake and candy booths represent interesting interpretations of everyday objects. Where scale is altered completely, the objects are not only humorous, but take on a new significance. From *Ladies' Home Journal,* November 1902; October 1907; November 1905; and November 1914.

THE CANDY-BASKET BOOTH COMPLETE

A Candy-Basket Booth for a holiday fair may be worked out in woven strips of red and green denim or paper, or the same effect may be more easily painted in. Bunches of holly tied with red ribbon ornament the corners and top of the handle. Green candy straws tied with red ribbon would carry out the color scheme on the counter.

DESIGNED BY P. W. HOLT
When the Cake is "Done"

room to look like a Saturday morning market. The peddler fair phenomenon reached what may be considered its ultimate conclusion in 1910 when the peddling women dressed as figures from familiar contemporary advertisements and hawked the products associated with them. Manufacturers were more than willing to donate goods for this kind of publicity.[82]

Retail merchants were also heavily involved with fundraising fairs in new, more direct ways. They frequently served on advisory boards. Mr. Lord of Lord & Taylor was on the executive committee of an 1885 fair held to endow a hospital ward for shopgirls, for example, and Isidor Strauss was president of the 1895 Hebrew Fair. Other officers of that event included Mr. Altman, Mr. Stern, Mr. Loeb, Mr. Sachs, and Mr. Bloomingdale; it is not surprising that the press referred to 1885 fair as "the largest department store in New York." Nineteenth-century merchants sometimes even named their stores "The Fair."[83]

There were also close relationships between the environments and display techniques of fairs and retail stores. Fundraising fair decorators sometimes borrowed scenery and props from local stores (see fig. 72). On the other hand, department stores

The giant jars for the preserve booth are made of barrels covered with brown paper

Fig. 69. The preserve booth suggested in *Woman's Home Companion* in April 1913 was another outsize interpretation of reality. Each mason jar flanking the central shelves was to be made of two vertically stacked paper-covered barrels. Alternately, preserves could be implied by pasting pickle-shaped cut-outs on paper covering a lath frame; if electric lights were installed inside, the silhouettes would stand out prominently.

were periodically decorated for thematic festivals like "Fete d'Automne," or "One Thousand and One Nights" that were themselves like huge fairs. By 1900 some stores featured theme rooms that were like large-scale booths—Marshall Fields had an "Elizabethan Room" for linens, for example, a "Louis Quatorze Salon" for gowns, and an "American Colonial Room." The stores had also added restaurants and other service amenities, and customers came to see them, like the fairs, as social centers where they might relax, eat, and browse.[84]

With all this emphasis on exciting commercial products, it is easy to forget that handwork was still an important part of the product line in many cases. Up to one hundred suffragists still met twice weekly before the 1886 Boston fair to make bags, cushions, and potholders and to baste items for still other women to take home to finish. Some small-scale fairgivers still eschewed manufactured goods and realized most of their profits from needlework. At its annual sales in the 1890s, for example, the woman's society of a wealthy Episcopal church near Wilmington, Delaware, averaged about half of its total profits from the fancywork table (the next most remunerative category was ice cream).[85] While we cannot reconstruct the specific sale items at this table, it was generally the case that women were under even more pressure to make their handwork appear "shoppy," and many of their items more closely mimicked manufactured goods. Sofa cushions had long been popular, for example, but by the new century they were frequently painted rather than embroidered, or were worked with "racy" sayings like "Nobody's Looking But

Sample Raffle Items at Turn-of-the-Century Fairs

Railroad Men's Fair,
Northampton, Massachusetts, April 1895

silver lantern	coal-hood
half ton of coal	clock
pair of slippers	2 doz. cans tomatoes
silver cup and saucer	box of cigars
year's subscription to paper	suit of clothes
barrel of flour	toilet set
rocking chair	rug
4 silk handkerchiefs	1 dozen cans of fruit
silver smoking set	copper kettle

Masonic Fair,
Atlanta, Georgia, December 1900

picture	sideboard
bolero jacket	ladies' desk
lamp	clock
centerpiece	cigar box
piece of cut glass	leather chair
tobacco holder	ladies' mackintosh
blankets	hat
watch	Masonic history [book]
white enameled bed	cushion
silver tea set	water set
card case	umbrella
table cover	set of Shakespeare
brass fire set	trousers
lounging robe	jardiniere
Masonic ring	Napoleon plate

the Moon." Doilies featured at a suffrage fair, similarly, were not crocheted or tatted, but decorated with indelible ink sketches. Personal items and sewing accessories like scarves and pincushions were sometimes replaced by travel accessories or stationery-type items like photograph frames, bookends, paperweights, and wastepaper baskets. While these were still domestic-sphere objects, they were less related to traditional women's work and less dependent on sewing skills. (A photo holder suggested in 300 *Decorative and Fancy Articles for Presents, Fairs, Etc.*, for example, was to be made from a wooden dish drain.)[86] They projected an image of an educated consumer who was busy reading, writing, and traveling and was thus more concerned with the affairs of the world than with sitting by the fireside sewing or knitting. The image reflected real changes in women's lives and reminds us that if we look closely at any aspect of the fair, we will find evidence about social and aesthetic conditions and concerns. It is certainly true that sewing skills were far less universal by the end of the century. Although reformers still supported Soho Bazaar–type sales outlets where poor women could support themselves through the production and sale of fine handcraft, they could no longer assume that all women had been inculcated with such "womanly" training. "Many girls in [Working] Girl's Clubs can hardly use a needle," complained the author of *The House and Home*. For this reason, she advised club leaders to put on plays or sponsor a decorative kirmess rather than hold a fair.[87]

DESIGNED BY ADRIENNE BRUGARD

AN OLD Lady With 100 Pockets, dressed in 1840 costume, will add to the amusement and financial results. As she walks around the patron chooses the pocket from which she wishes to purchase a five-cent or a ten-cent article.

The Handy-Holder Lady

Figs. 70 and 71. Variations on the "Pocket Lady" or "Walking Grab Bag" were particularly popular at fairs in the first quarter of the twentieth century. The women functioned as a type of mobile booth. "The Old Lady With 100 Pockets" was illustrated in *Ladies' Home Journal* in November 1914. "The Handy-Holder Lady," who dispensed potholders, was illustrated in the same magazine in October 1917.

The Anti-Bazaar Movement and New Fundraising Schemes

Not surprisingly, the commercialization and sensationalism of the turn-of-the-century bazaar resulted in a rash of criticism. Critics voiced varying grounds for disapproval. Some focused on the human energy that fairs cost; they claimed that women became exhausted or even sick and overwrought after their fairs were over and would have better spent their time doing "true" charitable work. Labor costs were taken into consideration for the first time; fairs were characterized as time consuming and inefficient because the cost of donations and women's energy were never factored in when profits were calculated. Other critics used older arguments, stating that fairs brought out jealousy and discordant emotions, and even ruined the young and innocent by teaching them to importune, wheedle, or beg. Many focused on gambling and playacting, saying that fairs turned churches from "houses of God" to "houses of merchandise" or "houses of Mammon" and created unfair competition for local tradesmen. Some observers specifically indicated that commercial merchandise bothered them; handmade items would have been acceptable, but mass-produced goods made the events suspect. Those who were afraid of rampant consumerism were particularly uncomfortable with the mixture of benevolence and business; they felt that a sensual embracing of commodities was "non-Christian," even devious and immoral. The criticism of fairs was often part of a broader critique of the interwoven pecuniary and social aspects of church life. Critics noted, for example, that "pure" entertainments or socials were rare; the great majority of church social activities had a fundraising component.[88]

In England, Lady Gwendolyn Cecil actually attempted to institute an anti-bazaar movement in 1897. No formal campaign was undertaken in America, but many of the sentiments were the same, and it was unusual to find vocal defenders of the fair concept. The *New York Times* printed a story in 1881 about a Brooklyn incident that illustrated this point. Soon after "Reverend Miss Anna Oliver" took charge of the Willoughby Avenue Methodist Episcopal Church, she announced she would not permit her congregation to participate in fair-type entertainments. She then tried to sponsor a debate, "Is It Right to Hold Church Fairs?" but no one was willing to argue the positive position. Several fictional stories from the period also make reference

Fig. 72. The close relationship between fairs and retail outlets is indicated in this fancywork display at a Nebraska fair. From *Ladies' Home Journal*, November 1906.

DRAPERIES of blue and white cheesecloth; paper chrysanthemums, suspended by white and blue ribbons; fern leaves and palms, formed the decorations of this fancy-work booth at an Omaha, Nebraska, fair. The scenery in the background was loaned by a local store.

to this kind of debate, and the *Chatauquan* carried the pro and con arguments for the topic in 1890. It is interesting to note that parallel outcries were also made about agricultural fairs at this time. There were journalistic campaigns against the abuses of the midway, for example, and about the fairs' loss of serious purpose. In Minnesota, an 1896 "anti-vice crusade" articulated many common complaints about the undue influence of gambling at state fairs.[89]

None of the criticisms had any long-term, serious effect. Advice columns about successful fairs proliferated, and the fairs remained ubiquitous. Two new types of fundraising schemes appeared at the turn of the century, however, that at first seemed less commercial and time consuming than the standard bazaar: the rummage sale and the benefit card party. Ironically, the rummage sale too was based on commercial or manufactured goods, and over time it became largely absorbed into the fair phenomenon. The card party was shorter lived.

The rummage sale, which featured donated used goods resold at inexpensive prices, was introduced about 1900. It caught on quickly, and for a time it threatened to actually replace the bazaar. *Outlook* magazine devoted a column to the subject, claiming the sales were "sweeping the country like a cyclone . . . sometimes striking three in a week in the same town." The author was delighted with this development:

Commentary on Raffling: The Masonic Fair, Atlanta, 1900

After dinner, the Masons invaded the fair proper. Their advent into the booth room was a signal for the young ladies with chance books. For several hours after that the bazaar resembled a clearing house on a busy day, or the stock exchange when 10-cent cotton is trembling on the rise.

There was one poor fellow who proved himself what Henry Wood termed "an easy mark." He had on an evening suit with a big red chrysanthemum for a boutennair [*sic*] and brought $10 just to spend. He bought a chance and sometimes two on everything in the room, and then went all over this programme again for an encore. At 10 o'clock he had just 7 cents left and wanted to find somebody who had a book of chances to take that amount.

Before he had really started on his mad career every girl in the room had him singled out, and if he overlooked one opportunity to take a chance it was not his fault. There is hardly a night that passes but other young men similarly inclined do not "take in the fair" and assist in putting the coin of the realm in circulation.

—*Atlanta Constitution*
December 8, 1900

"[I] have bought tickets for and spent money at about every kind of charitable entertainment hitherto known—fairs, strawberry festivals, kirmesses, tableaux, candy, doll, bag and apron sales, pink teas, pound parties and the rest. But this rummage sale was a surprise. . . . It is [cheap, picturesque] and simple—so thoroughly so that one wonders why nobody ever thought of it before."[90] Spot-checks of local newspapers from different areas of the country from the year 1900 confirm both the rapidity with which these sales caught on and the wide variety of causes they supported, including churches, schools, and benevolent and patriotic organizations. Their peak frequency seems to have been about 1905.[91]

Both the *Outlook* observer and the author of a 1903 *Atlantic Monthly* column credited women with the rummage sale idea, but rather than praise them for coming up with a less extravagant fundraising mechanism, they implicitly still criticized them for devising another potentially commercial institution. *Outlook* likened the donated goods to a secondhand department store. The *Atlantic* contributor felt it was a short step from rummage sale to manufacturer's sale, and the ladies of the future would "only have to sit in stalls gay with bunting and inscribed 'Eat Calkins' Breakfast Food for Red Cheeks."[92]

The benefit card party also seems to have emerged about 1900, and this too spread very quickly. In 1905, thirteen Madison parties were announced in the *Wisconsin State Journal*, and five Northampton area parties were noted in the *Hampshire Gazette*. One took place on the Smith College campus. The parties involved no sale products; profits were realized by "renting" tables for each game. The parties generally took place within private homes (exceptions will be discussed in the next chapter), and are outside the main subject of this study, but they do underline the constant search for novel fundraising ideas. In any case, both the rummage sale and card party were eventually integrated back into the fundraising fair. Secondhand booths were introduced as features of more traditional bazaars by about 1920 and have been common ever since.[93] Benefit card parties peaked in the interwar years, but they too were sometimes incorporated into fairs, for card tables could be set up almost spontaneously at any event.

The heyday of the fundraising fair climaxed, for most practical purposes, shortly after World War I. The theatricality, commercialism, and spectacle that characterized premodern fairs was brought to a feverish pitch in a last spate of dramatic events in the Jazz Age, but even then there were signs that significant change was imminent. The very excess of 1920s extravaganzas helped sow the seeds for a very different approach after the stock market crash, when the costumed carnivals were replaced by seemingly old-fashioned, no-frills sales. In the next chapter we will explore the interwar tensions that led to these changes and look more closely at the changing face of the fair.

CHAPTER SIX

Fairs during and between the World Wars

Three weeks before . . . the bazaar, there appeared in the local paper an intriguing little paragraph about a new Resort Hotel—Fir Tree Lodge. . . . There were no details, just enough to make outsiders ask questions. Followed in other issues short, snappy interviews with the manager, the "chef," the "Armenian" owner of the Gift Shop, the "Pro." Each had alluring suggestions of fishing, racing, dainty fancy work, delectable foods and renowned beauty specialties. Only the name, date and location were featured plainly. Over all else was a tantalizing mysteriousness . . . [that] created for the public a piquant atmosphere of expectancy.

—Ruby Phillips Bramwell, from
Dennison's Party Magazine, 1928

Descriptions of preparations for the Fir Tree Lodge bazaar indicate how matter-of-fact the 1928 fairgiver was about using the latest techniques in public manipulation to promote and execute her fairs. She was, to use Karal Ann Marling's words, "zooming forward" into the modern world. Within a matter of months, however, after the stock market crash, the typical fair was to once again stress domesticity, modesty, and stay-at-home values. These contrasting fair models reflect what Warren Susman characterizes as the essential cultural tension of the 1920s: it was a time caught between "rival perceptions" of the world, a view dominated on one hand by an older Puritan work ethic and, on the other, by the consumer culture of material abundance.[1] In the case of the woman's fair, the tension was resolved after the economic crisis in favor of the past. The slow erosion of women's distinctive power base discussed in relation to turn-of-the-century fairs was essentially complete by the 1930s.

Fairs during the Great War

Fig. 73. The Red Cross tent illustrated here was featured in a fair held in Plainfield, New Jersey. Red Cross bazaars were popular before the United States was officially involved in the First World War, but grew less common as the conflict wore on. Photograph taken from *Ladies' Home Journal,* October 1907.

Even before the United States officially entered the war in 1917, large numbers of American women were working for war relief. The socialites who had been running other kinds of charity fundraising events organized several major bazaars by involving coalitions of existing groups. The National Allied Relief Committee, the sponsor of events in New York, Boston, and Chicago, netted nearly one and a half million dollars for European Red Cross hospitals and organizations like the Workers for the French Wounded. (That sum was worth about fifteen times more then than it would be today, so this was a significant effort.) The Allied Bazaars included the usual mix of goods, entertainment, celebrities (in Boston this meant many literary personalities), and a lighthearted atmosphere. The newspaper from the Boston event captured the mood with cartoons, humorous remarks about relationships, and tongue-in-cheek articles. One, which played with "questions for discussion at women's clubs," asserted that the function of the fair was to lighten the strain of selecting Christmas gifts.[2]

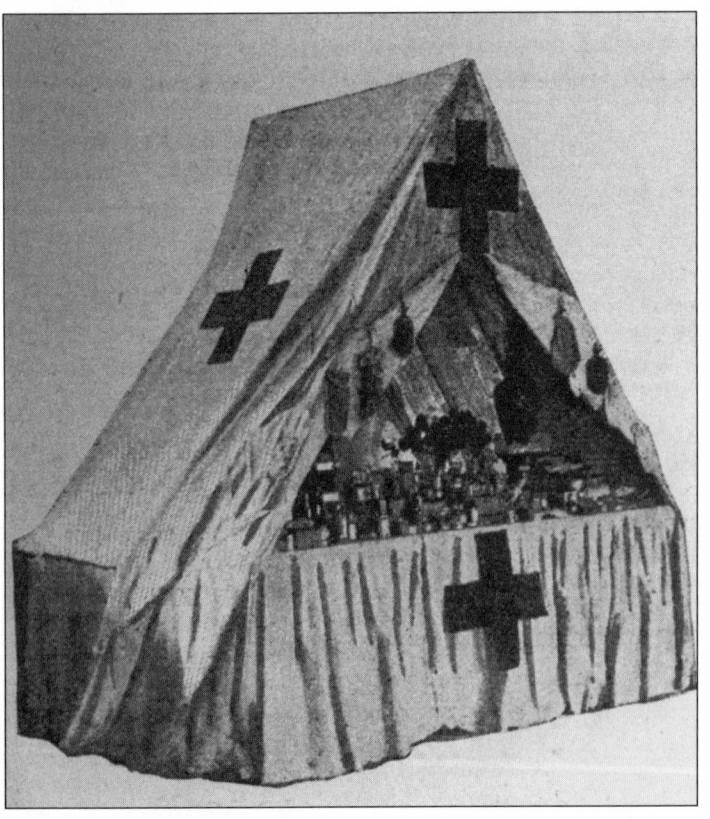

German Americans held a number of their own fairs for the relief of the widows and orphans of the Central Powers. Stressing both their American patriotism and their interest in U.S. neutrality, the sponsors of such a bazaar in Wilmington, Delaware, in 1916 stated they hoped to clear ten thousand dollars.[3]

War relief workers were drawn heavily from the middle class. Newspapers and magazines like *Ladies' Home Journal* and *Woman's Home Companion* encouraged even retiring readers who had not previously participated in such activities to join in the "great [relief] work" and not be a "parasite or sluggard." By the middle of the war, at least one-fourth of the female population worked with officially sponsored programs, while others contributed more informally. The strongest aid society was the Red Cross, which, significantly for our story of fundraising fairs, was the direct successor of the Sanitary Commission. In the northwestern region (Washington, Oregon, and Idaho) alone, there were 113 Red Cross chapters with an average membership of 7,400 per chapter, and an additional 279,000 young women enrolled in the junior auxiliary.[4]

Ladies' Home Journal included specific instructions for a Red Cross bazaar in July 1917, a few months after the country had officially declared war, and by October of that year such events were so taken for granted that an article in the same publication urged women to use a light touch in using red, white, and blue decorations and consider forgoing the usual booths representing the United States and the Allied countries. A Red Cross bazaar in Madison in December warranted front-page coverage in the *Capital Times*. Because Red Cross chapters were frequently run by influential local women—they were often drawn from the ranks of club officers, and many social clubs suspended their usual activities and reconstituted themselves as aid chapters—Red Cross fairs were usually still organized by those who had already been active in fairgiving. However, this was not always the case, because they were by this time also perceived as tried-and-true, appropriately womanly endeavors. A Red Cross fair in Pocatello, Idaho, for example, was organized by a mother and daughter who said they were not comfortable with fund drives or other public activities but still wanted to find a way to express their patriotic feeling. They considered a fair a suitably feminine method of raising money and contributed fifty pieces of needlework between them.[5]

Bringing the War Home to Americans: Hero Land and Other Extravaganzas

Once the United States entered the war, the kind of coalition events represented by the Allied Relief Bazaars became even grander in scale. As noted in the first chapter, for example, representatives of thirty war charities collaborated on New York's "Festa" in MacDougal Alley. The alley, which the *New York Times* referred to as the heart of Bohemian life in the city, was transformed into a "Neapolitan" street. Buildings were fronted with newly constructed facades which had been painted and decorated by resident artists. The length of the street was covered by a weatherproof red, white, and blue awning and filled with banners, lanterns, colored lights, and confetti. After they had made their way through the ballad singers, flower girls, fruit vendors, and loaded donkeys that roamed under the canopy, visitors could stop at artist's ateliers for a variety of entertainments. Gertrude Vanderbilt Whitney's three-story studio, notably, was made into an "al fresco dining room." Elsewhere was a lively "Red Cross Dance Hall," and games of chance were offered continuously. Following the familiar model of the fraternal fairs, different nights and afternoons were "dedicated," this time to various allied countries. Patrons were encouraged to return repeatedly for each new attraction. The Festa was another cleverly staged, highly organized event, in other words, and it was a group of highly visible socialites who were responsible. Its association with Society seems to have been taken for granted by the public. On one occasion the *New York Times* amusedly commented that debutantes were seen everywhere before the fair, "thrusting their little painted cashboxes under the chins of pedestrians." The affair was so successful that the streets were continually jammed and the Festa was extended an extra six days. Over sixty-two thousand dollars were raised.[6]

New York was also the site of two other major fairs in 1917. The Army and Navy Bazaar, held in late October and early November, created much ill feeling because the proceeds contributed to the war effort were pitiably small in proportion to the amount taken in, and city authorities saw fit to both investigate the managerial methods and initiate regulations for future events of the same sort. The organizers of "Hero Land," which opened shortly after in the same building (the Grand Central Palace), went out of their way to assure the city and the public that the previous fiasco would not be repeated. One hundred organizations, said to represent two million people, participated in Hero Land, and though there was a paid executive manager, a committee of several hundred women was in charge of daily operations. Once again, well-known social leaders were involved (Mrs. Woodrow Wilson headed the list of honorary patrons).[7] Planning meetings were held at the Ritz-Carleton, and the whole tone of the event, at least as represented in the press, was one of a professional entertainment. The Society section of the Sunday *New York Times* on November 18 stated, in fact, that Hero Land would be "society's rendezvous for days" and would "resemble somewhat the gay Winter season before the war." Junior League women worked as waitresses at the Red Cross tea room, where "persons of social prominence" reserved tables well in advance of opening day.[8]

Hero Land had its fancywork, embroidery, doll, candy, and toy booths, but it was certainly not an old-fashioned ladies' fair. Many of the handmade sale items were made not by women but by prisoners of war and by blinded soldiers. The stated object of the fair, in fact, was not just to raise money but "to bring the actualities of the war home to Americans." This was a new kind of goal, first expressed at the Allied Relief Bazaars of the previous year. In fact the war was turned into a great spectacle, which must have precluded any true taste of its horrors, but Hero Land was a long way from fairyland, and some of the "tawdriness" of the conflict had certainly begun to intrude on the fair. On display were war relics, including captured German helmets, thermoses from the trenches, sacks that carried flour to the destitute Belgians, even full-size planes and submarines. Fairgoers could also buy souvenirs like tobacco jars made of shells, pencils made of rifle bullets, and bullet-tipped "swagger sticks," or they could attend a dance pageant that dramatized the "spirit of the war" coming to disturb the calm and peaceful people of Poland. They could also listen to army generals' messages on phonograph recordings, or step into five different motion picture theaters to view films taken at the front.[9] Instead of tableaux of Mother Goose or Jack in the Beanstalk, Hero Land featured dioramas of battlefield scenes, the wreck of the Zeppelin, and "Armenians being struck down by Turks." The major attraction of the fair was a replica of a portion of the Hindenburg line, with life-size dug-outs and trenches and a daily demonstration of a charging tank. Staging this was a complex undertaking, as tons of bricks, mortar, sandbags, and lumber had to be brought in to create the right effect. The original plan had included the firing of actual machine guns over the trenches, but the Fire Department would not issue a permit. This was probably a wise decision, for as it was there were some accidents. On December 3, the tank charged the trench with too much speed and knocked down a large portion of it.

Hero Land included some activities that echoed the educational tone of a peacetime agricultural fair or trade exposition. The New York Police Department demonstrated new safety devices, for example, the blind demonstrated some of their equipment, and health workers provided information on nutrition and food conservation. However, there were also still many familiar amusements: costumed beauties and gypsy fortune tellers; "French" and "Old English" streets; "Bagdad," which covered an entire floor and included "black slaves," screeching peacocks, mysterious caverns and caves, and veiled young girls; and the reproduction of an early American village square. There were attractions for children, and boxing matches, sports programs, fashion shows, authors' readings, and other activities for adults. Hero Land was a huge undertaking, in other words, modeled on the large-scale international exposition, but it was also a pageantlike spectacle, based on a militaristic fantasy. The center of the "dream world" had shifted during the war from the never-never land of childhood to a more masculine, heroic adventure.[10]

It is difficult to evaluate how successful Hero Land was. Total attendance was about 250,000, but expenses were high and proceeds as reported on December 16 amounted to $400,000, rather than the $1,000,000 projected. This was almost the same figure raised at the Allied Bazaar held in the same city the year before; the additional great effort that went into Hero Land may not have paid off in a purely financial sense. The fair was a social and morale-building event, however, and contemporary writers spoke of it in glowing terms. D'ann Campbell concludes that the real contribution of women's volunteer work during World War I was to raise morale and keep up awareness of the war, and in this sense the energy that went into the fair was not wasted. No matter how much the serious purpose of the fair was masked by spectacle, moreover, it is important to remember the role of fellowship and the heartfelt feelings of organizers and participants about the cause they were supporting. Evelyn Pearly Coe, for example, who appears from her correspondence to have been working on both suffrage and war-relief bazaars in 1917, wrote to her friend Rosa Levis on October 25. It is not clear from her letter which cause she was referring to, but her devotion to both was clear. She told Levis she couldn't see her as planned because she had to meet a musician she hoped to engage for the bazaar. "Nothing but bazaar work would make me change the hour," she said to her friend. "We are going to have a magnificent bazaar and we are going to be [very] proud."[11]

Begging for Money: Direct Solicitation and the "Age of Drives"
A new phenomenon at the large 1917 bazaars was the direct solicitation of funds. At the Alley Festa, there was a novel twist to the expected sales ploy: costumed young women came up to people not to sell goods or raffle tickets but to ask for money outright. As we have seen, only dolls had been allowed to be so bold until this point.

Even more dramatic soliciting took place at Hero Land. On December 12, when the day's proceeds were earmarked for Halifax sufferers, visitors were met at the front entrance by two women dressed in mourning clothes who asked that they put money in a huge barrel. Liberty Bonds were also sold at fundraising fairs; five hundred thousand dollars' worth were sold at the Alley Festa alone.[12]

As the war went on, this kind of solicitation became even more common, and much of the energy that women first put into fairs was diverted to bond drives and related campaigns. These activities fostered a new kind of aggressive behavior. Several 1918 Liberty Loan campaigns brought women out to canvas, many for the first time. The organization most involved in these drives, the National League for Woman's Service, could mobilize members across the country on a week's notice, and once they were on the streets, the women were relentless. They literally accosted people on the sidewalks, in restaurants, and at the theater. In New York, they set up a special sales building dubbed the Liberty Bank and kept it and several auxiliary booths open from early in the morning until late at night. Soon every town with a National League branch had its own Liberty Bank. In Atlanta, "pink apron girls" situated themselves on one of the main thoroughfares, and in Nashville women solicited from a conspicuous tent set up on busy Capitol Boulevard.

These solicitors were in many cases the same people who worked for other relief organizations, and as they had for the Red Cross, pre-existing groups sometimes transformed themselves into National League chapters. Some of their strategies—building a boothlike bank building, appearing in colored aprons, and even some forms of soliciting—were familiar from previous fair work. As Bessie James, who chronicled the history of the National League, put it, many women "had the advantage of previous experience in selling chances on pianos, automobiles and sofa pillows at bazaars, festivals, and church entertainments."[13]

James christened the 1918 period a "new age—the age of drives" and, despite the credit she had given to bazaar experience, spoke rather belittlingly of the elaborate and entertaining type of fundraising the bazaar represented. She declared the fair dead, in fact; it "perished along with militarism and aristocracy in the war." James's dismissal was as inaccurate as her image of world politics, but her perspective was probably representative of the most active fundraisers of the war period:

> Bazaars had [formerly] been given in every part of the country for the benefit of one or another of the fighting nations. Once [we were well into the war], American women were much too busy to get up one of these grand affairs, and the spirit of celebration and public pleasure, moreover was swallowed in the seriousness of the business confronting the nation. Then too, much larger sums were to be raised than ever before for charitable purposes and it must be done in a business-like way. Old methods which gave the women opportunities to wear evening [dress] were not in order. Everyone was in uniform. Whereas a sale of sofa pillows and pincushions at the benefit fair had brought what was considered a nice sum in the old days, millions were required now.[14]

James may have been glib, but it is true that there was a waning of bazaar-type activities in 1918. The only suggestion for anything like a fair in *Ladies' Home Journal* that year was a "war-winning clothes bazaar," consisting of a display of articles made from leftovers and remnants, with instructions for making each of them. The articles were reclaimed by their makers when the event was over, and the only proceeds came from a five- to fifteen-cent admission charge. Not only the idea but the very tone of the article was subdued, and though the author referred to the event as a bazaar, it involved no frills and no retail sales of any kind. In Madison there were a few fairs held in support of churches, but only two events were devoted in any way to war relief. One was at the Memorial Reformed Church, where members were specifically asked to donate aprons and other useful items rather than fancy articles; this was called a "sale" rather than a bazaar, and it only lasted one afternoon. The other event was a Christmas bazaar sponsored by the Alpha Chi Delta sorority, held to support a French orphan the girls had adopted.[15]

Rummage sales and benefit card parties would generally fall into the no-frills fundraiser category that Bessie James approved, but it would be a mistake to assume such events were always simple. James herself did not see the contradiction in her description of a white elephant (rummage) sale in Seattle. She noted the interior of the room was "arranged like the bazaar district of a city of India," with ample oriental decorations. "Buzzing femininity" blocked the view of the loaded central table. The impulse for festivity and elaboration could not be easily suppressed, it seems, even in wartime. Festive fairs returned when the war was over, and for a time the type of spectacle that Hero Land represented grew even stronger. The patronizing attitude expressed by Bessie James in 1920 illustrates the new dichotomy and polarization that took place after the war, however, as the expanded experience of direct solicitation and operation in less "feminine" arenas gave some women a new model for fundraising and perhaps contributed to a different sense of self.[16] Those who saw themselves as fully "modern" and outgoing seem to have felt increasingly distant from those who were more home-oriented and identified with old-fashioned values. Eventually, as fundraising fairs became even more identified with the second group, the distancing affected the way fundraising fairs were perceived.

Bazaars in the Jazz Age: Youth Fairs and Sophisticated Carnivals

Direct solicitation did not take place in every community, and even where fairs were suspended during the war, it was not long before they re-emerged. In a small community in northwestern Wisconsin, for example, a Red Cross group quickly reconstituted itself as a community sewing circle that annually sponsored sales in the 1920s. In Boston bazaars were regularly given by such organizations as the Dorchester Community Health Association and the Boston Equal Woman's Suffrage Association, and by 1922 the city newspapers pointedly commented on the plethora of fairs. The Animal Rescue League, the Community Child Welfare Association, the Boston Dispensary, the All Soul's Church, and the Tide-Over League all held events in the first week of December; the "season of rummage sales, bazaars and their like" was proclaimed by the *North Shore Breeze* to be "most strenuous." There was no lack of willing workers, and according to the *Boston Traveller,* each affair seemed to succeed even beyond the expectation of its sponsors. This same kind of enthusiasm was reflected in the record books of Madison's Pilgrim Congregational Church women's guild, where the majority of 1920s entries refer to rummage sales and bazaars. The time and attention the women devoted to fundraising events was considerable, for in addition to holding two or three of their own in a single year, guild members brought goods to other groups that in turn sold them on a kind of commission basis at their own fairs. In 1929 the guild secretary remarked, "at every meeting [we] have worked joyfully on fancywork for our Bazaar."[17] Many of the trends seen before the war, in other words, reemerged with the fairs. They were still old standbys of church groups and a variety of charitable and reform associations and were still associated with both youth or children's groups and highly efficient socialites.

The youth trend was apparent in Madison. Some of the fairs were held by adults, but they expressly supported youth activities. Many public and parochial school activities were funded through annual fairs, for example, usually sponsored by parent-teacher associations. Even more often, it was young women and girls who actually gave the fairs under some sort of adult supervision. A 1929 Madison Girl Scout Bazaar was typical—it involved close to three hundred girls who had prepared sale goods and entertainment as part of their scouting activities. There were also fairs run by church youth groups, college sororities, and the YWCA (the latter two groups occasionally joined forces). Similar programming was evident throughout the country. A doll show suggested as a suitable girl's club activity in the 1922 issue of *Playground* magazine was said by the author to be based on a show put on by coeds from the University of Illinois. As in the prewar years, the Illinois girls arranged doll tableaux and dressed like dolls themselves.[18]

While the culture still emphasized youth in the Jazz Age, it was not quite with the same prewar refusal to grow up. Rather, as indicated by the events cited here, the primary concern was to provide young people with wholesome educational and leisure opportunities so they would mature into healthy and productive adults. The so-called recreation movement was at its peak; *Playground* magazine was in fact a publication for recreation workers who hoped to effect social change through youth programming. Such programming bled into school curricula, so it is not surprising that by the end of the war there were even articles like "Projects for the School Bazaar" in periodicals aimed at industrial arts teachers. It is significant to note that in a parallel fashion, youth programming also became the "life blood" of agricultural fairs in the 1920s through 4-H and Grange clubs. It was a time, in fact, when many activities that had originally been experienced as adult pastimes became more particularly associated with children. Nineteenth-century adult games became standard at twentieth-century children's parties, for example, and people began to think of them as something that would be outgrown. Pageants, which had originally involved people of different ages and classes and were seen as community-building, socially transformative activities, went through a similar progression. By the 1920s, they primarily appeared in the context of school and youth group programs and were simpler and more standardized (Prevots claims they were reduced to "trite spectacle[s] created and staged by amateurs").[19] Fundraising fairs became conceptually linked with schools and children's projects, then, even while they were in what was probably their most businesslike and "professional" phase.

The more professional face of 1920s fairs was especially evident in society circles in larger cities. Since most of the women who had fought to forge careers in the early years of the century remained single (only 12.2 percent of professional women were married in 1920) and married women were unlikely to seek paid employment (after the war the flood of returning servicemen created a particular backlash against working women), there was a pool of available talent for these undertakings. The privileged, well-educated, married women who were typically comfortable taking on authoritative public positions put more energy than ever into volunteer work. Charitable fundraising (mixed at times with fundraising for social reform) became for many of them an even more businesslike avocation, albeit one mixed inextricably with social obligation and persona.[20]

The personal papers of Marietta Pratt, a well-off Bostonian who worked tirelessly for many causes in the postwar years, offer a glimpse of the way this professionalization worked in a specific community. Marietta Hockness made her social debut before the war and in 1914 married Walter Pratt, a governor's aide and son of the former mayor. The young matron quickly assumed a prominent role in Boston social circles, and filled several bulging scrapbooks in the 1920s with newspaper clippings and papers documenting her many activities. The sheer volume of entries indicates how busy she was and implies a great pride and devotion to the undertaken tasks. Pratt used her social position in a variety of ways. In what appears to be 1919 (many clippings have no dates), for example, she initiated a chain of bridge parties to benefit disabled soldiers and raised $1,350 in six weeks.[21] She worked at the yearly fair for the Massachusetts Equal Suffrage Association from at least 1916 to 1922, sometimes taking a leadership role. (This organization became the League of Women Voters once suffrage was achieved.) The 1921 event, billed as a Harvest Fest and Thanksgiving Market, was held at the Copley Plaza, an elegant hotel. Pratt negotiated the site and coordinated donations, workers, and publicity. In 1922 she put additional energy into a Wonderland Fete for the league, and into a Serviceman's Ball and a "Caravan" for the Soldier's and Sailor's Club.

> ### The Atlantic City Boardwalk and Fairgivers as
> ### Publicity and Organizational Specialists

The next year Pratt had an even bigger challenge, as she was one of the organizers of a major regional event, the "Atlantic City Boardwalk." The League of Women Voters joined with numerous other institutions (see sidebar below) to stage this fair, which was set up as a re-creation, in a Boston hall and in the depths of December, of the New Jersey seaside resort. The stage set was imaginative. The walls were covered with full-scale murals of piers and waves, and a sand-filled play area was placed at ground level at one end of the room. In front of the sand there was a long wooden boardwalk, complete with the famous Atlantic City wheelchairs that fairgoers might ride in. Beach chairs and umbrellas, parades of "bathing beauties in the latest swimwear," and a suspended plane "hovering over the shore" completed the illusion. The booths themselves were a mixed lot: some featured handmade goods (everything from night-gowns and aprons to paper birds and "flapper dolls," and a wealth of foodstuffs); some featured exotic goods sponsoring organizations had procured elsewhere (Brittany china, Indian baskets, mahjong sets); and others were rented to commercial retailers from Boston and New York.[22]

The Boardwalk concept, scenery, and props were rented from Thomas Convey, a Chicagoan who had produced a similar event in his own city (net profits there were about ninety-two thousand dollars) and then formed Atlantic City Boardwalk, Inc., to stage Boardwalk theme fairs elsewhere. Groups in Nashville, St. Louis, Milwaukee, Louisville, Cleveland, and St. Paul had all used the company's services between 1919 and 1923, and it is probable that the same scenery was adapted to each location. Convey had also offered to produce "The Streets of Paris," but the Boston fundraisers felt the Boardwalk was more novel and a better way to improve upon "the old idea of a fair."[23]

As Pratt and her fellow organizers were part of Boston's "smart set" (other managers were from well-known local families with names like Channing, Elliot, Lodge, James, and Sumner), the Boardwalk, like comparable prewar events, was decidedly the social event of 1923. "Everyone, everywhere, seem[ed] to be talking about the Boardwalk," and the question of interest in society was "who's going to sell what," according to the *Boston American* on November 12. *Boston Advertiser* columnist Betty Alden gossiped on November 6, "I don't believe there's a single debutante of the season who isn't going to serve as an usher at the Boardwalk Theatre." Even in the summer preceding the fair, society columns mentioned the Boardwalk, noting that the usual diversions of the summer had been shared with the work of the fair.

The organizers handled publicity brilliantly. They began by distributing mysterious posters to pique the city's curiosity and by contacting merchandisers in a no-nonsense fashion with a flyer reminding them that two hundred thousand potential customers would be exposed to their line of goods at the fair. They ran a contest for the individual or organization that could sell the most advance tickets, offering a tempting new automobile as first prize. In October, one of the chairwomen posed with Mayor Curley in front of City Hall, exchanging a book of tickets for a key to the city. Chorus girls from a current production called "The Spice of '22" were also on hand to sell tickets to the crowd after the ritual exchange. On other occasions the women used Atlantic City wheelchairs for publicity stunts. A cavalcade of wheelchairs, each bearing a chairwoman with a hatful of tickets, buzzed around Harvard Square "at a great rate" on one afternoon, and every Monday, Thursday, and Saturday for several

Organizations Represented at Boston's Atlantic City Boardwalk

Animal Rescue League
Boston Children's Friend Society
Boston Music School Settlement
Boston YWCA
Cambridge YWCA
Children's Farm Home
Daughters of the American Revolution
Disabled Servicemen's League
Elizabeth Peabody House
Father's and Mother's Club
Florence Crittendon League
Francis Willard Settlement (for Its Home for Incurables)
Home of Mercy

Household Nursing Association
Massachusetts Association for the Blind
Massachusetts League of Women Voters
Mount Pleasant Home
New England Hospital for Women [and Children]
New England Peabody Home for Crippled Children
South End Music School
Talitha Cumi Maternity Home and Hospital for Unmarried Mothers
Tideover League
Travellers Aid Society
Tufts Alumni Association
Woman's Trade Union League

weeks thereafter the chairs were pushed about by uniformed soldiers on the Boston Common. The women saw that many photographs of these activities were printed in the local press, and newspaper professionals admitted that the women handled them with aplomb. A letter sent to Mrs. Pratt from Frank Sibley, an editor at the *Boston Globe*, stated, "It appears that half of the men in Boston are [doing publicity for you]. . . . The *Herald* yesterday threw up its hands altogether and declared editorially it could not find space for all the notices and letters you folks are sending out."[24]

Publicity of this type was encouraged in advice books of the day, and learning the tricks of the trade was a part of the apprenticeship for these quasi-professional benefit-givers in the Junior League and similar organizations (Mrs. S. F. Blodgett, a member of the executive committee at the Boardwalk, was said by the *North Shore Breeze* to have "won her spurs as an organizer" the winter before, when she "put over" a Copley Plaza fundraising event called Woman's Day). Lessons about the latest techniques of consumer manipulation developed in the burgeoning fields of advertising and public relations were actually provided to all kinds of women through the popular advice literature. Dayton and Barratt, whose *Book of Entertainments and Theatricals* was published in 1924, specifically stated that "stunts" must be thought of to keep attention going both before and after a fair, and if anything unexpected occurred fairgivers should "play [it] to the limit." Photographs of costumed saleswomen should be supplied to the press, they noted, and a publicity chairwoman should stay on her toes and be able to exploit all photographic opportunities. Emily Burt, who wrote *Make Your Bazaar Pay* in 1925 after many years as associate editor of *Woman's Home Companion,* offered much the same advice. Get people "on tiptoe" so they can hardly wait for the event, she said, and find ways to get illustrations published in the press. "Remember, this is a pictorial age," she noted. "If there are to be pretty girls helping in any capacity—and there always are—they can be photographed *ad infinitum.*" Three years later, *Dennison's Party Magazine* described the publicity scheme for the Fir Tree Lodge bazaar cited at the beginning of this chapter. Advice-givers assured women that soliciting was "part of the game," and they should "ask everyone for something." As Burt said, this was a "business proposition." In the Fir Tree Lodge, saleswomen dressed as maids to beg for money. If "guests" couldn't believe that maids were dependent on their generosity, noted writer Ruby Bramwell, "conspicuous placards on the wall made the appealing announcement." Connections with the advertising profession were quite explicitly acknowledged in prescriptive fair literature. In a 1929 "Buyway Bazaar," for example, the group in charge of the program was to be known as the "Advertising Committee" or "Agency."[25]

The wheelchair processions arranged to interest people in the Boardwalk were also *au courant* publicity strategies. Burt suggested using auto floats and other mobile advertising for fairs. *Woman's Home Companion* suggested an effective advertising ploy for a carnival-theme fair: the event would be heralded by two clowns riding through the streets on donkeys, followed by a decorated automobile with boys blowing horns and beating drums. The mobility theme had first been stressed just prior to World War I. The long-familiar Bazaar of All Nations theme, for example, was transformed to "personally conducted Trips to Foreign Lands" in several instances. At a church fair suggested in *Modern Priscilla* in 1916, fairgoers went to "steamship" offices to buy tickets, and "conductors" led them to subsequent country booths. A similar event featured a railway station piled with trunks, picture postcards, and a shoeshine boy. *Ladies' Home Journal* based a whole fair on the idea of traveling at about the same time. Each booth was a decorated truck, car, motorcycle or cart (figs. 74–76). "Take the booths and attendants anywhere you want them to go," proclaimed the headline of this feature. The mobile booths looked and even functioned like parade floats, which must have been even more in the popular consciousness after the war. The troops had been welcomed home from Europe with huge parades, and a rash of similar spectacles had followed, including the Thanksgiving parade sponsored by Macy's department store in New York. By 1923 the Dennison (Crepe Paper) Company indicated how closely linked booths and parades had become when it called its new instruction booklet *How to Decorate Halls, Booths and Automobiles.* The mobile fundraising fair booths embodied the same kind of fanciful, "innocent" costuming and feeling as floats in a children's parade, although that was somewhat anomalous compared with the almost aggressive, technological presence of the early vehicles themselves and the message about women's rights and capacities their female drivers implied.[26] Again, this anomaly embodied the salient quality of the 1920s fair: a romantic facade and humorous overall tone masking a sophisticated, businesslike organization and operation.

The Atlantic City Boardwalk, like other Jazz Age fairs, was unquestionably a major business undertaking. Large sums of money were involved in its staging: rental on the main building alone cost $10,000, and there were subsidiary buildings and fees for Mr. Convey's stage settings, electricity, insurance, and so on. Income came from profits on admissions, sales goods, and entertainments, supplemented by rental fees for commercial booths (the range was $250 to $1,000). The juggling of this kind of budget was demanding, but it was only one form of recordkeeping the organizers had to contend with. They solicited and then processed large numbers of donations (one committee alone sent out 4,000 postcards asking for goods). They also juggled large numbers of personnel: just one booth, a 12-by-12-foot shop for the Massachusetts Society for the Blind, involved 18 saleswomen each day, drawn from a total pool of 97. To handle this volume of work, most committees met almost daily for many weeks before the event. While the efficient operation of the fair may have been attributable to the organizers, it is important to remember that the success of the Atlantic City Boardwalk was dependent on these banks of workers. Immigrant and working-class women sometimes donated items and worked at the booths of "their" organizations; for example, former patients of the New England Hospital came to help out at the dispensary booth, often dressed in the finery of their native lands. Settlement house workers sometimes came with their "charges." Labor was also donated by women from other parts of the state. The *Springfield Republican* reported on September 29 that appeals to help out at the Boardwalk had already reached its clubwomen.[27]

Immigrant women could of course be organizers themselves. In Milwaukee in 1921, for example, German Americans brought disparate groups together to form a Charity Bazaar Association that sponsored a fair for the benefit of German and Austrian children. It was time, according to a letter from President Harding's office that was printed in the bazaar program, that "the asperities of the war" should be put aside. In addition to local organizations like the Milwaukee Maternity Hospital, participants in the association included German choral societies and clubs from elsewhere in Wisconsin and from the rest of the country—as far away as San Antonio, Texas. While the relative social status of the organizers of this fair is uncertain, the thick (128-page) program is filled with cameo-like photographs of 177 individuals, mostly directors and committee chairs. This kind of highlighted, self-congratulatory presentation was typically seen at the time in rotogravure sections and other society pages, and it is likely that these were the social leaders of the German community. While this constituency-based fair never reached the scale or the prepackaged quality of the Atlantic City Boardwalk, it too was a well-choreographed event with hundreds of musical performances and visually exciting attractions like "Electric Wonderland." Many of the booths gave an ethnic spin to popular themes—women posed at their spinning wheels in Swiss, German, and

Dutch costume; there were Hungarian, Saxony, and Wiener cafes—but some standard American favorites, such as a Martha Washington booth and a Country Fair booth, were also featured.[28]

Clubwomen may have been more likely to sponsor fairs in the 1920s than in any other period. Karen Blair argues, in fact, that a focus on fundraising may have been one reason for the decline of women's clubs after the war. She notes in *The Torchbearers* that many groups were forced to spend a high proportion of their time raising funds because they had chosen to build costly clubhouses and had to pay them off. *Dennison's Party Magazine* was suggesting fundraising schemes like bazaars "for your club or society" by the latter part of the decade, implying that this was a routine need for both types of groups. Even special-interest clubs became fairgivers. The Pasadena Shakespeare Club staged a "Spanish Fiesta" in 1925, for example, to raise money for a club auditorium.[29]

Figs. 74–76. (below and opposite) In November 1919, *Ladies' Home Journal* ran its last major feature on novel fair ideas. The new twist was a kind of mobile ("movie") bazaar, in which each "booth" was mounted on some kind of wheeled vehicle. These contrivances were close to parade floats and were designed to command attention.

Themes Stressing Leisure and Play

Some of the smaller fairs of the 1920s drew on familiar themes that had been popular at the turn of the century. The women's society of Madison's Christ Presbyterian Church held a festival of the seasons in 1924, for example, and *Eureka Entertainments,* an instruction book originally published in 1894, was reprinted almost without revisions in 1927, implying that long-familiar ideas remained useful in the modern age. The "Family Af-Fair" bazaar, hailed as a new idea in 1905, was still appearing in the popular press as a "novelty" in 1929. There were slight variations in the ways the booths were linked to family roles—the 1929 version that appeared in a Canadian farmer's magazine noted the mother's booth, which in 1905 was to feature "everything for housekeeping," was "naturally" a bakery table—but these were minor. What may be more notable is the progression of the feature, i.e., from a magazine catering to a largely well-off, urban audience to a farmer's publication.[30]

Even so, the profile of the fair was changing. Fairy tale themes were largely absent from adult-run fairs; doll tableaux, nursery rhymes, and similar images were primarily limited to fairs oriented to children or sponsored by youth organizations. The spectacle of the wartime Hero Land was transformed to a new dramatiza-

The Motorcycle Has a New Use as a Grab Bag

THE side car is converted into a huge flower-adorned crêpe-paper bag of mysterious packets.

tion of leisure and play—a theme perfectly embodied at the Fir Tree Lodge or the Atlantic City Boardwalk. Atlantic City was an adult playland, and the Fir Tree Lodge was "a fashionable resort"; these were places for vacation, relaxation, *not*-work. Even the *Farmer's Advocate* commented in 1928 that "the best thing to sell at a bazaar is amusement" and suggested a similar "Maple Leaf Lodge," complete with leisure activities like horseback riding, horse racing, and golf. Many larger fairs evoked what Dayton and Barratt called the new "combination of circus, Monte Carlo, and the Rue de la Paix" and reflected what some have referred to the "play-spirit" of the Jazz Age—an ethos of living for the moment, given the horror of the newly

understood potential of mass destruction. The fair still created an environment removed from the realities of everyday life, in other words, but the fantasy had changed from a childlike Never-Never Land to an adult amusement center.[31]

These themes were manifested in various ways. At many large bazaars there were amusement areas that mimicked the midways at prewar world's fairs. The Atlantic City Boardwalk included rides, racing monkeys, and a "Temple of Illusion," which featured daring staged escapes from torture pillories (like P. T. Barnum, the Boston fairgivers literally promised their customers a thrill every minute). "Uncle Sam's Market Place," a 1924 fundraiser that involved many of the same Boston socialites, also featured a midway and a plethora of wandering hurdy-gurdy girls. Both the Boardwalk and the German fair had a Monte Carlo section, with roulette wheels and other games of chance. The circus theme was also a leitmotif of the 1920s. This ranged from the 1923 "Carnival of Tent Cities and Military Tournament" staged by the Army and Navy Club of Boston (or its auxiliary) to smaller fairs run by more middle-class women. Carnivals and circuses were pointedly featured in the advice literature, and typically these included ideas for sideshow attractions. The theme was taken up across the country. In Madison, the 1929 YWCA Circus included an inter-sorority contest for the best sideshow booth, and snake charmers competed with fat ladies, bearded men, and sword swallowers. The sideshows were farcical in tone, almost like the mock art exhibits that had only recently fallen out of favor, but they had a harder edge, for they were often "freak" shows and made fun of people rather than including them in the joke. The "Fattest Baby in Captivity," for example, was to be represented by a fat boy who had extra excelsior stuffed around him.[32]

The YWCA bazaar and others like it were held indoors, but carnival themes could also be effectively worked into seasonal outdoor street fairs. Some fairs had been held outside since the 1890s (the Alley Festa and the Movie Bazaar suggested in *Ladies' Home Journal* both used the street), and outdoor trade fairs and pageants with carnival themes had been at the peak of their popularity just before World War I. It was in the early 1920s, however, that Dayton and Barratt referred to the street fair as the current bazaar craze. They spoke of the "piquant flavor" of a street fair—it was like a foreign carnival mixed with the thrill of a circus. Emily Burt thought the rise of interest in outdoor fairs was probably influenced by the recent increase in automobile traffic, and she may well have been correct. Wayne Neely also attributed the rise of the state and neighborhood agricultural fairs (at the expense of the county fair) to a proliferation of cars.[33]

Dayton and Barratt documented several New York area street fairs. At one held annually in support of crippled children, Park Avenue was closed to traffic, hung with lanterns and ribbons, and filled with stages, merry-go-rounds, pony and donkey carts, and booths of all descriptions. Outdoor fairs associated with Society were held in Southampton, Long Island (the theme of the 1923 fair in support of the local hospital was the Royal Gardens of Delhi); Greenwich, Connecticut (some of the Park Avenue scenery was borrowed); and Glen Cove, Long Island. Uncle Sam's Market

Place was also held outdoors; it was dubbed "Boston's Mammoth Street Fete" and featured canvas tents set up around Copley Square plaza.[34]

In addition to the circus, the 1920s outdoor fair drew some of its imagery from the agricultural fair. A popular attraction at the Greenwich event, for example, was "The Farm," which featured calves, pigs, and chickens that children could pet. Garden and grocery areas reminiscent of a country fair were featured in Uncle Sam's Market Place. Even indoor fairs frequently included "farmers" and country store booths. Farmers seemed to represent old-fashioned values and offered a wholesome counterpoint to modern cynicism and the worldliness of the city (over half the population was urban by this time), but even farmers were mocked, as they were often featured in the sideshow context. A Youngstown, Ohio, fundraising event called a Country Fair involved animals, a circus performance, and "many people dressed up as Rubes." This mockery was harder-edged than the gentle caricatures of the New England Kitchens, and it is significant that despite the prevalence of almost sacrosanct Colonial Revival imagery in 1920s popular culture, the old-fashioned hearth had disappeared from the 1920s fair.[35]

Aprons and Modernism: Practical Products and Streamlined Environmetnts

There was continued interpenetration between bazaars and retailing establishments in the 1920s, although this took different forms than it had at the turn of the century. Merchants were quick to take advantage of the opportunity to show their greatly expanded line of ready-to-wear garments at fundraising events, and they held many of their newly popular style or fashion shows among the fair booths. They had experimented with a number of venues for these shows, including agricultural fairs and expositions, but the fundraising fair, with its largely female clientele and its pointedly lighthearted atmosphere, was a particularly good setting. At the Atlantic City Boardwalk, every merchant who rented a booth was entitled to stage a fashion show. Retailers also helped fairgivers. *Woman's Home Companion* reported in 1925 on a "get together with the merchants," where milliners, dressmakers, and proprietors of clothing stores cooperated with organizers of a particular fair. In Madison, many bazaars were actually held in retail establishments, ranging from department stores to hardware or shoe stores and flower shops. Organizers also continued to retail goods that they themselves had procured at wholesale rates. This was true not only at grand bazaars (items at the Atlantic City Boardwalk ranged from cigarettes, sold by "50 beautiful socialite girls" dressed in Turkish harem costumes, to miniature Russian icons and other goods brought from Europe and the Near East), but also at small church fairs. The Italian women of St. Joseph's Church in Madison imported novelties from their home country and resold them at their Christmas sale in 1917. The women of Grace Episcopal Church sold novelties from India in 1924. The idea that women were perhaps more likely to be able to see themselves as entrepreneurs is suggested by a fair described in *Parties* in 1929. At the "Buyway Bazaar," the row of

Fig. 77. *(left)* The Fir Tree Lodge bazaar, featured in *Dennison's Party Magazine* in March–April 1928, was set up to imitate a resort hotel. Fairgoers could amuse themselves with games like "fishing," "horse racing," and "golf." Many of these amusements allowed middle-class individuals to play at fashionable leisure pastimes associated with the wealthy. Photograph by the author; used by permission of Avery Dennison Company.

Fig. 78. *(right)* The sketch represents a booth at "Carnival, 1923," discussed in the August issue of *Woman's Home Companion.* The Egyptian theme reflects the "Tutmania" that was sweeping the country after the discovery of the Tutankhamen tomb was made public. It would be easily adapted to the kind of outdoor carnivals or street fair that was popular in the 1920s.

"houses" (booths) facing a central street was changed to an arcade of shops. A proprietor would be chosen for each, "the point [being] to so enthuse each shopkeeper that her particular place will be her sole interest."[36]

Despite the cooperation with storekeepers and the emphasis on entrepreneurship, however, both the presentation of goods and the sense of their infinite possibilities were being toned down. Even as fundraising fairs reached a peak in terms of spectacle and complexity, then, they were transforming into a new phase where everything, including sale items, was more self-consciously "modern." While it is not possible to assign a specific date to modernity or the decline of the so-called commodity aesthetic, many scholars who have written about the allure of goods note a significant shift at the end of World War I.[37] A focus on rational consumption had been an integral part of the Progressive reform agenda, and proponents of the Arts and Crafts philosophy had espoused more spare, unemotional products that were functional rather than fanciful or exotic. By the 1920s, with the new cynicism engendered by the war, these ideas were pervasive. Educators spoke about the aesthetic value of ordinary objects and taught students to create "art in everyday life," and simplicity was a new watchword. Moreover, middle-class women were finding it increasingly necessary to take over more of the day-to-day upkeep of their homes, as the pool of individuals willing to work as domestic servants had shrunk dramatically. With more and more consumer products and objects in the typical home, the women increasingly needed to find a way to manage them. In sum, goods were no longer seen primarily as vehicles of transformation, but as objects to be controlled and put to use. Gordon and McArthur also argue that women's attention shifted in the modern era to products that helped them perceive their given social roles more positively. Once they had to do their own cooking, for example, kitchens and kitchen products became more attractive; kitchens illustrated in women's magazines in the 1920s, for example, "combined the attributes of a sitting room, boudoir, and a laboratory."[38]

Sale items at 1920s fairs—even those with spectacular circus or resort themes—tended to be far more practical and ordinary than those in preceding decades. While there was still interest in international merchandise like Brittany china, goods were often items that would be needed on an everyday basis. The grocery booths that have been previously mentioned were extremely common. At the 1929 version of the Family Af-fair, the grocery booth was associated with father, the provider. It sold fruit, vegetables, and canned goods. At Uncle Sam's Market Place in Boston, grocery items were integrated into a "Cape Cod Folks" booth that highlighted regional foodstuffs like scallops and cranberries. Even the cigarettes sold by the Turkish harem girls at the Boardwalk were everyday necessities in the 1920s. In discussing "Bazaars for Fun and Profit" in 1928, Dorothy Wright cautioned twice that the prime consideration in handmade goods should be practicality. Her recommendations included simple bags, book covers and similar items made from felt, and bibs, dusters, and aprons made from unpretentious unbleached cotton. She also suggested that fairgivers use sealing wax to decorate cost-free goods like old bottles or inexpensive purchased items such as glasses, ashtrays, or hairbrushes. In addition, she mentioned items that might be made by "the handyman": bookshelves and bookends, shoe stands, window boxes, and even "wedges for rattling windows." This is the first instance I have found where men's hand labor was even discussed in relation to fair sale products. Even here, Wright discusses the judicious amount of transformative paint that the woman who coaxed him to contribute would have to apply.[39]

Of all the items made for fairs in the 1920s, aprons emerged as the single most consistently mentioned category. They were among the primary contributions to the Atlantic City Boardwalk and were remembered by older interviewees more than almost any other articles. In the records of the Woman's Alliance of the First Unitarian Society in Madison, proceeds from the apron booth were given a separate listing of their own, perhaps because the aprons were the most profitable elements of the fair. In 1926 over $100 was realized from the sale of aprons, $63 from the sale of food, and only $25 from the "bazaar" booth. In 1927 the aprons yielded nearly three times the profit of the other handwork. These aprons were not ornate in the Victorian sense, and they did not "masquerade" as other items, but they were made to look attractive and festive; they were considered accessories suitable to be seen publicly. "Tea" aprons, specifically made for entertaining, were common. A woman who told me she made hundreds of organdy aprons for fairs kept reiterating details about their trim and manufacture, repeating, "they were so pretty!" *Ladies' Home Journal* played on this sentiment in 1925, when it assured its readers there was "nothing so appealing to the masculine eye as a dainty apron." Hand-trimmed lingerie and kitchen dining cloths, also popular at this time, must have had something of this same appeal. Again, the prevalence of practical objects with "homey" associations reflected a postwar emphasis on homemaking and a renewed insistence that (middle-class) woman's place was in the home. One woman I interviewed told me that her grandmother, born in the 1880s, would not be seen in an apron—she kept her domestic work hidden. Her mother, in contrast, was happy to be seen in an apron, and especially liked to dress up in attractive ones with funny sayings. She was part of the postwar generation that expected to be doing its own entertaining.[40] The popularity of the aprons reminds us of the stronger and stronger identification of fundraising fairs with the middle-class housewife. By the late 1920s items that alluded to wealthy lifestyles were increasingly out of place.

The same practicality that was evident in sale goods was also seen in the environments of fairs and related institutions in the 1920s. The lure of the department store had diminished; large stores were still prevalent, but they did not have the same emotional hold on the public, and despite the boom economy, profits dropped significantly. Retailers consequently began modernizing and streamlining both their interiors and their displays, and the formerly exciting and stimulating environments of the stores gave way to a more subdued, "logical" atmosphere that appealed to those concerned with rational consumption. International expositions changed in similar ways. Whereas prewar expositions had glorified conventional norms and highlighted the importance of goods and the intractability of progress, expositions of the 1920s and after focused on abstract concepts and technology. Their settings were streamlined and futuristic rather than formal, grand, and luxurious. Visitors were also less attracted by the existing world of goods than by the promise of modernism and sophistication that awaited them in the future.[41]

The same spareness and streamlining was also evident in the fair environment, even at the spectacular 1920s events. Booths and costuming were generally simplified and made suggestive rather than literal, and sensual stimulation was reduced as textures, sights, and sounds became less overwhelming. Some signs of change had been evident by the time of the war. At a "house sale" introduced in 1915, the enclosed playhouse-type booth of the turn-of-the-century era was replaced by a few props. The living room, where accessories such as pillows and tinware were sold, was implied by a few chairs, a table, and a lamp. The bedroom was furnished with a bed, dressing-table, and chair, over which sale negligees, boudoir caps, and other intimate garments were arranged.[42] This remained a staged setting, but perhaps reflecting the breaking down on an international scale of the old order, it was sparer and less bounded, contrived, and protected.

Booths built of lath frameworks were still discussed in the guidebooks of the modern era, but there were more suggestions for much simpler, uncovered tables—the word "tables" was reintroduced into the fair vocabulary, in fact, for the first time since the 1880s. An autumn cat-theme fair described in 1913 by Caroline French Benton called for tables "simply covered with dark cloth with painted designs" (fig. 79). Elaborate booth decorations were specifically discouraged, for they would detract from the cat idea; a token decor of cattails and unobtrusive signage was all that was recommended. At the Buyway Bazaar, decorations consisted only of strings of colored lights. Even when novelty booths were suggested in the World War I period, they were smaller in scale and had a more open quality. By the 1920s they had for the most part disappeared from the prescriptive literature, and those that were illustrated typically had simple upright posts (fig. 80), latticework, or open sides (often, they were a kind of pergola). There were no more closed-in, densely draped spaces that alluded to safe retreats.[43]

The popular outdoor settings also encouraged simpler decor. Costume might be used outdoors, but it need not bear a strong relationship to the tables. A "Brittany Summer Fair" described in *Woman's Home Companion* included romantic outfits for both women and girls (in the evening, the costumed participants were to form a slow procession around the fairgrounds [fig. 3]), but sale items could be set out on stands improvised with sawhorses and boards. The peddlers or "basket girls" first seen at the turn of the century were present at almost every fair by the 1920s, and this trend further reduced the necessity of elaborate structures.[44] The 1919 mobile or "movie bazaar" mentioned earlier symbolized just how thoroughly the enclosed, protective, and domestic quality of the turn-of-the-century booth had been broken.

We are reminded once again how the fairs functioned as a kind of microcosm of social and aesthetic trends when we see how closely the generally more streamlined look of fair booths in these decades corresponded to changes in house decoration and women's fashions. Contemporary decorators talked about removing clutter from the home, and were concerned with "charm" and "personality" rather than impressive spaces. Fashion underwent its greatest change between 1910 and 1920, the same time that the fair environment was becoming more spare. It was in this time period that women began to release themselves from body-distorting corsets and wear slimmer, simpler, and less encumbered dresses. This relationship between women's bodies and the design of the fair environment was not new. In the Victorian era, both walls and dresses had been "festooned," and proper tables, like proper ladies, wore skirts so their legs did not show. Like women who were outfitted by dressmakers, booths were draped with fabric. With the advent of easier styles and the availability and acceptability of ready-to-wear garments during and after World War I, women's very relationship to their clothes shifted dramatically. They were no longer personally and painstakingly draped or fitted in the same manner—rather, they were able to dress themselves quickly (they "got" dressed) in the newer, plainer clothing that came off the rack. Fair environments, which were in many ways extensions of the women themselves, began to echo or reflect this new relationship.[45]

The simplified or streamlined look of the fairs extended to iconographic imagery as well. The 1915 house fair described above, with its simple visual suggestion rather than literal representation of a house, was an early expression of this idea. By the 1920s much of the fair environment was suggestive and somewhat abstract; realistic reproduction was no longer highly valued. In their detailed chapter on fair decoration, Dayton and Barratt stated in 1924 that (decorative) license could be taken, for the "object [is] effect, not verity." "Merely suggestive" details were adequate. They described beach theme decor which was remarkably like the setting at the Atlantic City Boardwalk: the beach was represented by a simple backdrop, with a four-foot band of sand-colored paper topped by an eight-foot expanse of brilliant sky blue. Triangular sail-like shapes were applied over the horizon line, and to create a sense of depth a few large beach parasols were placed in front of the paper. Venice was similarly suggested by a mural dominated by a strip implying a watery canal on the bottom, overlaid by geometric shapes implying "tinted palazzos" against the sky. Several in-progress murals were illustrated in the book, and although their final effect was not clear, they appear to be made with cartoonlike outlines that suggest a mood rather than a realistic scene.[46]

Such suggestion was in keeping with other artistic trends of the day. The abstract shapes and geometric lines of cubism and the Art Deco style dominated the visual environment, just as the abstract cadences of jazz influenced music. Some fair environments may have had the hand of trained designers (the Atlantic City Boardwalk and its promoter's other offering, "The Streets of Paris," are cases in point), but most fairs were still volunteer events run by women who followed instructions from books and magazines. These tended to be extremely specific (Dayton and Barratt included such details as the number of 10-quart pails that would be needed to paint the booths in one of their suggested fairs), so that everyone could know how to create modern-looking, up-to-date environments. Dorothy Wright pointed out in the *Farmer's Advocate* that "modern art is kind to the amateur, since it depends so much on [geometric form]."[47]

The Thrift Shop and the Woman's Exchange

Two other institutions that were tangentially related to the fundraising fair and came to prominence in the 1920s must also be mentioned, for they help provide a segue into the discussion of the simplified fair of the 1930s. The first of these is the thrift shop, which served as a kind of permanent rummage sale. After sponsoring an extremely successful sale in 1918, the St. Louis chapter of the Junior League decided to open a freestanding resale shop in 1921. Other groups picked up on the idea, and soon Boston society columnist Betty Alden pronounced thrift shops the "latest wrinkle in philanthropic fashions." Junior League shops especially proliferated in the late 1920s, when fairs were less frequent, and many stayed open through the 1930s.[48] The second related institution is the Woman's Exchange. Woman's Exchanges were philanthropic organizations, akin to settlement houses, that were devoted to vocational and technical training; they were often run under the auspices of an industrial union. The first Woman's Exchange was founded in the nineteenth century, but they proliferated in the Progressive era and became quite common in the 1920s. They are relevant because they typically included both a restaurant and a handwork outlet where poor women's products could be sold. Women's Exchanges were closely related to the original London bazaars that functioned as outlets for handmade goods made by impoverished women, but even more to the point the volunteers who staffed them in the 1920s were often the same women who formerly or even simultaneously worked at fundraising fairs (college students were particularly often involved with both activities). In a sense, the thrift shops and Women's Exchanges drew energy away from fairs, and particularly in the case of the privileged socialites, put the fairgiver's attention elsewhere. By the time the stock market crashed and the country was in serious economic decline, the type of professional fairgiver who had so dominated the press in the turn-of-the-century era had generally turned to other pursuits, and the "grand" fundraising fairs had essentially disappeared.[49] The middle-class women who had been working in the background at fairs for decades became more visible and moved to center stage.

The Depression Era: Simplicity on All Fronts

Scaled-Down Bazaars, Sales, and Other Fundraising Schemes

With the onset of the Depression and the full identification of the fair with the "simpler" housewife, there was, as might be expected, a marked decrease in the number of elaborate or frivolous events. Women's magazines stopped running regular features about clever fairs; one of the few instructional references to bazaars I have found for the whole 1930s decade, in fact, appeared in *Needlecraft* and described a "penny fair" that young people might find amusing. The change was clearly noted in

Fig. 79. *(left)* In the decades following World War I, "booths" were often reduced to "tables" with an uncluttered appearance. From *Woman's Home Companion,* October 1913.

Fig. 80. *(right)* The generally open appearance of this simple popcorn booth illustrated in *Woman's Home Companion* in 1923 provides a strong contrast to the closed-in feeling of the Louisiana table at the 1893 Confederate Bazaar (see fig. 60).

the history of Madison's First Baptist Church. Prior to 1932, the women's guild raised missionary funds through regular public dinners, bazaars, and rummage sales. These activities were dropped completely at that time. It is significant in this regard that some of the fellowship formerly engendered at festive fairs was channeled into gatherings that had no pecuniary purpose. For example, "Around the World" parties given at churches followed the long-familiar fair theme, but no fundraising was involved. A statewide convention of the Wisconsin Business and Professional Women's Clubs, similarly, was set up as a "Pow-wow," and members came to the convention hall dressed in Indian costumes. These events were particularly frequent in the 1930s, perhaps as a counterpoint to the hard economic times.[50]

Other simpler types of fundraising were preferred. Thrift shops and rummage sales proliferated, and there were grassroots community efforts like the "Lord's Acre Plan" begun in North Carolina. Individuals there donated what they could for a community auction; farmers set aside the produce of one of their acres, laborers set aside the equivalent of the first hour of their week's wages, and so forth. Middle-class urban women perpetuated benefit card parties of the type set up by Marietta Pratt in Boston in the 1920s and attended them frequently. These were undemanding events that involved no preparation or clean-up and could be held almost anywhere. They reflected a more informal approach to leisure activities than had been typical in the 1920s. Card parties were extremely popular, but because many were purely social and others donated some money to charity, it is impossible to determine how many were actually held with fundraising in mind. The great frequency with which they occurred is indicated, however, in a tracking of card parties specifically listed in the Madison paper as "benefits." One benevolent group, the "Attic Angels," held thirty-four benefit card parties in 1933. In just two months in 1930, twenty-seven benefit parties were listed in the *Capital Times,* ten of which were sponsored by parent-teacher organizations. The majority of the elementary schools in the city were included in this sample.[51]

Card parties were sometimes combined with bake, candy, or food sales. The word "sale" was most prevalent; in fact, the section of the *Capital Times* that listed community events included a category called "Card Parties and Sales." (There was no longer a bazaar category.) "Sale" implied something simple, without booth decoration, games, or frivolity—i.e., a no-nonsense event that eliminated the amusement component of the fair. Terminology could be misleading, however, and this was not a clear-cut or absolute distinction. There were some "Christmas sales" that were really Christmas bazaars, and other events had double names like "Fall Sale and Bazaar." The words "sale" and "bazaar" were used interchangeably in the Pilgrim Congregational Church records, but in those of the First Unitarian Society, "bazaar" seems to have been synonymous with fancywork, as separate proceeds were listed for food, candy, bazaar, and apron sales on the same day. Sales were still held in public spaces. Madison groups continued to bring goods to downtown or neighborhood stores and hotel lobbies to set up temporary selling areas. All kinds of retail outlets were involved. PTA bake sales were often set up in grocery stores, as one case in point, and ladies' aid societies were invited to set up fancywork tables in prominent display areas of department stores. The Beldenville, Wisconsin, sewing circle even held sales in the County Home. Most newspaper announcements of sales listed only one sponsoring organization, but groups apparently joined forces and supported one another almost matter-of-factly. The minutes of the Woman's Guild of the Pilgrim Congregational Church indicated in 1930 that members voted to take the fancywork they had left from an earlier sale "uptown to sell." One member knew of a food sale that was soon to be given by the WCTU and thought they might bring their fancywork there. In 1931 the women brought their needlework to an "all church food sale."[52]

Those Depression-era events that did include amusements and could qualify as true bazaars seem to have been primarily "in-house" events; unlike their nineteenth-century predecessors, they were typically oriented to and attended by members of a particular organization. This was certainly true for the left-wing political groups that held bazaars for their own constituencies. Souvenir programs of two events held in Chicago, the "Red Election Bazaar" sponsored by District 8 of the Communist Party in 1932 and the "International Labor Defense Bazaar" held in 1935, give little indication of attempts to appeal to outsiders. On the contrary, the bazaars were almost like pep rallies, with activities (ethnic crafts and foods, "working class movies," music and singing at a "red election rally") designed to instill good feeling and pride among organization members. There were many events of this kind among labor organizations, and participants remember a strong community feeling. The bazaars were a kind of comrades' party.[53] These left-wing fairs remind us how fairs helped promote and sustain fellowship, but they also indicate how strongly the institution had now become associated with the working class, and how much of a closing-in there had been from the time when fairs were held to directly call attention to political and moral causes and hopefully recruit new converts.

About 10 percent of the 1930s bazaars I have found references to were held to support hospitals and clubs. Most of the remaining 90 percent were given by church groups. These often took place as part of other church activities; there would be a "Church Night" consisting of a dinner and bazaar, for example, or a bazaar scheduled to coincide with the regular meeting times of the church circles. The public was nominally invited, but outsiders accounted for only a tiny proportion of the attendees. There is one notable exception to this general rule: churches in summer resort communities held their fairs during the tourist season so as to attract a maximum number of customers. The fairs became part not only of the summer experience for residents, then, but also of the vacation experience for tourists. One place where there may have actually been an increase in fairs was in northern black churches. With the great migration of African Americans to northern cities, African American communities in cities like Brooklyn grew significantly. Black churches grew accordingly, and many used bazaars for fundraising. The women of Berean Baptist Church first held a bazaar in 1930, for example, and they repeated it every spring, throughout the Depression and the subsequent war. St. Phillips Protestant Episcopal Church, also in Brooklyn, held a three-day carnival in 1933 that included a popularity contest and social dancing. Clarence Taylor argues that the black bourgeoisie was not just imitating white society with its adoption of activities like bazaars; it was taking such activities on its own terms and making them its own. The heavy emphasis on social activity in African American churches in the interwar years was not a rejection of the spiritual, he claims, but an extension of it.[54]

Although they were greatly reduced in number, some fundraising events still maintained a light, carnival-like feeling or quality. At least in my limited sample, many of these were associated with Catholic churches. Annual fall festivals in Madison parishes included hearty meals, card or bingo parties, raffles, door prizes, games, and entertainment. Festivals of this type increased as the 1930s wore on and the most severe days of the Depression had passed. When fairs were thematic, they usually drew on tried-and-true international and historical ideas. A 1935 fair held at Madison's Christ Presbyterian Church was typical. Each woman's circle was asked to prepare a booth with a regional or historic theme, and the expected Dutch, Mexican, Scotch, Japanese, and Early American subjects emerged. The booths were decorated only symbolically, and even refreshments tended to be light. Both Holland and Japan were represented by simple tea and cookies, and Early America was represented by brown bread and baked beans. The only Depression-era book to discuss fundraising fairs in detail, *Financial and Social Success in Welfare Plans* (author Ansel Stubbs appears to have been a male youth worker), described a "Christmas Country Fair" jointly organized by a number of groups. It included a Japanese Tea Garden and a North Pole booth, but nobody resembling Lady Winter or Mistress Marigold was present; the North Pole featured only a Christmas tree and a merry Santa Claus. This event did have an element of lightheartedness—it featured a "trained animal exhibit" made of children's toys and an "Indian exhibit" that displayed items like Indian cornmeal and the Indian Paintbrush flower—but all of this was relatively low key, and unlike fairs of the premodern era, it did not play on the idea of childish stories or escapist fairylands.[55]

Even at the most elaborate fairs of the 1930s, fanciful environments were relatively rare. Stubbs expressly derided the kind of decor that had previously prevailed: he spoke of earlier fairs as too often overwhelmed by a "melange of palms, bunting and the inevitable crepe paper." He did say that the fair environment should be attractive, but he offered no instructional detail. When asked about decoration, a woman who ran many bazaars in eastern Wisconsin in this period replied, "We didn't do that. The things were so pretty they were decorations themselves." Another informant related, "If you had nice [sales goods] you didn't have to dress things up."[56] The simple environments are further indices of the changed role of the fundraising fair in the modern period. It would conceivably still have been possible to find escapist themes at fairs; many 1930s movies were characterized by highly imaginative, elaborate sets and costumes despite the deprivations of the "real" world. But fairs were no longer providing the kind of large-scale public entertainment that they had before the advent of visual mass media, and they were generally catering to a more home-oriented, self-referential audience.

These Aprons Will Go to Fairs

BY
STINE FERRY

n apron is one of those things with
no woman can well do without, apron
continue to be one of the most lucra-
urces of income at the fairs which the
and means committees of most char-
ations stage during the months im-
ceding Christmas, and each season
come more and more colorful because
tly increasing variety of patterned and
r material which is available.
s is the month of October when, here
and, at least, the hillsides are covered
ry of glorious autumnal coloring, the

AND
E. MARION ST

the lines to make them a bit more p
the short ones branching from them.
    To accompany this apron there is a le
of green gingham backed with brown,
about seven inches from tip to tip in
To make this holder, baste front and
with three or four thicknesses of fl
wadding between. Then outline v
threads of dark green stranded
through all the thicknesses, like qui
ing the needle up each time to meet t
as to form a line of backstitching on
work.

Left. No. 32 - 10 - 10.
Maple Leaf Apron
No. 32 - 10 - 11. Matching
Holder
Right. No. 32 - 10 - 12.
Flower Apron
No. 32 - 10 - 13. Matching
Holder
Top. No. 32 - 10 - 14.
Organdy Apron

Fig. 81. Aprons and potholders were among the most typical fair sale items of the 1930s. In this October 1932 *Needlecraft* feature, the items were presented as fashionable accessories that every woman desired.

Handmade Goods: Household Helpers and Cloying Cuteness

Elaborate goods almost disappeared from fairs and sales in the 1930s. Most manufactured products were both small and practical; I have found references to items like paring knives, kitchen "necessities," Christmas cards, fountain pens, and vanilla. More typically, fairgivers once again resorted to handwork. Handmade items were appreciated; Stubbs claims that the fancywork booth brought in the most money at his community fair. While some clothing or baby items and some toys and novelties were included on sale tables, housework-related articles were perhaps most important. Dish towels, place mats, and tea cloths were common, and aprons still sold well. A 1932 *Needlecraft* feature stated, in fact, that "apron booths continue to be one of the most lucrative sources of income at . . . fairs." "An apron is one of those things which no women can well do without."[57]

It is telling that these 1930s handmade items were often characterized by a rather saccharine and self-conscious cuteness. *Needlecraft* suggested a "busy bee" apron as a fair item that would make an appealing gift for a little girl; the garment was said to be so charming it would "thrill" any "Mary Jane." Similar items were also considered appropriate for adults. There were aprons with matching potholders, for example, that made housework seem picturesque and sweet (fig. 81). Other sale articles also implied that housework and cleaning were a game. Washcloths were made into "bouquets"; face cloths were made into flowers. *Needlecraft* described a "cute and useful" laundry doll dubbed "Miss Bridget," who was said to sell wonderfully at fairs. The doll's body was made from a cake of wax, purchased ready-made with a wooden handle, and the figure was given a painted face and dressed in a skirt and bonnet. The wax would eventually be used to help with the household ironing. Miss Bridget was, of course, a surrogate maid for the homemaker who had no one to work for her. "Oilcloth ladies," who kept doors open for their mistresses, similarly "peppered the eastern seaboard" in 1931.[58]

Figure 82 illustrates another "servant," represented as an African American rather than Irish woman. Her body is made with a whisk broom and potholder-covered strainer, and pastry brushes form her arms. Her clothing is fashioned from a dishcloth, tea towel, and handkerchief. This figure was created in 1940 for a bridal shower, but typifies the kind of item thought suitable at the time "for fairs or presents." She and Miss Bridget are telling about fair participants and their expectations and beliefs. The type of people who made and purchased these items were not wealthy women who could afford household help; rather, they were housewives themselves. They were probably white, and had absorbed the racist cultural assumptions about servants— that they would come from certain ethnic groups and that their portrayal was somehow humorous.[59] A doll of this type is similar in a sense to the "masquerading" fair items of the Victorian era, but her close relationship to the tedious household work of cooking and cleaning was something new. Ironically, this twentieth-century assistant can only be helpful if she is taken apart and used up.

Fig. 82. This "servant" was a wedding shower gift in 1940, but similar novelties were sold at fairs. She is made completely from kitchen and cleaning tools and is in the author's collection.

Amusement was coupled with a somewhat condescending or even self-mocking quality in other fair objects as well. *Ladies' Home Journal* ran a feature in 1938 called "Stuffies You Can Make" in which small stuffed animals were suggested for the next church bazaar. Each animal was tagged with a similarly cloying name: the rabbit was "Puffo," the pig was "Porko," the elephant was "Jembo," and so on. Words like "cute" and "jolly" were common in the periodicals at this same time, as were diminutive terms like "tiny" and "wee" and alliterative phrases like "made in a joyful jiffy!" A 1932 pattern for a fish-shaped scissors scabbard included the instruction "assemble their chubby anatomies." If the dominant iconography of the mid-nineteenth-century fair items was ephemeral and whimsical and turn-of-the-century imagery bore an "artistic" look, the mid-twentieth-century items were abstracted but self-consciously adorable. Anthropomorphic plants and animals prevailed. In addition to the fish and stuffies mentioned above, there were penguins, cuddly bears, and even personified flowers and vegetables like "Tillie Tomato" and "Otis Onion." The latter, which appeared in potholder form, were billed as "sure money-catchers."[60]

Fairs and Fundraising during World War II

With the outbreak of the Second World War in 1939 and the gradual involvement of the United States, much of the attention that had gone into other charitable fundraising was once again funneled into the war effort. In December 1941, just after America had officially entered the conflict, the society editor of Madison's *Wisconsin State Journal* asked her readers, "Do you remember, way back in 1939, when clubwomen used to nibble dainty lettuce sandwiches, sip jasmine tea, [and concern themselves with non-essential issues]? Times are different now." Once again women involved themselves in war bond campaigns, Red Cross work,[61] and miscellaneous individual efforts. Hazel Hansen, who was secretary of the Ladies Aid Society of Trinity Lutheran Church in 1941, recalled that when she learned of war-related starvation and deprivation in Norway, she suggested her group drop their plans for their usual fall bazaar and help with conditions overseas. The idea was overwhelmingly approved. The women turned their attention from the pillowcases, dresser scarves, and towels they usually made for the bazaar to warm and functional clothing for the needy.[62]

Once again, war relief shops that had many bazaarlike features and effectively substituted for fundraising fairs were set up in different parts of the country. When the British War Relief Society (the name is a misnomer, for the women were not British and did not work exclusively for English relief) opened a shop in Madison in time for the 1940 holiday season, the facility served as both a sales outlet and social center. Society members gathered to knit and sew on the premises, and while most of their products were shipped overseas, fancy items were donated directly to the shop. Entries such as "10 scalloped doilies" and "5 flannel egg warmers" are thus found in the shop records. The society also received donations of used items and at times featured special white elephant sales. International themes were incorporated in many instances. Members dressed up for events like open houses and highlighted Oriental products like Chinese table spreads, Japanese wall panels, and Korean prayer bells in their shop advertisements. A publicity photo in the *Wisconsin State Journal* illustrated old-fashioned "dressed" tables, some of which even had canopies made from Japanese umbrellas. Carnival elements like harmonica players, balloons, and grab-bags were all found in the shop in 1942. The Madison shop was not unusual. New York women also ran a war relief shop that functioned like a permanent fair; "Dickens' Muffin Bay," which was set up as a replica of a London street, opened on East 57th Street in 1941. Donations of goods, many of them handmade, were sent in from all over the country.[63]

Again, the wartime fairs that did take place were usually supporting churches. When the Berean Baptist Church held its fifteenth spring bazaar in 1944, it lasted six days and raised two thousand dollars. Most events were shorter and relatively simple, for given the rationing of sugar and decorating materials, it was difficult to create a festive enough fair environment or provide sweets. Even when a booklet with ideas for successful fairs was published just after the war, no instructions were included for decoration or presentation. (Illustrations showed tables with upright posts and some twined crepe paper, but these were not inspired booths that required planning, energy, or forethought.) Suggestion columns for fundraising fairs and related events were almost non-existent during the war years themselves, but the few I have found appeared in magazines that appealed to particularly conservative women. The magazines took a condescending tone and assumed their readers to be insecure and almost childlike. They were said to have "energy and gentleness of heart," for instance, and would "tenderly nurse" their projects, but they needed assistance. The Chairman [*sic*] of the Ways and Means Committee of the hypothetical woman's club discussed in an article in 1940 was "distracted," but, with the advice of the magazine, she might calm down. In 1941 *American Home* referred to its reader as "my little diplomat." Women were told to stand firm in arrangements with businessmen; a hotel manager would be likely to think women "fussy," but could be won over. "Don't worry—you can do it" was the underlying message of a 1945 entry.[64] This kind of rhetoric had not appeared before. Again, the fair was no longer firmly centered in the domain of the confident reformer or the wealthy social leader; it was now associated with the middle- or lower-class housewife who liked "cute" items for her home.

The assumption that women who work at fundraising fairs fit this stereotype may not be valid, but as a popular perception, it has not changed significantly in the last half of the twentieth century. Other aspects of the fair have continued to shift and evolve, however, and the focus on profit, which is perhaps the most significant change of all, has occurred in the most recent period. We will explore this and the still-changing settings, sales items, and meanings of the fair in the next chapter.

CHAPTER SEVEN

The Contemporary Fair: Developments since World War II

Chickens wrapped in cellophane and tied with red ribbons, platters of lettuce, spinach and radishes, and baskets of extra large fresh eggs were set up in another corner of the room, while baked goods, including tall cakes, filled cookies and pies of every kind weighted down two more tables. . . . As voices rose to signal bids [at the auction], some participants picked peanuts from the wonder peanut plant. Each peanut contained a slip of paper which told the player whether he'd won a set of hand-painted china, a box of soap made from pasteurized milk, baby clothes hangers, or some other item.

> —description of the Central Lutheran Church Harvest Festival, Madison, *Capital Times*, Nov. 1945

The Community Emphasis of the Postwar Years

Almost as soon as World War II ended, bazaars returned. As the rather lyrical description of the Harvest Festival indicates, Madison newspapers reported on church fairs in the 1945 holiday season with an unprecedented amount of detail. The prose lingered on images of festivity and plenty, almost as descriptions had in the antebellum era, for the events were treated as proof of a return to normalcy and ease. Two weeks later, the paper emphasized that over 1,000 people had come to a weeknight smorgasbord dinner at the Grace Episcopal Church fair. Terms of plenty were still used two years later to describe the 1,200 pounds of lutefisk and 2,000 lefse (Norwegian specialties) prepared for the Lutheran Church fair in nearby Stoughton.[1]

Articles with titles like "Make Your Church Bazaar a Huge Success" reappeared in a wider range of women's magazines, and it was again possible to purchase instruction books. *McCall's* published a full-length guide, *The Complete Book of Bazaars,* in 1955. "There has *never* been a money-making method so ideally suited to the capabilities of every . . . organization . . . as the bazaar," the introduction assured its readers. Postwar authors referred nostalgically to "old fashioned" fairs and festivals, implying that they belonged to the good times of the past.[2]

Church and community fairs were well received in this era that emphasized home, family, and community life; the prevailing sentiment was that fairs brought families and communities together and offered something to people of all ages. Some groups expanded their efforts in a more community-focused way. Individual circles of Madison's Pilgrim Congregational Church had run sales in the early 1940s, for example, but several guilds pooled their efforts for a single larger event in 1950. Other groups held fairs for the first time, and as the enthusiastic description of preparations for Madison's Temple Beth-El bazaar (1952) cited in chapter 1 implies, this was done in the spirit of community building.[3]

Another type of group that seems to have held fundraising fairs for the first time in the 1950s were the homemaker's clubs. In Wisconsin, their events were billed as Holiday Fairs, and were organized on a countywide basis, with each club taking responsibility for a specific food, craft booth, grab-bag item, or decoration. The cooperative extension agencies that sponsored such groups encouraged the fairs both as a way of raising money for club programming (since almost all fairgoers were club members, this was primarily a way of recirculating funds), and as a mechanism to facilitate community networking. Significant numbers of women must have been involved, as nationwide, over five hundred thousand individuals belonged to clubs of this type.[4]

The Involvement of Men and Children and the Withdrawal of "Society"

Club fairs catered to an almost entirely female constituency, but ironically the clear association between fundraising fairs and women began to become somewhat muddied in other arenas during the same period. Again because of the postwar emphasis on community, family, and "returning home," more men seemed willing to become actively involved. The Temple Beth-El Men's Club, for example, pitched in with a donor's dinner and raised seven hundred dollars for the bazaar in 1954. A photo of aproned men working in the kitchen at a church fair ran in *American Home* in the same year, with a caption stating that husbands, bachelors, and grandfathers were "scullery maids for a day." The event in question was a festival at St. Wendelin's Church in Butler County, Pennsylvania, and it was Rev. Linus Doemling, the pastor of the church, who was credited with making the fundraising event the success it was. A similar story was related regarding a fair in Annisquam, Massachusetts. Prewar fairs held at that town's Community Church had rarely grossed more than three hundred dollars and had sometimes made no profit at all. In 1947 Brig. Gen. James Cunningham and a local businessman stepped in. They determined to change the event into a thematic "sea fair" and to involve all segments of the community in its production. By 1954 there were thirty-eight standing committees representing both men's and women's groups and over three thousand dollars were raised. Illustrations accompanying this article showed males exclusively.[5]

Men were not actually responsible for these fairs—General Cunningham's first rule of thumb, in fact, was "don't worry about getting the men into the fair—sell the ideas to the ladies." This kind of reportage and publicity was, on the contrary, a legitimization of men's involvement in what was still seen as women's work; by making the men seem like knights in shining armor, this kind of prose "ennobled" their efforts. However, women's magazines still acknowledged the primacy of women's contribution. In 1961 *Ladies' Home Journal* asked, "What does the Christmas bazaar mean to America?" and concluded it meant giving of time, understanding, and womanly skills. "Millions of women prepare [the bazaars] . . . hope abideth because women *care*."[6] Men who turned their attention to the home front after the war became involved in the women's activities, however, and their very presence made those activities seem important.

Men were particularly likely to be involved in specific new or newly packaged attractions. They displayed and sometimes demonstrated their handwork at "hobby shows," for example, and were encouraged to work at "pet corners" or booths set up as fix-it and green-thumb shops. As they had in the Civil War era, professional artists also participated in "art shows." They donated pieces which were to be sold or even auctioned off, or, less often, they came in person to sell their work and donate some of the proceeds to the sponsoring organization. Unlike the nineteenth-century art galleries which were generally one feature of a larger women's fair, the 1950s versions were conceived (and perceived) as separate shows where art was the main draw. Nevertheless, they did typically include the sale of food and other festive activities. New York's Downtown Community School, a private, elementary institution, held the first of its art shows in 1947. A total of $250 was raised, primarily through the sale of paintings donated by artists who had children in attendance. The show was so well received that by 1957 gross profits were $36,000. By this time parents solicited artists for their work and asked gallery owners for contributions, and works by well-known artists (Shahn, Chagall, O'Keeffe, and even Matisse and Picasso) were represented. The *New Yorker* cited one of the "high-powered ladies in charge of the [1959] event" who claimed art sales of this sort were "becoming fashionable all over town."[7] New York was an art center with unusual resources, and this particular fundraiser was held at an atypical and elite institution, but it was not out of step with its time. Even in this case, community involvement was stressed. The magazine article focused on the school bus driver and neighborhood candy store owner who had built up art collections through their yearly connection with the fair and on artist Willem de Kooning's relationship with his daughter, who attended the nursery.

In the 1960s art shows became even more common fundraisers. Some were outlets for amateur Sunday painters, but, increasingly, "serious" high-quality work was needed to draw a crowd. In 1969 *Good Housekeeping* reflected the prevailing attitude by insisting that only the works of professional artists should be considered. These individuals could be located through local art associations and galleries, the magazine asserted, and the person in charge of the show should have a background in art. Someone else on the committee should be knowledgeable about insurance, liability, and related issues, even if the show were a simple event held to benefit a local parent-teacher organization.[8] This new manifestation of the professionalization theme was yet another example of the usurpation of what had been a woman's institution. Needlework and other women's products paled in comparison to the glamour of "high" art.

Men's participation in fairs and shows was paralleled by their new visibility in the charity fund drives that had markedly increased after the war. "Are Charity Fund Drives Driving You Crazy?" *American Magazine* asked its readers in 1954. "Are doorbell ringers and phone callers pestering you to death for donations?" The sentiment was repeated frequently throughout the decade. According to a 1958 report in *Harper's*, seventy different organizations were soliciting in Chatham County, Georgia, in a single season. Providence, Rhode Island, had an average of three charity drives a day. Magazines began to run features with titles like "Hints for a Volunteer Fund-Raiser," and individuals who came up with novel ideas were even highlighted as heroes. California barber Frank Sibilia was featured in *American Magazine*, for example, in 1952. He donated haircuts to a church building fund and persuaded friends in other professions to come up with similar contributions. Women were involved with charity fund drives also, but they rarely led them and were rarely featured in the limelight of their glowing publicity.[9]

Children and children's activities were often the primary focus of the fairs of the postwar period. "Get-togethers" that involve "grown-ups and youngsters" are "good for the whole," remarked the press. There were still such traditional children's activities as fishing ponds and Punch and Judy shows, but new, more dramatic diversions were also encouraged. Pony rides were supplanted by tank and jeep rides at a Winnetka, Illinois, children's fair in 1947. A few years later fairgivers were advised to rent movies and cartoons and show them on an ongoing basis and were told about a large city fair which featured cameo appearances by the cast of the popular Howdy Doody television show. Children, who were born in record numbers, were also symbolic of the return to normalcy and the promise of the future. As the center of community life, they stood at the heart of community fairs. They were also encouraged to become active participants. The chairman's report on the 1950 Temple Beth-El Bazaar proudly stated that the "children begged for work so they too could become a part of this tremendous project."[10]

The First Unitarian Society in Madison was not atypical when it went so far as to develop a special feature, the "Nutcracker Shop," at its annual holiday fair. This was set up as an area where children could buy items for themselves or buy presents for their parents. It was intended to make a "happy impression" and be an educational experience. Attention was given to small details—because young children could not read, for example, attendants were carefully trained in appropriate ways to approach and help orient them. Several pages of observations, ideas for future projects, and discussion of what the shop was all about were written up each year after the fair. The children's section of the annual fair of another church described in *Woman's Day* was so popular that it evolved into the major attraction of the fair and "became the tail that wagged the dog." In 1961 the Children's Fair was designated an Oriental Fantasyland, and participants came in costume. Children looked forward to the event each year, so much so that the organizer stated, "Fair Day ranks right along with birthdays and Christmas among our families."[11]

Older children—teenagers—were also still encouraged to work at adult fundraising fairs or, to a lesser degree, to sponsor fairs of their own. Their role in the scheme of things, according to the popular literature, was to add energy and enthusiasm to community events. "Teen Angels" in Desert Hot Springs, California, were said to be the "real stars" of a yearly Penny Carnival held for the Angel View Crippled Children's Clinic; even "oldsters and arthritics" "caught the youngsters' infectious initiative." The college students who painted and decorated furniture for the Winnetka, Illinois, Children's Fair were similarly called "invaluable and inspirational." Magazine editors advised clubwomen to turn to teenage volunteers, especially if services could be auctioned off. Young people's energy was stressed in suggested signage: "Fine, husky lad with good teeth guaranteed to do a good job on lawns. Girl with four eyes excellent for watching children. Exceedingly smart boy, who will see through anything, can do marvelous job on washing windows."[12]

College sororities and YWCA branches continued to hold bazaars and fairs, but their importance in the college community was considerably diminished, probably because fairs were no longer associated with "important" people. The University of Wisconsin YWCA chapter had sponsored a Christmas bazaar every year since 1914. The proceeds had originally been used for general organizational expenses, but by this era they were earmarked for limited specific purposes such as sending individuals to intercollegiate conferences or sending Christmas parcels to the needy overseas. The postwar fairs were both much smaller in scale and less involved. In 1927 booths had been elaborately decorated to follow a Dutch theme, and there were auxiliary activities like a "vaudeville swim meet." By 1952 the bazaar was a straightforward sale, with simple tables decorated only with a few silk-screened posters. Some sale items were made by the college girls, but others were donated by faculty wives, parents, and friends or taken on commission from area craftspeople or merchants. The bazaars afforded the students an opportunity to participate in the larger community, as they often went to private homes to make candy and knit and sew sale items, and solicited local "celebrities" like college professors to help them at the sales tables. The fairs seem to have been less associated with dating or a peer-oriented social life than they had been in earlier years.[13]

The society women who had been so strongly associated with fairs in the past were rarely involved after World War II. "Society" was in fact a less dominating social force after the Depression, and the booming postwar economy was marked by an emphasis on democratization, for it seemed that everyone could have a luxurious life. Rich women still worked at fundraising, and their activities still had some of the playfulness of the older fairs, but their involvement was generally limited to entertainments or activities in which they did not have to leave their own social set. Junior League members, for example, organized high-priced charity balls, dinner-dances, and benefit performances that drew small, select crowds. Since donations were tax deductible, each attendee could be depended on to spend a sizable amount of money. Upper-class charity fundraisers turned increasingly to corporate donors, also, as new tax laws encouraged their contributions. The New York Junior League, which held Mardi Gras balls for several years after the war, invited twenty large business firms to put up fifteen hundred dollars apiece for its 1955 event that supported one hundred different charities. The firms were able to advertise themselves in the process, for Junior League members came elaborately dressed as "Miss Fuller Brush," "Miss General Motors," "Miss Columbia Broadcasting," and other industrial icons. The Air France, Coty, and Cartier companies, similarly, all helped sponsor an "April in Paris" ball for various Franco-American charities in 1956. The individual merchants the wealthy women had worked with at the turn of the century were replaced by corporations, in other words, but fundraising was still an operation involving the power elite. Society galas were often given for the very organizations—the New York Mission Society, the Boy's Club, the New York Infirmary, Catholic Charities— that had formerly been supported by bazaars or fairs. Again, there was an ever-widening gap or distance between the "somebodies" who frequented the exclusive events (even celebrities like Ed Sullivan sometimes made appearances) and the "everybodies" who went to grassroots community fairs. The separation, which has continued to this day, contributed to the increasing trivialization of the fairs and furthered the association of fairs as unimportant events.[14]

Decorations and "Populuxe" Sale Products

Although the college students at the University of Wisconsin did not spend much energy on decor at their bazaar, environmental planning and design received a little more general attention in the postwar period. Advisors once again discussed color coordination, visual impact, and even the idea of an overriding theme. They suggested building booths with upright poles, canopies, and interesting shapes.[15] There was some interest, in other words, in resurrecting the festive, transformative atmosphere of the premodern fairs, but a full transformation was never realized, for the modern self-consciousness could not be completely suspended. Decoration was restrained, and environmental effects were suggestive rather than overwhelming. When illustrations accompanied magazine articles about fairs, they were usually in the form of quickly worked line drawings, which were not even always integral to the text. Iconography, too, was suggestive rather than literal, and visual importance was achieved with large-scale imagery and massing of color rather than with careful detail. Balloons—eye catching, inexpensive, and potentially dramatic—were suggested, as were printed posters, which were bright, filled space, and could be easily procured. Where decor was thematic, simplicity still prevailed. A Dutch Kitchen environment created at a Tarrytown, New York, fair in 1962 was characteristic. Said to be the most talked-about feature of the fair, the kitchen was merely suggested by a large mural-like back-drop. The painted motifs included an "old-fashioned" Dutch tile stove, copper kettles, and rows of abstracted cabinets filled with china, cooking utensils, and items suggesting a bountiful harvest, such as corn and pumpkins. Waitresses dressed in ordinary skirts and blouses, but each wore a Dutch cap and paper apron that suggested a costume (fig. 83).[16] This kitchen was clearly meant to be seen as a stage setting rather than as a re-creation of reality. It contrasts strongly with the attempted historical accuracy and literal interpretation of the Dutch or New England Kitchen of one hundred years before, and it indicates a far less reverent attitude toward the domestic domain that women were still identified with.

Although the stage setting was lighthearted, it lost its cloying tone, and the "cute" imagery common in pre–World War II sale items was generally directed toward the juvenile market by the late 1950s. A new type of rhetoric appeared in the literature, as adjectives like "glamorous," "luxurious," and "importance" were used to describe salable items. The desirable image of fair products, like other objects of the era, was sophistication. Thomas Hine coined the word "populuxe" to describe the blending of "popular" and "deluxe" that characterized 1950s American consumer products and their new promise of democratic luxury. Mass-produced goods from cleaning products to cars were designed in this era with allusions to a kind of suburban good life. These same qualities were seen in items made for fundraising fairs. *Ladies' Home Journal* featured purses made out of artificial fur and decorated with gold pins, for example, and suggested updating ordinary household objects with materials like leopard-skin print adhesive paper and gold braid. Although kitchen items were still recommended, they too had changed. Instead of aprons, favored items were place mats and potholders, presented as room accessories ("potholders make bright splashes for kitchen hooks") rather than fashionable extensions of the homemaker herself.[17] Pincushions and knitting bags were replaced by tote bags and desk or office items such as file boxes and phonebook covers. Even more than in the 1930s, the objects were crafted rather than sewn (spice racks and pencil holders were made with cardboard, a hanging ornament was made with lumber scraps). Sale items presented a somewhat new image of the fairgiver, in other words: she was still identified with the home, but was not primarily a domestic homebody; she was more of an overseer, and she was sophisticated, elegant, and gay.

The Sixties and Beyond: Boutiques and Craft Fairs

Despite their "unimportance," fairs were still significant fundraising mechanisms in the early 1960s. In 1961 *Ladies' Home Journal* claimed that women raised a half billion dollars every year at bazaars and fairs—a sizable portion of the eight billion dol-

Fig. 83. This "Dutch Kitchen" at a 1962 suburban New York bazaar is very different from the kitchens of the sanitary fairs one hundred years earlier. The kitchen is implied rather than realistically recreated, and does not involve antiques or relics of any kind. It is a more pointedly light-hearted play, with no element of veneration. Even this kind of environment was unusually elaborate at a fair at this time, and it was memorable to fairgoers in the area. From *Woman's Day*, September 1962; used by permission.

lars that represented all charitable contributions. Church bazaars were satirized for the first time since early in the century, indicating they were alive and well. Catholics even discussed instituting "silent bazaars" (periodic tithelike collections) because fairs had once again become so demanding.[18]

As the 1960s wore on and the insularity of the postwar years began to give way once again to a more global and socially aware consciousness, the fairs were packaged and presented differently. The old rubrics seemed tired, so familiar titles like "Christmas bazaar" were increasingly replaced with phrases like "holiday fair," and a new terminology began to appear. *Good Housekeeping* introduced the phrase "fund-raiser's fair" in 1963, for example, and the terms "art" and "fair" were put together for the first time in the 1960s. A "rumbazauc" (combination rummage sale, bazaar, and auction) held in Westchester, New York, was said to be a success because of its innovative name. By 1967 some fairgivers tried to update the image of their events by calling them "boutiques."[19]

The boutique concept, which implies a small shop with interesting and exclusive merchandise, could be adapted to both of the new thrusts of 1960s fundraising fairs. The pendulum did, on the one hand, swing back strongly to a focus on commercial goods. Many fairgivers eschewed local or handmade sale items altogether and, reflecting the new global awareness, concentrated on the sale of novel international merchandise. The University of Wisconsin YWCA had first introduced imported products purchased from a commercial firm called Crafts of the World in 1956 (the New York–based company advertised its products in *Intercollegian Magazine* and addressed its form letters "Dear Bazaar Chairman," so we can assume the Wisconsin chapter was not alone in adopting such objects), and by 1962 this bazaar was totally transformed into an International Gift Fair. Posters borrowed from a local travel agency replaced the handmade decorations, and Moroccan leather goods, Swedish egg cups, and African carvings replaced hand-stitched aprons and stuffed toys. Profits went up considerably. The gift fair was repeated until 1969, with local antiques occasionally added to the international-theme products. Once again, the emphasis on international merchandise paralleled similar developments in other forms of retailing, for department stores frequently held so-called "international festivals" in the late 1960s.[20] In their 1967 *Encyclopedia of Successful Program Ideas,* Dorothy and Clement Duran contrasted the "trite affairs" where goods were made by group members to sales of "exquisite merchandise." They described boutiques with items donated from up-scale shops like Bergdorf Goodman or from well-known individuals such as politician Bella Abzug. The confusion of terms and the interpenetration of different kinds of retailing concepts was also indicated by a 1976 event that featured no handmade goods, but was still referred to as an "Auction Bazaar." The strong focus on goods was also noted in the prescriptive literature. *McCall's* reminded its readers that the merchandise was "the real star of the [bazaar] show."[21]

The products featured at a boutique could, on the other hand, be handmade, and the second and sometimes seemingly contradictory thrust of fairs in this era was a focus on craft. In this sense, bazaars or fairs reflected the burgeoning contemporary interest in creative self-expression and in "making things"; the handcraft revival that had begun in the 1950s had taken on almost epidemic proportions by the late 1960s.[22] Fundraising and program manuals suggested holding craft demonstrations (bookbinding, picture framing, needlework, etc.), and many organizations followed this advice. There were demonstrations at homemaker's club holiday fairs, for example, and at the University of Wisconsin YWCA bazaar, which shifted its focus one last time before it died out completely in 1972. In its final incarnation it was an arts and crafts fair, with local craftspeople working in various media from candlemaking to weaving and decorating plates. After this particular event, 10 percent of the proceeds was given to the YWCA. The craft emphasis was also reflected in a new rash of books and articles that provided instruction for projects rather than help with organizational structure, publicity, and related matters. This trend became more and more pronounced; by the 1980s, publications about fairs were essentially instruction books with titles like *Country Bazaar Crafts* and *McCall's Big Book of Bazaar Crafts.* The author of *The Great Bazaar* even addressed her reader as "dear craftworker."[23]

"Crafted" items were seen as something different from ladies' fancywork or needlework. "Craft" drew upon older traditions, but was more gender-neutral and associated with new ideas; craftspeople of the 1970s identified more with the back-to-the-land, do-it-yourself philosophy influenced by the youth counterculture than with traditional feminine roles and pursuits. Some sale objects might still be sewn, but even they were seemingly transformed by their new context, and older associations were

Fig. 84. "Home Sweet Home," worked with lace and calico on an embroidery hoop, embodies the nostalgic feeling of fairs today. This sales item was photographed at a Madison fair in 1988.

downplayed. Since male contributors were always in the minority, even if they were highly visible, it was not their presence that accounted for this shifting identification. Rather, the shift reflected a change in women's activities (it was no longer as routine for women to be proficient sewers, and more women were entering the workforce) and a feminist questioning of the traditional homemaker image.[24]

The fact that the University of Wisconsin YWCA linked the terms "craft" and "art" in its fair is significant; the "arts and crafts fair" epithet does not seem to have been used much before 1972. A somewhat broadened definition of art is implied, and it is certainly the case that while some contemporary bazaars are billed as art fairs, their sale items are rarely paintings or sculpture. Hand-turned bowls, beaded or silver jewelry, and custom-made sweatshirts are often labeled as art in the fair environment, largely because they are one-of-a-kind items. Their functionality would have formerly kept them in the craft category, but these distinctions began to blur somewhat in the 1970s, as both scholars and practicing artists questioned the standard definitions. In other words, even the way that art has been defined and featured in the fundraising fair has changed in accordance with evolving cultural norms and ideas. In the mid-nineteenth century art was "uplifting," "grand," and inspiring. At the end of the century it was mocked in comical galleries that were part of a fairylike amusement center. In the 1950s art shows highlighted the work of professionals—usually male painters—and served to remind women that they were to play a supportive role. In our own time, fundraising fair art is typically associated with a sense of homeyness and domesticity. It is typically accessible, pleasant, and relatively inexpensive, and it is usually functional.[25]

Crafted Sale Items

"Craft" involved new media and techniques, which, ironically, were often dependent on commercial products. There were novel materials that sped up production time; a single 1971 magazine feature on fair projects, in fact, relied on a variety of such products, including instant papier-mâché (packaged paper pulp), plaster bandages, and melt-in-the-oven plastic crystals. Instruction books also stressed using everyday commercial household items in novel ways. In the 1970s, this was presented almost as a form of recycling. "Helpers will have fun converting such items as cake pans and

egg cups into pretty [sales articles]," enthused *Ladies' Home Journal*. Baby food
jars were turned into decorative spice
containers, plastic margarine tubs became
candy dishes, and crayon stubs were melted
down into candles. A wire whisk covered
with a piece of velvet became a hanging
pincushion, plastic bread and dry cleaners'
bags were cut into Christmas wreaths, and
old phonograph records were heated and
fashioned into nut dishes. Natural materials like pine cones and milkweed pods were
also worked into ornamental items, as were
kitchen staples like macaroni, peppercorns,
and dried beans.[26]

Fig. 85. Calico and vaguely
country-looking imagery
prevailed at bazaars in the
1980s. This small (ten-inch)
"peasant" doll was purchased
at a fair in upstate New York
in 1987.

By the late 1970s the focus shifted
from recycling used goods to the adapta-
tion, embellishment, or individualization of
new commercial products. In a sense, then,
the two types of goods—commercial vs.
handmade—had merged. Dorothea Britton's
Complete Book of Bazaars was the first instruction book to expressly feature several
items of this kind. Her "Night-Light Lady," for example, consisted of a purchased
plug-in night-light, dressed up with fringe, rickrack, and felt. She also featured
dressed-up flyswatters and brooms and promoted music boxes made from parts
purchased in hobby shops and novelty stores. In 1980 *Better Homes and Gardens*
featured such items as "bandanna babies," each made with two new scarves; pillows made from newly purchased cowboy shirts; and keepsake books made from
photograph albums. Lesley Linsley's 1981 *The Great Bazaar* pictured embellished
versions of products like anklets, combs, barrettes, T-shirts, and stools. The 1983
Woman's Day Bazaar Best Sellers went so far as to list "Storebought and Decorated" as a category in its table of contents, and another category, "Recycled and
Decorated," was in fact a foil for the same thing. The use of commercial products
was so ingrained and automatic that the misleading use of the term "recycled"
was not even noticed, and by 1987 no truly recycled items were included. Popular
items in the mid-1990s included purchased dish towels with hand-crocheted loops
at the top, allowing them to be hung on a belt. This blurring of handmade and
manufactured is even reflected in the kinds of booths that are seen at contemporary fairs. At a recent Madison "craft sale," for example, one of the booths featured "personalized children's books." No handwork or craft was involved, for a
computer was used to insert a particular child's name into the hero's role. The
almost complete blending of commercial and handmade goods reflects what some

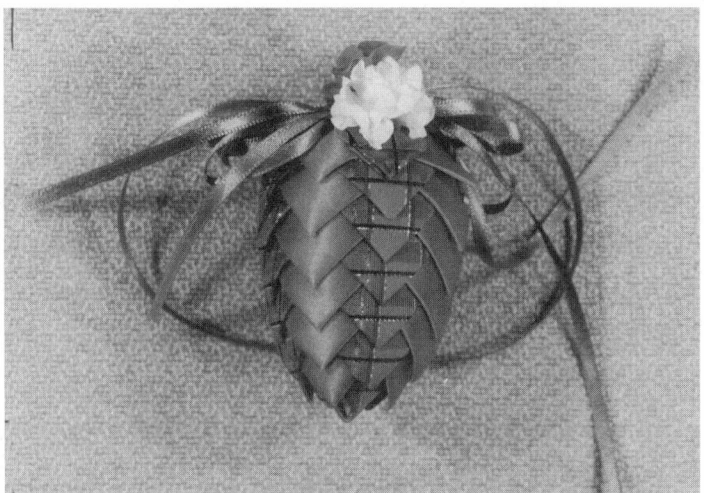

Fig. 86. *(left)* Christmas ornament from the 1995 bazaar season. The plaid fabric and flower preclude the pine cone from looking too realistic; although life-size, it is a cheerful *tour de force.* Author's collection.

Fig. 87. *(right)* This little "fancy," popular in fairs in 1986, was quickly made and likely to be purchased as a spur-of-the-moment token for a loved one. It was usually worked in red and white yarn and included a "kiss" wrapped in green foil. In subsequent years the kiss was packed in other shapes, including footballs and abstracted animals. Puns have been part of the fair environment throughout the history of the institution. Author's collection.

scholars have posited as a postmodern concern with individual lifestyle, defined or symbolized by a constantly changing set of symbolic material goods. There is no longer a clear dividing line between the personal and commercial.[27]

Sale items always expressed the flavor of their immediate time. In the 1970s they were often made with flamboyant, colorful fabrics and motifs, and at the time of the Bicentennial they included patriotic images. In the 1980s and early 1990s the focus was on soft, romantic, "heartwarming" items that emphasized the comforts of home and reflected the trend of what came to be called "cocooning." There was an abundance of calico, lace, and homey, "folk" imagery that played on a sense of nostalgia for the imagined good old days of the past. The fifty best-sellers featured by *Better Homes and Gardens* included patchwork images of familiar, traditional houses and friendly farm animals, and a cross-stitched sampler featuring the phrase "Home Sweet Home" (fig. 84). The 1980s decade was particularly filled with instructions for patchwork and calico-covered checkbook covers, memo pads, and tissue boxes, and objects like embroidered and stenciled hearts, tulips, ducks, teddy bears, and dolls in long dresses.[28] The "country look" imparted a fresh image to the bazaar and contrasted strongly with the image of runaway greed that many associate with the Reagan years. In some senses it resurrected the counterpoint between the "dangerous" public marketplace and the comfort, safety, and goodness of the private home, and it evoked the fantasized countryside without the mocking tone of the 1920s. "Country" provided a positive context and seemingly new meaning for the kind of domestically oriented sale items that had been standard for many years.[29] The country look did not disappear as the 1990s wore on, but it became less overwhelming. Many other items had a more self-consciously clever or humorous facade, which implied a different kind of urbane sophistication (see below), and popular preoccupations like a fascination with angels were reflected by crisply starched white crocheted figures with wings.

Ironically, given the nostalgia for the old days, many of the most popular sales items of recent years imply pampering and leisure rather than usefulness or hard work. Some kitchen standbys like potholders and napkin rings are popular, but there are barely any more aprons (with the exception of barbecue or chef's aprons, which do not belong in the same sense in the woman's kitchen). Decorations (especially Christmas ornaments), accessories for the home (especially items for the desk and "comforts for bed and bath" like sachets, decorated soaps, padded hangers), toys, and embellished clothing frequently prevail.[30]

Many of the contemporary items once again evince a kind of masquerade: a pincushion is made in the form of a toadstool, a cactus, or a slice of layer cake; a Christmas stocking is made in the form of a roller skate. Unlike the Victorian items discussed earlier, these are tongue-in-cheek. The impulse behind the Victorian's knitted mosses and rabbit penwipers was an imitation of reality. Today's imitations, on the other hand, are commentaries, statements *about* reality. They are thought of as "soft sculpture" (this word, which came into popular usage in the 1970s, is even used in some of the instruction books for bazaars), artwork that almost mocks the original form by taking it out of its original context and making it playful. A tissue holder fashioned out of plastic needlework canvas (the plastic mesh always remains visible) and made in the shape of a football helmet cannot be mistaken for the real thing. The objects show the slightly bemused and sophisticated stance of both maker and purchaser, thus adding a contemporary touch to the lighthearted quality of the fair.[31]

Another trend in contemporary fair items that reflects this same kind of self-conscious humor is an emphasis on written messages. Articles of all kinds are "marked" or personalized—plastic adhesive letters, handpainting, and even embroidery are applied while customers wait at the booths—and slogans or sayings are added to make items more interesting. A Christmas stocking is marked with the words, "Fill Up"; a tooth-shaped cushion is labeled "Tooth Fairy Pillow." Sometimes words are entirely or almost the point of little sale articles. A 1994 bazaar featured plaques with messages like "This house protected by killer dust balls!" for example, and an item popular from

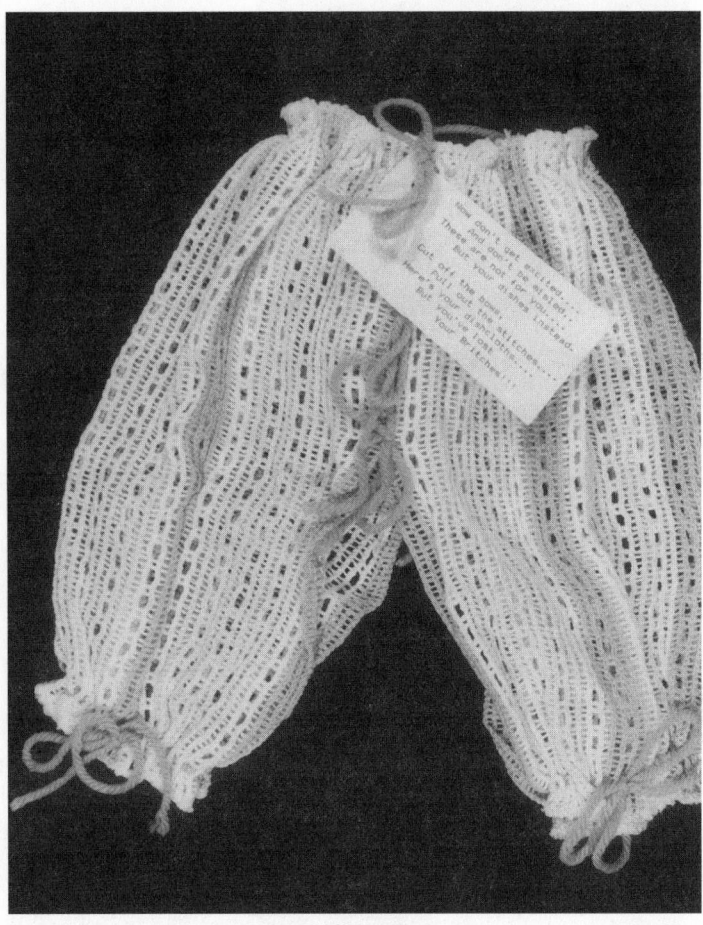

Fig. 88. Practical items like dishcloths are transformed into amusing fair gifts by a few pieces of yarn and a typed message. Many fair sales items are similarly made to be used up or consumed. Author's collection.

at least 1986 through 1995 was a diminutive lip-shaped, needlepoint-covered reticule that opened to reveal a chocolate Hershey's Kiss and a slip of paper with the typewritten words, "A Kiss For You" (fig. 87). Another novelty seen at several different midwestern fairs in 1994 relied on its poem to communicate its purpose and its cleverness (fig. 88). The typed message read:

> Now don't get excited . . .
>   And don't be misled . . .
> These are not for you . . .
>   But your dishes instead.
> Cut off the bows,
>   Pull out the stitches . . .
> Here's your dishcloths . . .
>   But you've lost
>   Your Britches!!!

Baked goods have remained standbys at most bazaars, but I have seen a trend in the last few years that reflects increased commercialization even in this area. It is becoming common at Christmas season fairs (which now typically take place well before Thanksgiving) to see "cookies by the pound," where, rather than purchasing a paper plate filled with five or six cookies, one comes up to a bakery store–type display and buys in bulk. The cookie room at a 1994 Madison fair featured long tables with organized displays of different cookie varieties, all selling at five dollars a pound. It was serviced by about twelve plastic-gloved workers helping customers fill up their plastic boxes and proceed to the scale and cashier near the exit door. The cookies were all handmade, but the assembly-line approach obscured any sense of individual donations or bakers. Nevertheless, the abundant display helped create a feeling of well-being and pleasure (so *many* cookies!), and the fact that they were homemade made them different from those found in a regular store. Customers were expected to freeze and later serve them when entertaining for the holidays, perpetuating the feeling of an old-fashioned Christmas.

In sum, contemporary fair items reflect a somewhat new relationship to goods. They are no longer experienced as inherently exciting, and expensive luxury items are not necessarily the point; nor are they exclusively practical. Rather, goods are used to create comfort and good feeling. The implied customer is nostalgic for an imagined simpler time in the past, but embraces the commercial world of the present and uses the latter to advantage. She approaches this world in a somewhat tongue-in-cheek fashion, but is caught up in it nevertheless. If we consider the abundance of goods in contemporary American society—not only the new products surrounding us in retail stores and mail-order catalogues, but also the plethora of used items at the ubiquitous yard sale, rummage sale, and flea market[32]—we see why the fairgoer's attitude toward sale items would indeed have been likely to change. This profile of the fairgoer reflects the prototypical American consumer, and we are reminded again of the many ways in which the fair serves as a mirror of the changing culture of which it is a part.

Local Versions of a National Culture

One last and related point that may be made about contemporary fairs is that they are local events (I know of no more regional bazaars), but they reflect a broad-based national culture. Ideas for fair themes, attractions, and sale products are discussed in books and magazines, but they are also spread informally from one area to another. This has always been the case to some extent, but it is especially pronounced now that people travel so extensively. A woman who initiated a community calendar for a Madison church fair told me she had seen similar products in many places, including North Carolina, Michigan, and Florida. The Florida connection is important, for retirees who have second homes in the Sun Belt are particularly likely to spread ideas throughout the country. A minister's wife who has lived in many states said that wherever she went she witnessed a similar scene: a woman would arrive at a committee meeting, pull out an object or newspaper clipping, and say, "*Here's* an idea we might use! Let's just change this one part here. . . ." While ideas certainly cross international boundaries as well, they don't translate completely. A book of English bazaar bestsellers, written in 1987, has a different feel to it than its American counterparts. The English sale items were far less dominated by the country look, and there was more emphasis on recycled products than had been common in the United States for some time.[33]

Profit Making and the Contemporary Fair

Entrepreneurial Salespeople

The contemporary emphasis on crafted projects is also tied to perhaps the most important shift in the fundraising fair, one which marks the beginning of a new phase in the history of the institution. As indicated in chapter 1, the kind of professional artist or craftsperson who was first invited into the fair after World War II—the outsider who makes a personal profit from the sale of her wares but gives a set percentage of the earnings to the sponsoring organization[34]—has now become a fair fixture. At a 1994 event, for example, the schedule of the bazaar was dominated by the "vendor list." This arrangement was first evident in Madison at the 1971 YWCA fair, but it only became common between 1977 and 1981, when many groups found they could no longer generate enough contributions from members to fill sale tables with handmade goods. Craftspeople lent an air of interest and importance to the fairs, but their presence was the result of necessity rather than preference. Some Madison bazaar workers greeted this innovation with relief, as they felt they would be less personally pressured to produce sale items, but there was also a sense of loss, a nostalgia for the time when it was really *their* group that was able to meet the fundraising task with the products of its labors.[35] The loss of identity or group cohesiveness was in fact something I observed in the late 1980s and in the 1990s. At one church "Craft Sale" where most booths were run by nonmembers, for example, the only place where I noticed relaxed conversation and chatter was the luncheon area, which was run by the women's guild of the church.

Fundraising events with this kind of professional participant are markedly different from their predecessors, not only because of the reduced community interaction, but also because they emphasize the element of private profit. The community group does benefit, but only in proportion to the benefit afforded the individual entrepreneurs, whose participation has a pecuniary motivation. In addition, the presence of outsiders may further reduce the impetus for organization members to devote their time and energy to make objects voluntarily for the fairs. Ironically, there are even cases where the very same individuals who once donated their goods to their church groups and similar organizations are now selling them there on commission. This inevitably changes their relationship with the group, for they are involved in a businesslike arrangement and must approach it in a more calculated fashion.[36]

The intermixing or blurring between the fundraising bazaar and the for-profit craft sale or fair is also evidenced in other ways. In 1981 Lesley Linsley, a professional designer who owned a craft company and created kits and patterns for magazines like *Family Circle*, wrote *The Great Bazaar* for the "many people involved with the world of bazaars and crafting." She often interchanged fundraising bazaars and profit-oriented fairs in the text. Although she claimed the book was written for those working on the familiar, "homegrown" type of bazaar, for example, she defended the importance of bazaars by quoting a profit-oriented artisan speaking about the role of craft fairs. Several bazaar organizers I spoke with, furthermore, mentioned they had recently found themselves competing with other kinds of art or craft fairs, as many of the items that were formerly found primarily at charitable holiday fairs are now available elsewhere at all times of the year. One woman said she knew several people who used to shop for handcrafted items at Christmas bazaars, but no longer did so because they were so easy to find. She herself stopped painting cups because similar items were seen at stores and craft fairs, and they were no longer very salable.[37]

A recent development that makes the situation even more complex is the Christmas craft boutique. This is typically a for-profit sale, run by a group of craftspeople on a cooperative basis. The merchandise is nearly identical to that found at a fundraising bazaar, and sometimes there is even an overlap in personnel. The Christmas boutique phenomenon is only about two decades old, but it seems to have taken a firm hold. *How to Have a Successful Craft Show in Your Home*, published in Chicago in 1981, created enough interest to warrant a second printing two years later,[38] and the number of these events increases annually. The boutiques are held in a variety of spaces, including private homes, restaurants, historic buildings, office complexes, and even country clubs. Some have catchy titles, much as the fundraising fairs do, and some are even called "bazaars." It is not easy to discern which events have a charitable purpose ("Most Mem-bear-able Crafts" and "Country Crafts Bazaar" were profit-making sales; "Hope Country Fare" was a fundraiser). There is even further confusion because there can be an actual overlap of profit and charitable functions: organizers of the for-profit events sometimes sponsor a charity raffle or volunteer a small portion of their proceeds to a community cause such as a camp scholarship fund or the public library.

"The Bazaar Calendar," a supplement that appeared in the *Ann Arbor (Mich.) News* in September 1992 listed 102 upcoming events that involved the sale of handmade items.[39] Of these, thirteen were profit-making boutiques (names like "Old Friends Holiday in the Country" belied their pecuniary intent, and phrases like "7th [8th, 10th] Annual" implied that they were already community traditions), and seven were craft/art sales with no apparent charitable cause. There were also three open houses at profit-making businesses, although in one case a percentage of the proceeds was to be donated to a community cause. At least nineteen other events held to benefit schools, hospitals, churches, and groups like the Bird Rescue Society also involved artisans selling their wares.[40] Tellingly, church bazaars were least likely to feature the "professionals" (only five of thirty-four church events clearly included profit-making vendors). They were also most likely to feature meal service, which may have facilitated the kind of leisurely visiting and sociability described above. Of the thirty-one events that indicated that a meal would be served, twenty-six were church-sponsored.

With the exception of the already existing communities that would be drawn to the church bazaars, the contemporary public does not seem to make a strong distinction between profit and nonprofit events. While the idea of a charitable fair is still appealing (the four publicity photos included in the Ann Arbor calendar all featured volunteers), individuals still flock to profit-making sales boasting "crafters in a country store atmosphere offering baskets, quilts, candles" and similar items.

Both the consumerist orientation of the fairgoer and the more central role of profit making in the fair itself are tied to the dramatically changing profile of women in the workforce. Not only is there a decrease in available voluntary labor,[41] but also, as indicated earlier, there is a shift in the perception of time and its value,[42] resulting in a different attitude about making and donating handmade goods. Even if an individual woman is not currently working outside the home, she has probably done so in the past, or expects to in the future. Because she has this experience and orientation, she looks at her time in relation to an hourly wage and values it in economic terms. Almost every woman I interviewed made some kind of remark about time. The most telling, perhaps, was that "time was nothing in those days—when time [to make things] didn't count, everything we earned was found money." Women's time *does* count now; women count the number of hours that go into making a particular product and calculate the eventual return. When labor time is factored in, the numbers are often so low that the fair seems ludicrous. More and more women are coming to feel that the effort is not worthwhile. Unlike their nineteenth-century foremothers, today's women do have money of their own, and they often prefer to donate cash to whatever

cause is at hand. Even some homemakers' groups, which represent the most traditional constituency, have recently disbanded their bazaars and now raise funds through
donations. The groups that still hold fairs often encourage profit making, for individuals spend time making sale items when they can realize a direct return.

The semiprofessional artisan has even had an impact on the decoration and physical environment of the contemporary fundraising fair. The visual emphasis is now directed toward the goods, much as it would be at a profit-making craft fair, and the
public has come to expect the kind of unrelated individualized displays that would be
common at a craft fair. Linsley expressly suggested in her 1981 book that bazaar organizers visit craft fairs for display ideas, and individuals I have spoken with indicate that
they do just that. Recent bazaar instruction books sometimes even suggest the kind of
portable displays that work well for craftspeople who have to set up repeatedly in different places: items might be hung on ladders, clothes drying racks, or chicken wire.[43]

Fairs Given by Those Outside the Workforce

Given the time-as-money perception, it is not surprising that senior citizens are heavily
involved with the contemporary fundraising fair. Many older women functioned outside the wage economy most of their lives; others may have counted their time in
financial terms in the past, but no longer need to do so. These "seniors" are perhaps
the primary contributors to church bazaars still relying entirely on donated items.
Madison's United Methodist Church "Fall Faire," for example, was for many years
spearheaded by an energetic retired librarian who met regularly with others who were
all well over fifty, many of whom said that this was something they "finally had
time for." Women involved with hospital auxiliary bazaars typically have a similar
profile.

Bazaars are also thriving in seniors' clubs and retirement and nursing homes. Madison has a nonsectarian senior citizens' center with six hundred members, for example,
that has been holding a Christmas boutique since the early 1970s. Work for the boutique is integrated into ongoing activities; at regular craft classes, students (both men
and women) are encouraged to make at least two of every project—one for themselves
and one to be sold at the annual event. The boutique thus becomes an extension of the
center's program, giving form and meaning to day-to-day get-togethers of group members. The classes are led by paid and volunteer workers. A similar situation prevails in
group homes. The items made in these settings are especially likely to be small and
able to be completed in a single work session (e.g., Christmas ornaments), and because many are designed with a craft class in mind (e.g., molded ceramic pieces
that can be individually hand-painted), they do not tend to be inspired or innovative.[44]

Madison's senior center was in step with national trends when it inaugurated its boutique in the early 1970s. *Retirement Living* published a feature in 1976 with money-
raising ideas for senior citizens' clubs, including the observation that a "boutique" was
a workable and enjoyable plan. Since "so many [retired] people" were currently making hand-crafted items, according to the magazine, that was a logical type of activity.[45]

The seniors' bazaars in many ways parallel the events sponsored by youth organizations; both evolve from institutional programmatic needs rather than from the needs, wishes, or initiation of the constituency (though interest and enthusiasm must exist within the group for the events to continue), and both involve individuals who are marginal to the labor economy. Some of the same individuals who belonged to youth organizations that ran fairs in the earlier part of this century may now belong to the seniors' groups. Today's youth are much less likely to be involved in full-scale bazaars (simple bake sales are more common), and when they are, they tend to be younger. College students (now thought of as women rather than girls) do not participate, but preteen girls' groups like scouts sometimes do. Students from private or church-related schools are perhaps the most likely to be involved, for parent groups from parochial schools hold fairs more regularly than their public school counterparts. There were three parochial school fairs on one Saturday alone in Milwaukee in November 1988.[46]

A Community of Consumers

Two other trends evident in contemporary bazaars or fairs are also related to the reduced pool of women willing to work as volunteers and the increasing difficulty in getting ever busier people to even come to the event. Some organizers have created high visibility for their events by reversing the usual order of things and moving the bazaar "to the people": they are holding the bazaars in shopping malls. The manager of one of the malls in Madison had been asked repeatedly by different groups if they might set up tables in the central public area. When he suggested the groups get together and hold their sales on the same day, the "Community Bazaar" was born. An individual who had been spearheading the fair at her own small church agreed to act as coordinator, and she remained in that role more than fifteen years. Between fifteen and thirty organizations participate yearly. Most are church groups, but other nonprofit organizations such as service sororities, Girl Scouts, Drum and Bugle Corps, and some nursing homes are also involved. The Madison mall manager said he has had inquiries from his counterparts in many other areas, and he felt the practice was spreading rapidly.

The mall setting has meant that groups do sell their handwork, but there are trade-offs and some less positive consequences. In order to preclude competition with the surrounding retailers and restaurateurs, the mall allows only handmade items and simple baked goods to be sold at the Community Bazaar; not only elaborate meals but even offerings of tea or coffee are eliminated. Consequently, much of the informal conversation and socializing that typically characterizes the church fair is missing (there is nowhere to sit), and like the for-profit boutiques, the event is more of a straightforward sale.[47] Although it is billed as a community event, there are no activities other than buying and selling, and interaction is limited to the kind of casual conversation that takes place during sales transactions. The community is reduced to something fleeting and illusory: it is a community of consumers. The individuals who work at this bazaar are not concerned with personal profit, but the whole environment of the shopping mall is one where profit making is paramount.[48]

Where people do have to come to a fair, organizers occasionally still resort to dramatic themes and gimmicks or rely on gaming and amusement. Episcopal church groups sometimes hold old English theme fairs with mock battles, singing boy choirs, bagpipe players, and wandering costumed "lords and ladies." A large Madison congregation holds such an event every few years. High tea is served, and brass rubbings and "old-fashioned" smocked dresses are among the sales items. The church is adorned with large banners borrowed from the British consulate. At a nearby Catholic parish, the fair is regularly built around a theme such as "Puttin' on the Ritz," where decorations feature evocative images like the debonair Fred Astaire and penguins in "tuxedos." People migrate to the casino and beer garden area for blackjack, roulette, poker, and other games, or dance to bands playing everything from polkas to rock music. A third Madison event takes place outdoors in the early fall. "Edgefest," which raises money for a church school and has been held annually since 1971, has much of the quality of a county fair. There is continuous entertainment, a midway with roller coasters and rides, a games area, and buttery corn, cotton candy, and other walk-along foods. Many Madisonians wait all year to shop at the enormous resale (rummage) tent; I know one woman, in fact, who takes off from work on the Friday afternoon that Edgefest opens so she can be among the first to go through the clothing racks. There is also a book sale and many craft booths that follow the usual commission arrangements. Interestingly, the "Granny's Kitchen" area, where sale goods are donated and all profit is given to the school, is well removed from most of the frenzied activity, so much so that it is never even seen by most of the visitors. Edgefest is highly profitable, but it is the carnival aspect of the event that makes it so; the importance of the donated handcrafts is negligible. Recent prescriptive literature encourages this commercial approach. In *Fundraising Events: Strategies and Programs for Success* (1988) the authors indicate a contemporary preoccupation with time-as-money when they speak of "feasibility analysis" and suggest contracting with professional advertising agencies. They insist that even at simple sales, refreshments, raffles, and other entertainments be added to make it worthwhile for visitors to attend.[49]

We have been looking at the myriad details of women's fairs held from the early part of the nineteenth century to the end of the twentieth—at the sale objects, the carefully planned atmosphere of the hall, and the practices and politics of fairgiving. In the following chapter, we will pull all this together and draw conclusions about the developments and meanings of the fundraising fair phenomenon.

CHAPTER EIGHT

Conclusions

When I interviewed fairgivers, I asked them what first came to their minds when they heard the words "bazaar" or "fair." Their responses varied widely. Some said that fairs were "a lot of hard work" or that they promoted "working with friends." Others replied "homemade things," "sewing and baking," or "getting good things at low prices." One individual joyously exclaimed, "Knowing that I could really pull it off!" The answers were highly personal and immediate, in other words, but implicitly referred to the explanations offered in the first chapter for the fairs' tenacity. The comments alluded to the social and aesthetic aspects of the fair, and to the idea that familiar domestic skills and considerable donated time and effort was involved. Even my assertion that the successful management of this kind of complex undertaking brings a sense of satisfaction and accomplishment was confirmed by the interviewees' replies. The comments remind us that the fundraising fair must always be considered with a kind of double vision or perspective: it is an *institution* that can be analyzed in a general, historic context; but it is also an *experience* involving real individuals, which can best be understood on a more personal level through particular stories, images, and memories. As Michael Robertson pointed out in his article "Cultural Hegemony Goes to the Fair," people mold their experiences of mass culture to their own needs; they do things for their own reasons and see "reality" through their own filters.[1] As we review what the fair has been and assess where it may be going, we must continually shift from one perspective to another, stepping back to see the bigger, overall picture, but simultaneously stepping forward into the personal space where fairs were actually experienced.

As an institution, the fundraising fair has been a significant social phenomenon. Hundreds of thousands of people have been involved in "producing" fairs, contributing countless hours and an enormous amount of psychic energy. Even more people have participated as part of the fair "audience." The fair has served many functions over the last century and three-quarters. It has been a means by which groups could raise money and work for a perceived greater good; a social meeting ground and entertainment center where pleasant feelings, amusement, and the sense of community could thrive; a place for political and social networking; an aesthetic outlet and showcase of art; a shopping center; and a training ground where individuals could develop skills in each of these other arenas. The fair has been an integral part of the "background history" described in the introduction and of the American social fabric. As such, it offers a window through which we can examine broader cultural patterns and ideas. I have used that window in this book—I have studied the institution of the fair much as others have studied institutions like the theater. I have also approached it as a form of creative expression, much like architecture, fashion design, or painting (each of these other expressive forms has been incorporated into fairs, but the gestalt of the fair is more than the sum of its parts). Moreover, since the fair was so strongly identified with and controlled by women, I have further approached it as an institution that offers valuable insights about women's changing lives.

In most cases, these woman-identified institutions were completely up-to-date and in tune with the spirit of their times. The women's approach to goods accurately reflected changing consumer attitudes, for example, and their sale products and sale environments were in keeping with contemporary commercial goods and other types of retailing establishments (see table 2). Current cultural ideas and values were evident as well. In the Victorian era, sentimentality, a sense of self-importance, and confidence in progress were all evident in realistic pincushions and historic kitchens and in diorama-like settings in horticultural halls. At the turn of the century a more free-floating sense of self was reflected in more ethereal, sensual, playlike fairylands. With their emphasis on color, light, and fantasy, these environments were akin to dreamy contemporary books like *Peter Pan* and the images of illustrator Maxfield Parrish, or the canvases of painters like Renoir and Gaugin. By the 1920s, fair settings and goods were abstracted and "suggestive"; they only alluded to reality. Like the jarring abstract planes of cubist paintings and the stylization of jazz rhythms, they reflected a new, more cynical and less literal sense of what was real or permanent. Contemporary approaches to art were themselves expressed at fairs, as we have seen in the shift from the serious, quasi-religious attitudes expressed in the Civil War era to the humorous treatment at the turn of the century and the emphasis on community context after World War II.

New types of cultural expression were even *introduced* at fairs. Historic reenactments and period rooms can be traced to the New England Kitchens and the living tableaux of the sanitary fairs, where many of the standard icons and themes of the Colonial Revival were actually pioneered. Elements later seen in early-twentieth-century civic pageants and folk dance festivals, similarly, were rooted in nineteenth-century bazaars. Imaginative theme-based merchandising strategies—e.g., selling

Table 2
Characteristic Sale Goods, Attitudes toward Goods, and Related Retail Establishments

	Handmade Goods: Dominant Types and Presentation	Handmade Goods: Imagery	Presence of Commercial Goods	Attitudes toward Goods	Developments in Related Retail Establishments
1830–1850	practical items such as aprons, potholders, blankets prevail	unknown	few	primarily practical—means to an end	country store is major retail outlet
1850–1885	fanciful but ostensibly useful items most favored sewing-related goods predominate	"masquerade" and ephemeral imagery	begin to proliferate; important part of Civil War fairs	goods become exciting, with transformative properties; commodity aesthetic begins	department stores like "marble palaces" are opened
1885–1920	more stationery and kitchen/dining items; often less whimsical but transformed by contextual setting	"artistic," lighter, more straightforward	very important—large fairs almost like department stores	last pattern continues, but after about 1900 excitement subsides; goods are put to use, managed	department stores proliferate with elegant, evocative settings; often thematic presentations
1920–1947	increase in items that assist housework; generally functional presented as extension of the woman	"cute" and cloying; some cartoonlike imagery home-oriented (e.g., with Colonial Revival references)	less important—handmade goods prevail (other than reasale)	consumers use goods to find satisfaction, not so much to become someone "new"	department stores more streamlined, less extravagant or fanciful
Post WWII	more "upbeat" and "crafted" rather than sewn items presented as extension of home regularly incorporate commercial goods into handmade	reflect time: "sophisticated" in cold war era, colorful and recycled in 1970s, "folk" or homey country in 1980s masquerade returns in tongue-in-cheek fashion	generally, handmade goods prevail (other than resale)	celebration of goods renewed in "lifestyle" context	wide range of stores have extravaganzas—like amusement parks; some evoke the past

goods in a "garden of Allah" or a "pirate's den"—which have become an important part of the modern experience, were also first seen at fundraising fairs, as was the idea of providing music to make shoppers feel relaxed and happy. Sanitary fairs also influenced the future development of art museums and public parks. A wide range of new attractions and products, in fact, was introduced and/or experienced at fundraising fairs, just as it was at commercial and agricultural fairs. Sometimes these were amusements—think of the Christmas tree at the antebellum fair—but just as often they were novel consumer items like imported china, or they were new technologies, ranging from craft materials to telephones.

In a very real sense, women's fairs played an integral role in the development of the American culture of consumption. This phrase refers not just to a culture where people buy quantities of goods, but to a culture where goods become infused with meaning and a seeming power to make dreams come true. From their inception the fairs were special kinds of markets, where sale items were transformed and intensified by virtue of a pleasurable setting and context. Even before large department stores and international expositions played with costuming and theatrical display, these ideas were experimented with at fundraising fairs. The dreamlike quality of the late-nineteenth-century fair, in particular, helped imbue goods with a sense of promise and transformative possibility and contributed to the cultural shift from a Protestant ethos emphasizing self-denial to a consumer or "therapeutic" ethos of self-realization and self-fulfillment. More tangibly, fairgivers worked cooperatively with manufacturers, wholesalers, retailers, and other types of "culture brokers" who collectively helped effect this new view of reality by making the necessary pieces fall into place.[2]

In large part, the institution of the fundraising fair furthered prevailing class and race structures and stereotypes. We have stressed the leadership role of the white middle- and upper-class fairgivers in the premodern period, and how, even in its original form, the charity bazaar was essentially elitist (those who can afford to "do" charity by definition affirm their own elevated social standing). Fairgivers also reinforced cultural stereotypes through international theme booths that confirmed an evolutionist view of race. Many of these individuals were associated with social and reform movements—mission societies, settlement houses, the Arts and Crafts movement—that helped perpetuate hegemonic assumptions about the social order. Their beliefs permeated every aspect of the fair; the repeated references we have cited to "pickaninnies" and black servants indicate how ingrained their assumptions were. At the same time, however, fairs were also used by many nondominant, non-WASP groups—African Americans, and waves of white ethnic immigrants including Jews, Catholics (Irish, Italians, Polish), Czechs, Germans, French, etc.—for their own ends; they were embraced and elaborated by each population in turn and adapted to their particular needs, circumstances, and values.[3] The fair may actually have been one of the mechanisms by which immigrant groups negotiated their assimilation into mainstream American society. It was in any case such an adaptable institution that it cannot be simply identified with one class, race, or ethnic affiliation.

When it comes to gender, however, the identification of the fair is un-equivocal, and the subject of gender roles lies at the heart of this book. We have seen that women also used fairs for their own purposes. They held them for causes they expressly wanted to support, including, in some cases, the advancement of their own rights. Even beyond this instrumental use, however, was a more dynamic and symbolic one. Women used fairs to play with and against their assigned roles. They often literally dramatized the so-called domestic sphere, turning it into both an icon and an entertainment. This was the case in the sanitary fair kitchens, where the great domestic hearth was simultaneously venerated and gently mocked. It was true at the turn of the century when domestic objects like cake pans were blown up into the stuff of fantasy and playhouse-type booths created protective yet amusing spaces for sales transactions. It was true in the 1930s when housewife-helper dolls were favored sales items, and it was still true in the 1980s when popular articles included house blessings or objects embroidered with scenes of houses or sweet, domesticated animals. The fair was an institution that, like the domestic sphere itself, was simultaneously socially constructed *for* and *by* women; it was both imposed upon women from without, and defined, embraced and continually negoti-ated by the women who were working within it.[4]

In some senses the domestic kitchen serves as a primary symbol of the woman's fair. The kitchen represents a rather timeless image of the female role, for no matter what its accouterments, it remains a place for cooking and nurturing and for fam-ily. Women who are represented in it function as actors in an intimate and "natural" domestic context rather than in a public or social one.[5] This message diverges consid-erably from—is almost the antithesis of—the underlying message of the agricultural or trade fair, which is by definition associated with science and progress, forces that can seemingly overcome nature. The fair kitchen did in fact change somewhat over time, and by the modern era it was no longer presented as an "important" space, but the strong identification between the fundraising fair and timeless do-mestic values nevertheless remained constant. The inclusion of children as contributors to or participants in fundraising fairs also marks the institution as do-mestic. Children did not routinely participate in this way in other types of fairs be-fore the twentieth century, and their involvement with bazaars is another indication of the institution's symbolic identification with the domestic domain, for children are also generally considered to belong there.

Women's traditional domestic skills like cooking, baking, and sewing have always taken center stage at fundraising fairs, for even when carnival games and expensive commercial merchandise were included in the mix, no fair was complete without handwork. Even today, when women are no longer generally judged by their com-petence in the "domestic arts," it is those arts that are proclaimed and celebrated at fairs. The attitudes toward the women who exercise these skills, on the other hand, *have* shifted over time. The women were more fully appreciated when the dominant cultural ideology was against their working for wages. Now that women's outside labor is valued and women, like men, are judged by their professional work, handwork, baking, and related talents are appι ciated, but are seen as "extra," almost superfluous amenities. The central position of these amenities or skills at fundraising fairs contributes to the contemporary perception that fairs themselves are trivial and superfluous.

The changing perception of the fair is also related to the way women used fairs in the premodern era to play with—or against—their sexuality. When it was still uncommon and unseemly for women to act "aggressive," they were able to be quite forward in the context of the fair, both as salespeople and flirtatious romancers. Men made much of their bold behavior and of their sexual presence, but the women made use of these qualities for their own purposes: they played up the puns about their "fair" presence, composed slightly risqué missives for post office letters, and advised using pretty girls to advantage. They wore alluring costumes to rivet fairgoers' eyes on them and ensure that they would remain the center of attention. Such a display was particularly titillating in an age when the only life-size mannequins were found in cheap "curiosity" museums.[6] Since women were knowingly "consumed" in this way, the fair also played on the distinction between the consumer and the consumed. The play with sexuality is completely missing in the contemporary fair, for women and bazaars no longer represent the same kind of danger to contemporary mores that they once did. Furthermore, concepts like luxury and desire, which were from the beginning associated with bazaars, have been totally redefined in our consumer culture. In the earlier era dominated by the Puritan work ethic, desire and luxury represented the antithesis of goodness. In our time, these terms have not only lost their negative connotations, but are sometimes even seen as sources of strength and affirmations of success and the good life. Once the qualities lost their negative power, the bazaar that was associated with them in turn seemed less alluring and essentially harmless. It is this cultural shift that explains the paradox of an institution that at first seemed to embody the risqué and sensual, but is now primarily thought of in relation to old-fashioned moral values and propriety.

This discussion brings us back to the argument that the premodern fundraising fair served as the "woman's fair"—as a gendered manifestation of the broader fair phenomenon. All fairs are characterized by play, festivity, ritual, and inversions or transformations of everyday reality. They involve the "grotesque" or "lower" body, the body of desire, as they emphasize food, drink, sexuality, and longing. They function as a place where usual rules may be suspended, and in middle-class culture in particular, where the "other" may be embraced. Women's fairs involved all of these elements. They offered tempting foods, music, dance, games, theater, and costume, and considerable play with normal and expected roles. In their earliest form, they turned conventional expectations on their end because they involved women in business—women "selling themselves"—and class mixing. They embodied the dangers of the unruly marketplace and its potential for greed, and they referred, either obliquely or quite explicitly, to exotic other places and peoples. In the modern era when none of this seemed so extraordinary or unusual because it had been fully incorporated into everyday life, women's fairs lost their seeming power and, again, their perceived significance.

The issue of male and female participation is one instance where the fundraising fair diverges from other types of fairs and American social institutions. Kathy Peiss demonstrates that much of nineteenth-century socializing was homosocial: men socialized with other men, and women socialized with other women. She documents one of the major shifts that occurred around the turn of the century, when there was an increasing tendency toward heterosocial mixing.[7] In the case of the fundraising fair, the situation was almost reversed. Although nineteenth-century fairs were homosocially based in that they originated in women's groups, men were always drawn in as part of the "audience"; they were needed because they were the ones with the money. Men were increasingly involved in the later part of the century when it was their organizations that directly benefited from fairs, but they fell away after World War I when women had more money of their own and other types of institutions brought opportunities for coeducational mixing.

The emphasis on theatricality and play is a significant part of the story of the woman's fair, and my examination of this phenomenon opens up a previously unexplored chapter in the history of American entertainment. Fairs played an important role in the social life of the premodern age, particularly before the advent of theme parks, motion pictures, and other forms of mass entertainment. Especially in the antebellum era when the very idea of entertainment was considered questionable, fairs offered morally laudable opportunities for amusement. Great numbers of people attended, often coming from great distances. They dressed festively, much as they would for a dance or a night at the theater, for they were going to a social event where they would see and be seen, and where flirtatious behavior and a play between the sexes was expected and safely ritualized. In many cases, going to a fair functioned as a kind of courtship ritual. In our present era when few young men even go to bazaars, it is easy to downplay the significance of this part of the fair experience in the past. The fact that the fair functioned as a social center is also evident in the variety of entertainments that were offered, in the routine inclusion of fair goings-on in society columns of late-nineteenth- and early-twentieth-century newspapers, and in the public appearances of celebrities like actresses and president's wives. The fair remained a social meeting ground and center until about 1930, when it was usually reduced to a simpler "sale." Its social quality was resurrected after World War II, but it was changed to a meeting ground for women and middle-class families; for the most part, the young men and the socialites went elsewhere.

Play was such a central quality of the fair experience that it colored much of what

Table 3
Trends in Design of Fair Environments

Time Period	Overall Design Concept	Booth and Sale Areas	Wall, Ceiling Treatment	Costume	Salient Materials	Other
Early Fairs: 1830–1860	"decoration" tables typically placed around side of room	plain tables, no framework	evergreen foliage some banners for color	not stressed	evergreen most popular	sales items and saleswomen attract attention
Civil War Era: 1861–1870	whole buildings erected for large fairs, allowing centralized plan; some have long, continuous "avenues" most booths are simple tables, although some frameworks are seen	beginning of theatrical theme booths	abundant bunting, banners, evergreen	international- or historical-themed costumes seen at some booths	cloth bunting and heavy drapery natural materials: plants, minerals, even animals	stress literalness horticultural environments at some fairs, like interior mini-parks with picturesque habitats
1870s	space conceived of as a whole with central area of interest, frequently a floral bower		ceiling beams, walls covered with drapery and greens	increasingly important	cloth, natural plants and flowers	necessary to "transform" a room—aesthetic quality discussed and rated parasols popular
1880s	visual unity through "matching" (color, fabric, etc.)	booths begin to be individually conceived, often have frameworks and draping	not stressed	very important; sometimes more than booths	new materials and textures; e.g., thatch, shell, palm	fairs seen as tableaux

Period	Concept	Booths/Structures	Walls	Costumes/Themes	Materials	Other
Turn of the Century: 1890–1915	conceptual (thematic) unity; booths as individual "stage sets"	booths have novel shapes: often high, peaked, or hooped frameworks; booths often houselike forms, enclosed spaces; some booths are literal interpretations of sale items	not stressed	very important; often fanciful and based on "fairy" themes (flowers, fairies, nursery rhyme characters); international themes still important; costumed peddlers like mobile booths	paper, especially crepe paper, important; cloth less so	ever increasing need for novelty; contrived allusions to the natural world; electric light and color important
WW I and Postwar: 1915–1930	no single conception prevails but conceptual themes remain and space is again conceived of as a whole	tendency toward simplification: booths with simpler frames or tables without frames	sometimes used for signage and mural-like backdrop; fair moves back into its containing space	importance decreases and costume simplifies; peddlers continue	crepe paper; some natural materials brought in	more outdoor, "street" fairs; instructions for fair environments very specific; effects less literal, more suggestive ("the object is effect, not verity")
Depression and WW II: 1930–1947	little information available	generally straightforward; covered tables	no information	none indicated	crepe paper	
Cold War: 1948–1965	return to feeling of festive environment; no single conception prevails	some shaped booths reappear	posters and signage on walls	not stressed; simplified costumes consist of suggestive details like caps		balloons, large-scale designs and massed color
1966–Present	focus on goods, not environment; influence from craft fair model: booths designed by individual entrepreneurs	simple covered tables; hanging display areas made from chicken wire, clothes dryers, etc.	not stressed	not stressed		outdoor fairs again popular

went on. Everything from "doing good" to selling was turned *into* play, and when it became a game, the women had great control and power. There was play with scale, and with time, space, and reality—other eras, places, and worlds (i.e., identities) were all "playacted" and "tried on." In this context, nothing was too serious or overwhelming; all ideas and phenomena were brought to the same humorous level. While there was a clear hierarchical order in the presentation of artifacts and countries at international expositions, for example,[8] women's fairs reduced Shakers, American Indians, Turks, Russians, and even Yankee ancestors to equally funny characters in a playful dramatic game. At other types of fairs, environments and staging often stressed progress and abundance (e.g., a palace made of corn, a tower made of apples or butter),[9] but at the fundraising fair this was generally not the point; what mattered was the creation of an alternate, transformative reality. Even costuming was used in the real spirit of play—as "dress-up" rather than symbolic allegory. Dress-up allowed the women to further "domesticate" or control that which was different from themselves and transform it into something they knew and understood. Costume and dress-up is largely absent from fundraising fairs today because fairgivers have less need to try on a different reality in order to experience a sense of control; they can buy and sell, solicit, and deal with the world without taking on an alternate persona.[10]

Play and dress-up, which are intimate, sensual experiences, relate too to the theme of aesthetic elaboration. In the self-defined woman's space of the fair, this was celebrated and unabashed. The importance of an attractive hall and appealing sales goods was commented on at some of the earliest antebellum fairs; it was the sensual delight of the glittering Christmas tree, once again, that helped draw crowds to the Boston antislavery event. Once the environments were further elaborated, they provided stimulation for all the senses and thus provided fairgoers with a strong aesthetic experience. Often, textural detail was particularly stressed. I believe this must have created an especially immediate, accessible sensation, and I find it interesting to contrast it with developments at department stores at the turn of the century. Leach describes the way merchants reduced the open flow of traffic in their retailing spaces and developed glass showcases to highlight goods.[11] The glass kept the goods at a distance and eliminated the customer's experience of smell and touch, so it was the visual sense, which is the most intellectual or "mediated," that was most stimulated. Much of the fair environment subverted the hard-edged masculine view of the world and offered an alternative, intimate perspective. Elaborate environments have also been far reduced in fairs of the modern era because the need for sensual stimulation seems to be filled through other outlets such as travel, television, and movies, but attractive presentation is still of concern. Although attention is primarily centered now on the goods themselves, the interest in—the need for—aesthetic elaboration and creative expression has not diminished. It is telling that some of the twentieth-century fairgivers' strongest memories still relate to aesthetic details such as the prettiness of aprons, the smell of cookies, or the look of recently completed objects sitting in the sun.

The "feminine" preoccupation with aesthetic detail and domestic and playful presentation in no way negates or precludes the fact that fairs afforded women a chance to strengthen their skills and their sense of competence and importance. The events functioned as training grounds for the young; children held doorstep fairs in the Civil War era and begged for work in the 1950s, and young women learned to take on adult responsibility through fairgiving. Even more important was the role of the fair in the lives of adults, who learned about things like community organizing, personnel management, publicity, wholesaling, construction techniques, and design principles. Stories of the sanitary fairs, the large consortium events like the Atlantic City Boardwalk, or even a contemporary event like Madison's Edgefest show us just how effective this training might be, and how much women could do when they worked together. In the premodern period and particularly in the early days of the fundraising fair, the strength and efficacy of women working together was well recognized. The editor who told the organizers of the Atlantic City Boardwalk that the newspapermen of Boston had thrown up their hands over their onslaught of fair publicity was recognizing this, as were the veterans and fraternal organizations that turned to women's groups to help them raise their very buildings. Even more pointed was the manager of a Massachusetts agricultural fair who asked women for their help in the 1850s, fearing that his event might not succeed without such assistance. The antebellum "ladies" who impatiently waited for men to complete the Bunker Hill Monument were completely confident that they could raise the money themselves by holding a fair, and did so in order to see the job done. In general, the women's contribution—and the distinct nature of *women's* organizing efforts and institutions—was acknowledged and valued in the nineteenth century; even though it was mocked and satirized by the male establishment, it was taken as a force to be contended with. Unfortunately, fairs (and perhaps women's associations and activities in general) are not looked upon with the same pride or respect today. They are no longer discussed in the press, and no individuals are credited for their efforts by the society at large. The unapologetic, even boastful tone of Mary Livermore's description of her sanitary fair work would not likely be heard from a contemporary fair organizer.

We have established that this lack of respect is due largely to the changing demographic profile of fairgivers. The community leaders and later the socialites who gave a certain amount of visibility and glamour to fundraising fairs are for the most part no longer involved. The young people who participate are now generally quite young indeed—children rather than young adults—and again, few unmarried or youthful men are present. Fairs are increasingly identified, in fact, with older, retired people who have the time to devote to making them happen. All of these factors have reduced the romance of the fair experience and the opportunities for networking and getting to know new people. While in the nineteenth and early twentieth century people of different religious denominations and community groups with different philosophies and agendas sometimes worked together to sponsor fairs and fairgoers occasionally mingled with individuals outside their own social class, today's events are generally more parochial, both sponsored and attended by people who are already identified with a given group. Where there is a broader audience, it is often little more than a community of consumers.

The dominance of the profit motive is, we have seen, perhaps one of the most critical variables in the new face of the fair. Profit making was probably first introduced in the late nineteenth century when fair organizers rented out commercial space to interested merchants. The practice was extended to individuals when artisans were invited to fairs and shows during the twentieth century, especially after World War II, and it has now become a relatively ubiquitous phenomenon. With profit making and the emphasis on sales goods more pointed than ever, charity and good works are no longer even perceived as the primary function of a fundraising fair, even when proceeds go to worthy causes. Ironically, just as the laudable associations have diminished, there is no more questioning of the morality of the fair, and few remember the impassioned feelings of the anti-bazaar movement.

It is important that the picture of the contemporary fair not seem unduly grim or barren. The comments about fellowship and community cited in chapter 1 came in many instances from individuals who are still working at fairs, and while there may be less flirting, hoopla, or even heterosocial mixing, it is still a highly social experience for those involved. While there are few ritual reversals, and environments and costuming are greatly simplified, and while sensual stimulation is reduced at contemporary events, these elements are not missing entirely. When fairgivers still turn to themes like "Puttin' on the Ritz," they remind us that there is much in the human spirit that yearns for festivity, play, and aesthetic elaboration. When books featuring cheerful handmade bazaar items still sell briskly, we are also reminded of the creative urge to "make things."

The contemporary fair has a new function, related to the practice of inviting artisans to sell their wares: it is providing artists who are only beginning to sell their work a new outlet and economic opportunity. They have a chance to earn extra money, and a familiar, nonthreatening context in which to gain experience in the exhibiting and selling process. For these individuals, the fundraising fair may contribute to a deeper sense of self and confidence in their artistic endeavors. This outlet is found for the most part within the women's community and is primarily affecting women, although there are a small number of men involved.

What is the future of the fundraising fair? It is difficult to make pronouncements or predictions. Like Bessie James who wrote during the World War I era, we might be tempted to proclaim the age of the fair past, and point to remaining examples as vestiges of a dying breed or as inauthentic or impure events. Such proclamations would be unwise. The popular press is still stating that bazaars are booming, and more instruction books with the word "bazaar" in the title have been published in the last twenty years than ever before. It is true that many organizations have stopped holding fairs, but others have started new fair traditions, and when a bazaar is disbanded, its regular contributors easily find other outlets for their work. The coordinator of a hospital auxiliary bazaar remarked that she is getting more donations every year and sees no end in sight.

The very nature of community, and certainly the communities that individuals identify with, are undergoing change. One interviewee noted that people in her church are turning less to fellow members for support than they did in the past. The church circle used to be one of the primary places where women could talk over their concerns and problems, she told me, but with the new prevalence of crisis centers and organizations like Alcoholics Anonymous, individuals have more places to turn. While working together on a group project like a fair still engenders fellowship and mutual understanding, organization members may be less likely to even initiate such projects because their involvement with one another is less constant and more diffuse. These may be temporary shifts, however, and even if they are not, the fair may simply be adapted to new circumstances. The need for fellowship and community has not abated, and the fair may be used in the future by the new kinds of communities. We must not forget the enormous flexibility of this institution. When novel fundraising schemes like secondhand (rummage) sales were introduced, it seemed they would spell the demise of the fundraising fair that demanded so much more preparation time. Nevertheless, it wasn't long before rummage booths were incorporated into fairs, and the two forms coexisted comfortably. When amusements like movies and midway rides began to compete with fundraising events, fairgivers incorporated them as well. The irrepressibility of the fair is tied to the fact that it gives people an opportunity to turn an endeavor with a serious underlying purpose into a festive, playful, and pleasurable event. The nature of the pleasurable activities can continue to change without disturbing the essential institution.

It is likely that the element of private profit will remain a part of the fair of the future, for even this institution associated primarily with women has been fully integrated into the labor economy and its construct of time-as-money. It is further likely that the fair will be even more closely identified with the community of retirees who can afford to donate their labor and who will be present in increasing and unprecedented numbers.

Whatever the future holds for the fundraising fair, the past is a rich tapestry of stories and experiences, incorporating millions of people, millions of objects, and millions of hours of work. Of all fairs in America, it was the most common type—it was held most often and in the greatest number of places. I have tried in this book to bring this ubiquitous, seemingly unremarkable institution into the foreground and to explore its actually rather remarkable legacy. I hope I have paved the way for further exploration of the subject and have added to the appreciation of the "fair ladies" of yesterday, today, and the days to come.

Notes

Introduction

1. Robert Darnton, *The Great Cat Massacre and Other Episodes in French Cultural History* (New York: Basic Books, 1984).

2. Janice Radway, *Reading the Romance: Women, Patriarchy, and Popular Literature* (Chapel Hill: Univ. of North Carolina Press, 1984).

3. Kenneth L. Ames, "Anonymous Heroes: Background History and Social Responsibility," *Museum News* (Sept./Oct. 1994): 34–35. Mary Daly's ideas are spread through her many books, but are perhaps articulated most succinctly in *Gyn/Ecology: The Metaethics of Radical Feminism* (Boston: Beacon Press, 1978).

4. Regarding women's contributions to world's fairs, see Jeanne Madeline Weimann, *The Fair Women: The Story of the Women's Building of the World's Columbian Exposition, Chicago 1893* (Chicago: Academy Press, 1981); Virginia Grant Darney, "Women and World's Fairs: American International Expositions, 1876–1904" (Ph.D. diss., Emory Univ., 1982). Earlier study of American fundraising work discounted women's contributions almost completely. In Scott M. Cutlip's 1965 book, *Fundraising in the United States: Its Role in America's Philanthropy* (New Brunswick, N.J.: Rutgers Univ. Press, 1965), for example, fundraising fairs are discussed, but women's highly significant role is not explored or even credited. A few recent studies have considered women's work at fundraising fairs, but only in particular, narrow contexts. See Virginia Gunn, "Western Reserve Women and the U.S. Sanitary Commission, 1861–1865," *Western Reserve Studies* 3 (1988): 75–85; "Art and Artists at the Civil War Sanitary Fairs," a panel of papers presented at the American Studies Association conference, Nov. 8, 1992, by Jean Attie, Charlotte Emans Moore, and Elizabeth Kornhauser; Debra Gold Hansen, *Strained Sisterhood: Gender and Class in the Boston Female Anti-Slavery Society* (Amherst: Univ. of Massachusetts Press, 1993); Lee Chambers-Schiller, "'A Good Work Among the People': The Political Culture of the Boston Antislavery Fair," in *The Abolitionist Sisterhood: Women's Political Culture in Antebellum America*, ed. Jean Fagin Yellin and John C. Van Horne (Ithaca: Cornell Univ. Press, 1994); William D. Moore, "Funding the Temples of Masculinity: Women's Roles in Masonic Fairs in New York State, 1870–1930," *Nineteenth Century* 14, no. 1 (1994): 19–25; Barbara Kirshenblatt-Gimblett, "The Moral Sublime: The Temple Emanuel Fair and its Cookbook, Denver, 1888," *Rocky Mountain Jewish*

Historical Notes 13, nos. 1/2 (Spring/Summer 1995): 1–7. There has been consideration of the English fundraising fair, although again only selected aspects are addressed. In *Women and Philanthropy in Nineteenth Century England* (New York: Oxford Univ. Press, 1980), Frank Prochaska provides an excellent summation of the financial and social contribution of the English bazaar, but he does not examine the qualitative experience of the event. Analysis of men's responses to charitable fairs also appears in Gary R. Dyer, "The 'Vanity Fair' of Nineteenth Century England: Commerce, Women, and the East in the Ladies' Bazaar," *Nineteenth Century Literature* 46, no. 2 (Sept. 1991): 196–222.

5. For example, see Robert W. Rydell, *All the World's a Fair: Visions of Empire at American International Expositions, 1876–1916* (Chicago: Univ. of Chicago Press, 1984); Karal Ann Marling, *Blue Ribbon: A Social and Pictorial History of the Minnesota State Fair* (St. Paul: Minnesota Historical Society Press, 1990); Leslie Prosterman, "The Aspect of the Fair: Aesthetics and Festival in Illinois County Fairs" (Ph.D. diss., Univ. of Pennsylvania, 1982).

6. Germaine Greer, *The Obstacle Race: The Fortunes of Women Painters and Their Work* (New York: Farrar, Strauss, and Giroux, 1979).

7. Undue credit was given to men in many different eras. Men's contributions were highly touted during the Civil War, at the end of the nineteenth century, and even in the 1950s and 1960s. Specific instances of this kind of activity are discussed in the ensuing chapters.

8. One serious omission in my discussion of fairs is a thorough treatment of their foodways. This represents another, equally important dimension of the fair, as well as an important part of the background history I have been discussing, but it is largely outside my area of expertise and I did not originally set out to include it. I have been unable to give foodway practices the full treatment they deserve.

9. See note 4. The work on abolitionist and Masonic fairs came out in print in 1993 and 1994.

10. Jules David Prown, "Mind in Matter: An Introduction to Material Culture Theory and Method," *Winterthur Portfolio* 17, no. 1 (1982): 1–19; Katherine C. Grier, *Culture and Comfort: People, Parlors and Upholstery 1850–1930* (Rochester, New York: Strong Museum, 1988); Kenneth Ames, *Death in the Dining Room and Other Tales of Victorian Culture* (Philadelphia: Temple Univ. Press, 1992).

11. J. Huizinga, *Homo Ludens: A Study of the Play-Element in Culture,* trans. R. F. C. Hall (London: Routledge and Kegan Paul, 1949 [orig. German edition 1944]), 5, 173; Ellen Dissanayake, *Homo Aestheticus: Where Art Comes From and Why* (New York: Free Press [Macmillan], 1992); Yi-Fu Tuan, *Passing Strange and Wonderful: Aesthetics, Nature and Culture* (Washington, D.C.: Island Press, 1993); Michael Owen Jones, *Exploring Folk Art: Twenty Years of Thought on Craft, Work and Aesthetics* (Ann Arbor: UMI Research Press, 1987), esp. 169, 173; Thomas Moore, *The Re-Enchantment of Everyday Life* (New York: Harper Collins, 1996), ix.

12. I know of no one who has specifically addressed the topic of aesthetic meaning in women's lives other than myself and one of my close colleagues. Joy H. Dohr spoke to the issue in a paper entitled "A Framework for Examining Aesthetic Meaning in Women's Lives," presented at Univ. of Wisconsin–System Women's Studies Conference, Oshkosh, Sept. 1986. I developed the ideas in one of my earliest examinations of the fundraising fair, "Aesthetic Meanings in Women's Turn-of-the-Century Fundraising Fairs," *Turn-of-the-Century Women* 3, no. 1 (Summer 1986): 15–28. I suggest this kind of analysis of aesthetic meaning may be considered a potentially important tool for the study of women's history.

13. For a good overview and discussion of relational theory, see Christina Robb, "A Theory of Empathy," *Boston Globe Magazine* Oct. 16, 1988. Primary sources include the following: Jean Baker Miller, *Toward a New Psychology of Women* (Boston: Beacon Press, 1976); Carol Gilligan, *In a Different Voice: Psychological Theory and Women's Development* (Cambridge: Harvard Univ. Press, 1982); and Mary Field Belenky et al., *Women's Way of Knowing* (New York: Basic Books, 1986).

14. Barbara Leslie Epstein, *The Politics of Domesticity: Women, Evangelism and Temperance in Nineteenth Century America* (Middletown, Conn.: Wesleyan Univ. Press, 1981); Mary P. Ryan, *Women in Public: Between Banners and Ballots, 1825–1880* (Baltimore: Johns Hopkins Univ. Press, 1990); Nancy F. Cott, *The Grounding of Modern Feminism* (New Haven: Yale Univ. Press, 1987); Karen J. Blair, *The Clubwoman as Feminist: True Womanhood Redefined, 1868–1914* (New York: Holmes and Meier, 1980);

Karen J. Blair, *The Torchbearers: Women and Their Amateur Arts Associations in America, 1890–1930* (Bloomington: Indiana Univ. Press, 1994); Kathleen McCarthy, *Women's Culture: American Philanthropy and Art, 1830–1930* (Chicago: Univ. of Chicago Press, 1991).

15. William Leach, *Land of Desire: Merchants, Power and the Rise of a New American Culture* (New York: Pantheon, 1993); T. Jackson Lears, "Beyond Veblen: Rethinking Consumer Culture," in *Consuming Visions: Accumulation and Display of Goods in America 1880–1920*, ed. Simon J. Bronner (New York: W. W. Norton [for Winterthur Museum], 1989); Richard Wightman Fox and T. J. Jackson Lears, eds., *The Culture of Consumption: Critical Essays in American History 1880–1980* (New York: Pantheon, 1983).

One. The Many Meanings of the Fundraising Fair and an Overview of Its Development

1. Peter Stallybrass and Allon White, *The Politics and Poetics of Transgression* (Ithaca: Cornell Univ. Press, 1986), 18–43.

2. The realities of the Eastern bazaar have little bearing on this perception. Especially ironic in the Western fantasy is the sense that sensual women—odalisques—are waiting to lure the unsuspecting man. Women were rarely even allowed in the public spaces of the Near Eastern bazaar, and women associated with royal harems were literally prisoners of the men who "owned" them.

3. Donald Smalley, ed., introduction to Frances Trollope, *The Domestic Manners of the Americans* (New York: Vintage Books, 1966), xli–xlv. Several scholars have explored the exciting late-nineteenth-century bazaar-like markets and their role in the development of a consumer culture based on a sense of restlessness, longing, and wish-fulfillment. See the discussion of the bazaar in Lears, "Beyond Veblen," 73–88.

4. There were also a handful of men working at charitable bazaars. Joseph Nightingale, an 1816 observer, counted two who worked alongside their wives at Soho (this was out of a total of two hundred salespeople). An 1818 account listed six men: a jeweler, watchmaker, gunsmith, hatter, and shoemaker. See Joseph Nightingale, *The Bazaar: Its Origin, nature and objects explained, and recommended as an important branch of political economy* (reprint of letter to Hon. George Rose, M.P., May 4, 1816) (London: Davies, Michael & Hudson, 1816); *A Visit to the Bazaar* (London: J. Harris, 1818; facsimile edition published as part of the Osborne Collection of Early Children's Books, Toronto, London and Sydney: The Bodley Head, 1981); Dyer, "Vanity Fair," 208–10.

5. Dyer, "Vanity Fair," 201, 203. Dyer also claims the upper class feared the potentially polluting effects of mixing with the poor. Significantly, Nightingale's *The Bazaar* was an attempt to both defend the respectability of Trotter's bazaar and to argue its economic benefit to England.

6. Dyer, "Vanity Fair," 205. The institution did have considerable traffic: Nightingale estimated there were about 2,500 visitors a day (*The Bazaar*, 16).

7. See Prochaska, *Women and Philanthropy*, 48–49; *A Visit to the Bazaar*.

8. Actually Dyer conflates three types of bazaars: the charitable/commercial establishments; the strictly commercial establishments, like Frances Trollope's; and the temporary women's sales or fairs.

9. Dyer, "Vanity Fair," 208, 213. Leach, *Land of Desire*, 104–10, also discusses attitudes towards the bazaar.

10. Hansen, *Strained Sisterhood*, cites the antebellum reformers and does not question the distinction.

11. *Harper's Bazar* [sic], Nov. 2, 1867, 2. Here and throughout, I am rendering the spelling as "Bazar" when it originally appeared that way.

12. Lears, "Beyond Veblen," 87–88.

13. Mary Elizabeth Maxwell Braddon, *Like and Unlike* (London: Simpkin, Marshall, 1887), 150.

14. In some cases, the women's domestic labor may not have been their own. Lee Ann Whites documents a time when the women at an Augusta, Georgia, fair served a hot supper that was actually prepared by their servants. It is unclear how common this practice was. Because both the servants and the fairgivers were women, however, it does not affect the argument about gender. See Whites, "The

Charitable and the Poor: The Emergence of Domestic Politics in Augusta, Georgia, 1860–1880," *Journal of Social History* 17 (Summer 1984): 601–16.

15. Ryan, *Women in Public*, 39.

16. There are numerous examples of this phenomenon, and many scholars have addressed the topic. One good study is Kathleen D. McCarthy, ed., *Lady Bountiful Revisited: Women, Philanthropy and Power* (New Brunswick, N.J.: Rutgers Univ. Press, 1990). McCarthy argues that charity and reform associations gave women a point of access to public roles.

17. McCarthy, *Women's Culture*, 23. In *West of Everything: The Inner Life of Westerns* (New York: Oxford Univ. Press, 1992), Jane Tompkins provides a compelling explanation of the appeal of the twentieth-century American western that also casts light on the dismissal of the bazaar. She argues that the western, which men identify with strongly, valorizes the quality of living on the edge and facing life-and-death choices that are a test of will and strength. This quality is contrasted with the quality in activities like shopping, which are repetitive and "secondary."

18. See Kenneth Luckhurst, *The Story of Exhibitions* (London and New York: Studio Publications, 1951), 12; Robert Chambers, *Chamber's Journal*, Aug. 6, 1887, 497. Note that the Soho Bazaar was also set up in this same manner of streetlike rows of booths.

19. See Prochaska, *Women and Philanthropy*, 49–50. Margaret Andere, in *Old Time Tools and Toys of Needlework* (reprinted as *Old Needlework Boxes and Tools: Their Story and How the Collect Them* [New York: Drake, 1971]), makes the assertion about the earlier date (see p. 69). This is impossible to confirm, however, and because Prochaska has done a thorough literature search and comes up with the nineteenth-century time frame, it is reasonable to conclude that her date is too early.

20. Luckhurst, *Story of Exhibitions*, 12; Lawrence Blair, *English Church Ales With a Note on Church Fairs* (Ann Arbor, Mich.: Edwards Brothers, 1940), 1–27; Chambers, *Chamber's Journal*, 497.

21. Wayne Caldwell Neely, *The Agricultural Fair* (New York: Columbia Univ. Press, 1935), 21, 20, 89. See also Luckhurst, *Story of Exhibitions*; Colin Simkin, *Fairs Past and Present* (Hartford: The Travelers, 1939); Helen Augur, *The Book of Fairs* (New York: Harcourt, Brace, 1939), 245; "Notice on Cattle Show and Fair," *Northampton Democrat*, Sept. 26, 1843; *Hampshire Gazette*, Oct. 6, 1850.

22. Prochaska claims that the English "exported" the fundraising fair to North America and other parts of the world (*Women and Philanthropy*, 56). Since in places like Africa and India the events were held by Englishwomen who were there as officer's wives or missionaries, colonial fairs probably did not have much local leadership or flavor. American fairs, on the other hand, evolved independently.

23. This characterization is based particularly on a profile of the women who organized early fairs in Northampton and on the profile of the abolitionist fairgivers provided by Lee Chambers-Schiller and Debra Hansen (see chap. 2). Mary P. Ryan further clarifies that most members of antebellum female charity associations were wives and daughters of the prosperous and professional (*Womanhood in America: French Colonial Times to the Present* [New York: Franklin Watts, 1983], 151). Nancy Hewitt observed that the elite men in Rochester, New York, even helped provide their family members with legitimacy by donating space in public buildings for their fundraising events and exhibitions. See *Women's Activism and Social Change: Rochester, New York, 1822–1872* (Ithaca: Cornell Univ. Press, 1984), 50–51.

24. Hewitt explains that by the 1850s there was a shift in basic thinking about benevolence work (*Women's Activism*, 149). Reformers were typically less concerned with perfectionism and more with amelioration and prevention of specific, local problems. This made participation possible even for women who had formerly been hesitant.

25. This phrase was used by Rebecca Gratz, who was working for a fair for a Jewish Home in Philadelphia. See David Philipson, ed., *Letters of Rebecca Gratz* (New York: Jewish Publication Society, 1929; reprint, Arno Press, 1975), 407–8. The comment about temperance is based on Ruth M. Alexander, "We Are Engaged as a Band of Sisters: Class and Domesticity in the Washingtonian Temperance Movement 1840–1850," *Journal of American History* 75, no. 3 (Dec. 1988): 763–85. For black women's fairs, see Dorothy Sterling, ed., *We Are Your Sisters: Black Women in the Nineteenth Century* (New York: W. W. Norton, 1984), 114–24.

26. L. P. Brockett and Mary C. Vaughn, *Woman's Work in the Civil War: A Record of Heroism, Patriotism and Patience* (Philadelphia: Zeigler, McCurdy, 1867), 67. See also Barbara Berg, *The Remembered Gate: Origins of American Feminism: The Woman and the City, 1800–1860* (New York: Oxford Univ. Press, 1978), 150–69. The conversion from 1860s dollars to today's is based on tables in Scott Derks, ed., *The Value of a Dollar: Prices and Income in the United States* (Detroit: Gale Research, 1994), esp. 2.

27. Abba Gould Woolson, "Charitable Fairs," in *Woman in American Society* (Boston: Roberts Brothers, 1873), 143–45.

28. Several scholars have previously shown that women were able to use and reinforce domestic values after the war, but pushed them in new directions related to health and general welfare. Ruth Bordin concluded that women were drawn to the 1873 temperance crusade because it corroborated the values of "true womanhood" and the ideology that woman's place was in the home, but gave them an external, public forum for their ideas. Lee Ann Whites found that women in Augusta, Georgia, were similarly able to bring many parts of their formerly private domestic lives into the public arena in the 1870s. Anne Firor Scott explained that in the postwar period women's voluntary associations were able to greatly expand in both religious and secular directions. See Bordin, "A Baptism of Power and Liberty! The Woman's Crusade of 1873–1874," in *Woman's Being, Woman's Place: Female Identity and Vocation in American History*, Mary Kelley, ed. (Boston: G. K. Hall, 1979), 287–90; Whites, "The Charitable and the Poor"; Scott, "Women's Voluntary Associations: From Charity to Reform, in *Lady Bountiful*, 35–46.

29. Charlotte M. Yonge, in her novel *The Long Vacation* (New York: Macmillan, 1895), noted that fairs had "advanced since their early days, from being simply sales to the [current] grand period of ornaments, costumes, and anything to attract" (182).

30. A similar observation was made by Susan G. Davis about the evolution of the public parade in nineteenth-century Philadelphia. Parades and ceremonies had been largely noncommercial, community events in the antebellum period, she maintains, but commercial traditions, tied to new patterns of consumption and advertising, developed after the Civil War. Department stores sponsored parades in the latter part of the century, further mixing the traditions of ceremony, commerce, and spectacle. See *Parades and Power: Street Theatre in Nineteenth Century Philadelphia* (Philadelphia: Temple Univ. Press, 1986), 17–18, 170.

31. Woolson, "Charitable Fairs," 143–45. For commentary on women's role in public life, see Christine Stansell, "Women, Children and the Uses of the Streets: Class and Gender Conflict in New York City, 1850–1860," in *Women's America: Refocusing the Past*, ed. Linda Kerber and Jane DeHart-Mathews (New York: Oxford Univ. Press, 1987), 94; Ryan, *Women in Public*, 182–83; Lynn Weiner, *From Working Girl to Working Mother: The Female Labor Force in the United States 1820–1980* (Chapel Hill: Univ. of North Carolina Press, 1985), 3; Ann Douglas, *The Feminization of American Culture* (New York: Avon Books, 1977), 169. For criticism of women's wheedling, see Robert Louis Stevenson, "The Charity Bazaar: An Allegorical Dialogue," in *Letters and Miscellanies of Robert Louis Stevenson: Sketches, Criticisms, etc.* (New York: Charles Scribners, 1898), 603–5.

32. A popular *Ladies' Home Journal* column that regularly featured reports about successful fairs was tellingly called "The Minister's Social Helper."

33. A new publication, inaugurated in the 1890s and aimed especially at the clergy, was called *The Monthly Social*. For discussion of the sociability of the church, see Alfred E. Myers, *The Sociable, the Entertainment and the Bazaar: A Discussion of Church Customs* (Philadelphia: Presbyterian Board of Publications, 1882); Ian Maclaren, "The Candy-Pull System of the Church," *Ladies' Home Journal*, Oct. 1899, 19; William Bayard Hale, "A Study of Church Entertainments," *The Forum*, Jan. 1896, 576; William Bayard Hale, "Another Year of Church Entertainments," *The Forum*, Dec. 1896, 396–405. For the increasing importance of packaged amusement, see Rossiter Johnson, ed., *A History of the World's Columbian Exposition* (New York: D. Appleton, 1898); John F. Kasson, *Amusing the Million: Coney Island at the Turn of the Century* (New York: Hill and Wang, 1978); Neil Harris, "Museums, Merchandising and Popular Taste: The Struggle for Influence," in *Material Culture and the Study of American Life*, ed. Ian M. J. Quimby (New York: W. W. Norton, 1978).

34. Lina Beard and Adelia B. Beard, *The American Girls' Handy Book: How to Amuse Yourself and Others* (New York: Charles Scribner's Sons, 1893).

35. Leonore Davidhoff, *The Best Circles: Society, Etiquette and the Season* (Totowa, N.J.: Rowman and Littlefield, 1973), 56–57; Janet Gordon and Diana Reische, *The Volunteer Powerhouse: The Junior League* (New York: Rutledge Press, 1982), esp. 31–47; Doris Gold, "Women and Voluntarism," in *Woman in Sexist Society: Studies in Power and Powerlessness,* ed. Vivian Gornick and Barbara K. Moran (New York: Basic Books, 1971), 384–400.

36. This was seen most dramatically in the case of Bertha Palmer, manager of the Woman's Building at the Columbian Exposition in Chicago in 1893. Palmer, the wife of a wealthy industrialist, was the reigning "queen" of the city. In order to raise money for the underfunded Woman's Building and its auxiliary, the Children's Building, Palmer held a fundraising fair at her home. The public jumped at the opportunity to see her famous house, and the fair was a phenomenal success. Proceeds for the three-day event were over $48,000, with $14,000 coming from admission fees alone on the final day. See Weimann, *Fair Women,* 333.

37. For the Festa, see *New York Times,* June 3–11, 1917. The information on the Atlantic City Boardwalk is gleaned primarily from the scrapbooks of Marietta Pratt, the organizer of the Boston event. Pratt's papers are housed in the Archives of the Schlesinger Library at Radcliffe College. See also Sophronisba P. Breckinridge, *Women in the Twentieth Century: A Study of Their Political, Social and Economic Activities* (New York: McGraw Hill, 1933; reprint, Arno Press, 1972), 37.

38. One exception to this is that there were fairs sponsored by members of labor organizing groups. However, these seem to have been strictly "in-house" affairs that were put on for the group's own membership rather than for the public at large. See chap. 6 for details.

39. The association with the working class may also be related to the fact that Catholics were especially likely to sponsor church fairs, even during the Depression. Many parishes had predominantly working-class constituencies.

40. The "Chairman" of the Ways and Means Committee of the hypothetical woman's club discussed in an article in 1940 was "distracted," but with the advice of the magazine, she might calm down. In 1941 the magazine referred to the reader as "my little diplomat." Women were told to stand firm in arrangements with businessmen; a hotel manager would be likely to think women "fussy," but could be won over. See Harriet R. Curtis, "And One for You," *American Home,* Sept. 1940, 31, 85; "This Month It's Raising Money for a Cause," *American Home,* May 1941, 14–21; Jean Cowles, "Make Your Church Bazaar a Huge Success," *American Home,* Aug. 1945, 70–72.

41. Better Homes and Gardens, *Country Bazaar Crafts* (Des Moines, Iowa: Meredith, 1986); *McCall's Big Book of Bazaar Crafts* (Radnor, Pa.: Chilton Books, 1984). Lesley Linsley, the author of *The Great Bazaar,* even addressed her reader as "dear craftworker." (New York: Delacorte Press, 1981), 174.

42. I am aware of the irony inherent in this word; although I am talking primarily about women and a woman-dominated institution, I am using a term based on male bonding. The only term I could think to substitute, however, is "sisterhood," which has a much more specific meaning, and which I use in more precise contexts throughout the text.

43. Chapman cited in Ronald G. Walters, *The Anti-Slavery Appeal: American Abolitionism After 1830* (Baltimore: Johns Hopkins Univ. Press, 1976), 24; Mary Lowe Dickinson, ("Pro" position on bazaar), "The Pro and Con of the Church Supper, Bazar, and Fair," *Chataquan,* Nov. 1890, 229–30; Mrs. James Anthony, "A Defense of Church Bazaars," *Homiletic Review,* Nov. 1924, 380–81.
It is noteworthy that commentators on world and state fairs continually stressed this same point. See Melton A. McLaurin, "The Nineteenth Century North Carolina State Fair as a Social Institution," *North Carolina History Review* 59 (July 1982): 213–29; "Point of View," *Scribner's,* Oct. 1914, 552–53; Elsie Singmaster, "Big Thursday," *Century Magazine,* Jan. 1906, 364–79; "The Country Fair as an Exhibition Center: The Story of One Held in a New England Village Street," *Craftsman,* Sept. 1911, 581; Mary A. Whedon, "State Fairs: Intelligent Promoters of the Various Interests of Rural Women: Outlets for Their Activities and Meeting Grounds for Social Intercourse," *Craftsman* 25 (Oct. 1913): 86–91; John R. Christiansen, Hans C. Groot, and Donald E. Johnson, *Wisconsin County and District*

Fair Study, Preliminary Report 1: *Background of the Study* (Madison: Center of Applied Sociology, Univ. of Wisconsin Cooperative Extension, 1971), 20.

44. Interviews with Hazel Talbot, Madison, Wisconsin, Sept. 1987; Georgeanne Cusick, Madison, Wisconsin, Aug. 1986; Eileen Pickett, Madison, Wisconsin, Oct. 1986; Dorothea Britton, Scarsdale, New York, Dec. 1986. Unless otherwise noted, all interviews were conducted by the author.

45. A similar conclusion was reached about the meaning of American civic pageants in the early twentieth century. Naina Prevots talks about the pageant as emphasizing process as much as product, and about the ways a community might bond together through such an endeavor. See *American Pageantry: A Movement for Art and Democracy* (Ann Arbor: UMI Research Press, 1990), 1, 13.

46. Sometimes groups even evolve special items that become identified with them. In Madison, for example, one church had great success with the sale of a toy designed by a community member. The "Drummer Boy" had been featured at the annual fair for several years and had become so popular that numerous people were put to work making enough to meet the demand. In 1986 thirty toys were sold within seven minutes of the opening of the bazaar, even with a thirty-dollar price tag. The Drummer Boy became the symbol of the bazaar. It was featured on local television when a sample was donated to the auction of the public station, and its image was used as the logo for all fair publicity. A Minneapolis church group was impressed enough to write and ask for the pattern, but the Madison group decided not to share it. Interview with Eileen Pickett.

47. Ryan argues that women first developed their own public rituals by the middle of the nineteenth century; she notes they claimed the winter holidays as their own. This is congruent with the developments of the fundraising fair (*Women in Public,* 39–40).

48. See Alessandro Falassi, *Time Out of Time: Essays on the Festival* (Albuquerque: Univ. of New Mexico Press, 1987), 3–6. Mary Grew is cited in Walters, *Anti-Slavery Appeal,* 24.

49. It is relevant that admission fees to fairs seem to have generally been disbanded by the turn of the century, when other forms of mass entertainment were more generally available. Ten-cent admission tickets were still typical in the late nineteenth century (see, for example, the *Baltimore Morning Sun,* Dec. 10, 1870; Dec. 12, 1870), but after that time, admission was only likely to be charged for specific attractions, if at all.

50. *Balloon Post* (Newspaper for the Fair to End the Suffering in France, Boston), Apr. 13, 1871, 6.

51. "Annual Bazaar Held," *Los Angeles Examiner,* Nov. 30, 1913; "Railroad Men's Fair," *Hampshire Gazette,* Apr. 9, 1895; Mary Dawson, "An Operatic Bazaar," *The Ladies World,* May 1911, 25; specific references to dances include: "Crowd at Hero Land Breaks All Records," *New York Times,* Nov. 30, 1917; "Red Cross Bazaar," *Wisconsin State Journal,* Dec. 15, 1917.

52. Souvenir Program distributed at the St. Barnabas Hospital Fair, Essex County, New Jersey, Dec. 1908; *Woman's Journal,* Dec. 18, 1909, 205.

53. At Charlton Fair, patrons dressed in horned headdresses and clothes of the opposite sex. See Luckhurst, *Story of Exhibitions,* 13; Edo McCullough, *World's Fairs Midways* (Carnivaland Enterprises, 1966; reprint, Arno, 1976), 18; Simkin, *Fairs Past and Present,* 14; Samuel McKechnie, *Popular Entertainment Through the Ages* (London: Sampson, Low, Marstone, 1932), 31.

54. On "author's carnivals" see Ellye Howell Glover, *Dame Curtsey's Book of Party Pastimes for the Up-to-Date Hostess* (Chicago: A. C. McClurg, 1912; reprint, 1921), 14–16; Blair, "What to Do for the Fair," *The Delineator,* Feb. 1894, 173; Alma E. Fowler, "The Fete of the Heroines," in "Planning the Church Fair," *Ladies' Home Journal,* Sept. 1903, 34; "An Author's Carnival, *New York Times,* Dec. 10, 1890; Kate Douglas Wiggin, "How We Attracted 2,000 People to a Country Fair," *Ladies' Home Journal,* July 1912, 15. Helen Hoover Santmeyer reminisced in *Ohio Town* (New York: Berkley Books, 1985; orig. ed., Columbus: Ohio State Univ. Press, 1956), 216. Note that actual literary figures were also sometimes heralded as fair attractions, much as popular entertainers might be; autograph signings featuring authors such as Nathaniel Hawthorne (1865) and Kate Wiggin (1910) were noted in fair publicity.

55. See Karen Halttunen, *Confidence Men and Painted Women: A Study of Middle Class Culture in America 1830–1870* (New Haven: Yale Univ. Press, 1982); Blair, *The Torchbearers,* esp. chaps. 3, 6.

56. In her semiotic analysis of the institution of the quilting bee, Susan Roach showed how the bee became a kind of holiday occasion that ritually drew the quilting group together. See "The Kinship Quilt: An Ethnographic Semiotic Analysis of a Quilting Bee," in Rosan A. Jordan and Susan J. Kalcik, *Women's Folklore, Women's Culture* (Philadelphia: Univ. of Pennsylvania Press, 1976), 59.

57. Ellen Dissanayake, *What Is Art For?* (Seattle: Univ. of Washington Press, 1988), 78–92.

58. Santmeyer, *Ohio Town,* 215–16.

59. Interviews with Evelyn Huggins, Dorothea Britton, Ethel Huiskamp; Maude Ward Elliot, *Memories of the Civil War, 1861–1864* (Boston: privately printed for the Red Cross, 1945). (Manuscript in the Massachusetts Historical Society Archives.)

60. Caroline French Benton even suggested that a small boy might sit inside the windmill booth to turn the blades. See *Fairs and Fetes* (Boston: Dana Estes, 1912), 101.

61. For examples of stimulating environments of this type, see Theresa Wolcott, "Fair of the Good Fairies: A New Idea in Church Bazaars," *Ladies' Home Journal,* Oct. 1916, 28; Margaret Nourse, "Suggestions for Fairs," *The Delineator,* Feb. 1895, 266; Caroline Benedict Burrell, "Church Fairs," *Harper's Bazar,* Aug. 1905, 772–75; "In a Pink Bower," *New York Times,* Dec. 11, 1890; "To Be the Finest Fair," *New York Times,* Jan. 28, 1889; *Wisconsin State Journal,* Jan. 21, 1895; "Twenty New Ideas for Church Fairs," *Ladies' Home Journal,* Nov. 1903, 34; Theresa H. Wolcott, "Eight New Fair Booths," *Ladies' Home Journal,* Nov. 1904, 27.

62. Margaret Mitchell, *Gone With the Wind* (New York: Macmillan, 1936), 66. The scene is set, of course, in the 1860s rather than the 1930s, but Mitchell must have had enough of an experience of the smells of the fair to include it in her novel.

63. "Fancy Fairs and Bazaars," *The Delineator,* July 1889, 59. Perfume booths were especially common from about 1900 to 1930.

64. "Church Bazaars for Eastertime," *Ladies' Home Journal,* Apr. 1904, 49.

65. In *Women in Public* (44–66), Ryan identified a mid-nineteenth-century trend whereby the physical attractions of the daughters and wives of prominent male citizens were exhibited in increasingly scant attire. Susan G. Davis also referred to the temporary breakdown of social boundaries provided by humorous costume and makeup in *Parades and Power: Street Theatre in Nineteenth Century Philadelphia* (Philadelphia: Temple Univ. Press, 1986), 161. A concise review of the influence of clothing and accustomed role or behavior is provided in Susan B. Kaiser, *The Social Psychology of Clothing and Personal Adornment* (New York: Macmillan, 1985), 125–53.

66. James M. Barrie, "Bazaars," in *Potpourri: Gifts Literary and Artistic, Contributed as a Souvenir of the Grand Masonic Bazaar in Aid of the Annuity Fund of Scottish Masonic Benevolence,* ed. W. Grant Stevenson (Edinburgh, 1890), 95–98.

67. In her study *American Pageantry,* Prevots argues that the grassroots desire to "make art" can be traced throughout the twentieth century. My argument is of course that this desire can be documented long before this.

68. "Seaside Booth," *Harper's Bazar,* Aug. 1892, G59.

69. Alice Meredith, *Godey's Lady's Book,* Aug. 1875.

70. Dissanayake, *What Is Art For?* 84; *Wisconsin State Journal,* July 11, 1915, 5. Note that Huizinga (*Homo Ludens,* 128–29) also talks about poetry as play.

71. *The Oxford English Dictionary* (New York: Clarendon Press 1933; reprint, 1961) 4, 60–62, lists several definitions for *fancy* that clarify some of its underlying meanings or associations. The first is a "fantasy or mental conception, an illusion of the senses or a hallucination"; in early use, the term was synonymous with *imagination.* It is also defined as a whim or supposition resting on no solid ground; as something that pleases or entertains; an invention, and as something "bred" or made into a more beautiful form. Something "fancied" to be like something else, lastly, is something that is transformed. I have addressed the meanings of fancywork and its elements of masquerade and transformation in my article, "Victorian Fancywork in the American Home: Fantasy and Accommodation," in *Making the American Home: Women and Domestic Material Culture, 1840–1940,* ed. Marilyn Ferris Motz and Pat B. Browne (Bowling Green, Ohio: Bowling Green State Univ. Popular Press, 1988), 48–68.

72. "Some Hints for Charity Fairs," *Harper's Bazar,* Dec. 13, 1879, 790–91; "A Carnival of Mimic Commerce," *New York Times,* Dec. 16, 1884; "Newspaper Men Banqueted by Officers of Masonic Fair," *Atlanta Constitution,* Dec. 16, 1900; "Fifth Regiment Fair," *New York Times,* Dec. 21, 1880; "Hebrew Fair," *New York Times,* Dec. 12, 1880. Jane Przybysz comments in "Quilts, Old Kitchens and the Social Geography of Gender," unpubl. ms prepared for the Nov. 1989 Winterthur Museum (Wilmington, Del.) conference, *The Material Culture of Gender/The Gender of Material Culture,* that playacting with "uncouth" speech at theatrical enactments at fairs was "likely to have contributed to the spirit of play and communitas."

73. Helena Smith Dayton and Louise Bascom Barratt, *The Book of Entertainments and Theatricals* (New York: Robert M. McBride, 1924), 126; Dorothea Britton, "Peeking Through the Holly—or Thirty Tears of Christmas Nonsense," flyer distributed to author's bazaar workshop participants, n.d. (1970s). Britton's associational process is a classic example of the kind of free-form thinking that is characteristic of creativity.

74. An excellent discussion of the art hierarchy is found in Roszika Parker and Griselda Pollock, *Old Mistresses: Women, Art and Ideology* (New York: Pantheon Books, 1981), esp. chap. 4. The impact that a well-designed needlework piece might have was summarized by Patricia Mainardi. Good needleworkers were "known throughout their area, fine craftswomanship and design influenced other women who returned home stimulated, . . . and [design] ideas were disseminated from one area to another" ("Quilts: The Great American Art," *Feminist Art Journal* [Winter 1973]: 3).

75. *The Craftsman,* the acknowledged mouthpiece of the Arts and Crafts movement in the United States, ran an article on the fair as an exhibition center for women's art and craft work in 1916. In "Women's Interests at the Country Fair," an article in the Canadian magazine *The Farmer's Advocate* (Feb. 18, 1926), author Ethel M. Chapman mentioned how women were attracted to the sewing and fancy work: "We walk around and 'take notes' of the way other women do things, and examine closely some piece of handiwork with a view to future activities" (236). For a discussion of women's work at agricultural fairs, see Marling, *Blue Ribbon,* esp. 64, 95, and Prosterman, "The Aspect of the Fair." For a discussion of women's work at international expositions, see Weimann, *Fair Women;* Darney, "Women and World's Fairs." See also Barbara Brackman, "Fairs and Expositions: Their Influence on American Quilts," in *Bits and Pieces: Textile Traditions,* ed. Jeanette Lasansky (Lewisburg, Pa.: Oral Traditions [Union County Historical Society], 1991).

76. Nourse, "Suggestions for Fairs," 264.

77. Shirley Dare, *Art Amateur* commentary reprinted in *The Knapsack,* Dec. 4, 1879. See Helen Kenney, "Church Fair Booths," *Harper's Bazar,* Dec. 1911, 561; Mary Dawson, "A Wonderland Bazaar," *Ladies' World,* May 1911, 25. I have seen references to ceramic pieces from the Rookwood and Marblehead Potteries and for crewelwork from the Deerfield Blue and White Society. See "Fair for Kossuth Monument," *New York Times,* Feb. 10, 1894; "Nu Gamma Chi Fair," *Hampshire Gazette,* Dec. 14, 1909.

78. Bulletin, Temple Beth-El, Madison, Wisconsin, 1952 (month unclear). Archives, State Historical Society of Wisconsin.

79. *Balloon Post,* 6.

80. Ibid.

Two. The Tensions of the Antebellum Fair

1. The first epigraph that opens this chapter comes from the earliest detailed description I have found of an American fair.

2. *The Ladies Fair: A Poem in Aid of the Funds of the Ladies' Scrap Society of Christ Church, North Hempstead* (Brooklyn: By the Author, 1836); F. M. Adlington, untitled poem in *The Liberator,* Jan. 7, 1842, 3; *Northampton Courier,* Apr. 29, 1835; May 6, 1835.

3. While historians sometimes disagree about the ultimate meaning and repercussions the separate

sphere ideology had for women, most concur as to its general contours and pervasiveness. The classic work on the ideology of domesticity is Nancy F. Cott, *The Bonds of Womanhood: "Woman's Sphere" in New England, 1780–1835* (New Haven: Yale Univ. Press, 1977), 126–40. See also Epstein, *Politics of Domesticity,* esp. 4–5, 7, 67. Some of the controversy about the separate sphere ideology relates to Barbara Welter's argument that women's activities were guided by the precepts of the "cult of true womanhood" (see "The Cult of True Womanhood: 1820–1860," *American Quarterly* 18, no. 2 (Summer 1966): 151–74). One of the main critics of this argument, Frances B. Cogan, argues in *All American Girl: The Idea of Real Womanhood in Mid-Nineteenth Century America* (Athens: Univ. of Georgia Press, 1981) that competing ideals coexisted with the image of the fragile woman. Cogan does not dispute the principle of the separate spheres, however; her Real Woman specifically based her concept of self on the notion of a separate gender-determined role.

Cott argues that women turned to the church not only for religious reasons, but because through it they could experience a sense of community or sisterhood with one another and could exercise a range of moral, intellectual, and physical powers. The church became, in other words, a vehicle through which women could define and order their lives.

4. The idea that the fair was experienced as an entertainment is supported by the fact that the antebellum public was willing to pay an admission fee just to get into it. The Northampton Young Ladies' Benevolent Society charged twelve and one-half cents to adults who came to their 1831 fair, for example, and six and one-quarter cents to children. The same fees were charged ten years later. A fair in Richmond, Virginia, was more expensive: twenty-five cents was charged in 1831, and no reduced fee was listed for children. (*Northampton Courier,* Oct. 26, 1831; *Northampton Democrat,* Dec. 14, 1841; *Richmond Compiler,* Dec. 15, 1831).

5. The Baltimore fair is mentioned in Cutlip, *Fundraising in the United States,* 9; Sarah Josepha Hale, editorials in *The Ladies Magazine,* 1831; "Ladies Fair in Boston [from the *Boston Centinel*]," *Northampton Courier,* May 8, 1833; "Articles at the Fair [from the *Boston Advocate*]," *Northampton Courier,* May 22, 1833; "Ladies' Fair," *Northampton Courier,* Apr. 24, 1833. Note that "fashionable" had a different connotation in the United States than in England, where the queen's presence was not uncommon. See Prochaska, *Women and Philanthropy,* 50–51.

6. Review of "*An Address to the Citizens of Philadelphia on the Subject of Fancy Fairs*" (Philadelphia: M. Fithian, 1834). A scan of newspapers did not yield a single reference to a fair in the Charleston, South Carolina, newspapers in 1835 or in 1840. In a discussion in the *Richmond Compiler* (Dec. 15, 1831), the reporter defended the ladies of the Humane Association by referring to them as "most respectable" and wondering why anyone would object to an undertaking of this sort. See also *Baltimore Morning Sun,* Dec. 23, 1837.

7. The terms "fragment" and "scrap society" also have a Biblical origin, from the injunction to "gather fragments together." For information on benevolent and reform groups, see Ryan, *Womanhood in America,* 150; Mary Ryan, *Cradle of the Middle Class: The Family in Oneida County, New York, 1790–1865* (Cambridge: Cambridge Univ. Press, 1981), 53–54; Florence Hayes, *Daughters of Dorcas: The Story of the Work of Women for Home Missions Since 1802* (New York: Board of National Missions, Presbyterian Church, 1952); Marjorie Drake Ross, "A Brief History of the Fragment Society, 1812–1962," typescript, Forbes Library Collection, Northampton, Massachusetts, 2; Maria Kleinbund Baghdadi, "Protestants, Poverty and Urban Growth, New York and Boston, 1820–1865" (Ph.D. diss., Brown Univ., 1975), 101–6.

Society meetings had a social component that was sometimes criticized by outsiders—see Baghdadi, "Protestants, Poverty and Urban Growth," 104–6, and Frances Trollope, *Domestic Manners of the Americans* (1832; reprint ed. Michael Sadler, London: Billings and Sons, 1927), 240–41. However, they also did considerable work. For example, the Dorcas Society of the First Church of Northampton, founded in 1809, lists in its records dozens of sewing projects and large amounts of bedding and clothing distributed to local families and indigent women. See Josiah W. Parsons Jr., "Dorcas Society, 1809–1984—175 Years," typescript, Northampton Historical Society Archives, 2–3.

8. *The Liberator,* Nov. 22, 1834, 187; *Report of the Boston Female Anti-Slavery Society* (Boston, 1836), 77.

Lee Chambers-Schiller commented that sewing circles provided a kind of "captive audience for anti-slavery education." See "Good Work," 254.

9. *Northampton Courier,* Mar. 4, 1835; Catherine McCarthy, ed., *The Ladies Benevolent Society of the Church of Christ in Phillips Academy* (Andover, Mass.: Phillips Academy, 1961); *Northampton Democrat,* Dec. 14, 1841. The most common causes funded by the earliest fairs were education and bible societies, libraries, and institutes for the blind. It was not until 1841 that the Northampton papers listed the town "destitute" as recipients of fundraising fair proceeds. Unlike their counterparts in Britain, American fairs at this time did not generally fund church buildings. The Oxford Movement, initiated in 1833 to revitalize the Church of England, had stimulated the building of more beautiful and inspiring churches. Because building funds were needed in every local parish, this movement contributed to the proliferation of British fairs. (Bea Howe, *Antiques From the Victorian Home* [London: B. T. Batsford, 1973], 140). I have not investigated fairs in other European countries, but I know they did exist. My impression is that they were particularly vital in Germany, at least by the second half of the nineteenth century.

10. Ryan claims in *Womanhood in America,* 128, 150–53, that charity organizations could be found throughout the Ohio Valley, deep into Virginia, and as far west as Illinois by the 1840s. Charitable endeavors had become a strong enough component of the urban social system to offer women an almost "full-time career." Bostonian Susan Harrington, for example, belonged to seven different organizations, including a maternal association, an education society, and a group overseeing the Female Orphan Asylum. Even rural areas were well represented by benevolent organizations, as women everywhere found the "lady bountiful" role brought them a sense of self-importance, and their work with other women in voluntary organizations fostered a sense of sisterhood and community. See also Barbara Berg, *The Remembered Gate: Origins of American Feminism: The Woman and the City, 1800–1860* (New York: Oxford Univ. Press, 1978), 155, 224; and Blanche Glassman Hersh, *The Slavery of Sex: Feminist Abolitionists in America* (Urbana: Univ. of Illinois Press, 1978). On pp. 3–4 Hersh provides a cogent and concise summary of differing views of the relationship between the cult of true womanhood and moral reform work.

11. Trollope, *Domestic Manners,* 240–41.

12. Regarding the issue of class, see Stansell, "Women, Children and the Uses of the Streets," 133; Hewitt, *Women's Activism,* 39; Cogan, *All American Girl,* 13–14.

13. *Northampton Democrat,* Jan. 4, 1842; Thomas Wentworth Higginson, "Anti-Slavery Days," *Outlook,* Sept. 3, 1898, 52–53.

14. Catholics were to become very avid fairgivers, but most were new immigrants at this time and were not heavily involved before this date. One of the earliest references to Jewish fairs I have found comes from David Philipson, ed. *Letters of Rebecca Gratz* (New York: Jewish Publication Society, 1929; reprint, Arno Press, 1975).

15. *The Liberator,* Dec. 20, 1834, 203; Hewitt, *Women's Activism,* 42, 143. Note that the less reformist Ladies' Anti-Slavery Society was not interested in this kind of racial mixing. See ibid., 176.

16. Sterling, *We Are Your Sisters,* 114–24; Hewitt, *Women's Acitivism,* 42. The Orphan Asylum had been founded by white women, but it was the North Star Association that sponsored the fair and made the money to support it.

17. She introduced this term in "Women's Antislavery Activism in Rochester, New York," in *Women, Families, and Communities: Readings in American History,* 2 vols., ed. Nancy Hewitt (Glenview, Ill.: 1990), 1:151–53. It was subsequently adapted by Chambers-Schiller, "Good Work."

18. Chambers-Schiller, "Good Work," 252–53.

19. Hansen, *Strained Sisterhood,* 128–31. Chapman came from middle-class New England stock, but as a young woman lived with a wealthy English uncle and was well trained in cultural pursuits. Her husband was a merchant, although he was by no means conservative; he was the one who got her involved in the abolitionist cause. See Alma Lutz, entry on Chapman in *Notable American Women, 1607–1950: A Biographical Dictionary* (Cambridge, Mass.: Belknap Press, 1971), 1:324–25. Hewitt's analysis of the Rochester abolitionists also supports the class distinction and further illuminates the strategies

adopted by the two groups. She explains that the political suasionists came from urban merchant families, while the moral suasionists came from Quaker agricultural families ("Women's Antislavery Activism," 149–53). The agriculturalists were used to a system of seasonal cooperation among household members, but the capitalists were used to a strict division between men's and women's work.

20. Detailed descriptions of the contrasting fairs are provided in Hansen, *Strained Sisterhood*, and Chambers-Schiller, "Good Work."

21. Public spaces in Northampton ranged from an empty room above a downtown shop to the court room or town hall. In larger cities, public gathering places were used: examples are Faneuil Hall or the Armory in Boston and Samson Hall in Philadelphia. In her study of women's activism in Rochester, Hewitt noted that well-connected husbands sometimes facilitated the procurement of these spaces, seeing for example that the women could have a hall rent-free for the duration of a fair ("Women's Antislavery Activism," 50). It is unclear to me how often rental fees were necessary or waived. I have found references to fees in some cases, but I don't know if these are representative.

22. "Ladies' Fair in Boston," *Northampton Courier*, May 8, 1833; "Ladies' Fair," *Northampton Courier*, July 10, 1833; "Springfield Fair," *Northampton Courier*, May 8, 1833.

23. Maria Weston Chapman, "Sketches of the Fair: The Christmas Tree," *The Liberator*, Jan. 27, 1843, 15.

24. "Articles at the Fair," reprinted from the *Boston Advocate*, *Northampton Courier*, May 22, 1833.

25. Harvey Green, "Popular Science and Political Thought Converge: Colonial Survival Becomes Colonial Revival, 1830–1910," *Journal of American Culture* 6, no. 4 (1983): 4.

26. H. F., letter to William Schouler, from *The Lowell Journal*, Dec. 28, 1842, reprinted in *The Liberator*, Jan. 20, 1843, 7.

27. *Northampton Courier*, Jan. 8, 1846; "Paul Pry's First Epistle to his Country Friends About the Bazaar," [National Anti-Corn Law League] *Bazaar Gazette* no. 12: 5–6 and 16; "Grand Festival of the Buffalo Benevolent Association," *Frank Leslie's Illustrated Newspaper*, Feb. 26, 1860, 204; *Charleston Daily Courier*, Dec. 9, 1850.

28. H. F. letter to Schouler; Chapman, "The Eighth Massachusetts Fair"; Hewitt, *Women's Activism*, 251.

29. The earliest reference I have found to an auction is in *The Ladies Fair: A Poem In Aid of the Ladies' Scrap Society of Christ Church, North Hempstead, New York* (Brooklyn: F. G. Fish, 1836), excerpted in the sidebar at the beginning of this chapter. Auctions were somewhat controversial in later years, but there is no indication of controversy at this early date.

30. I have been unable to document dollar equivalencies for the 1830s, but an estimated or rough number is that this might buy about twenty times what it would buy today—i.e., $3,000 would be worth about $60,000.

31. *Northampton Courier*, Nov. 2, 1831; Nov. 3, 1830; May 8, 1833; July 10, 1833; May 7, 1834; Oct. 17, 1832; Sept. 9, 1835. The lack of precision or specificity in reported earnings was also true in England. Prochaska reports that small-scale country fairs were usually not advertised at all in the newspapers (word of mouth and posted notices were sufficient), and receipts of fairs were reported only sporadically at best. Only a very vague or rough estimate of the amount of money raised at the fairs could be calculated (*Women and Philanthropy*, 53–54).

32. *The Weal-Reaf: A Record of the Essex Institute Fair* (Salem, Mass.), Sept. 11, 1860, 49.

33. *The Ladies Fair: A Poem*.

34. "Old Maidish," *Northampton Courier*, Apr. 23, 1834; *The Ladies Fair*; "The Monument Fair;" H. F. letter to Schouler; Chapman, "The Eighth Massachusetts Fair;" *Boston Transcript*, Sept. 26, 1840. I have seen references to "Gentleman's Horror" exhibits beginning in 1840 and continuing throughout the century.

35. *Northampton Democrat*, Jan. 4, 1842.

36. It is possible, of course, that the young women did talk among themselves in this way. Most of the letters and commentary come from the fair organizers.

37. "The Monument Fair"; "To the Women of Great Britain," flyer announcing the National Anti-Corn-Law-League Bazaar, London, 1845; *Bazaar Gazette* no. 8, 2–3; *Northampton Courier*, June 6, 1843; Archibald Prentice, *History of the Anti-Corn Law League*, 2 vols. (London: W. and F. G. Cash, 1853; reprint, London: Frank Cass, 1968), 296–301.

38. The layout of the hall reflected the structural organization of the fair in a literal sense. The Charlestown table sat in the center under the rotunda, and the tables of the satellite communities ringed the hall. *Northampton Courier,* July 29, 1840; Aug. 18, 1840; Aug. 26, 1840.

39. In 1843 English contributions to the Philadelphia fair, including fancywork, clothing, drawings, and paintings, amounted to about $400 worth of goods. See N. Orwin Rush, "Lucretia Mott and the Philadelphia Antislavery Fairs," *Friends Historical Association Bulletin* 35 (Autumn 1946): 71; Kathryn Kish Sklar, "Doing the Nation's Work: Florence Kelley and Women's Political Culture, 1830–1930," typescript draft, chap. 2 of *Florence Kelley and the Nation's Work* (New Haven: Yale Univ. Press, 1995), 24–25.

40. This subject is addressed in Chambers-Schiller, "Good Work," 265. She also cites a similar observation in Suzanne Lebsock, *The Free Women of Petersburg: Status and Culture in a Southern Town, 1784–1860* (New York: Norton, 1984), 225–30.

41. Although it took place in Britain and is thus technically outside the parameters of this study, it is instructive to look at the organizational structure of the Anti-Corn-Law-League [Free Trade] Bazaar, held in 1845 in support of a political movement working to repeal grain taxes that favored landholders at the expense of the working people. The flyer announcing this event stated that the first organizational step was the formation in each town of a Ladies Local Committee which would communicate with a central council in London, but be responsible for its own table. A committee of men was to be formed in each community as well, and its major task would be to solicit contributions of fabrics that could be made into salable items by the women. The flyer was written by the male secretary of the organization, but he assured the women that it was other ladies who formed the central committee and suggested that women be called upon to help. See "To the Women of Great Britain"; *Bazaar Gazette* no. 8, 2–3; Prentice, *History of the Anti-Corn Law League,* 296–301.

42. The authors say the homes were nominally run by men, but day-to-day operations were taken care of by women. The men were relegated to legalistic audits, contracts and similar "limited if essential tasks." See Patricia Rook and R. L. Schnell, "The Rise and Decline of British and North American Protestant Orphan's Homes as Woman's Domain, 1850–1930," *Atlantis* 7, no. 3 (1982): 22–35.

43. *The Liberator,* Nov. 19, 1841, 188 (and subsequent issues); Jan. 13, 1843, 12; Oct. 1, 1842, 152; "The Monument Fair."

44. This was before the split in the organization; it was Chapman's group that made the request.

45. *Northampton Courier,* Apr. 24, 1833; Oct. 29, 1834; Nov. 25, 1835; Aug. 26, 1840; *Report of the Boston Female Anti-Slavery Society,* 9. The 1831 Richmond, Virginia, fair was also held just before Christmas (*Richmond Compiler,* Dec. 15, 1831).

46. *Northampton Free Press,* Dec. 11, 21, and 28, 1864; *Hampshire Gazette,* Oct. 6, 1850, Dec. 17, 1850.

47. This tradition also parallels the contemporary custom of the quilting bee.

48. Rush, "Lucretia Mott," 72; Sklar, "Doing the Nation's Work," 16. Rochester antislavery activists also met regularly (alternate Wednesdays) for their annual December event. See Hewitt, *Women's Activism,* 136, 141.

49. David Mollenhoff, *Madison: A History of the Formative Years* (Dubuque: Kendall/Hunt, 1982), 45; *Secretary's Record Book,* Ladies Benevolent Society, Grace Episcopal Church, Madison, Wisc., Dec. 16, 1846, Jan. 20, 1847, Nov. 10, 1846; letter from Rebecca Gratz to Ann Boswell Gratz, Dec. 3, 1857, in Philipson, *Letters of Rebecca Gratz,* 407–8.

50. See, for example, Kate Sutherland, "The Fancy Fair," *Peterson's Magazine,* Apr. 1848, 135–39. The "Articles for Fancy Fairs" feature ran eighteen times in *Godey's Lady's Book* between 1856 and 1861. Its featured items were similar to others that appeared in the magazine both before and after this period, but the 1856 column was the first time the fair designation was made explicit.

51. Luckhurst, *Story of Exhibitions,* 83–118. Note that six million people attended the Crystal Palace Exhibition.

52. There was at least one large-scale fair in Massachusetts in 1843, when Martha Washington societies from throughout the state netted $1,684. The temperance groups generally abandoned "rescue work" in the late 1840s, however, and functioned less and less as benevolent societies that needed to raise money. *Northampton Courier,* May 3, 1842; July 12, 1842; Alexander, "We Are Engaged," 763–85.

53. Andrew Jackson Downing, editorial, *The Horticulturalist and Journal of Rural Art and Recreational Taste*, July 1848, 157. When the Greenfield, Massachusetts, women raised $400 in 1855 for a local cemetery, they were also responding to this call. See *Hampshire Gazette*, May 9, 1855.

54. *The Weal-Reaf*, McCarthy, *Women's Culture*, 23.

55. *Northampton Free Press*, Dec. 21, 1860; *Hampshire Gazette*, Jan. 2, 1855; William J. Petersen, "Strawberry Time," *Palimpsest* 49 (Mar. 1968): 93–94. Note that some of the objections to the frivolities of a fair or festival were bypassed when the event was merely advertised as a "sale." When the Philadelphia Female Anti-Slavery Society first proposed holding a fair based on the Boston model, there was objection among the Quakers until the term "sale" replaced the word "fair" (Rush, "Lucretia Mott," 69).

56. Ladies' sales were listed in conjunction with this fair until the early 1850s. See "Notice on Cattle Show and Fair," *Northampton Democrat*, Sept. 26, 1843; *Hampshire Gazette*, Oct. 6, 1850. The articles exhibited and sold at the agricultural fair included handwoven blankets, quilts, rugs, shawls, and other articles of clothing, and pillows, tidies, antimacassars, mats, and artificial flowers. See "Agricultural Fair," *Northampton Courier*, Oct. 18, 1845.

57. Ironically, the fancywork seems to have been passed over by the male attendees. The *Courier* went on to chide the men for this attitude. "We are disposed to find fault with some of our friends who hurry over this department of the exhibitions, as too trivial for more than a hasty glance, and who would confine their paneygerics [*sic*] altogether to the Cotton Bale and Bundles of Hay. There are few things, alas! too few, that our young ladies generally can or will do in the way of industrial pursuits" ("The Editor's Table," *The Ladies Companion*, Oct. 1844, 298; "The Fair at the South Carolina Institute," *Charleston Daily Courier*, Nov. 20, 1850). Note that women's magazines also discussed Institute Fairs regularly; they were fully of interest to both sexes.

58. "Doesticks Attends a Ladies' Fair," *Hampshire Gazette*, Mar. 13, 1855. It is true that some critics still felt it was unseemly for women to act as sales clerks, whatever their age. Even in the next decade Union General William Sherman wrote his wife, "I don't approve of ladies selling things at a table. So far as superintending the management of such things, I don't object, but . . . it merely looks unbecoming for a lady" (cited in Agatha Young, *The Women and the Crisis: Women of the North in the Civil War* [Obolenski, N.Y.: McDowell, 1959], 310.)

59. Sutherland, "Fancy Fair," 135–39.

60. Hersh, *Slavery of Sex*, 11–15; *Report of the Boston Female Anti-Slavery Society*; Rush, "Lucretia Mott," 69–75; Otelia Cromwell, *Lucretia Mott* (Cambridge, Mass.: Harvard Univ. Press, 1958), 155–56; *The Liberator*, Dec. 20, 1834, 203. In the early days of the movement there were also apparently some "in-house" sales of fancywork among abolitionist women. A letter from Sarah Forten to Angelina Grimke dated Apr. 15, 1837, included the note, "I presume there will be a sale of fancy articles at the Ladies [anti-slavery] convention, as we were requested to send some of our work" (cited in Sterling, *We Are Your Sisters*, 125). Antislavery "stores" were later opened in eleven locations in western New York in the last half of 1848. These apparently functioned as gathering places, and included reading rooms where sympathizers could meet and work together. See Hewitt, *Women's Activism*, 136.

61. The Massachusetts fair ran from 1834 to 1857. (I am counting the time when they competed with the evangelicals by holding a separate "Fair of Individuals.") Many observers felt Chapman ran the fair almost single-handedly (see, e.g., Hansen, *Strained Sisterhood*, 126), and I am sure this was generally the case. Lutz claims Chapman moved to Europe from 1848 to 1855 in order to have her children attend school there, but that she kept up with her antislavery work (Chapman entry, *Notable American Women*, 325). Because many of the reports from those years bear her name and there are many references to her activities, I believe she must have spent at least part of each year in the United States.

62. *The Liberator*, Dec. 10, 1834, 203; Chambers-Schiller, "Good Work," 260.

63. In Utica, New York, according to activist Paulina Wright in 1844, the antislavery fair was "more opposed than anything that had been started" in that city for years. See Hewitt, *Women's Activism*, 226.

64. *The Liberator*, Dec. 17, 1841, 203ff.; *The Liberty Bell* (Boston: Massachusetts Anti-Slavery Fair, 1833–58); Cromwell, *Lucretia Mott*, 74–75. In her discussion of *The Liberty Bell*, Hansen notes that Chapman "used her influence, connections, and sheer boldness to procure original pieces" from these writers

(*Strained Sisterhood,* 134–35). Chambers-Schiller claims that owning a copy of *The Liberty Bell* became a symbol of one's involvement with the cause ("Good Work," 258). Note that for one year, 1841, the rival Massachusetts Female Emancipation Society tried publishing its own giftbook, *The Star of Emancipation.* This was a more modest publication, with contributions from sympathetic clergymen and society members. See Hansen, *Strained Sisterhood,* 134–35.

65. Hansen, *Strained Sisterhood,* 127–28, 132; Chambers-Schiller, "Good Work," 268–73. Note that Chapman's 1858 subscription campaign was in the form of a "salon" which Chambers-Schiller feels was once again filled with the necessary female symbolism (272–73). The campaign was short-lived because the Female Anti-Slavery Society was disbanded after the Emancipation Proclamation.

66. The $1,000,000 figure and all other dollar equivalents are based on tables in Derks, *The Value of a Dollar.* The $60,000 figure was my approximate calculation determined by adding proceeds listed for each year available and extrapolating probable proceeds for the missing years. It was impossible to determine an exact amount, for in addition to missing data, some reported figures appear to have been net profits while others were gross profits. There were also small fairs that contributed their proceeds to the society, but were inconsistently included in the annual reports. Hansen claims the 24 Massachusetts Female Anti-Slavery Society fairs raised over $65,000 (*Strained Sisterhood,* 138). Note that the listed profits peaked about 1850 at approximately $3,000, but after that date more small fairs took place, so the figures may be misleading. It is unclear if sales of *The Liberty Bell* are or are not included in these numbers.

The Philadelphia Anti-Slavery Fair, which was smaller than the Boston events, raised approximately half as much. Rush estimates the total earnings in Philadelphia amounted to about $32,000 ("Lucretia Mott," 72). Sklar calculates the figure to be somewhat over $28,000 ("Doing the Nation's Work," 2–19).

67. Chapman expressly stated the fairs provided an opportunity for sympathizers in outlying towns, who "usually stand aloof from meetings," to get actively involved. Maria Weston Chapman, "The Eighth Massachusetts Anti-Slavery Fair," *The Liberator,* Jan. 14, 1842; Nov. 19, 1841, 188.

68. Massachusetts Anti-Slavery Society, *Annual Report,* 1848, 58; 1849, 63. The personal relationship and involvement of those involved in the cause is indicated by an interaction between Chapman and an English donor in 1845. "Miss Hildritch" labeled her items "Gift of your Sister to the Bazaar." Chapman thanked Hildritch personally, telling her the sisterly inscription stirred the American fairgoers so much that the goods were purchased with great eagerness (she also enclosed a copy of *The Liberty Bell* and *The Liberator* report of the fair with her thank-you note).

69. Chapman, "The Eighth Massachusetts Anti-Slavery Fair," 3; Dec. 25, 1856, diary entry in Ray Allen Billington, ed., *Journal of Charlotte L. Forten* (New York: Dryden Press, 1953), 74–75; Antoinette Brown, letter to Lucy Stone, Dec. 30, 1850, reprinted in Carole Lasser and Marlen Deahl Merrill, eds., *Friends and Sisters: Letters Between Lucy Stone and Antoinette Brown Blackwell, 1846–1893* (Urbana: Univ. of Illinois Press, 1987), 99–100.

70. Chambers-Schiller, "Good Work," 256.

71. Hewitt, *Women's Activism,* 140.

Three. The Excitement and Lasting Legacy of the Civil War Sanitary Fairs

1. Frank B. Goodrich, *The Tribute Book: A Record of the Munificence, Self-Sacrifice and Patriotism of the American People During the War for the Union* (New York: Derby and Miller, 1865), 31–50.

2. The group published the appeal for the formation of the group that day, and it was quickly implemented. Note that the Board of Management of the organization listed twelve men and twelve women; although the principal officers were men, women held responsible positions. Elizabeth Blackwell, who had formal medical training, chaired the group that organized medical personnel. She was responsible for employing the first female nurses in the army.

3. Goodrich, *Tribute Book,* 70–81; J. Christopher Schnell, "Mary Livermore and the Great Northwest-

ern Fair," *Chicago History* n.s. 4 (Spring 1975): 36. L. P. Brockett and Mary C. Vaughn, *Women's Work in the Civil War: A Record of Heroism, Patriotism and Patience* (Philadelphia: Zeigler, McCurdy and Co., 1867), claim that over 12,000 separate groups worked with the Sanitary Commission (67), but Charles Stille, *History of the United States Sanitary Commission* (Philadelphia: J. B. Lippincott, 1866), puts the number at 7,000 (172). The discrepancy must be due to what was counted as a group, as some were more informal than others.

4. The branches provided cloth and yarn at cost for those who were willing to make needed garments, and patterns for those unaccustomed to preparing such items. Garments and other supplies that came in to the offices were sorted, packed, and given a commission stamp, and subsequently shipped to central distribution depots. See Goodrich, *Tribute Book,* 84–86; Mary A. Livermore, *My Story of the War: A Woman's Narrative of Four Years Personal Experience* (Hartford, Conn.: A. D. Worthington, 1889), 133. See also Beverly Gordon, "Textiles and Clothing of the Civil War: A Portrait for Contemporary Understanding," *Clothing and Textiles Research Journal* 5 (1987): 41–47.

5. The original Alert Club, from the town of Norwalk, Ohio (population 2,000), collected $560 in seven months. See Frances McTeer and Minnie Dubbs Millbrook, *Michigan Women in the Civil War* (Lansing: Michigan Civil War Centennial Observance Commission, 1963), 123; Goodrich, *Tribute Book,* 87–88; Brockett and Vaughn, *Women's Work,* 67. Sometimes the children's contribution involved several different steps. In 1864 girls in one Massachusetts town worked together on a quilt, then raffled it to the highest bidder. They used the $17 profit to buy supplies, which they donated to the Sanitary Commission. See Robert Lester Reynolds, "Benevolence on the Home Front in Massachusetts During the Civil War" (Ph.D. diss., Boston Univ., 1970).

6. Still other charitable causes, such as relief for those who were widowed and orphaned after a particular skirmish of the war, were also supported separately. Sometimes a local donation was divided between several recipients. On December 20, 1861, for example, a Northampton shipment of socks, mittens, and drawers was sent directly to the hometown boys, but a $50 cash donation which could be used wherever it was most needed was sent to the commission. *Northampton Free Press* Apr. 30, 1861; assorted issues May 1861; July 26, 1861; Aug. 2, 1861; Dec. 20, 1861; June 13, 1862; July 8, 1862; Sept. 2, 1862; Sept. 5, 1862.

7. The story was similar elsewhere. Women in both Boston and Lexington, Massachusetts, for example, each raised $1,000 (perhaps $15,000 today) for the soldiers in 1862. See Francis Phelps Weisenburger, *Columbus During the Civil War,* Ohio Civil War Centennial Commission Series 12 (Columbus: Ohio State Univ. Press for Ohio Historical Society, 1963), 17; Reynolds, "Benevolence on the Home Front," 262–66, 298–304; Robert H. Bremner, *The Public Good: Philanthropy and Welfare in the Civil War Era* (New York: Alfred A. Knopf, 1980), 62; *Northampton Free Press* Dec. 10, 1861; June 27, 1862; July 1, 1862; Dec. 1, 1863; Dec. 23, 1863.

   Caroline Gardiner Curtis described 1860s "Levees": "they combine a social gathering with a side show of dolls and pincushions, and later on a supper for which you pay to have a chance to display the superiority of your own cooking. . . . They were entirely feminine arrangements. The men were allowed to come in the evening to eat and buy, but the only male help that ever offered itself to us was Mr. Brown, who kept the shop and Post Office below the town hall where these events took place." See *Memories of Fifty Years in the Last Century* (Boston: Privately printed, 1947).

8. Goodrich, *Tribute Book,* 158–59.

9. Livermore, *Story of the War,* 409–17.

10. Ibid., 412.

11. Mary Ashton Livermore (1820–1905) had been a teacher when she married a Universalist minister and started writing for religious periodicals. As a young woman, she had been active in the antislavery movement and may well have worked at Chapman's fairs. When she moved to Chicago she met Jane C. Hoge (1811–1890), whose roots were in respected social circles in Philadelphia and Pittsburgh. Hoge's husband ran an ironworks. Before the two women became associate directors of the Chicago branch, they worked as Sanitary Commission agents for Dorothea Dix. Both had traveled to the battlefields in 1861. See entries in *Notable American Women,* vol. 2.

In every city, the women who spearheaded the fairs had previously been active in reform work and fundraising. In Rochester, for example, the leaders of the Soldiers' Aid Committee had previously worked with the Ladies Anti-Slavery Society, the Industrial School, and the Home for Friendless and Virtuous Females. See Hewitt, *Women's Activism.*

12. Goodrich, *Tribute Book,* 158–59.

13. *History of the North-Western Soldiers' Fair* (Chicago: Dunlop, Sewell and Spalding, 1864), 3, 152–55, 159. The original record of donations kept by the Receiving Committee of the fair is in the Chicago Historical Society Archives. Individual donations are listed by state, community, and individual.

14. Ibid., 20.

15. Ibid., 71–177.

16. Ibid., 15–18, 23–32, 71–177; *Chicago Tribune,* Oct. 29, 1863.

17. *History of the North-Western Soldiers' Fair,* 6, 25–27, 36, 39–40, 46.

18. The one exception to this was the Christmas Bazaar held in Rochester (the women of the Ladies Hospital Relief Committee reported much of the same resistance and "adverse counsel"), but this fair was in preparation at the same time as the Northwest fair, so the positive results had not yet been felt. See *Report of the Christmas Bazaar, December 14–22* (Rochester: Benton and Andrews, 1864).

19. Gunn, "Western Reserve Women," 75–85.

20. Goodrich, *Tribute Book,* 171–78; *Report of the Christmas Bazaar,* esp. 14–17. The tableaux idea was not completely new at the sanitary fair, although that was certainly the first time it was used on such a large scale. In 1858, a reconstruction of Ben Franklin's birthplace was set up at a fair held to raise money for the building fund for the Boston YMCA. Costumed volunteers performed tableaux and led visitors in singing. *Boston Post,* Dec. 15 and 21, 1858, cited in Jane C. Nylander, *Our Own Snug Fireside: Images of the New England Home, 1760–1860* (New York: Alfred Knopf, 1993), 16. It should be noted that there were many items for sale in the Rochester booths that did not really match the particular national theme. The list of donations to the Russian booth, for example, not only includes numerous skating caps and knitted scarves, but also baby clothes, tidies, cushions, and other standard bazaar items. Retailers' donations, such as skates, cigars, and brooms, were mixed in with donations from individuals.

21. On some nights the tableaux had to be canceled because the hall was too crowded. See *Report of the Christmas Bazaar,* 17–19.

22. "The Bazaar and Its Arrangements," *The Canteen,* Feb. 22, 1864, 1.

23. I refer here to fundraising fairgivers in the aggregate since the sponsors of the Boston YMCA fair preceded the Rochester women with this kind of innovation.

24. Halttunen, *Confidence Men,* 153–90; Jack W. McCullough, *Living Pictures on the New York Stage* (Ann Arbor: UMI Research Press, 1981). Tableaux were carefully distinguished from scenes given by "model artists." The latter were more sensational and titillating scenes of the female body.

25. In contemporary usage, an old folks' concert did not necessarily imply elderly singers; it meant that the songs themselves were from an earlier time.

26. "The Holland Booth," *The Canteen,* Mar. 1, 1864, 86; *History of the Brooklyn and Long Island Fair, February 22, 1864* (Brooklyn: The Union, 1864), 73–78; *Northampton Free Press,* Mar. 11, 1864. Note that the portrayal of American Indians was completely in accordance with dominant racist attitudes. In describing the wigwam in the Metropolitan Fair, the *Record of the Metropolitan Fair in Aid of the U.S. Sanitary Commission, Held at New York, April 1864* (New York: Hurd & Houghton, 1867) noted that "it bore no traces of civilization" (50).

27. Despite its name this was a fundraising event, held in support of the religiously oriented Christian Commission rather than the Sanitary Commission, but similar to a sanitary fair in every respect.

28. *History of the Brooklyn Fair,* 77; *Chicago Evening Journal,* Apr. 24, 1865; *Voice of the Fair,* June 17, 1865. A discussion of the New England Kitchen phenomenon is in Rodris Roth, "The New England, or 'Olde Tyme' Kitchen Exhibit at Nineteenth Century Fairs," in *The Colonial Revival in America,* ed. Alan Axelrod (New York: W. W. Norton, 1985), 159–83.

Maria Lydig Daly, the wife of a prominent New York judge, was asked if she would serve as one of the attendants in the Knickerbocker Kitchen at the Metropolitan Fair or alternately impersonate the Washington Irving heroine Katrina Van Tassel at the book booth. She refused, writing in her diary that she did "not particularly fancy the idea of being seated in cap, short gown and petticoat, pouring out tea for all the rabble." See diary entries for Mar. 17 and 18, 1864, in Harold Earl Hammond, ed., *Diary of a Union Lady 1861–1865* (New York: Funk and Wagnalls, 1962), 280–81.

29. Elizabeth Fries Ellett's *Domestic History of the Revolution* (New York: Baker and Scribner, 1851) reflected women's sense of purpose and self worth. It was "written to portray the . . . experiences of a class not usually noticed" (39). See also Roth, "New England Kitchens"; Jane E. Przybysz, "Quilts, Old Kitchens," 14. On heroic deeds in domestic spaces, see Kenneth Ames's introduction to Axelrod, *The Colonial Revival in America*, 12.

30. Among those who have credited the influence to the Centennial Exhibition are William Seale, *The Tasteful Interlude: American Interiors Through the Camera's Eye, 1860–1917* (Nashville: American Association of State and Local History, 1980), 20–21, and Green, "Popular Science and Political Thought," 18. Rodris Roth's "New England Kitchens" is one of the only scholarly treatments that does credit the sanitary fairs.

31. I have developed the subject of nineteenth-century attitudes about the past at length in my article "Dressing the Colonial Past: The Nineteenth Century Looks Back," in *Dress in American Culture*, ed. Patricia Cunningham and Susan Voso Lab (Bowling Green, Ohio: Bowling Green State Univ. Press, 1993), 109–39.

32. Goodrich, *Tribute Book*, 444–48, 286. The battleships were featured at the Pittsburgh fair, the National Sailor's Fair in Boston, and the second Northwest fair (the Soldiers' Home Fair) in Chicago.

33. Mark Twain (Samuel Clemens), *Roughing It* (American Publishing Co., 1871; reprint, New York: Harper Bros., 1913), vol. 2: 26–31. War relics were particularly likely to make the rounds. A letter from the Wisconsin Quartermaster's office to the organizers of the second Northwest fair requested they return Wisconsin flags which were needed for the upcoming Soldiers' Home Fair in Milwaukee. See Mary Clark Brayton, "General History," in *Our Acre and Its Harvest: Historical Sketches of the Soldiers' Aid Society of Northern Ohio*, pt. 1 (Cleveland: Fairbanks, Benedict, 1869), 135–36; *Rochester Union*, Dec. 22, 1863, cited in *Report of the Christmas Bazaar*, 20; *Chicago Tribune*, June 1, 1865; Letter from J. M. Synch, Quartermaster's Office, June 14, 1865, in the Chicago Historical Society Archives.

34. Brayton, *Our Acre*, 180–86; Goodrich, *Tribute Book*, 247, 252–54; *Home Fair Journal*, June 29, 1865.

35. Letter from unidentified sender to Mrs. Hunter, Mar. 1, 1865, Chicago Historical Society Archives; Goodrich, *Tribute Book*, 278.

36. *History of the Brooklyn Fair*, 80–81.

37. Editorial, *Albany Evening Journal*, Dec. 17, 1863, quoted in *Report of the Christmas Bazaar*, 13; Charles Brandon Boynton, ed., *History of the Great Western Sanitary Fair* (Cincinnati: C. F. Vent, 1864), 244; Brayton, *Our Acre*, 148–52, 204–5; Goodrich, *Tribute Book*, 248–50, 286–87. See also illustrations in William C. Davis, ed., *Shadows of the Storm*, vol. 1 of *The Image of War 1861–1865* (Garden City, N.Y.: Doubleday, 1981), 400.

38. Seven thousand of these purchased a separate printed catalogue.

39. M. E. B. [Mary Elizabeth Braddon], Letter to the Editor, *Arthur's Home Magazine*, June 1864, 302; Livermore, *Story of the War*, 442; *History of the Brooklyn Fair*, 60; "Description of the Fair," *Spirit of the [Metropolitan] Fair*, Apr. 14, 1864, 180.

40. *Report of the Christmas Bazaar*, 19; *Our Daily Fare*, June 1864, 38; [Milwaukee] *Home Fair Journal*, July 3, 1865, 2; *The Voice of the [Chicago] Fair*, June 3, 1865, 3; *Record of the Metropolitan Fair*, 98; Hammond, *Diary of a Union Lady*, 286.

41. *Home Fair Journal*, July 1, 1865, 2; July 3, 1865, 2; *Voice of the Fair*, June 3, 1865, 3; *Report of the Christmas Bazaar*, 21; M. E. B. [Mary Elizabeth Braddon], "The Great Central Fair," (Report to the Editor), *Arthur's Home Magazine*, Aug. 1864, 97.

42. "The Art Gallery," *Our Daily Fare*, June 20, 1864, 69. See also the *Chicago Tribune*, June 4, 1865, 2.

43. Works by Church, Bierstadt, Gilbert, Gignoux, Gifford, and Kensett were among the painters listed most frequently in gallery catalogues.

44. Livermore, *Story of the War,* 441; *Chicago Tribune,* June 4, 1865; M. E. B., Letter to Editor, 302–4; Hammond, *Diary of a Union Lady,* 286; Boynton, *Great Western Sanitary Fair,* 403–4.

45. *History of the North-Western Soldiers' Fair,* 35; Goodrich, *Tribute Book,* 223; Livermore, *Story of the War,* 441; Hammond, *Diary of a Union Lady,* 286.

46. Hammond, *Diary of a Union Lady,* 291; *Spirit of the Fair,* Apr. 19, 1864, 100; "Letters from Sally Popcorn to her Sister Betsey in Pumpkinsville," 3, *Spirit of the Fair,* Apr. 23, 1864, 195–96.

47. Goodrich, *Tribute Book,* 194, 223. Given the phenomenal price of the Bierstadt painting and the sheer size of the gallery at the Metropolitan Fair, the $25,000 figure is high rather than representative. At the opposite extreme, the net profit of the art gallery at the Cincinnati fair was $350 (Boynton, *Great Western Sanitary Fair,* 404). See also Brayton, *Our Acre,* 190–92.

48. *Report of the Christmas Bazaar,* 21.

49. *Northampton Free Press,* Aug. 29, 1866, Nov. 4, 1867, Nov. 28, 1871, Jan. 6, 1872; Edward P. Alexander, *Museums in Motion: An Introduction to the History and Functions of Museums* (Nashville: American Association of State and Local History, 1979), 30–32. The Art Institute of Chicago was funded in part by the proceeds from the art gallery of the Chicago Interstate Exposition. The express purpose of that gallery was to fund a permanent art museum in the region. See Stefan Gerner, "Pictures at an Exhibition," *Chicago History* 16 (Spring 1987): 4–30.

50. Brayton, *Our Acre,* 180–86.

51. Goodrich, *Tribute Book,* 252.

52. Ibid., 247, 252–54; *Voice of the Fair,* June 9, 1865, 4; *Chicago Tribune,* May 30, 1865.

53. *Chicago Tribune,* June 8, 1865; *Home Fair Journal,* June 3, 1865; *Chicago Evening Journal,* June 3, 1865.

54. Unfortunately, the identity of the designers is not clear; they were uncredited in fair reports and in the press, except in the case of Chicago's Floral Hall, when both a local architect and a Rockford gardener were mentioned. See *Voice of the Fair,* June 5, 1865.

55. The influential landscape designer Frederick Law Olmsted was the general secretary of the Sanitary Commission for over two years, and while there is no evidence that he had any direct role in the design or implementation of the sanitary fair landscapes (his involvement with the commission was an outgrowth of his antislavery activism, his duties were related to organizational management and transport services, and he had resigned his post well before these landscapes were made), his ideas did strongly influence them. Olmsted and partner Calvert Vaux's "Greensward" design for New York's Central Park was being implemented at the time of the fairs, and it had been generally well publicized and discussed. See Stille, *History of the Sanitary Commission;* Julius Fabos, Gordon Milde, and Michael V. Weinmayr, *Frederick Law Olmsted, Sr.: Founder of Landscape Architecture in America* (Amherst: Univ. of Massachusetts Press, 1968); *Voice of the Fair,* June 5, 1865, 2. For a complete discussion of the way the interior environments matched Olmsted's ideas, see Beverly Gordon, "The Interior Landscapes of the Civil War Sanitary Fairs," unpublished paper, 1986.

56. Frederick Law Olmsted Jr. and Theodora Kimball, eds., *Forty Years of Landscape Architecture: Being the Professional Papers of Frederick Law Olmsted, Sr.: Central Park as a Work of Art and As a Great Municipal Enterprise 1853–1895* (New York: Knickerbocker Press, 1928), 175; G. B. Tobey, *A History of Landscape Architecture: The Relationship of People to Environment* (New York: Elsevier, 1973). The quote is from "The Influence of Exhibitions in Improving the State of the People," *Voice of the Fair,* June 9, 1865, 2; *Voice of the Fair,* June 21, 1865, 2.

57. *Philadelphia Public Ledger,* June 11, 1864, June 23, 1864.

58. Olmsted and Kimball, *Forty Years of Landscape Architecture,* 178.

59. James R. Buckler, "Victorian Horticulture: The Smithsonian Approach," *Nineteenth Century* 7 (Spring, 1981): 53–61. The judgment about relative imaginativeness is based on the author's comparison of the sanitary fair environments and the Centennial environment. The latter is based on a description in James D. McCabe, *The Illustrated History of the Centennial Exhibition* (Philadelphia: National Publishing, 1876), 507–16.

60. Ann P. Hosmer, "Reminiscences of Sanitary Work," handwritten mss., recorded Jan. 1882. Chicago Historical Society Archives.

61. Goodrich, *Tribute Book,* 221; *The Voice of the Fair,* June 8, 1865, 2, and June 21, 1865, 2. Barbara Kirshenblatt-Gimblett cites the practice of buying votes in this way as another example of the inversion of the woman's fair. See "The Moral Sublime," 5.

62. *The Voice of the Fair,* May 4, 1865, 4; Livermore, *Story of the War,* 152–53; Goodrich, *Tribute Book,* 288.

63. *Chicago Tribune,* June 9, 1865, 4. According to Roth ("New England Kitchens," 167), African Americans also served the food at the Metropolitan Fair's Knickerbocker Kitchen.

64. According to New York City newspapers, Mrs. David Dudley Field and Mrs. Caroline Kirkland, both members of the Executive Committee of the Metropolitan Fair, sacrificed their lives to "overwork at the fair." It is true that both women took ill at that fair, but both were elderly, and might have succumbed under any strain. Hammond, *Diary of a Union Lady,* 2.

65. Livermore, *Story of the War,* 435–36. There were many other incidents that contributed to Livermore's radicalization. She and Hoge also learned during the course of the fair that they had no legal claim on minor children, for example, which led to a "new world of insight and feeling." After the war Livermore founded (with Lucy Stone and others) the American Woman's Suffrage Association. She edited the suffragist newspaper *The Woman's Journal* from 1869 to 1872 and then went on the lecture circuit for several decades. In 1892 she and Frances Willard coauthored a book profiling the lives of notable women. Hoge worked with the Woman's Education Association of Evanston, Evanston College for Ladies (later part of Northwestern University), and headed the (Presbyterian) Board of Foreign Missions in the Northwest. See *Notable American Women* entries.

66. *Report of the Christmas Bazaar,* 7, 10; Hammond, *Diary of a Union Lady,* 289.

67. Goodrich, *Tribute Book,* 96–104.

68. This was not missing entirely. A cartoon in *The Drumbeat,* the newspaper of the Brooklyn and Long Island Fair, for example, showed a husband eyeing a pretty saleswoman lasciviously. See Przybysz, "Quilts, Old Kitchens," 19.

69. Another piece of evidence about the wealthy women who contributed to Civil War fairs is provided by the diary of affluent Boston matron Elizabeth Crowninshield Hammond. Her entries from December 1863 make constant reference to making items for the fair and buying others at multiple visits. The diary is in the Schlesinger Library, Radcliffe College, Acc. No. 82-M24.

70. *Report of the Christmas Bazaar,* 3; Alvin Robert Kantor and Marjorie Sered Kantor, *Sanitary Fairs: A Philatelic and Historical Study of Civil War Benevolence* (Glencoe, Ill.: SF Publishers, 1992), 38, 147.

Four. Other Fairs of the Civil War and Reconstruction Periods

1. Sometimes proceeds from the local fairs were donated to the organizing committees of upcoming sanitary fairs. At other times, contributions were made directly to the commission treasury.

2. Columbus women seem to have been particularly active fairgivers. As indicated in the previous chapter, they had also organized two other bazaars in the preceding ten months. See Weisenburger, *Columbus During Civil War,* 18.

3. The Springfield Fair was in many respects like a full-scale sanitary fair, but all profit went to the hostel. *Northampton Free Press,* Mar. 21, 1865.

4. *Northampton Free Press,* Jan. 12, 1864, Jan. 13, 1865, Feb. 7, 1865, Feb. 14, 1865; Bremner, *Public Good,* 295–96.

5. Reynolds, "Benevolence on the Home Front," 253; *Northampton Free Press,* Feb. 7, 1865.

6. The only confederacy-wide relief society I have seen referenced is the Association for Relief of Maimed Soldiers, later called the Women's Relief Society of the Confederate States. See Kantor and Kantor, *Sanitary Fairs.*

7. Mary Elizabeth Massey, *Bonnet Brigades* (New York: Alfred A. Knopf, 1965), 37; *Charleston Daily Courier,* Apr. 25–May 14, 1862.

8. Twenty males were also listed as the members of the "Junior Manager Committee," but this must have been a group of boys, too young to be at the front.

9. *Charleston Daily Courier,* Apr. 25–May 14, 1862. Because the value of Confederate scrip fluctuated widely, I am unable to determine present-day equivalents for this figure or any other from the wartime South.

10. The story of South Carolina's Great Bazaar is taken from the following: Nell S. Graydon, *Tales of Columbia* (Columbia: Nell Graydon [R. L. Bryan], 1964), 131–32; Helen Kohn Henning, *Columbia: Capital City of South Carolina, 1786–1936* (Columbia: Columbia Sesquicentennial Commission [R. L. Bryan], 1936), 32; Earl Schenck Miers, ed., *When the World Ended: The Diary of Emma Le Conte* (New York: Oxford Univ. Press, 1957), 12–13; Grace Elmore, "The Last Bazar," Mrs. T. Taylor, Smythe, Kohn, et al., eds., *South Carolina Women of the Confederacy: Experiences During the Civil War* (Columbia: The State Co., 1903), 243–45; *South Carolinian,* Jan. 18, 1865, cited in *New York Herald,* Jan. 29, 1865; Soldiers' Relief Association, *To The Friends of the Southern Cause at Home* (Columbia, 1864), 2.

11. Their activity could be intense. The July 11, 1864, *Philadelphia Inquirer* reported that schoolchildren worked so hard on their projects for the Great Central Fair that they neglected their studies, and examinations had to be dispensed with.

12. Livermore, *Story of the War,* 152–53; Brockett and Vaughn, *Women's Work,* 68; Goodrich, *Tribute Book,* 101.

13. Livermore, *Story of the War,* 153–54.

14. Goodrich, *Tribute Book,* 487.

15. The Chicago fairs all took place in a fortnight. Livermore called the $300 a "handsome sum" to come from events taking place outdoors in hot weather (*Story of the War,* 153). The Boston fair, according to Reynolds ("Benevolence on the Home Front," 266) was also "held in the home of one of [the city's most] prominent citizens. See also *History of the Brooklyn Fair,* 165.

16. "At the Fair Cafe," *The Mayflower* 10 (Nov. 2, 1872): 1.

17. Woolson, "Charitable Fairs," 143–45; "My Experience at the Fair," *Godey's Lady's Book,* Aug. 1875, 288. Robert Louis Stevenson in an 1868 piece called "The Charity Bazaar: An Allegorical Dialogue," in *Letters and Miscellanies,* 603–5, also referred disdainfully to the shopkeeping aspect of the fair. "You play at shopping awhile," he wrote, "and in order to keep up the illusion, sham goods do actually change hands."

18. According to the secretary's records, on November 2, the Rhode Island group wanted a table at the bazaar for its own benefit. The vote on this proposal was undecided; it was to be left up to the Rhode Island Convention. All of the information about this fair is taken from this document, marked "Records, Woman's Suffrage Bazaar Association," with entries from early October to December 27, 1871. It was found in Alice Blackwell's house and is now in Radcliffe's Arthur Schlesinger library.

19. Records, Suffrage Bazaar.

20. *The Woman's Journal,* Oct. 30, 1886, 45.

21. Livermore, *Story of the War,* 128–29, 476–530; Elizabeth Blackwell, *Pioneer Work in Opening the Medical Profession to Women: Autobiographical Sketches* (New York and London: Longmans, Green & Co., 1896); Mary Roth Walsh, *Doctors Wanted: No Women Need Apply: Sex Barriers in the Medical Profession, 1835–1975* (New Haven: Yale Univ. Press, 1977), 83–90; Lasser and Merrill, *Friends and Sisters,* 167. Zakrzewska also was actively involved with the suffrage fairs held in Boston in subsequent years. *The Woman's Journal* reported at length on her suggestions for effective marketing in 1886.

22. The discussion of the NEHWC fairs is taken from New England Hospital for Women and Children *Annual Reports,* 1864–79, located in the Sophia Smith Collection, Smith College Library, Northampton, Massachusetts.

23. The titles of the sponsoring groups of the hospital fair, headed as they are by the word "ladies,'" indicate that these organizers could probably be characterized as politically moderate. Note that "electrifying orator" William Cullen Bryant, who also spoke at agricultural fairs in this era, delivered the opening address. "The Homeopathic Hospital Fair," *New York Times,* Apr. 11, 1875; Apr. 13, 1875.

24. "For the Sake of Charity," *New York Times,* Dec. 8, 1875. Manuscripts relating to the bazaar of the Hahnemann Hospital Attending League are in the archives of Northwestern Univ., Evanston, Illinois.

25. According to Ann Douglas, *The Feminization of American Culture* (New York: Avon Books, 1977), it was in the decade after the war that serious gains were made in women's education (69). See also *Northampton Free Press*, Dec. 17, 1869; *Northampton Free Press*, Nov. 1, 1867; *Wisconsin State Journal*, Sept. 22, 1870; "Woman's Work for Women," *New York Times*, Apr. 29, 1875.

26. Douglas, *Feminization of American Culture*, 69; Myers, *The Sociable*; *Northampton Free Press*, Nov. 17, 1871; "Catholic Fair," *New York Times*, Dec. 1, 1878; "Church of the Holy Trinity Grand Bazaar," *New York Times*, Dec. 10, 1877; *Northampton Free Press*, Oct. 17, 1874; "Fair for Paulist Fathers, *New York Times*, Dec. 18, 1877; Kantor and Kantor, *Sanitary Fairs*, 281.

27. "Bazaars," *New York Times*, Nov. 21, 1875; "Women's Foreign Missions," *New York Times*, Nov. 30, 1875; "St. Ann's Fair," *New York Times*, Apr. 24, 1875; May 3, 1875; *Wisconsin State Journal*, Dec. 4, 1875; *Northampton Free Press*, Feb. 16, 1869, Dec. 5, 1874, Apr. 19, 1872, Feb. 25, 1868, June 10, 1868; "Bazaar for Benefit Station Mission School," *New York Times*, Oct. 27, 1875; "Masonic Temple Bazaar," *New York Times*, Oct. 27, 1875; "Bazaar for Camp Mission," *New York Times*, Nov. 16, 1875; "A Novel Bazaar," *New York Times*, May 3, 1874.

28. Hoge also worked with Frances Willard of the Women's Christian Temperance Union. While contemporary observers usually think of the WCTU and the suffragists as two different camps, it is noteworthy that Livermore also worked with Willard; they co-authored a book on notable women in the 1890s. See entries on Jane Hoge and Mary Livermore in *Notable American Women*, 2: 200–201.

29. Patricia R. Hill, *The World Their Household: The American Woman's Foreign Mission Movement and Cultural Transformation, 1870–1920* (Ann Arbor: Univ. of Michigan Press, 1985), 100–102.

30. Wartime relief work was itself international. In 1863, for example, Americans sent a shipload of supplies to unemployed factory workers in the British Isles. In 1866 the British reciprocated, and they, along with French and Cuban sympathizers, contributed to the Southern Relief Association Fair in Baltimore. See Goodrich, *Tribute Book*, 383–86; Bremner, *Public Good*, 122.

31. Cutlip, *Fundraising in the United States*, 18; *Report of the Executive Committee of the Fair for the Relief of Suffering in France* (Boston: Rand, Avery and Co., 1872); "Fair of the Swiss Benevolent Society," *New York Times*, Mar. 27, 1879; Goodrich, *Tribute Book*, 371–73; *From the Slavery of 1776 to the Freedom of 1876: An Account of the Labors of the Ladies Charitable Association of Boston* (Boston, 1876); Association for Befriending Children and Young Girls, *Annual Report* (New York: Catholic Publication Society, 1874); Alice B. Keith, "White Relief in North Carolina, 1865–1867," *Social Forces* 17, no. 3 (Mar. 1939): 337–55. Note that $50,000 was reserved for special cases at the Baltimore fair.

32. *Northampton Free Press*, Aug. 4, 1871, Nov. 28, 1871.

33. I have seen one reference to a Grand Army of the Republic benefit performance in Northampton in 1870 (*Northampton Free Press*, Apr. 5, 1870), but it was not until about a decade later that GAR "grand fairs" became common. See "Soldier's Bazaar," *Hampshire Gazette*, Dec. 16, 1879; "Koltes Post GAR Fair," *New York Times*, Sept. 16, 1878; *The Knapsack: Daily Journal of the Seventh Regiment New Armory Fair*, vols. 1–12 (New York: Nov.–Dec. 1879).

34. Bordin, "A Baptism of Power and Liberty"; Blair, *The Clubwoman*; Ryan, *Women in Public*, 51.

35. The same general effect was created five years later at the Hahnemann Hospital Fair when an avenue of palms led to a central Rose Bower.

36. "The Homeopathic Hospital Fair," *New York Times*, Apr. 11, 1875, Apr. 13, 1875, Apr. 18, 1875; "The Hahnemann Fair," *New York Times*, Apr. 12, 1880; "The Grand Army Fair," *Hampshire Gazette*, Jan. 20, 1885.

37. *The Knapsack*, Seventh Regiment Armory Fair, no. 8 (Nov. 25, 1879): 2; "Fifth Regiment Fair," *New York Times*, Apr. 29, 1875; "Swiss Fair," *New York Times*, Mar. 27, 1879; "Minnie Hauk Selling Bouquets," *New York Times*, Oct. 20, 1882; "Y.W.C.A. Fair," *New York Times*, May 3, 1876; "Dances of Different Nations," *New York Times*, Apr. 15, 1885.

38. David Glassberg, *American Historical Pageantry: The Uses of Tradition in the Early Twentieth Century* (Chapel Hill: Univ. of North Carolina Press, 1990), 26; "The Hahnemann Fair"; "For the Sake of Charity."

39. *Report of the Christmas Bazaar*, 18. William Leach has suggested that turn-of-the-century fairyland

environments were designed to eliminate the literal character of merchandising space. This would be equally true of the earlier fairylands. See Leach, *Land of Desire,* 53.

40. "For the Sake of Charity"; "Woman's Work for Women"; "A Novel Bazaar"; "Homeopathic Hospital Fair."

41. The Northampton Good Templars Festival included a popular Old Folks Kitchen (*Northampton Free Press,* Dec. 28, 1866). See also *Report of the Executive Committee, French Suffering,* 3, 72; *Wisconsin State Journal,* Dec. 22, 1870; "Bazaars and Fairs," *New York Times,* Nov. 21, 1875; "The Fair," *New York Times,* Apr. 18, 1875. The Centennial has been credited with instigating the new passion for Orientalia and everything Japanese that swept the country in the last quarter of the century; with stimulating interest in a revival of pre-Revolutionary architecture, furniture, and decorative arts; and with furthering interest in international customs, people, and goods. See Clay Lancaster, *The Japanese Influence in America* (New York: Walton H. Rawls, 1963); Seale, *The Tasteful Interlude,* 20–21. While the far-reaching influence of the Centennial is not being disputed, it is important to credit the earlier models provided by the fair-organizing women.

42. Serious wartime letters received a sanitary fair stamp, but were later taken to a regular post office for mailing. In Philadelphia, the chairman of the post office booth was actually the city's postmaster. Prewritten letters, like other sanitary fair attractions, were sometimes used repeatedly. At the Springfield Soldier's Fair, mock letters were redeposited in the mailbox once they had been "delivered" and drawn again. Kantor and Kantor, *Sanitary Fairs,* 12, 116, 168.

43. Curiously, this same woman had written 2,000—twice as many—letters 37 years before for the Post Office at the Bunker Hill Monument Fair. See "A Boston Woman as Letter-Writer," *New York Times,* Dec. 23, 1877.

44. Regarding lemonade stands, see "Woman's Work for Women"; "The Homeopathic Hospital Fair"; "For the Sake of Charity." Occasionally lemonade was portioned out by women representing other nationalities. At the stand in Northampton's Edwards Church Festival in 1869, for example, a "bonnie Scotch lassie in Highland costume" was substituted (*Northampton Free Press,* June 18, 1869). Other references in this paragraph are taken from *Northampton Free Press,* Nov. 6, 1867; "The Fair," *Northampton Free Press,* Apr. 28, 1871.

45. *Wisconsin State Journal,* Jan. 28, 1875; "St. Raphael's Fair," *Wisconsin State Journal,* Jan. 11, 1871; "For the Sake of Charity"; "Catholic Cathedral Fair," *New York Times,* Dec. 1, 1878; "Close of St. Francis Xavier Fair," *New York Times,* Dec. 8, 1880; "Fair of Festival of the Spirit of Forty Lodge, IO of GT," *Northampton Free Press,* Dec. 14, 1866, Dec. 3, 1867; *Wisconsin State Journal,* Jan. 11, 1871, Mar. 14, 1871; Kirshenblatt-Gimblett, "The Moral Sublime," 5.

46. Art galleries were even included at fundraising events with ostensibly very different emphases, such as the Los Angeles Flower Festival. Jane Apostol, "They Said It With Flowers: The Los Angeles Flower Festival Society," *Southern California Quarterly* 62 (1980): 68. *Report of the Executive Committee of the Fair, French Suffering;* "A Novel Bazaar"; "Homeopathic Hospital Fair," *New York Times,* Apr. 11, 1875; "[M.E.] Church Fair," *New York Times,* Dec. 8, 1880; "Another Church Fair," *New York Times,* Dec. 2, 1880; *The Knapsack,* Seventh Regiment New Armory Fair, New York (Nov. 24, 1879, and Nov. 18, 1879). Note that in reporting on the YMCA event, the *New York Times* gave as much space to the donors of the paintings as to the artists.

47. Mary Ryan similarly observed that women themselves had become the focus of attention at parades after the Civil War (*Women in Public,* 46).

48. The very word that was used to describe these items, "fancywork," embodies a similar contradiction in terms and, like the "useful and ornamental" epithet, reflects an ambivalent Victorian attitude toward women and work. Women, of course, did work, but given the strong distinction and separation made at the time between the outside world of work and the inside world of the home, women were by definition not "workers," and their tasks carried other names. The only work that was acknowledged as such was light, ornamental, and nonpecuniary—i.e., needlework or fancywork. Fancywork features in the periodicals were called "work sections," "work departments," or "work baskets." Cooking and cleaning advice columns were never referred to this way—they were "household" depart-

ments—and since childrearing was considered more a holy mission than a job (a woman was a "bene-diction" for her children; the home she made for them was an "altar" or a temple"), the word "work" also did not appear in commentary about mothering. At mid–century agricultural fairs, "Woman's Work" displays included the familiar pincushions, stool covers, needlecases and ornamental wreaths, and local newspapers printed lists of these objects under the same heading. Women may have milked the cows or otherwise tended the livestock, in other words, and they may have contributed signifi-cantly to the crops, but such outside activities were man's work, and woman's work was done inside, with a needle. I have discussed this topic in "Victorian Fancygoods in the American Home: Fantasy and Accommodation" in *Making the American Home,* 48–68.

49. See Beverly Gordon, "Woman's Domestic Body: The Conceptual Conflation of Women and Interi-ors in the Industrial Age," *Winterthur Portfolio* 31, no. 4 (Winter 1996), 281–301.

50. Abby G. Shaw, "A Quilting Party," *The Ladies Floral Cabinet and Pictorial Home Companion,* Dec. 1875, 18; Laura C. Holloway, *The Hearthstone; or, Life at Home: A Household Manual* (Chicago and Philadelphia: L. P. Miller, 1888), 421–24; Woolson, "Charitable Fairs," 145–46. The sentiment about elaborate nothings had been expressed before, but it was strongest at this point in time.

51. "Some Hints," 790–91. In the records of the 1871 Woman's Suffrage Bazaar, the secretary indicated some discussion about whether or not merchants should be able to sell goods on commission. There was no consensus at that meeting and no further entry to indicate how the matter was resolved.

52. "Methodist Church Fair," *New York Times,* Dec. 14, 1878; "The Hahnemann Fair Opened," *New York Times,* Apr. 13, 1880; "French Fair," *New York Times,* Apr. 25, 1882; "G.A.R. Charity Fair," *Hampshire Gazette,* Jan. 27, 1885; "Soldier's Bazaar"; "At the Waldorf," *New York Times,* Dec. 17, 1896; "Congre-gational Church Fair," *Wisconsin State Journal,* Dec. 12, 1880.

53. Davis, *Parades and Power,* 17–18; William Leach, "Transformations in a Culture of Consumption: Women and Department Stores, 1890–1925," *Journal of American History* 71, no. 2 (Sept. 1984): 319–42; and Leach, *Land of Desire,* 322; Jean Gordon and Jan McArthur, "American Women and Domestic Consumption, 1800–1920: Four Interpretive Themes," *Journal of American Culture* 8, no. 3 (Fall 1985): 35–36; Fox and Lears, *The Culture of Consumption;* Russell Lewis, "Everything Under One Roof: World's Fairs and Department Stores in Paris and Chicago," *Chicago History* 12, no. 3 (Fall 1983): 32; Harris, "Museums, Merchandising," 151–54.

54. Interview with Dorothea Britton, Scarsdale, New York, Dec. 1986; Elmore, "The Last Bazaar"; Mihaly Csikzentmihalyi and Eugene Rochberg-Halton, *The Meaning of Things: Domestic Symbols and the Self* (Cambridge: Cambridge Univ. Press, 1981), 8; Beverly Gordon, "The Souvenir: Messenger of the Extraordinary," *Journal of Popular Culture* 20 (Winter 1986): 135–46.

55. This observation was made by Walters, *Antislavery Appeal,* 24–25.

Five. The Heyday of the Fundraising Fair

1. William Leach, "Strategists of Display and the Production of Desire," in *Consuming Visions,* 99–132; Leach, *Land of Desire;* Jean-Christophe Agnew, "The House of Fiction: The American Interior and the Rise of a Commodity Aesthetic," paper presented at the "Accumulation and Display: The Devel-opment of American Consumerism, 1880–1920" symposium, Henry Francis DuPont Winterthur Mu-seum, Wilmington, Delaware, Nov. 7, 1986.

2. Michael B. Miller, *The Bon Marche,* cited in Lewis, "Everything Under One Roof," 36.

3. Johnson, *A History of the World's Columbian;* Miles Orvell, *The Real Thing: Imitation and Authenticity in American Culture 1880–1940* (Chapel Hill: Univ. of North Carolina Press, 1989), 34–36; Kasson, *Amusing the Million;* McCullough, *World's Fairs Midways;* T. J. Jackson Lears, *No Place of Grace: Anti–Modernism and the Transformation of American Culture 1880–1920* (New York: Pantheon, 1981), esp. 55, 300; Davis, *Parades and Power,* 170; Kathy Peiss, *Cheap Amusements: Working Women and Leisure in Turn-of-the-Century New York* (Philadelphia: Temple Univ. Press, 1986), 121, 134, 136.

4. Joan Jacobs Brumberg, "Zenanas and Girlless Villages: The Ethnology of American Evangelical

Women, 1870–1910," paper delivered at the Berkshire Women's History Conference, Vassar College, Poughkeepsie, New York, June 1981, 21–22; John Neubauer, *The Fin-de-siecle Culture of Adolescence* (New Haven: Yale Univ. Press, 1992); Leach, *Land of Desire,* 53–54, 85–88; Rodney Engen, *Kate Greenaway: A Biography* (New York: Schocken Books, 1981); Walter Crane, *The Masque of Flowers* (London: Cassell & Co., 1895); Crane, *The First of May: A Fairy Masque* (Boston: James R. Osgood, 1881). Lears even ties the period fascination with medieval and Egyptian themes to the childhood of the race idea, since these were seen as earlier stages in Western culture (*No Place of Grace,* 98, 143–46, 188). Regarding the beginnings of the fields of anthropology and folklore, see Jane S. Beeker and Barbara Franco, eds., *Folk Roots, New Roots: Folklore in American Life* (Lexington: Museum of Our National Heritage, 1988); Simon J. Bronner, *American Folklore Studies: An Intellectual History* (Lawrence: Univ. Press of Kansas, 1986).

5. For example, women worked independently for the 1876 Centennial Exhibition, forming their own organization and creating a separate Woman's Pavilion, where women's work and achievements were exhibited. Many of the same women continued to work together after the Centennial and formalized their group into the New Century Club for Women. Darney, "Women and World's Fairs"; Weimann, *Fair Women,* 1.

6. For general information on women's clubs, see Blair, *The Clubwoman,* 60–71, 77, 98.

7. Sophonisba P. Breckenridge, *Women in the Twentieth Century: A Study of Their Political, Social and Economic Activities* (New York: McGraw Hill, 1933; reprint, Arno Press, 1972), 19–32.

8. Women had made inroads into the public arena, but sadly this had in many cases contributed to a loss of female solidarity and identification, a greater class polarization, and a diminished sense of self. The Victorian ideal had posited women in the domestic sphere, but placed them as the undisputed arbiters of that sphere. They were genuinely thought of as powerful and necessary in their moral and educational influence. Many women were dissatisfied with their limited options, but few expressed self-doubt or insecurity about their importance and value in the overall scheme of things. This sense of security began to wane as the Victorian era drew to a close.

9. The professions women were entering were mostly service oriented, such as teaching, nursing, and settlement house (social) work. There were also more women working in clerical and sales positions, and though they were not well paid, they did have a degree of financial and concomitant social independence. Such individuals were portrayed in the popular media as new, more liberated women. Most females who worked in these jobs were single (approximately 85 percent of the female labor force was unmarried at the end of the century). See Hill, *The World Their Household,* 116–17; Epstein, *Politics of Domesticity;* Barbara Ehrenreich and Deidre English, "The Manufacture of Housework," *Socialist Review* 5 (Oct.–Dec. 1975): 14; Joan Jacob Brumberg and Nancy Jones, "Women in the Professions: A Research Agenda for American Historians," *Reviews in American History* 10 (June 1982).

10. New England Hospital for Women and Children *Annual Reports,* 1864–1910, in Archives, Sophia Smith Collection Library, Smith College, Northampton, Massachusetts.

11. Mary Mumford, "The Place of Benevolence in Club Work," in *Women's Cycle* 1, no. 8 [Association of Federated Women's Clubs Convention Number] May 15, 1890, 39–40.

12. Lorraine Bucklin in ibid., 12, 16; see also Emmeline Wells, *Charities and Philanthropies: Woman's Work in Utah* (Salt Lake City: George Q. Cannon and Sons, 1893), 25–54; Faustina Nenno, *Placentia Round Table Club: The First Thirty-five Years, January 1902–December 1937* (Placentia, Calif.: Placentia Courier Publishing, 1938), 55–56; Sadie Boyd Saxton and Elizabeth Bowman, "Stages and Highlights of Ossoli Circle's History," *Chronological History,* 1885–1960 (Knoxville: Ossoli Circle, 1960), 24–26; Ellen Henrotin, *The Attitude of Women's Clubs and Associations Toward Social Economics* (Washington: Bulletin of the Department of Labor, no. 23, July 1899). Of the 1,283 women's clubs listed in this bulletin, less than 10 percent claimed philanthropic or charitable activities as part of their function.

13. Apostol, "They Said It," 67–76.

14. Blair, *The Clubwoman;* Peiss, *Cheap Amusements,* 168–69. The Round Table Club of Placentia, California, was one that abandoned its annual market in 1915 when members agreed that they preferred and were able to pay dues (Nenno, *Placentia Round Table Club,* 1915 records). The idea that women's

clubs generally represented a middle-class hegemony is also reflected in Breckenridge's comment (*Woman in the Twentieth Century*, 70) that farm women were poorly represented.

15. Blair, *The Clubwoman*, 193; *Woman's Journal and Suffrage News*, Dec. 1, 1906, 188.

16. Members of the Massachusetts Woman Equal Suffrage Association seemed overwhelmingly enthused in 1886 when Mary Livermore was still president of the bazaar, but they stopped holding fairs altogether in 1901. They tried to resurrect the tradition in 1908, but unfortunately there was a devastating fire in Chelsea when their fair was about to open, and the "benevolent part of the public" was too busy assisting the homeless to come to the fair. Profit was barely $500. See *Woman's Journal*, Apr. 25, 1908, 66.

17. *Woman's Journal*, Dec. 18, 1886, 404; Feb. 10, 1891, Oct. 13, 1900, Nov. 3 and Nov. 10, 1900, Dec. 9 and Dec. 15, 1900; *Souvenir*, National Suffrage Bazaar, 1900; Elaine Hedges, "Stitches in Time: Sewing, Gender and the Politics of Femininity at the Ends of Two Centuries," typescript of paper presented at the American Studies Association, New York, Nov. 1985, esp. 6–9.

18. Susan Reynolds Williams, "In the Garden of New England: Alice Morse Earle and the History of Domestic Life" (Ph.D. diss., Univ. of Delaware, 1992); Hazel T. Craig, *The History of Home Economics* (New York: Practical Home Economics, 1945). Ruth Bordin points out that some of the same women who had worked with the temperance cause in the 1870s had moved into settlement house work and the suffrage cause by the 1890s. See "'A Baptism of Power and Liberty': The Women's Crusade of 1873–1874," in *Woman's Being, Woman's Place*, 151.

19. "Hebrew Fair"; *New York Times*, Dec. 12, 1880; "Vacations for Working Women," *New York Times*, Dec. 12, 1885; "A Fair for Saleswomen," *New York Times*, Apr. 18, 1885; "Fairs for Charitable Purposes," *New York Times*, Dec. 16, 1885; "Rest for Working Girls," *New York Times*, Dec. 10, 1886; "Many Handsome Dolls," *New York Times*, Dec. 11, 1886; "A Very Unique Fair," *New York Times*, Dec. 16, 1887; "To Aid the Ladies Hospital," *New York Times*, Apr. 10, 1888; "In a Pink Bower," *New York Times*, Dec. 11, 1890; "Red Cross Bazaar," *New York Times*, Dec. 20, 1896; "Silver Cross Nursery Fair," *New York Times*, Nov. 18, 1896; "Fair for Wayside Nursery," *New York Times*, Nov. 19, 1896; "An Easter Market," *New York Times*, Mar. 11, 1894; "The Social World," *New York Times*, Dec. 13, 1893; "In Aid of Worthy La Creche," *New York Times*, Apr. 14, 1893; "Dolls Sold for Charity," *New York Times*, Nov. 27, 1892; "Letter Carriers' Fair," *New York Times*, Nov. 13, 1892; "A Pretty Doll Bazaar," *New York Times*, Nov. 29, 1890; "Christmas Sale for Charity's Sake," *New York Times*, Dec. 14, 1889; "A Scene of Beauty," *New York Times*, Dec. 20, 1888; "Our Lady of the Rosary's Fair," *New York Times*, Nov. 2, 1890; "Fair by Women for Charity," *New York Times*, Feb. 17, 1894. The title of a publication put out by the Presbyterian church missionary society was *Women's Work for Women*. See Brumberg, "Zenanas," 1–9; Hill, *The World Their Household*, 55.

20. James Roland Coates Jr., "Recreation and Sport in the African-American Community of Baltimore, 1880–1920" (Ph.D. diss., Univ. of Maryland, 1991), esp. 77.

21. "For the Alumne [*sic*] Library," *New York Times*, Dec. 4, 1887; "Vis Unita Fortior's Fair," *New York Times*, Mar. 12, 1893; "Library Fair," *Hampshire Gazette*, Feb. 10, 1885; *Hampshire Gazette*, Dec. 25, 1900; *Milwaukee Journal*, May 7–16, 1896; "For Their Loved Poet," *New York Times*, Nov. 18, 1895 and Dec. 25 1895; "Festival of the Danes," *New York Times*, Apr. 1, 1893.

22. William Leach discusses the German tradition of *Gemütlichkeit*, or "pure comfort," which may have predisposed the German American community to particularly high-spirited, festive events. See *Land of Desire*, 139–41.

23. *Souvenir*, German Hospital Fair, New York City, Feb. 1889; "To Aid the German Hospital," *New York Times*, Dec. 9, 1888; "Harvest Bazaar," *Wisconsin State Journal*, Oct. 11, 12, 14, 21, 1895; "The Turnverein Fair," *New York Times*, Mar. 23, 1880; "Marnerchor Fair," *New York Times*, Oct. 9, 1888; "Turner's Fair," *Wisconsin State Journal*, Nov. 30, 1880; "To Have a Monster Fair," *New York Times*, Apr. 3, 1896; "The Great Cuban Fair," *New York Times*, May 14, 1896; "The Big Fair for Cuba," *New York Times*, May 16, 1896; "For the Irish Societies," *New York Times*, Dec. 27, 1896; "The Great Hebrew Fair," *New York Times*, Nov. 10 and Dec. 8, 1895; "The Hebrew Fair," *New York Times*, Dec. 10, 1895. I suspect the $225,000 figure may be a gross rather than net number. Kirshenblatt-Gimblett, "The Moral Sublime," 2–3.

24. Moore, "Funding the Temples," 19–25.

25. Peiss, *Cheap Amusements*, 18.

26. "Letter Carriers' Fair"; "Teacher's Pension Benefit," *New York Times*, Dec. 8, 1890. At the teacher's fair, student's work was displayed at booths set up by teachers from various city wards.

27. "Koltes Post GAR"; *The Knapsack* nos. 1–8, 1879; "Relief Fund of the 11th Regiment," *New York Times*, Nov. 25, 1880; "In Aid of a New Armory," *New York Times*, Mar. 27, 1883; Moore, "Funding the Temples," 22; "Grand Army Fair"; "The GAR Charity Fair," *Hampshire Gazette*, Jan. 27, 1885; "Plans Completed for Masonic Fair," *Atlanta Constitution*, Nov. 9, 1900; "Opening the Pythian Fair," *New York Times*, Apr. 18, 1893; Program, Odd Fellows Home Fair, Lenox Lyceum, New York City, Apr. 18–27, 1895; "Railroad Men's Fair," *Hampshire Gazette*, Apr. 9, 1895.

28. On male bonding in fraternal organizations, see Peiss, *Cheap Amusements*, 18. *Atlanta Constitution*, Dec. 11 and 12, 1900; "G.A.R. Charity Fair"; "Railroad Men's Fair"; "The Great Cuban Fair"; "Big Fair for Cuba."

29. "St. Benedict's Home Fair," *New York Times*, Apr. 7, 1896; "Few Extra Charges," *Milwaukee Journal*, May 11, 1896; "For Their Loved Poet"; "Fifth Regiment Fair"; "St. Leo's Church," *New York Times*, Dec. 8, 1882; "Charity in a Pleasant Guise"; "With a Brilliant Opening," *New York Times*, Nov. 10, 1885; "Grand Army Fair"; "Close of the Fair," *New York Times*, Dec. 19, 1886; "Close of St. Francis Xavier Fair"; "Railroad Men's Fair"; "Grand Fair, Westside Relief Association," *New York Times*, Dec. 12, 1876; "To Enlarge a Home," *New York Times*, Dec. 9, 1878; "Fifth Regiment Fair."

30. Lewis O. Saum, "The Broom Brigade, Colonel Donan and *Clementine*," *Missouri Historical Society Bulletin* 25, no. 3 (1969): 192–200. The broom brigade idea was discussed in print a few years later in a book with suggestions for fundraising fairs. The marches were to be in uniform costume, "as coquettish as you please." The quoted verses are taken from Lucretia Hale and Margaret E. White, 300 *Decorative and Fancy Articles for Presents, Fairs, etc.* (Boston: S. W. Tilton, 1885), 166–68. A broom drill was still featured years later in Edna J. Witherspoon, *Fancy Drills for Evening and Other Entertainments* (London and New York: Butterick, 1894) Metropolitan Pamphlet Series 3, no. 1 (Mar. 1894).

31. *Atlanta Constitution*, Dec. 11–12, 1900; Announcement flyer, The Confederate Relief Bazaar, 1885; Moore, "Funding the Temples," 23.

32. "Masons High and Low Attend Fair's Opening," *The Brooklyn Times*, Apr. 14, 1903.

33. Moore, "Funding the Temples," 20–21; "Everything Ready for Big Bazaar of Masons," *Atlanta Constitution*, Nov. 25, 1900; "Masonic Fair Had Large Profits," *Atlanta Constitution*, Dec. 22, 1900; "A Great Fair," *New York Times*, Apr. 7, 1889; "For Sweet Charity's Sake," *New York Times*, June 17, 1894.
    At an 1899 trade carnival in Chillicote, Ohio, the sponsoring organization even claimed its Streets of India were better than the Streets of Cairo at the World's Fair, because its oriental dancing girls were the "real thing." Many cities mounted street fairs to promote themselves and attract business and outsider visitors. "Profits to Agents," *Hampshire Gazette*, May 16, 1905; "Everything Ready for Big Bazaar," 8; Marling, *Blue Ribbon*, 129; Program, Elk's Street Fair and Trade Carnival, Chillicote, Ohio, May 29–June 3, 1899.

34. "Profits to Agents"; "Our Boston Letter: Charity Benefits That Do Not Benefit Charity," *Hampshire Gazette*, Nov. 26, 1893; "Bazaaring for War-Relief Funds," *The Survey*, Dec. 1, 1917, 252.

35. Benton, *Fairs and Fetes*, 160; Beard and Beard, *Handy Book*, 413–27; Lina Beard, "How to Give a Girls' and Boys' Fair," *The Delineator*, Jan. 1906, 122–24, and Feb. 1906, 304–6. Lina and Adelia Beard specifically saw the *Handy Book* as a girls' guide that would contrast with contemporary sports and amusement guides for boys. Lina Beard was a leader in girls' recreation (in 1905 she published *Handicraft and Recreations for Girls*), and she and Adelia were undoubtedly related to Dan Beard, the author of the 1882 volume *What to Do and How to Do It: The American Boys' Handy Book*, and a leader in the development of the Boy Scouts. He also contributed to both *Ladies' Home Journal* and *Woman's Home Companion* columns on amusements for boys. Between 1891 and 1893 the "Children's Corner" section of *The Delineator* often featured things to make for fairs.

36. Ladies' Aid Society Record Book, Pilgrim Congregational Church, Madison, Wisconsin, Dec. 13, 1904; "St. Ann's Church Fair," *New York Times*, Mar. 31, 1880; "Sunday School Junior Aid Society, Our Savior's Church," *Wisconsin State Journal*, Nov. 30, 1910; "Literary Carnival," *Wisconsin State Jour-*

nal, May 3–4, 1900; "Bazaar and Social," *Wisconsin State Journal,* Oct. 21, 1910; "Merrie Makers Work for Charity," *New York Times,* Mar. 17, 1894; "YWCA and YMCA," *Hampshire Gazette,* Nov. 11, 1890; "Haydenville: A Successful Fair," *Hampshire Gazette,* Feb. 24, 1885; "A Mystery Social," *Hampshire Gazette,* Mar. 19, 1895. It is probable that a contemporary scholar like myself cannot even recognize all the fairs that were run by youth groups. A fair "under the auspices of the library association" in Haydenville, Massachusetts, for example, was actually a youth project.

37. "Bazaar," *Dallas Morning News,* Dec. 3, 1900; "St. John's Church Guild," *Hampshire Gazette,* Dec. 11, 1900, Dec. 4, and Dec. 25, 1900; "Nu Gamma Chi Fair,"; "A Successful Sale," *Hampshire Gazette,* Dec. 14, 1909; "University YWCA Fair," *Wisconsin State Journal,* Nov. 29, 1915, Dec. 5, and Dec. 11, 1915; "For the Free Kindergarten," *New York Times,* Nov. 12, 1892; "Homeopathic Hospital Fair," *New York Times,* Apr. 7, 1885; "A College Bazaar," *New York Times,* Mar. 17 and 22, 1889.

38. "Merrie Makers Work for Charity"; *Woman's Journal,* Dec. 11, 1886, 396; "Episcopal Church Fair," *Hampshire Gazette,* Nov. 24, 1885; "For Sweet Charity's Sake"; Louise E. Dew, "A College Fair," *Entertainment for All Seasons* (New York: S. H. Moore, 1904), 114–15. In *Alma Mater: Design and Experience in the Women's Colleges from Their Nineteenth-Century Beginnings to the 1930s* (New York: Knopf, 1984), Helen Lefkowitz Horowitz discusses how strongly the image of college life dominated popular culture at the turn of the century.

39. For examples of fairs held in these locations, see "For Sweet Charity's Sake"; "Charity in Fashionable Garb," *New York Times,* Dec. 10, 1884; "American Industry for the Blind," *New York Times,* Dec. 10, 1886; "Railroadmen's Fair"; "A Pretty Doll Bazaar," *New York Times,* Nov. 29, 1890; "Snow Festival and Doll's Fairyland," *New York Times,* Nov. 27, 1894; "Charity Made Attractive," *New York Times,* May 26, 1886; "A Fair to Help Children," *New York Times,* Dec. 6, 1896; "Red Cross Bazaar," *New York Times,* Dec. 17, 1896. For a discussion of the nouveaux riche interest in elite fairs, see Davidhoff, *The Best Circles,* 56. See also Cutlip, *Fundraising in the United States,* 33; "Diet Kitchen Fair," *New York Times,* Nov. 22, 1887; "Fair and Loan Exhibit," *New York Times,* Nov. 26, 1893. See also "For Working Girls," *New York Times,* Dec. 11, 1889.

    Note that there were also more and more suggestions as the nineteenth century gave way to the twentieth for fairs in outdoor settings. See "For St. Mary's Hospital," *New York Times,* May 27, 1889; "German Hospital Fair," *New York Times,* Jan. 16, 1889; "Tis the Season of Fairs," *New York Times,* Dec. 7, 1893; "Staten Island Kirmess," *New York Times,* May 8, 1887; "For Sweet Charity's Sake," *New York Times,* May 27, 1887; "Bazaar in the Orchard" [Minister's Social Helper column], *Ladies' Home Journal,* Aug. 1908, 31; Nellie F. Heath, "A Fair in an Orange Grove," *Ladies' Home Journal,* Sept. 1903, 34; Wolcott, "Eight New Fair Booths," 27.

40. *The Gentlewoman,* a magazine geared to the upper-class British woman, listed more than fifty bazaars in a six-month period in 1904 and indicated who was on hand to "open" each one. Some titled women traveled from one to another, putting in only a brief appearance at each. See also Prochaska, *Women and Philanthropy,* 65. American fairs were "opened" by celebrities, political leaders, or even well-known leaders of a given ethnic group. Social leadership was determined not only by class, but also by context. At some of the New York fairs of the 1890s, for example, the unquestioned patronesses and leaders were Jewish women. These women had great status in their own community, but might not have been courted as social leaders of the city as a whole. For a general discussion of the socialites' role, see Davidhoff, *The Best Circles*; John Mayer, "Private Charities of Chicago, 1871–1915" (Ph.D. diss., Univ. of Minnesota, 1978), 486–95. Lawrence W. Levine's *Highbrow/Lowbrow: The Emergence of Cultural Hierarchy in America* (Cambridge: Harvard Univ. Press, 1988) is helpful for a general understanding of the social conditions that engendered this kind of "society."

41. "The Great Cuban Fair"; "Big Fair for Cuba"; "Colonial Supper and Sale," *Wisconsin State Journal,* Feb. 21, 1895; "Bedford St. Church Fair," *New York Times,* Nov. 18, 1877; "A Novel Church Fair," *New York Times,* Jan. 22, 1880; "Kirmess and Flower Fete," *New York Times,* Mar. 26, 1894; "An Easter Market"; "For the Brooklyn Orphan Asylum," *New York Times,* Nov. 15, 1889; "A Brilliant Fair," *New York Times,* Apr. 12, 1889; "Vis Unita Fortior's Fair"; "Silver Cross Nursery Fair"; "A Scene of Beauty," *New York Times,* Dec. 20, 1888; "A Very Pretty Festival," *New York Times,* Nov. 13, 1890; "A Dairymaid's Reception," *New York Times,* Dec. 9, 1887; "Fair for the Normal College Library," *New*

York Times, Dec. 7, 1888; "A Very Unique Fair"; " A Paradise of Gypsies," *New York Times,* Oct. 13, 1887; *Hampshire Gazette,* Nov. 24, 1885; Peiss, *Cheap Amusements,* 121.

42. Weimann, *Fair Women,* 333. The women of St. John's Church in Northampton had sponsored a "World's Carnival" in 1890 (*Hampshire Gazette,* Oct. 28, 1890), but Palmer's Chicago event may have been the first fundraising fair with the "All Nations" title. Other bazaars with this name followed in short order. Periodicals featuring suggestions for fairs just after the turn of the century referred to the Fair of All Nations as a standby theme that would be familiar to everyone. See "An Easter Market"; coverage of Bazar of All Nations, *Milwaukee Journal,* May 7–16, 1896; "The Minister's Social Helper," *Ladies' Home Journal,* Oct. 1907, 31; Caroline Benedict Burrell, "Church Fairs," *Harper's Bazar,* Aug. 1905, 774.

43. Weimann, *Fair Women,* 1, 132; "An Easter Market"; *Hampshire Gazette,* Oct. 14, 1890. The interpenetration between agricultural, educational, and fundraising fairs continued as well. Women's associations continued to sell handmade goods at agricultural fairs in both Northampton and Madison. Fancywork and food booths were also evident at the "Pharmacy Fair," held in Boston in 1895 (see *Boston Transcript,* May 1, 1895). This was an educational exhibit sponsored by a state commission on pharmaceutical affairs, which featured daily lectures and demonstrations of scientific principles, home nursing, nutrition, and physical fitness. However, ladies representing the Charity Club Hospital, the Lend-a-Hand Hospital, and the Soldier's Home sold fancywork to raise money for their respective charities. To complicate matters even further, there was a complete miniature reproduction of the recent world's fair at this event, and there were band concerts and other entertainments in the evenings. It was impossible to say where one type of fair began and the other left off.

44. Rydell, *All the World's a Fair,* esp. 29.

45. "Fancy Fairs and Bazaars"; Wolcott, "Eight New Fair Booths," 27; "The Bazar on the Lawn," *Ladies' Home Journal,* July 1912, 50; "Japanese Street," *New York Times,* Dec. 8, 1892; "Christmas Bazaar," *Los Angeles Examiner,* Nov. 28, 1913. Japanese tea gardens were also popular no matter what the ostensible theme of the fair, and almost every fair had a selection of paper fans and parasols for sale. Regarding the associations made between Japan and the aesthetic, see Lancaster, *Japanese Influence,* 48–54; Jane Converse Brown, "Fine Arts and Fine People: The Japanese Taste in the American Home, 1876–1976," in *Making the American Home,* 121–22.

46. Regarding European fairs, see *The Knapsack,* Nov. 17, 10; Nov. 19, 4; "Peasant Costumes at a Fair," *New York Times,* Dec. 14, 1880. Brumberg discusses the "masses of American women" who embraced the study of ethnology as early as the 1870s ("Zenanas," 2). This trend was evident in women's activities at the world's fairs. Lists of the exhibit items at the Woman's Building of 1893 indicate inclusion of many objects produced by non-Western women, and at the 1905 Louisiana Purchase Exposition women were said by one of the lady managers to be the undisputed leaders in anthropological research used in fair preparation. See Weimann, *Fair Women,* 135; Board of Lady Managers of the Louisiana Purchase Exposition, *Report to the Louisiana Purchase Exposition Committee* (1905), 242; Peiss, *Cheap Amusements,* 121.

47. The word "kermes" may be of Turkish origin. In Turkey, bazaar-type sales are still known by this name (they do not involve costumes or dancing). Personal conversation with Bilon Gurayman and Serim Denel, Istanbul, June 1992.

48. "Dances of Different Nations," *New York Times,* Apr. 15, 1885; "The Kirmess in New York," *New York Times,* Apr. 14, 1885; "Kermiss Festival," *Wisconsin State Journal,* May 10 and 11, 1900; "Souvenir of Kirmess," Richmond, Virginia, 1896 (Valentine Museum Collection, 30.39; see also Valentine Museum photograph 43.8.7.51); Women's City Relief Association *Annual Report* (Boston, 1897). In a discussion of ways that girls in clubs might earn money, one advice-giver noted that the "kermess or kettledrum" was a simple solution. She described an event where refreshment tables were staffed by girls in costume, but there was no dancing. *The House and Home: A Practical Book* (New York: Scribner's Sons, 1894), 205; Glassberg, *American Historical Pageantry.*

49. "A Paradise of Gypsies." At a similar fair held in Northampton, a king and queen were selected from the local "gypsies" (*Hampshire Gazette,* Nov. 24, 1885).

50. "Who Will Aid the Fair," *New York Times,* Dec. 2, 1887; "Great Throngs at a Fair," *New York Times,*

Dec. 7, 1886; *Souvenir,* Fair at the Hotel Vendome for the Benefit of the New England Hospital for Women and Children (Dec. 4–9, 1899). Ann Uhry Abrams, "Frozen Goddess: The Image of Woman in Turn-of-the-Century-Art," in *Woman's Being, Woman's Place,* 93–108, describes the general idealized artistic image of woman in this era. Abrams argues this idealization, which put women on a pedestal and removed them from daily life, was a reactionary counterforce in a time when women's position was rapidly changing.

51. "To Have a Monster Fair"; "French Fair," *New York Times,* Apr. 28, 1882; "Some Hints," 790. The actual dates of this kind of design shift may have varied, but the progression was consistent. The 1886 suffrage bazaar in Boston still featured booths representing town chapters or leagues, and most featured much of the same merchandise. No costumes were effected. By 1908, their bazaar tables, attendants and products were all color-coordinated in a rainbow theme. See *Woman's Journal,* vols. 12 and 39.

52. "A Festival of the Year," *New York Times,* Apr. 17, 1887; "Pretty Things in a Bazaar," *New York Times,* Dec. 3, 1890; "Real Folks' Fair," *Hampshire Gazette,* Dec. 7, 1909; "The Unitarian Success," *Hampshire Gazette,* Dec. 10, 1895; "Edwards Church Rainbow Tea," *Hampshire Gazette,* Feb. 11 and 18, 1890; "Rainbow Bazaar," *Wisconsin State Journal,* Jan. 19 and 21, 1895.

53. "Congregational Church Market," *Wisconsin State Journal,* Dec. 12–13, 1895; "Aided by Sister Churches," *New York Times,* Dec. 2, 1889; "Christmas Sale for Charity," *New York Times,* Dec. 4, 1895; "Unitarian Church Sale," *Hampshire Gazette,* Dec. 18, 1900; "Nu Gamma Chi Fair"; "Kirmess in New York"; Nourse, "Suggestions for Fairs," 265. Theresa Wolcott, author of the "Fair of the Good Fairies" article in *Ladies' Home Journal,* Oct. 1916, 28, credited fairy tale books and children's literature as the source of her booth ideas. See also "The Minister's Social Helper," *Ladies' Home Journal,* 31; Theresa H. Wolcott, "All Sorts of Church Fairs," *Ladies' Home Journal,* Nov. 1905, 23; Mary Dawson, "New Plans for Fairs and Bazaars, *The Ladies World,* May 1911, 25; "A Paradise of Gypsies." I have been unable to learn Mrs. Roosevelt's first name.

54. Glassberg, *American Historical Pageantry,* 26–27; Jack McCullough, *Living Pictures,* 121. Susan Stewart argues that the fairy world is usually seen as a female one. See *On Longing: Narratives of the Miniature, the Gigantic, the Souvenir, the Collection* (Durham: Duke Univ. Press, 1993), 112.

55. The temperance fair was under the sponsorship of the National Christian League, which was raising money for a training school and country retreat for unemployed women. "Temperance Bazaar," *Hampshire Gazette,* Oct. 22,1895; "Fair by Women for Charity," *New York Times,* Feb. 17, 1894; "Woman's Slavery to Fashion," *New York Times,* Feb. 23, 1894.

56. The first discussion of a mock art gallery appeared in "Some Hints," 790–91; it is from this reference that the "Sweet Seventeen" feature is taken. The "mystery" gallery was reported in "A Carnival of Mimic Commerce," *New York Times,* Dec. 16, 1884. Mockeries of this type were based, of course, on a solid understanding of practices and conventions of the art world. This was made particularly explicit in instruction books of the 1920s, where the "common catches" were referred to as "classic." See Albert M. Chesley, *Social Activities for Men and Boys* (New York: Associated Press [with the YMCA], 1921), 78–81. For information on burlesque tableaux, see McCullough, *Living Pictures,* 103, 118–21.

57. Stewart, *On Longing,* 117–25; quotation on p. 123.

58. "Beautiful but Dumb," *New York Times,* Dec. 4, 1886; "Babies' Day at the Dress Congress," *New York Times,* Feb. 25, 1894; "Japanese Street"; "Dolls to Wed for Charity," *New York Times,* Nov. 16, 1892; "A Doll Wedding," *New York Times,* Nov. 19, 1892; "St. Valentines Market," *New York Times,* Feb. 5, 1889; "Actresses Open Their Fair," *New York Times,* Dec. 16, 1893; "Charity Doll Show," *New York Times,* Dec. 8, 1890; "Seaside Sanitarium Fair," Nov. 30, 1881; "Christmas Bazaar," *Wisconsin State Journal,* Dec. 4–5, 1895; "Doll Fete," *Wisconsin State Journal,* Dec. 11–12, 1900; "Many Handsome Dolls," *New York Times,* Dec. 11, 1886; Hale and White, 300 *Decorative and Fancy Articles,* 171; "Restaurant and Bazaar," *Atlanta Constitution,* Dec. 20, 1900; "A Doll Bazaar of 1894," *Hobbies: The Magazine of Collectors,* Dec. 7, 1900, 9.

A doll presented to an earlier suffrage fair by First Lady Ida McKinley was brought back to a

1909 event for the same cause, re-dressed as a Norwegian (women had just won the vote in that country). *Woman's Journal,* Dec. 8, 1909, 205. In an interview in Madison in 1986, Evelyn Huggins discussed her memories of doll booths at church fairs. Milliners sometimes dressed the dolls, she told me, but it was also exciting for teenagers to do so. She had been in charge of a doll booth at a Janesville, Wisconsin, fair in 1915, when she was twelve.

59. Ennis Baldwin Coffey, "A Dolls' Department Store" ("Planning the Church Fair"), *Ladies' Home Journal,* Sept. 1903; "Doll Convention," *Wisconsin State Journal,* Dec. 4–5, 1900; Burrell, "Church Fairs," 772–75.

60. "Aided by Sister Churches." References to tableaux are legion. See, for example, the *Hampshire Gazette,* Feb. 18, 1890. Wall and ceiling decoration was still highlighted in the fair environment in the 1880s, but after that time it was only referred to in the context of a background setting, such as when the hall was decked in green for a flower theme fair. See "Aiding Hebrew Orphans," *New York Times,* Nov. 27, 1888; Beard and Beard, *Handy Book,* 413, 493; "Church Bazaars for Eastertime." The one reference I have seen to wall decor after the turn of the century is from 1904, when strings of popcorn caught up in ears of corn were suggested as wall adornment for a harvest festival. Anna Wolf Davis, "Harvest Time in the Church," *Ladies' Home Journal,* Oct. 1904, 22. This was an atypical arrangement, and it was much lighter in feel than the dense evergreen wreaths and drapery of the nineteenth century.

61. Beard and Beard, *Handy Book,* 413.

62. Stewart, *On Longing,* 61–62. Several other scholars also allude to the idea that enclosure was related to control (see Orvell, *Real Thing,* 35), or was a principle or strategy favored by turn-of-the-century women. Susan Williams discusses ("In the Garden of New England") the way that Alice Morse Earle used enclosure to ensure intimacy and help create a corrective for contemporary problems. Leslie Mina Prosterman discusses the idea of an ideal, stylized environment in "The Aspect of the Fair," 264–265.

63. See Michael I. Shoop, "A History of the Museum of the Confederacy, Richmond, Virginia, and its Library, 1896–1946" (Master's thesis, Univ. of North Carolina, Chapel Hill, 1983), 18. On cozy corners, see Katherine C. Grier, "The Decline of the Memory Palace: The Parlor After 1890," in *American Home Life, 1880–1930: A Social History of Spaces and Services,* ed. Jessica H. Foy and Thomas J. Schlereth (Knoxville: Univ. of Tennessee Press, 1992), 59–62; Mary H. O'Conner, "Some Original Suggestions, Useful and Decorative, for Historical Cozy Corners," *The Home Decorator and Furnisher,* May 1898, 56–57. Remarkably similar-looking dressing tables appear in "Good Points in Dressing Tables," *The Home Decorator and Furnisher,* Apr. 1898, 26–27.

64. Dawson, "New Plans for Fairs and Bazaars," 2; "To Have a Monster Fair"; "Japanese Street"; "Has Your Church Had Fairs Like These?" *Ladies' Home Journal,* Nov. 1906, 21.

65. "The Minister's Social Helper," *Ladies' Home Journal,* 31.

66. Wolcott, "All Sorts of Church Fairs," 23; "For the Big Bazaar," *Milwaukee Journal,* May 4, 1896.

67. An excellent discussion of the meaning of porches in women's lives is found in Sue Bridwell Beckham, "The American Front Porch: Women's Liminal Space," in *Making the American Home,* 69–89.

68. Gabrielle Rosier, "A Garden Fair for Summer," *Woman's Home Companion,* Aug. 1913, 19.

69. Stewart, *On Longing,* 46; Gaston Bachelard, *The Poetics of Space,* trans. Maria Jolas (New York: Orion Press, 1964), esp. 6–10, 150. The subject of control and scale is also addressed in Alton J. DeLong, "Phenomenological Space-Time: Toward an Experiential Relativity," *Science* 213 (July 1981).

70. For references to enlarged booths, see "The Minister's Social Helper," 31; Wolcott, "All Sorts of Church Fairs," 23; Ann Lawrence, "A Big Candy-Basket Booth" [Ideas for Church Socials], *Ladies' Home Journal,* Nov. 1902, 27; "The New Fair Booths," *Ladies' Home Journal,* Nov. 1914, 21; Caroline French Benton, "A Birthday Fair and Cake Sale," *Woman's Home Companion,* Mar. 1914, 31; "Has Your Church Had Fairs Like These?" 21; Wolcott, "Eight New Fair Booths," 27; "For Sweet Charity's Sake," *New York Times,* June 17, 1894. Stewart claims that miniaturization is associated with the female and enlargement with the male (*On Longing,* 112). I believe the male association would in some senses be neutralized when mixed with images of food and domesticity.

71. "For Fairs and Bazaars," *Ladies' Home Journal,* Nov. 1900, 21; Heath, "A Fair in an Orange Grove," 34; Kenney, "Church Fair Booths," 561; Mary Dawson, *Money-Making Entertainments* (Philadelphia: D. McKay, 1911), 183–84; "All Sorts of Church Fairs," 23; Wolcott, "Eight New Fair Booths," 27.

72. Emma C. Hewitt, *Queen of the Home—Her Reign From Infancy to Age, From Attic to Cellar* (Oakland, et al.: H. J. Smith, 1889), 331; Orvell, *Real Thing,* 50.

73. Dew, *Entertainments,* 97–98, 101, 105–6; "The Bazar on the Lawn," 50; Wolcott, "All Sorts of Church Fairs," 23; Beard and Beard, *Handy Book,* 417–19; "Festival of the Danes." Crepe paper was generally simpler and less expensive to work with than muslin, mosquito netting, or other kinds of cloth, and it was available in an array of pleasing hues. A novel type of crepe paper mentioned in *The Delineator* in 1895 had a tinted border, but readers were told that an industrious woman with a box of water colors could easily "wash in a similar effect" (Nourse, "Suggestions for Fairs," 264). Both the Butterick and Dennison Crepe Paper companies published booklets with instructions for making decorations, costumes, and fancy articles from working with the new material. See *How to Make Paper Costumes; How To Make Crepe Paper Flowers* (Framingham, Mass.: Dennison Co., n.d.). By 1913 *Woman's Home Companion* even commented it was wiser to buy paper flowers than to make them (the reason was not specified), but there is no indication that they were available in ready-made form much before that date.

74. Women were believed to be especially capable of developing their artistic nature, and it was agreed that they should do so because art was by definition uplifting, moral, and good. See Roger B. Stein, "Artifact as Ideology: The Aesthetic Movement in its American Cultural Context," in *John Ruskin and Aesthetic Thought in America, 1840–1900* (Cambridge: Harvard Univ. Press, 1967), for a full development of this thesis. Janet E. Ruutz-Rees contended in her 1881 guide, *Home Decoration: Art Needlework and Embroidery, etc.* (New York: Appleton, 1881), that "taste and skill in decoration are faculties which can be cultivated, and which once awakened, will rarely sleep again" (5). Margaret Payne, "Knick-Knacks and Necessaries," *Peterson's Magazine,* Sept. 1890, stated that "pretty things are more necessary than ever these days because feminine taste generally has been educated to a point where ugly or inartistic surroundings become an actual pain to endure" (453).

   The training of aesthetic sensibility was seen as an integral part of women's development, so much so that it was incorporated into female-identified organizations of all kinds. The Camp Fire Girls, for example, did not just engage girls in outdoor and group activities, but did so in appealing uniforms. The outfit consisted of cascades of long, loosened, or braided hair and a ceremonial gown that was supposed to imply an Indian maiden. See Charles E. Strickland, "Juliette Low, the Girl Scouts, and the Role of American Women," in *Woman's Being, Woman's Place,* 259. Women's colleges routinely sponsored picturesque ceremonies with strong aesthetic appeal. The entire student body at Vassar was involved in a "daisy chain procession" at the college's graduation ceremonies in 1902. Students marched in double rows, with long ropes of daisies undulating between them. Girls at Smith and at Wells College participated in similar processions, and sometimes also performed Maypole dances. Activities of this sort were illustrated in a *Ladies' Home Journal* series entitled "What a Girl Does at College," and were held as the ideal for the most educated and refined women of the day. See Carolyn Halsted, "The Close of the College Girls' Term," *Ladies' Home Journal,* May 1902, 26–27.

75. *Record Book,* Pilgrim Congregational Church, Madison, Wisconsin, Nov. 18, 1897, Archives, State Historical Society of Wisconsin; Robert S. Lynd and Helen Merrill Lynd, *Middletown: A Study in Modern American Culture* (New York: Harcourt, Brace & World, 1929), 239. The Lynds also said that 367 of 391 girls they surveyed in Muncie read such magazines.

   Ideas discussed in the magazines were usually derived from events that had already taken place. If we track a particular theme, we often see that it was reported in community newspapers before it appeared in national magazines or instruction books. For example, rainbow fairs were reported in Northampton in 1890, in Madison in 1895, and in New York in 1894 (there it was proclaimed to be no longer novel), but the first time the theme appeared in a magazine was in *Harper's Bazar* in 1905. The first year the Fair of the Nations was listed in the periodicals was also 1905. As we have seen, such a fair had first taken place at least twelve years before. "Edwards Church Rainbow Tea"; "Rainbow Bazaar"; "For Sweet Charity's Sake," *New York Times,* June 17, 1894; Helen Landon, "The Church

Sociable," *Harper's Bazar,* Oct. 1905, 1050; Marjorie Williams, "Novel Ideas for Fairs," *Harper's Bazar,* Dec. 1910, 722; "The Minister's Social Helper," *Ladies' Home Journal,* 31. The very abundance of the turn-of-the-century prescriptive literature also indicates the pressure to come up with ever novel, interesting attractions.

76. Other such stories abound. Singer Minnie Hauk worked at the floral booth at a fair for St. Vincent's Hospital and was "constantly surrounded by a huge throng." See "Mrs. Cleveland at the Fair," *New York Times,* May 23, 1890; "For the Free Kindergarten"; "Red Cross Bazaar," *New York Times,* Dec. 20, 1896; "To Aid a Hospital," *New York Times,* Nov. 5, 1896; "Lehmann at Fair," *New York Times,* Feb. 25, 1889; "Minnie Hauk Selling Bouquets."

77. "Campanini at a Fair," *New York Times,* Nov. 28, 1880; "President Taft to Open Actor's Fund Fair," *New York Times,* May 8, 1910.

78. "The Great Cuban Fair."

79. Moore, "Funding the Temples," 21; Coffey, "A Dolls' Department Store," 34.

80. See especially "Plans Completed for Masonic Fair"; "Great Crowds at Masonic Fair," *Atlanta Constitution,* Dec. 6, 1900.

81. Moore, "Funding the Temples," 21. Note that one place raffling was not found was at the suffrage fairs; the *Woman's Journal* made a point of the suffragist's forbearance (Dec. 11, 1886, 396).

82. "A Genial Company of Curios," *New York Times,* Dec. 15, 1887; "A Very Unique Fair"; "A Paradise of Gypsies"; "Pilgrim Congregational Church," *New York Times,* Dec. 15, 1882; "Confederate Bazaar," *The Atlanta Constitution,* Apr. 9, 1893; "St. Valentine's Market," *New York Times,* Feb. 10, 1889. On peddler's fairs, see Williams, "Novel Ideas," 722; Burrell, "Church Fairs," 772. Note that in at least some cases, the peddler's fair must have been akin to the "peasant" fair, for wealthy women "played" at a classic lower-class occupation.

83. "A Fair for Saleswomen"; "Endowing a Hospital Bed," *New York Times,* Mar. 27, 1889.

84. *Atlanta Constitution,* Apr. 2, 1893; Lewis, "Everything Under One Roof," 36–41; Harris, "Museums, Merchandising," 151–54; Leach, "Transformations in a Culture of Consumption," 322. Customers had to be compelled to stay for some time at both stores and fairs and had to feel comfortable enough to spend money generously. Late-nineteenth-century stores offered customer services and amenities such as sitting, reading, and letter-writing rooms, restaurants, and cafes, and sometimes even child-care facilities and showers. See also Robert Hendrickson, *The Grand Emporiums: The Illustrated History of America's Great Department Stores* (New York: Stein and Day, 1979), 46; Leach, *Land of Desire,* 111–12.

85. *Woman's Journal,* Nov. 13, 1886, 364; personal account book kept by Mary Pauline du Pont (including records of the St. Mary Society of Christ Church, Christiana Hundred, Delaware), 1891–98. Note that this was a church with a very wealthy congregation. The notebook is in the du Pont family archives, Hagley Museum and Library, Wilmington, Delaware.

86. *Woman's Journal,* Dec. 4, 1886, 308; Hale and White, 300 *Decorative Articles.*

87. McCarthy, *Women's Culture,* esp. 60–76; Eileen Boris, *Art and Labor: Ruskin, Morris, and the Craftsman Ideal in America* (Philadelphia: Temple Univ. Press, 1986), esp. 122–30; *House and Home,* 204–5.

88. Harriet North, "The Fair That Never Was," *Woman's Work for Woman and Our Mission in the Field* (New York Presbyterian Church), Sept. 1886, 216–18; Harry Davies, "The Bazaar Party Outflanked," *Good Words* (London), July 1903, 512–15; Louisa Twining, "Are Bazaars a Form of True Charity?" *Murray's Magazine,* Jan. 1888, 230–37; "Opposed to Church Fairs," *New York Times,* Feb. 26, 1881; "The Pro and Con of the Church Supper, Bazaar and Fair," (Woman's Council Table) *Chatauquan,* Nov. 1890, 227–33; "For the Good of the Church," *Ladies' Home Journal,* Mar. 1908, 26; untitled column, *Ladies' Home Journal,* Mar. 1902, 40. On criticism of church life, see Myers, *The Sociable.*

89. "The Spectator," *Outlook,* Sept. 29, 1906, 257; "Opposed to Church Fairs"; Davies, "Bazaar Party," 512–13; "The Pro and Con," 227–33; "The Great Bazar in Freeville," *Harper's Bazar,* Feb. 13 1875, 115; *Chatauquan,* Nov. 1890. "Pro" arguments for fairs included the familiar idea that they provided an opportunity for people to both develop and learn to appreciate their own and one another's skills, and they provided women who had no other way of contributing to a cause a means to do so. On criticism of agricultural fairs, see Neely, *Agricultural Fair,* 190–210; Marling, *Blue Ribbon,* 66.

90. "The Spectator," *Outlook,* Dec. 7, 1900, 781–82.

91. *Wisconsin State Journal,* Dec. 6 and 14, 1900, Apr. 29, 1905, Apr. 30, 1910; *Hampshire Gazette,* Nov. 13, 1900, Dec. 4, 1900, Dec. 18, 1900; Ladies Aid Society Record Book, Pilgrim Congregational Church, 1900–1910, Madison, Wisconsin; *Atlanta Constitution,* Apr. 1903; Dover [New Hampshire] Women's Club *Yearbook,* 1905–6.

92. "The Spectator," *Outlook,* Dec. 7, 1900, 781–82; "On Progress" ["The Contributor's Club"], *Atlantic Monthly,* Sept. 1903, 430–31.

93. *Hampshire Gazette,* Mar. 21, and other misc. entries, 1905; *Wisconsin State Journal,* misc. entries, 1905.

Six. Fairs during and between the World Wars

1. Warren I. Susman, *Culture as History: The Transformation of American Society in the Twentieth Century* (New York: Pantheon, 1984), xx; see also *American Heritage History of the 1920s and 1920s* (New York: American Heritage, 1970), 39. The phrase from Karal Ann Marling is taken from the keynote address she gave in November 1990 at the McFaddin Ward House (Beaumont, Texas) conference on the arts in the American home. Much of her talk was summarized in "From the Quilt to the Neoclassical Photograph: The Arts of the Home in an Age of Transition," in the book she edited with Jessica H. Foy, *The Arts and the American Home, 1890–1930* (Knoxville: Univ. of Tennessee Press), 1–13, although her "zooming forward, looking backward" epithet was not repeated there.

2. *The Bazaar Daily* [National Allied Bazaar], nos. 1–9, Boston, Dec. 9–18, 1916.

3. Souvenir program, *Charity Bazaar for the Widows, Orphans and Red Cross of the Central Powers of Europe,* Turner Hall, Wilmington, Delaware, June 12–17, 1916. Understandably, the tone of this event was unusually subdued; although the list of committee members indicated that the usual kind of bazaar booths would be available, the program did not expressly discuss festivities.

4. D'ann Campbell identifies the women as middle class. She claims that black and Hispanic women had little time to devote to volunteer activities. See *Women at War with America: Private Lives in a Patriotic Era* (Cambridge, Mass.: Harvard Univ. Press, 1984), 66–69. The Red Cross was so important that it functioned as a symbol of the good women who contributed to the war effort. Even in advertisements for everyday consumer goods, images of Red Cross nurses were routinely included. See Nancy J. Rowley, "Red Cross Quilts for the Great War," *Uncoverings* [American Quilt Study Group] 3 (1982): 43–44; Jo Ann Ruckman, "Knit Knit and Then Knit—The Women of Pocatello and the War Effort of 1917–1918," *Idaho Yesterdays* 26, no. 1 (1982): 28; Amy Aldrich, *Fifty Years Ago: Early Days of the Cosmopolitan Club* (Stamford, Conn.: Overbrook Press, 1959), 14–15.

5. Ruckman, "Knit, Knit," 29–31; Elizabeth Bissell, "A Patriotic Bazaar," *Ladies' Home Journal,* July 1917, 33; Virginia Hunt, "The New Bazaar Features With Timely Touches," *Ladies' Home Journal,* Oct. 1917, 105; "Red Cross Bazaar," *Capital Times,* Dec. 15, 1917; Ida Clyde Clarke, *American Women and the World War* (New York: D. Appleton and Co., 1918), 413–14. Red Cross chapters also engaged in other kinds of fundraising. They arranged benefit performances and dances, card parties, and quilt auctions.

6. "Artists to Have Festa," *New York Times,* June 3, 1917; "Want to Change Alley," *New York Times,* June 5,1917; "Rag Fair at Festa," *New York Times,* June 6, 1917; "Little Ball Rolls at Alley Festa," *New York Times,* June 7, 1917; "Alley Festa Has No Gambling Now," *New York Times,* June 8, 1917; "Alley Festa is Extended," *New York Times,* June 9, 1917; "Alley Festa With Sunday Left Out," *New York Times,* June 11, 1917; Clarke, *American Women and World War,* 414; Dayton and Barratt, *Book of Entertainments,* 129–30.

7. Jewish women of New York were particularly well represented as chairs of the various committees and were at the same time running other fundraising events, such as a bazaar for Jewish war sufferers held in Adolph Lewisohn's Fifth Avenue house. It is difficult to say if Jewish matrons were disproportionately involved in these activities, or if this impression is created by the special attention their participation received in the *New York Times.* The *Times* did report that Jews had collected twelve

million dollars for relief since the beginning of the war, and it is clear that they were assiduous fundraisers. See "Jewish Relief Day Crowns Hero Land," *New York Times,* Nov. 29, 1917.

8. The story of Hero Land is taken from the following: "Swan to Rid City of Bazaar Impostors," *New York Times,* Nov. 25, 1917; "Milking the Public," *The Bellman,* Dec. 29, 1917, 706–7; "Heroland," *New York Times,* Oct. 28, 1917; "Plans for Hero Land," *New York Times,* Oct. 19, 1917; "Prepare for Hero Land," *New York Times,* Nov. 4, 1917; "Hero Land Drive Starts," *New York Times,* Nov. 9, 1917; "Prepare for Hero Land," *New York Times,* Nov. 11, 1917; "Hero Land Gates to Open Tonight," *New York Times,* Nov. 24, 1917; "Society in War Relief Work," *New York Times,* Nov. 18, 1917; "An Author's Fund," *New York Times Book Review,* Nov. 1917, 479; "Expect Hero Land to Yield a Million," *New York Times,* Nov. 18, 1917; "Hero Land Opening a Blaze of Beauty," *New York Times,* Nov. 25, 1917; "Brittany Day Draws Many to Hero Land," *New York Times,* Nov. 28, 1917; "Jewish Relief Day Crowns Hero Land," *New York Times,* Nov. 29, 1917; "Crowd at Hero Land Breaks All Records," *New York Times,* Nov. 30, 1917; "Possibility Extending Hero Land," *New York Times,* Dec. 1, 1917; "This is Serbian Day at Hero Land Fair," *New York Times,* Dec. 3, 1917; "Hero Land Hears Pleas for Serbia," *New York Times,* Dec. 4, 1917; "Hero Land Pageant Revives Old Poland," *New York Times,* Dec. 5, 1917; "Hero Land Pays Homage to Belgian Minister," *New York Times,* Dec. 6, 1917; "Hero Land Closes Russian Street," *New York Times,* Dec. 7, 1917; "Russian Ambulance Still Out of Bazaar," *New York Times,* Dec. 8, 1917; "Armenia and Syria Have Hero Land Day," *New York Times,* Dec. 10, 1917; "Hero Land to Assist Halifax Sufferers," *New York Times,* Dec. 12, 1917; Dayton and Barratt, *Book of Entertainments,* 130–31.

9. At Boston's Allied Relief Bazaar, actress and decorator Elsie de Wolfe showed stereopticon pictures of the "miracles" performed by overseas doctors treating soldiers who had suffered gas burns. There were also relics from the *Lusitania,* and souvenirs from fighting soldiers. These included postcards made by men in the trenches and embroideries made by recovering soldiers in the Red Cross hospital at Netley, England. The *Bazar Daily* belied the class bias of its editors when it stated that the latter had been made by "rough soldiers, some of them with but one hand. . . . They show an aesthetic sense astonishing in men of this class" (no. 9, Dec. 19, 1916).

10. In *No Place of Grace,* T. J. Jackson Lears discusses the ways the militarist ideal offered the "promise of authentic experience" in the early twentieth century (98–105). Note that the dance pageant was typical of those at civic festivals at this same time. See Glassberg, *American Historical Pageantry.*

11. "Profit $400,000," *New York Times,* Dec. 16, 1917; Clarke, *American Women and the World War,* 414; Campbell, *Women at War with America,* 71; letter from Evelyn Pearly Coe to Rosa Levis, Oct. 25, 1917, in Rosa Levis papers, Archives, Arthur M. Schlesinger Library, Radcliffe College, Cambridge, Massachusetts.

12. "Alley Festa Has No Gambling Now"; "Hero Land to Assist Halifax Sufferers;" "Hero Land," *New York Times,* June 13, 1917.

13. Bessie James, *For God, For Country, For Home: The National League for Woman's Service* (New York: G. P. Putnam's Sons [Knickerbocker Press], 1920), 200–205.

14. Ibid., 233–34; Roy Lubove, *The Professional Altruist: The Emergence of Social Work as a Career, 1880–1930* (Cambridge: Harvard Univ. Press, 1965), 215.

15. "A War-Winning Clothes Bazaar," *Ladies' Home Journal,* Nov. 1918, 130; "Society," *Capital Times,* Mar. 20, 1918; *Capital Times,* Dec. 16, 1918; "What Folks Are Doing," *Capital Times,* Nov. 28 and Dec. 4, 1918. Madison did have a War Relief Shop, a permanent outlet with a downtown storefront location, and there were several sales that took place on its premises. This shop, along with rummage sales, local art sales, and card parties, supported the activities of the Red Cross and the cause of the French orphans.

16. James, *For God, For Country,* 235–36. Robert Lubove notes that many of those who worked on World War I fundraising drives became professional fundraisers after the war (*Professional Altruist,* 215). It is unclear how many of the individuals he refers to were women.

17. Minutes, Hill and Valley Club Community Sewing Circle, Beldenville, Wisconsin, Apr. 7–June 13, 1921, Archives, State Historical Society of Wisconsin; handwritten notes and miscellaneous clippings

in personal scrapbooks, Marietta Pratt papers, Schlesinger Library, Radcliffe College, Cambridge, Mass.; *Boston Traveller*, Dec. 1, 1922; *North Shore Breeze*, Dec. 2, 1922; Pilgrim [Congregational Church] Women's Guild, Record Book, Madison, Wisconsin, 1919–35.

18. References from the *Capital Times*: Apr. 13, 1920; Dec. 1, 1920; Dec. 3, 1920; Nov. 26, 1924; "Society News," Nov. 29, 1924; Dec. 17, 1924; Dec. 18, 1924; Nov. 28, 1925; Nov. 30, 1925; Dec. 5, 1925; "Stage Side Show at Girl Scout Bazaar," Dec. 10, 1929; "Girl Scout Bazaar," Dec. 6, 1929; Dec. 4, 1929; "Yuletide Spirit Pervades Crowds at YWCA Bazaar," Dec. 4, 1924; "Six Sororities Are Conducting Booths at YWCA Circus," Dec. 3, 1929; "Girl Scout Exhibit and Bazaar," Dec. 3, 1929. See also Helen Rand, "Doll Shows for Girls' Clubs," *Playground* 16 (Apr. 1922): 16–17.

19. Glassberg, *American Historical Pageantry*, esp. 52–55, 233; *American Heritage History*, 81; Donna R. Braden, "'The Family That Plays Together Stays Together': Family Pastimes and Indoor Amusements 1890–1930," in *American Home Life*, 145–61; Bonnie E. Snow, "Projects for the School Bazaar: Permodello Modeling," *Industrial-Arts Magazine*, Jan. 1919, 49; Neely, *Agricultural Fair*, 130–44. Note that those identified with the playground or recreation movement were often among the most avid sponsors of community pageants in the years immediately preceding the war. Pageants used many of the same kinds of costuming, processions, and other features that had long been popular at fairs (they were particularly akin to the kermiss version of the fair). See Blair, *The Torchbearers*; Prevots, *American Pageantry*, 9.

20. The 12.2 percent figure is taken from Gordon and Reische, *Volunteer Powerhouse*, 60, but their definition of "professional" woman is not clear. The editors of *America's Working Women* have compiled a chart indicating that 23 percent of working women in 1920 were married, but many of these held unskilled jobs. See Rosalyn Baxandall, Linda Gordon, and Susan Reverby, eds., *America's Working Women* (New York: Random House, 1976), 405. In *The Best Circles*, Leonore Davidhoff claims that World War I "destroyed" the social season system and there was a hectic attempt to resurrect it when the conflict was over. The socialites' activities at fundraising fairs would corroborate this.

21. Each player agreed to "entertain" four other players in a single week, collecting $1.25 from each. The additional players in turn agreed to continue the chain and find four others to play with them.

22. The information about Pratt's activities is taken from her scrapbooks of newsclippings and handwritten notes, kept from approximately 1920 to 1925. The clippings are from local Boston newspapers and papers from other Massachusetts cities (the *Boston Globe, Boston Herald, Boston Transcript, Boston American, Sunday Advertiser, North Shore Breeze, Worcester Telegram,* and *Springfield Republican*). Because the clippings were cut out and pasted in the books, no page numbers (and sometimes no dates) are available for the stories. As many of the clippings were taken from the women's press releases and are nearly or literally identical, I do not cite specific references unless they offer a unique perspective. Note that department stores also featured play areas for children in this era. In Chicago's Boston Store, a playground was made to look like an "immense forest." See Leach, *Land of Desire*, 138.

23. *Boston Globe*, July 16, 1922; *Boston Transcript*, Oct. 16, 1922; Glassberg, *American Historical Pageantry*, 258. It is unclear whether Convey's outfit specialized in benefit fairs or also produced community or commercial pageants.

24. Clippings, Pratt scrapbooks.

25. Dayton and Barratt, *Book of Entertainments*, 135–36; Elizabeth Bissell, "The Buyway Bazaar: A Money-Making Project for Any Town," *Parties*, May–June 1929, 42; Emily Rose Burt, *Make Your Bazaar Pay* (New York: Harper and Brothers, 1925), 14, 18, 24; Bramwell, "Opening of Fir Tree Lodge," 19. Regarding advertising, see T. J. Jackson Lears, "From Salvation to Self-Realization: Advertising and the Therapeutic Roots of Consumer Culture, 1880–1930," in *The Culture of Consumption*.

Just as they had in the sanitary fair days, women came from other areas of the country to learn the tricks of staging fundraising events. One of the first people to visit a Boston fair in 1924, for example, was a woman who spent her winters in Jamaica and wanted to use the same theme in a fair for a children's hospital in that country. Officers of the National League of Women Voters, similarly, came to the Atlantic City Boardwalk to see if such a bazaar was a suitable means to "solve the financial problems of the organization in other states" (miscellaneous clippings, including *Christian Science Monitor,* Dec. 5, 1922, Pratt scrapbooks).

26. Burt, *Make Your Bazaar Pay;* Pansy Meek, "Little Journeys in Foreign Lands," *The Modern Priscilla,* Feb. 1916, 55; Caroline French Benton, "Festival of Travel," *Fairs and Fetes* (Boston: Dana Estes, 1912), 129; Elizabeth Simons Tilton, "Come to the Big Carnival," *Woman's Home Companion,* Aug. 1923, 73; Elizabeth Bissell, "The New 'Movie' Bazaar," *Ladies' Home Journal,* July 1919, 36; Leach, *Land of Desire,* 324–33; *How to Decorate Halls, Booths and Automobiles* (Framingham, Mass.: Dennison Manufacturing Co., 1923).

27. Clippings, Pratt scrapbooks. See especially the *Brookline Chronicle,* Nov. 25 and 26, 1922; *Springfield Republican,* Oct. 6, 1922.

28. Program, Wohltatigteits Bazar (Charity Bazaar Association). Fruhlingsfest der Nachstenliebe Zum Besten der notleidendem Jugend in Deutschland und Oesterreich (Spring Festival for the Benefit of German and Austrian Children), Apr. 16–24, 1921. Note that most of the program is in German, but the patriotic American features were listed in English.

29. Blair, *The Torchbearers,* 193; M. Jamison Trachsel, "Making Money for Your Club or Society," *Dennison's Party Magazine,* Mar.–Apr. 1928, 33.

30. Dorothy Wright, "A Family Af-Fair" ["Ingle Nook" column], *The Farmer's Advocate,* Aug. 1, 1929, 1186; Burrell, "Church Fairs," 772. It is also interesting to trace the way this feature was credited over time. Not only were there two different authors listed in this twenty-four-year period, but the same theme was discussed in *Dennison's Party Magazine* in Oct.–Nov. 1927, 28, credited to Mary D. Webster. *The Farmer's Advocate* version was almost identical to the *Dennison* version, even including the same line drawing. The Dennison company must have sold or leased it to the Canadian publication, because while Dennison was not explicitly credited, readers could send to the *Advocate* for the company's instruction booklets. The fact that Wright could hold a byline on the feature remains unexplained.

31. "Society News," *Capital Times,* Nov. 29, 1924; *Eureka Entertainments* (Philadelphia: Pennsylvania Publishing Co., 1894, 1895, 1927), 36, 84–96, 104; Mary W. Jewett, "An Old English Fair with a Tavern and Shops" *Woman's Home Companion,* Oct. 1929, 87; Dayton and Barratt, *Book of Entertainments,* 121–22. Marling talks about the play spirit as a way of warding off ennui in the modern age. See *Blue Ribbon,* 130. On the underlying doctrines of the 1920s, see also Lears, *No Place of Grace; American Heritage History,* 81–82.

32. Clippings, Pratt scrapbooks; Tilton, "Big Carnival," 73; Burt, *Make Your Bazaar Pay,* 44; "Society," *Capital Times,* Nov. 8, 1920; "Stage Side Show at Girl Scout Bazaar," *Capital Times,* Dec. 10, 1929; "Six Sororities"; Trachsel, "Making Money for Your Club," 21. Note that the image of the clown appeared even in seemingly unrelated contexts. The Little Sister's Table of the Family Af-fair bazaar described in *The Farmer's Advocate* was dominated by a large circus clown (Wright, "A Family Af-Fair," 1186).

33. Dayton and Barratt, *Book of Entertainments,* 126–29; Burt, *Make Your Bazaar Pay,* 4–6; clippings, Pratt scrapbooks; Neely, *Agricultural Fair,* 119; Souvenir: Official Program, Madison's Grand Carnival and Street Fair (Madison, Wisconsin, Oct. 16–19, 1900); Program, Elks' Street Fair and Trade Carnival (Chillicote, Ohio, May 29–June 3, 1899); Neely, *Agricultural Fair,* 119.

34. Dayton and Barratt, *Book of Entertainments,* 126–31; Pratt scrapbooks.

35. Burt, *Make Your Bazaar Pay,* 128; Program, Wholtatigteits Bazar; clippings, Pratt scrapbooks; Chesley, *Social Activities,* 85–88. Regarding the popularity of country fairs, see Lears, "From Salvation," 10; Singmaster, "Big Thursday," 364–79; Arthur Ruhl, "At the County Fair," *Collier's Weekly,* Aug. 16, 1913, 20–21, 34; Richard Lloyd Jones, "The Significance of State Fairs," *Collier's Weekly,* Oct. 1, 1910, 16–17, 41–43; "Memories of the Fall Fair," *Canadian Magazine,* Aug. 1908, 381–83; "The Spectator," *Outlook,* Nov. 12, 1910, 578–80; "The Point of View," *Scribner's,* Oct. 1914, 552–53; Mary A. Whedon, "State Fairs: Intelligent Promoters of the Various Interests of Rural Women: Outlets for Their Activities and Meeting Grounds for Social Intercourse," *The Craftsman,* Oct. 1913, 86–91; William C.

Chilman, "The Feel of Fall in Old Bar Harbor," *New England Galaxy,* Fall 1977, 3–14; *Centennial Year, Mayne Island Fall Fair,* Aug. 14, 1971.

36. Marling, *Blue Ribbon,* 102; Dayton and Barratt, *Book of Entertainments,* 133–35; Burt, *Make Your Bazaar Pay,* 24; Gertrude Ellis-Skinner, "'Twas Up to the Ladies' Aid," *Woman's Home Companion,* Apr. 1925, 63; *Capital Times,* Dec. 4, 1929; Dec. 19, 1924; "Society News," *Capital Times,* Nov. 29, 1924; *Capital Times,* Dec. 15, 1923, Nov. 20, 1925, Dec. 8, 1925; clippings, Pratt scrapbooks; "Society," *Capital Times,* Dec. 12, 1917; "Society News," *Capital Times,* Nov. 29, 1924; Bissell, "The Buyway Bazaar," 42.

37. Leach's study, "Transformations in a Culture of Consumption," ends in 1925, and both the 1986 Winterthur conference, "Consuming Visions," and Gordon and McArthur cover the period through 1920. See Jean Gordon and Jan McArthur, "American Women and Domestic Consumption, 1800–1920: Four Interpretive Themes," in Marilyn Ferris Motz and Pat B. Browne, eds., *Making the American Home: Middle Class Women and Domestic Material Culture, 1840–1940* (Bowling Green: Bowling Green State Univ. Popular Press), 41–42.

38. In Muncie, Indiana, in 1928, women were only half as likely to have servants as they had been in 1890. See Lynd and Lynd, *Middletown,* 169. Regarding rational consumption and new attitudes to objects, see Lears, "Beyond Veblen," 73–98; Gordon and McArthur, "Women and Domestic Consumption," 41, 43; Harriet and Vetta Goldstein, *Art in Everyday Life* (New York: Macmillan, 1925). Note that *Ladies' Home Journal,* which was a strong proponent of rational consumption, stopped discussing fairs after the war.

39. Clippings, Pratt scrapbooks; Wright, "A Family Af-Fair," 1186; Dorothy Wright, "Bazaars for Fun and Profit," *The Farmer's Advocate,* Aug. 1, 1929, 1186. The "handyman" concept was itself taken from contemporary ideas about the value of craft and hobbies. It was influenced by the Progressive emphasis on manual training, and related to an increased amount of leisure time for men.

40. Treasurer's Account Book, Woman's Alliance, First Unitarian Society, Madison, Wisconsin, 1925–36 (Archives, State Historical Society of Wisconsin); interviews with Alice Huibitsge and Georgeanne Cusick, Madison, Wisconsin, Oct. 1986; *Ladies' Home Journal,* Dec. 1925, 67; Deirdre Beddoe, *Back to Home and Duty: Women Between the Wars 1918–1939* (London: Pandora, 1989). See also "To Wear or to Sell at Bazaars: Suitable Aprons of All Kinds," *Ladies' Home Journal,* Oct. 1916, 29.

41. Harris, "Museums, Merchandising," 157, 161–62.

42. Alice Belding, "A House Sale," *Woman's Home Companion,* Feb. 1915, 27. A very similar household bazaar was still suggested forty years later; see "Money-Making Bazaars," *Good Housekeeping,* Sept. 1956, 137.

43. Caroline French Benton, "At the Sign of the Cat," *Woman's Home Companion,* Oct. 1913, 31; Wolcott, "Fair of the Good Fairies," 28; Bissell, "Buyway Bazaar," 42; "The New Fair Booths," *Ladies' Home Journal,* Nov. 1914, 21; Benton, "A Birthday Fair," 31.

44. "The Bazaar on the Lawn," 50; Caroline French Benton, "A Brittany Summer Fair and Festival," *Woman's Home Companion,* Aug. 1914, 21; Ellye Howell Glover, *"Dame Curtsey's" Book of Party Pastimes for the Up-to-Date-Hostess* (Chicago: A. C. McClurg, 1912, 1921), 249; Burrell, "Church Fairs," 712; Dew, *Entertainments,* 113–44; Williams, "Novel Ideas," 722; clippings, Pratt scrapbooks.

45. For a concise discussion of the development of fashion in this era, see Elizabeth Ewing, *History of Twentieth Century Fashion* (Totowa, N.J.: Barnes and Noble, 1974, 1986), 62–91. See also Beverly Gordon, "Dress and Dress-up at the Fundraising Fair," *Dress* 12 (1986): 61–72; and Gordon, "Woman's Domestic Body," 281–301.

46. Dayton and Barratt, *Book of Entertainments,* 74–79, 64.

47. Burt's *Make Your Bazaar Pay* not only gave instructions for fabricating crepe paper and provided specific measurements and supply lists for booths and other projects, but advised readers about the best menus and the best hours to serve particular meals. Both Burt (45–85) and Dayton and Barratt (*Book of Entertainments,* 77) included discussions of fire regulations and other legal matters. Jewett, "An Old English Fair," 87; Dorothy Wright, "Planning Booths for the Church Fair," *Canadian Magazine,* Sept. 1929, 23; Dorothy Wright, "A Maple Leaf Bazaar," *The Farmer's Advocate,* Sept. 20, 1928, 1393.

48. Gordon and Reische, *Volunteer Powerhouse,* 86. Rummage sales were themselves often large in scale at this time. A 1922 Boston sale held by the Tide-Over League netted over $3,500. "Practically all of the

prominent women of the North Shore" were involved. (Clipping from the *North Shore Breeze*, Dec. 2, 1922, in Pratt scrapbook).

49. Frances E. Lanigan, "Women's Exchanges," *Ladies' Home Journal*, May 1900, 38; Henrotin, *Attitude of Women's Clubs*, 510; *Capital Times*, Oct. 24, 1925; Pauline Meyer, *Keep Your Face to the Sunshine: A Lost Chapter in the History of Woman's Suffrage* (Edwardsville, Ill.: Alcott Press, 1980), 15; College Settlement of Philadelphia, Commemorative Number, *Fifty Years, 1892–1942*, n.p.; John P. Rousmaniere, "Cultural Hybrid in the Slums: The College Woman and the Settlement House, 1889–1894," *American Quarterly* 22 (Spring 1980): 45–66.

    Products sold in 1925 at the Madison Woman's Exchange (which seems to have grown out of a temporary War Relief Shop) included baked goods and needlework from "mountain women of Kentucky," indicating that volunteers were not always attending to local relief.

50. "A Penny Fair," *Needlecraft*, July 1932, 2; *History of the First Baptist Church, Madison, Wisconsin, One Hundredth Anniversary, 1847–1947*; Scrapbook, Wisconsin Business and Professional Women's Club (undated), both in the Archives, State Historical Society of Wisconsin. Many of the women's magazines had stopped promoting fundraising fairs by the 1920s; they discussed them only in passing and in the most matter-of-fact manner.

51. Gordon and Reische, *Volunteer Powerhouse*, 86; Harriet Hawes and Eleanor Edelman, *McCall's Complete Book of Bazaars* (New York: Simon and Schuster, 1955), 13–14; Robert S. Lynd and Helen Merrill Lynd, *Middletown in Transition* (New York: Harcourt, Brace, 1937), 249; *The Attic Angels Association, 1889–1949* (Madison: Democrat Printing, 1948), 76; *Capital Times*. In their first book, *Middletown*, the Lynds noted that working-class women often picked up on activities that "business class" women had done a generation ago (281). I believe the burgeoning number of card parties in the 1930s reflects this phenomenon.

52. Annual Reports, First Unitarian Society, Madison, Wisconsin, and Minutes, Hill and Valley Club, Beldenville, Wisconsin, 1937–39; Annual Reports, Pilgrim Women's Guild, Pilgrim Congregational Church, Madison, Wisconsin. All are in the Archives, State Historical Society of Wisconsin.

53. Souvenir Program, International Labor Defense Bazaar, Chicago, Dec. 13–15, 1935; Program Souvenir, Communist Party District 8 Three-Day Red Election Bazaar, People's Auditorium, Chicago, Oct. 21–23, 1932; interview with May Katz, New York City, Aug. 1989. A four-month survey of the *Daily Worker* in 1934 indicated that there were regular bazaars of this type. The Scandinavian Workers Club held a bazaar in October in Chicago, and the International Labor Defense Bazaar and the Red Election Bazaar were both repeated in the same city in December. The New Jersey Communist Party held its "third annual statewide bazaar" that year, and the "fifteenth annual" bazaar of the local chapter of the party was held in Boston. There was also a party event in Cleveland and a Press Bazaar, designated to benefit the *Daily Worker, Young Worker,* and *Morning Freiheit,* in New York.

54. Eveline D. Johnson, "Novelties to Tempt the Tourist," *Needlecraft*, July 1932, 6; Clarence Taylor, "Black Churches of Brooklyn from the Early Nineteenth Century to the Civil Rights Movement" (Ph.D. diss., City Univ. of New York, 1992), esp. 139.

55. "Season of Bazaars Is at Hand, Foretelling Advent of Gift-Giving Period," *Capital Times*, Dec. 1, 1935; Ansel Hartley Stubbs, ed., *Financial and Social Success in Welfare Plans* (Kansas City: Inter-Collegiate Press, 1932), 79; Alma V. Lorimer, "The June Fete" ["Money in the Making"], *Ladies' Home Journal*, Nov. 1933, 33.

56. Stubbs, *Financial and Social Success*, 84; Julia Anne Rogers, "Larks in Latimer Street," *Recreation*, July 1939, 238, 252; personal interview with Alice Huibretsge and Mary Mack, Madison, Wisconsin, Aug. 1986.

57. Christine Ferry and E. Marion Stevens, "These Aprons Will Go to Fairs," *Needlecraft*, Oct. 1932, 7. Note that cutlery and similar household products were also sold at agricultural fairs in this period. Other functional items might be devised when there was a particular audience. A woman who worked at church fairs in Sacramento, California, said her group catered to state employees in nearby offices and specialized in handmade neckties. Interview with Evelyn Huggins, Madison, Wisconsin, Oct. 1986. In their 1939 study of Muncie, Indiana, the Lynds found that one in sixteen of both working-

class and business-class women replied they would do fancywork when they were asked what they would do with extra leisure time (*Middletown in Transition*, 310).

58. Johnson, "Novelties to Tempt the Tourist," 6; Florence R. Casey, "Aprons Are So Pretty!" *Woman's Home Companion*, Sept. 1949, 116; "For Bazaar or Gift List," *Woman's Home Companion*, July 1940, booklet advertisement; Brigham, "For Summer Sales," 7; Anna G. Bailey, "First Aid in the Laundry," *Needlecraft*, Nov. 1923, 17.

59. This particular doll belonged to Marian DeLong, who lived in Cleveland Heights, Ohio. All the gifts at Miss DeLong's "dolly shower," given to her by co-workers from a local public school, were humorous "helpers" of this sort. This is the only one that is still intact over fifty years later. When asked to provide information about this figure, Marian DeLong Merrill was aware of the racial stereotype that was embedded within it. She was quick to point out that "no one thought anything" of such a portrayal fifty years ago (handwritten note to the author, Mar. 1988).

60. Marian Hagen Schiff, "Stuffies You Can Make," *Ladies' Home Journal*, Jan. 1938, 62; *Woman's Home Companion*, Feb. 1934, 128; Lydia Brigham, "For Summer Sales or Fall Bazaars," *Needlecraft*, Aug. 1932, 7; Johnson, "Novelties to Tempt the Tourist," 6; Casey, "Aprons," 116; "Half a Dozen Money Catchers for Church, School or Club," *Woman's Home Companion*, Nov. 1934, 138. The condescending tone was actually beginning to be evident in the late 1920s; similar rhetoric was common, for example, in *Dennison's Party Magazine*.

61. In Wisconsin's Dane County alone, more than 150 organizations, including church, club, and PTA groups, were working with the Red Cross; 3,237 individuals were involved in a single month.

62. Louise C. Marston, "Clubwoman's Business Serious Now," *Wisconsin State Journal*, Dec. 31, 1941; interview with Hazel Hansen conducted by the East Side Oral History Project, Madison, Wisconsin, Mar. 31, 1981, typescript in Archives, State Historical Society of Wisconsin.

63. Miscellaneous clippings in British War Relief Fund scrapbooks, Archives, State Historical Society of Wisconsin, Madison, Wisconsin; "Dickens' Muffin Bay Now Rings Bell in City," *New York Herald Tribune*, Nov. 6, 1941, 13.

64. Curtis, "And One for You," 31, 85; "This Month It's Raising Money for a Cause," 14–21; Cowles, "Make Your Church Bazaar," 70–72.

Seven. The Contemporary Fair

1. *Capital Times*, Nov. 22, 1945; *Capital Times*, Nov. 2, 1950; *Capital Times*, Dec. 5, 1945.

2. Ruth H. Brent, "The Big Club Bazaar," *Good Housekeeping*, Sept. 1956, 142; Janet Suzanne Benton, "A Modern Story of Loaves and Fishes," *American Home*, Sept. 1954, 12, 14–15; Cowles, "Make Your Church Bazaar," 70–72; *Make Your Church Bazaar a Success*, booklet offered by *American Home*, mentioned in Cowles, ibid., 72; "Money Making Ideas for Fairs," offered by Good Housekeeping Institute, mentioned in *Good Housekeeping*, Nov. 1949, 185 [I have not found original editions of either of the last two references]; Hawes and Edelman, *McCall's Complete Book*.

3. Records of the Women's Guild, Pilgrim Congregational Church, Madison, Wisconsin; *Annual Reports* and *Bulletin*, Temple Beth-El, Madison, Wisconsin. (Both documents in the Archives, State Historical Society of Wisconsin). Goods were also celebrated in a family-oriented context in other retailing outlets. Many of the attractions of the world's fairs were transferred to the new suburban shopping centers, which were designed to appeal to entire families. The Great Western Shopping Center in Columbus, Ohio, which opened in 1955, featured replicas of the "wonders of the world," including the Taj Mahal, the Grand Canyon, and the Pyramid of Cheops. Department stores also sponsored thematic events with international overtones. Daytons held an annual flower show with titles like "Scheherazade: Exotic Gardens of Morocco"; Gimbels held a Dutch fair in 1950 that drew over 15,000 people to the Philadelphia store on the first day. See Robert Hendrickson, *The Grand Emporiums: The Illustrated History of America's Great Department Stores* (New York: Stern & Day, 1979), 273; "Dutch Dollar Fair at Gimbels," *Business Week*, May 13, 1950, 121–22.

4. The clubs were set up through the extension services of land grant universities. As such, they were

particularly prevalent in the Midwest. Interview with Carol Anderson, president, Wisconsin Extension Homemakers' Council, Nov. 1988; *Semi-Centennial History,* Pleasant Valley Homemaker's Club, 1933–83, and Minutes, Pleasant Valley Homemaker's Club, Hammond (Pierce County) Wisconsin, 1941–82, Archives, State Historical Society of Wisconsin.

5. Annual Report, Temple Beth-El, 1954; Benton, "A Modern Story," 12–15; Robert West Howard, "Squam's Fair Balances the Budget," *American Home,* July 1954, 24–25.

6. Howard, "Squam's Fair," 24; "What Does the Christmas Bazaar Mean to America," *Ladies' Home Journal,* Nov. 1961, 58.

7. Toni Taylor, "Spring Festival That Brings Good Will," *Woman's Home Companion,* May 1953, 32–33; Eva Beard, "Fair Play for Woodstock's Library," *American Home,* Aug. 1953, 20–22; Toni Taylor, "Home-Front Victory," *Woman's Home Companion,* Apr. 1951, 21–25; "Money Raising," *New York Times,* Apr. 18, 1959; "Money Raising," *New Yorker,* Apr. 18, 1959, 34.

8. "Twelve Helpful Fundraising Ideas for Your Club," *Good Housekeeping,* Nov. 1969, 198–99; Dorothy Siegel, "From Boutique to Barn Sale," *Parent's Magazine,* Aug. 1971, 46–47.

9. Joseph Donaldson, "Are Charity Fund Drives Driving You Crazy?" *American Magazine,* Apr. 1954, 26, 85–88; Marion K. Sanders, "Mutiny of the Bountiful," *Harper's,* Dec. 1958, 23–28; Ralph Lee Smith, "Is This Charity?" *American Mercury,* Dec. 1958, 94–101; Grace Hegger Casanova, "Hints for a Volunteer Fund-Raiser," *Good Housekeeping,* Sept. 1950, 58, 187–88; "Raising Money for Your Organization," *Changing Times,* Sept. 1954, 37–38; "Hire a Professional Fund Raiser?" *Changing Times,* Aug. 1954, 29–20; Joseph E. Sullivan, "Fundamentals of Fund-Raising," *America,* Oct. 12, 1957, 41–42; Max Gunther, "Eight Fundraising Ideas," *Coronet,* Aug. 1961, 79–81; "Good Clipper," *American Magazine,* Aug. 1952, 56. Many of the fundraising organizations of this period were in fact bogus, and there were numerous scandals about fundraising rackets. Honest groups began to band together and coordinate their appeals with professional fundraisers. The United Fund campaigns emerged as a response to these problems.

10. Ruth W. Lee, "Children's Fair," *American Home,* May 1947, 22–23; Carol Brock, "For the Hostess: Come to the Fair," *Good Housekeeping,* Nov. 1949, 151; Hawes and Edelman, *McCall's Complete Book,* 25, 56; Taylor, "Spring Festival," 33; Annual Report, Temple Beth-El, Madison, Wisconsin, 1950.

11. "Comments and Suggestions on the Nutcracker Shop, 1961–1965," miscellaneous papers from the First Unitarian Society, Madison, Wisconsin, Archives, State Historical Society of Wisconsin; Hilda Cole Espy, "How to Make a Success of Your Church Fair," *Woman's Day,* Sept. 1962, 97, 104.

12. Interestingly, this amusing sign was suggested as part of an Old English Fair. Ye Pastry Shoppe, Petticoat Lane, Oxford Street, and other such features were no different from features of adult fairs of the past. Lee, "Children's Fair," 23; Christmas Fundraising Ideas for Clubs," *Good Housekeeping,* Nov. 1965, 176; F. A. Rockwell, "Teenagers Capture a Town, *American Mercury,* Nov. 1960, 144–48; "Try a Fair . . . for Fame and Fortune," *Recreational Digest,* Sept. 1961, 373–74 [reprinted from Edythe and Davie De Marche, *Handbook of Co-Ed Teen Activities* (Associated Press, 1958)]; Gunther, "Eight Fundraising Ideas," 79–81.

13. In general, the students learned to emulate adult women and take on the homemaker role. However, they also reinforced their own childishness and still dependent status at these bazaars. The best-selling items in the 1950s were small stuffed animals made by a woman from a nearby community. The girls snatched up "Goosey Gander," "Honey Bunny," "Gingham Dog," "Snoozum," and "Little Necko" year after year. They also liked fishing pond grabs (geared to college students, not young children). Ultimately, they were not completely responsible for the fair, as the paid youth leader was actually in charge. Univ. of Wisconsin YWCA papers, 1961, Univ. of Wisconsin–Madison Archives.

14. "Trade Mardi Gras," *Time,* Feb. 28, 1955, 80; "Spring Benefits," *Vogue,* Apr. 15, 1956, 94; "How to Raise $400,000 for Music," *Look,* May 3, 1955, 22–24. The galas are still given for these organizations today; the incidence and exclusivity of these events has only increased over time. So-called "guilt dinners" are held at elegant places like the Waldorf-Astoria and the Metropolitan Museum of Art, and ironically many of these events rely as much on elaborate decoration and costuming as any of the earlier fairs. "People want to live in a fantasy for a few hours, not a cafeteria," explained Chris Graftos,

head of social events at the Metropolitan Museum of Art. See Sandra Oddo, "How to Raise Money for a Good Cause and Have a Good Time Doing It," *House and Garden,* Nov. 1976, 144; Bernice Kanner, "Guilt Dinners," *New York,* Dec. 5, 1983, 127–41; Ellen Hopkins, "Our Ladies of Charity," *New York,* Oct. 13, 1986, 46–53.

15. Brent, "The Big Club Bazaar," 142; Hawes and Edelman, *McCall's Complete Book of Bazaars,* 36–38; Helen K. Knowles, *How Groups Raise Funds* (Freeport, Maine: Bond, Wheelwright, 1955, 1961), 25; Marjorie Fatt Chester, *McCall's Book of Fundraising Ideas* (New York: Prentice-Hall, 1963), 55–59.

16. Espy, "How To Make a Success," 44–45, 96. Interestingly, the description and illustration of the Tarrytown kitchen are not completely consistent. In the illustrations, for example, the waitress's aprons are not white but dark. In the sense that the suggestive decor of the 1950s and 1960s was meant to create a feeling, but not overwhelm the sale items, the fair environments of the mid-twentieth century were akin to the environments of the antebellum period.

17. Margo Garrity, "More than 100 Bazaar Best Sellers!" *Better Homes and Gardens,* Sept. 1963, 60–63; "What Does the Christmas Bazaar Mean to America"; Thomas Hine, *Populuxe* (New York: Alfred Knopf, 1986); *Ladies' Home Journal,* Nov. 1961, 58–63.

18. "What Does the Christmas Bazaar Mean to America," 58; "The Christmas Bazaar," *Christian Century,* Nov. 21, 1962, 1435; "Catholics Adopt 'Silent Bazaars,'" *Christian Century,* Nov. 14, 1962, 1379.

19. Carol Brock, "Fund-Raiser's Fair," *Good Housekeeping,* Sept. 1963, 144; Hadassah, "Fund Raising Round Up," typescript, n.d. Technically, an art fair would be a direct exhibition, with artists displaying their artworks; an art show would involve an intermediary person who acted as a curator and artists would not necessarily be involved. Leonard Lieberman and Leslie Lieberman, "What Is an Art and Craft Fair?" paper presented at the Popular Culture Association Conference, Toronto, 1984.

20. YWCA papers. In 1968 three New York stores held simultaneous foreign fairs: Macy's sponsored a Festival of Britain; Gimbels featured a "Euro-fair" that had the look and feel of an Italian castle; and Sterns hosted an Irish-Israeli festival. Bloomingdales set out to create an ongoing "fantasy-like world, a quasi-amusement park . . . that buil[t] a 'crescendo of excitement.'" See "All's Well that Fairs Well," *Publisher's Weekly,* Sept. 16, 1968, 63; Mark Stevens, *Like No Other Store in the World: The Inside Story of Bloomingdales* (New York: Thomas Y. Crowell, 1979), 2–7.

21. Dorothy B. Duran and Clement A. Duran, *The New Encyclopedia of Successful Program Ideas* (New York: Associated Press, 1967), 347; untitled section of "Around the Town," *New Yorker,* Oct. 30, 1971, 42; Robert Jacobson, "Viewpoint," *Opera News,* Jan. 10, 1976, 5; *McCall's Big Book.*

22. Regarding the craft revival, see Beverly Gordon, "The Fiber of Our Lives: Trends and Attitudes About Women's Textile Art as Reflected in the Literature in America, 1876–1976," *Journal of Popular Culture* 10, no. 3 (Winter 1976–77): 553–54. The new emphasis was reflected in the title of an instruction book distributed by RIT dye company in the 1960s, *The Craft and Bazaar Book*—"craft" had top billing; "bazaar" was in second place.

23. Chester, *McCall's Book of Fundraising Ideas,* 53; Brock, "For the Hostess," Nov. 1949, 151–52; Rosemary C. Hutchinson, "Greek-Style Christmas Village: A Bazaar for 4,000," *Better Homes and Gardens,* Dec. 1978, 92–95; YWCA papers; Siegel, "From Boutique to Barn Sale," 46–47, 89–90; Better Homes and Gardens, *Country Bazaar Crafts*; Linsley, *Great Bazaar,* 174.

24. Ironically, the true back-to-the-lander or radical feminist was unlikely to work for fundraising fairs at this time. The Vietnam War era was marked by strong polarizations between the "establishment" and alternative cultures. Because bazaars were associated with the former, they were generally eschewed by the latter.

25. For a good discussion of the history of the art/craft dichotomy, see Parker and Pollock, *Old Mistresses.* For an ongoing discussion of the debate, see *Craft Horizons* (changed to *American Craft* in 1979), 1965–85. Note that many of the handmade objects sold at contemporary fairs fall into a category that has been designated "art/craft"; that is, they reflect craft concerns such as beauty, skill, utility, and respect for medium, and yet follow art concepts of individual expression and uniqueness. See Jerry Neopolitan, "The Art/Craft Object: Its Style and Conventions," *Sociological Spectrum* 5 (1985): 231–43. Note that the contemporary fair would not logically feature works of avant-garde or well-established

artists, even if the public museum had not been with us for more than a century: the sky-high costs of the art market have made temporary art showings difficult, and liability costs are exorbitant.

26. Morley B. Smith, "Bazaar: Dozens of Ingenious Things to Make and Bake," *Better Homes and Gardens,* Sept. 1971, 70–75; "What Does the Christmas Bazaar Mean to America," 61; interview with Ethel Stiempke.

27. Dorothea S. Britton, *The Complete Book of Bazaars* (New York: Coward, McCann and Geoghan, 1973), 141, 159, 200, 143–45; Jackie Vermeer and Marian Lariviere Frew, *The Bazaar Handbook* (New York: Van Nostrand Reinhold, 1980); Nancy Lindemeyer and Ann Lerne, "Fifty Quick and Easy Bazaar Best Sellers," *Better Homes and Gardens,* Sept. 1980, 95–101; Linsley, *The Great Bazaar;* Jule Houston, ed., *Woman's Day Bazaar Best Sellers* (New York: Sedgewood Press, 1983), 17, 103; *Better Homes and Gardens Blue Ribbon Bazaar Crafts* (Des Moines: Meredith, 1987). The phenomenon of lifestyle self-definition and material goods has been discussed at length by individuals like Stuart Ewen in *All Consuming Images: The Politics of Style in Contemporary Culture* (New York: Basic Books, 1988) and Mike Featherstone in *Consumer Culture and Postmodernism* (London: Sage Publications, 1991).

28. Lindemeyer and Lerne, "Fifty Quick and Easy"; *Better Homes and Gardens Country Bazaar Crafts* (Des Moines: Meredith, 1986); *Better Homes and Gardens Blue Ribbon Crafts,* 86–87, 102–3. The latter book included an "up-to-the-minute" wall-hanging idea that was conceptually based on the binary system of the computer, but appeared as a long-familiar patchwork design (names and other messages could be "programmed" by varying arrangements of light and dark triangles). Patchwork pillows and bears, needlepoint mottoes, and dried flower wreaths were among the most common sale items I observed at bazaars in the late 1980s and early 1990s.

29. The evocation of a seemingly simpler, happier, more carefree time associated with a wholesome, warm, and family-oriented lifestyle was evident in other retailing establishments as well. In Macy's (New York) cellar, for example, there was in the 1980s a replica of a nineteenth-century pharmacy. The store took on the same kind of interpretive, quasi-historical museum role that the fundraising fair did during the Civil War; a small-town, slower-paced setting was implied.

30. Houston, *Woman's Day Best Sellers,* 107; personal observation. I was told unequivocally by several bazaar participants that aprons no longer sell and that contributors are discouraged from bringing them in. The popularity of aprons may vary to some extent regionally. In 1984, *McCall's Big Book of Bazaar Crafts* still claimed that the apron booth was the "runaway best seller at almost every bazaar" (11). I did not observe this to be the case. Crocheted sweaters and knitted booties, similarly, often remain on the sale tables at the end of the fair; they are still made by some of the older women, but do not have the same widespread appeal they once did.

31. Houston, *Woman's Day Best Sellers,* 124; *Easy Bazaar Crafts,* 9; Vermeer and Frew, *Bazaar Handbook,* 22; *McCall's Big Book of Bazaar Crafts,* 14; Beverly Gordon, "Soft Sculpture: Old Forms, New Meanings," *Fiberarts* 10 (Nov.–Dec. 1983): 40–41, 60.

32. While rummage sales are typically still associated with not-for-profit groups, individuals who participate in flea markets and yard sales usually expect to earn money for themselves. A few scholars began to look at flea markets in the 1970s, indicating that these privatized version of the resale had already been thoroughly integrated into the culture at large. See Jeffrey J. Gordon, "Toward a Theory of Recirculation: The Case of the Periodic Flea Market in the Northeastern United States" (Ph.D. diss., Syracuse Univ., 1978); Robert Maisel, "The Flea Market as an Action Scene," *Urban Life and Culture* 2, no. 4 (Jan. 1974): 488–505.

33. Interview with Evelyn Ferch, Madison, Wisconsin, Sept. 1986; Jean Greenhowe, *Jean Greenhowe's Bazaar Bestsellers* (Devon: David and Charles, 1987).

34. These artisans are professional in the sense that they are charging money for their work and reaping personal profit from its sale, but many work only part-time at their craft and may be earning only marginal amounts of money. Some of these outsiders are drawn from much the same group of people who formerly had donated their handmade items to the fairs. The term "semiprofessional" or "amateur artist" might be more appropriate, although both seem somewhat condescending and are not always accurate descriptors. Ironically, other observers have referred to these same individuals as "amateurs." See

Neopolitan, "Art/Craft Object"; F. Maurice Ethridge and Jerome L. Neopolitan, "Amateur Craft-Artists: Marginal Leisure Roles in a Marginal Art World," *Sociological Spectrum* 5 (1985): 53–76.

35. Program, 10th Annual American Business Women's Association Craft Sale/Bazaar, Oct. 15, 1994, DeForest, Wisconsin; Personal interviews with bazaar workers from Madison churches, Sept.–Nov. 1986.

36. There are some cases where a profit system seems to stimulate members' participation. In the case of Extension Homemaker clubs, members formerly sent handmade items to a sale at the annual national conference of the organization, much as they donated goods to their county holiday fairs. Profits were returned to each state council. The national organization found it more and more difficult to get donations for this sale, and at the 1988 conference in North Carolina, it established a new policy. Member homemakers who sent in goods were allowed to make a profit on their items; they gave a percentage to the organization, but kept most of the proceeds. With this system, donations went up so much that the profit for the individual state organizations increased significantly. Interview with Carol Anderson, Nov. 1988.

37. Linsley, *The Great Bazaar*, 8, 21, 25, 31; interviews with bazaar workers.

38. Anne Patterson Dee, *How to Have a Successful Craft Show in Your Home* (Deerfield, Ill.: Daedalus Publications, 1981, 1983).

39. *Ann Arbor News*, Sept. 30, 1992, Sect. F, 1–8. The actual total of listed events was 106. The remaining four, which I considered outliers from the bazaar/craft sale prototype, included a book sale at the public library, a craft demonstration at the historical museum, a sale of cloth bags at the recycling center, and an auction of commercial goods held to benefit a nursery school. It is nevertheless significant that the editors saw fit to include these activities in the calendar; while they were not really bazaars, they did involve institutions or organizations that were themselves perceived to be nonprofit and oriented to public service.

40. This number is based on the wording of the descriptions of each event—e.g., "arts and crafts vendors" were counted as profit-makers, as were "craftspeople displaying" items at an arts and crafts fair whose proceeds were donated to a school or PTO endowment fund. The count is, therefore, somewhat impressionistic, and is used advisedly. I believe the actual number of events where individuals made a profit may have been higher, but the organizations did not broadcast the fact in their publicity information.

41. Dorothea Britton told me she was able to get additional contributions from volunteers in the 1970s when working women were provided with "kits" they could work on in their homes in the evenings.

42. In *No Place of Grace,* Lears noted that people in the premodern era "passed" the time, but now we save it, spend it, and package it in units (11).

43. Linsley, *Great Bazaar*, 31; *McCall's Big Book of Bazaar Crafts*; Vermeer and Frew, *The Bazaar Handbook*; Britton, *Complete Book of Bazaars.*

44. Interview with Della Koester, Madison, Wisconsin; observation in Madison at XYZ Center, Oakwood Retirement Home, St. Mary's Day Health Center, and Colonial Manor Nursing Home.

45. "Ten Money Raising Ideas for Your Club," *Retirement Living,* Mar. 1976, 28.

46. See "Bake Sales: Turning Your Dough into Dollars," *Teen,* July 1983, 42–43; "Money-Making Baking," *Seventeen,* Sept. 1981, 148. The events sponsored by the three Milwaukee-area schools were listed in the "Holiday Bazaars" column, *Milwaukee Journal,* Nov. 13, 1988.

47. Interview with Maria Thomas, Madison, Wisconsin, Nov. 1986; phone interview with administrative secretary, West Towne Mall, Madison, Nov. 1986. The mall bazaar is in some ways similar to the "downtown" food or fancywork sale that had been held in retail stores in the 1930s and 1940s.

48. Some people argue that the shopping mall is the "town square" of the modern age. Ironically, this very concept was tested in Madison in 1984, when an antinuclear group staged a "street theater" protest in the mall. Individuals who were arrested for interfering with customers defended themselves in court with the town square argument, stating that freedom of expression was guaranteed in such public spaces. They lost their case; the Wisconsin State Supreme Court ultimately ruled in 1987 that the mall was not a public space but privately owned property.

49. Descriptions of the Madison events are based on personal observation. See "Bazaar Calendar 1992," for a description of another English theme fair held in an Episcopal church; Ralph Brody and Marcie Goodman, *Fundraising Events: Strategies and Programs for Success* (New York: Human Services Press, 1988), 15–30, 162.

Eight. Conclusions

1. Michael Robertson, "Cultural Hegemony Goes to the Fair: The Case of E. L. Doctorow's *World's Fair,*" *American Studies* 93 (Spring 1992): 31–44.
2. The therapeutic concept comes from Lears, *No Place of Grace.* For a discussion of culture brokers, see Leach, *Land of Desire.*
3. It was possible to just change a few symbolic parts of a fair feature to make it fit a given group. For example, a Jewish fair might include a pageant called "Tabernacle Illustrative of Old Jewish Ceremonials"; an Irish fair might have a pageant showing scenes of "Old Ireland." As indicated in the introduction, I am uncertain if the adaptability was equally true in certain other communities, such as among Asian Americans and Latin American immigrants.
4. See Linda Kerber, "Separate Spheres, Female Worlds, Woman's Place: The Rhetoric of Women's History," *Journal of American History* 75 (June 1988). Kerber explains that the separate spheres construct has interchangeably been used to denote "an ideology *imposed* on women, a culture *created by* women, and a set of boundaries *expected to be observed* by women" (17). In the case of the fairs, all three uses of the term are sometimes valid in turn.
5. David Glassberg discusses the idea of a timeless domestic space in relation to twentieth-century pageants; he argues that women were presented as the "emotional essence of community." See *American Historical Pageantry,* 135.
6. Leach, *Land of Desire,* 64.
7. Peiss, *Cheap Amusements,* 6.
8. See Rydell, *All the World's a Fair,* 14.
9. Karal Ann Marling discusses this idea in *Blue Ribbon,* 52. The primary time abundance was stressed in fundraising fairs was in the early antebellum era, before these other types of fairs had become so prevalent. It was also stressed briefly during the Civil War and after World War II.
10. For a discussion of socialites' attraction to nonwhite and working-class subjects, see Davidhoff, *The Best Circles,* 26. Historic costume worn at fundraising fairs was more "democratic" than that worn at costume or fancy dress balls in the premodern era. It was wealthy people who were most likely to be at these balls in the first place, and they often vied for the most elaborate, expensive outfits. In some cases they wore actual old garments that came down to them through their families as a sign of their social pedigrees. The fundraising fair costume was not inherently expensive or valuable, since it was just a stage prop. See Gordon, "Dressing the Colonial Past," 109–39.
11. Leach, *Land of Desire,* 60–62.

Selected Bibliography

Organizational Records and
Miscellaneous Archival Materials

Annual Reports and Bulletins. Misc. dates in the 1950s and 1960s. Temple Beth-El, Madison, Wisconsin, Archives, State Historical Society of Wisconsin (hereafter referred to as SHSW).

British War Relief Fund. Undated scrapbooks. Madison, Wisconsin, SHSW.

College Settlement of Philadelphia. Commemorative Number, Fifty Years, 1892–1942.

Dover [New Hampshire] Women's Club Yearbook, 1905–6.

First Unitarian Society. Miscellaneous papers. Madison, Wisconsin, SHSW.

First Church, Northampton, Massachusetts. Miscellaneous papers, Northampton Historical Society Archives (hereafter referred to as NHS).

Hadassah, Fund Raising Round Up. Typescript, n.d., SHSW.

Hammond, Elizabeth Crowninshield. Diary, Dec. 1863, Arthur M. Schlesinger Library, Radcliffe College, Cambridge, Mass (hereafter referred to as SL).

Hill and Valley Club Community Sewing Circle Minutes. Beldenville, Wisconsin, SHSW.

History of the First Baptist Church. One Hundredth Anniversary, 1847–1947, Madison, Wisconsin, SHSW.

Hosmer, Ann P. "Reminiscences of Sanitary Work." Handwritten mss., recorded Jan. 1882, Chicago Historical Society Archives (hereafter referred to as CHS).

Interview with Hazel Hansen conducted by the East Side Oral History Project, Madison, Wisconsin, Mar. 31, 1981. Typescript, SHSW.

Ladies Aid Society Record Book. Pilgrim Congregational Church, Madison, Wisconsin, SHSW.

Letter from J. M. Synch, Quartermaster's Office, June 14, 1865, CHS.

Letter from unidentified sender to Mrs. Hunter, Mar. 1, 1865, CHS.

Levis, Rosa. Miscellaneous papers, SL.

Pleasant Valley Homemaker's Club Minutes. Hammond (Pierce County) Wisconsin, 1941–82, SHSW.

New England Hospital for Women and Children, Annual Reports, 1864–1910. Sophia Smith Collection, Smith College Library, Northampton, Massachusetts (hereafter referred to as SSC).

Parsons, Jr., Josiah W. "Dorcas Society, 1809–1984—175 Years." Typescript, NHS.

Personal account book. Mary Pauline du Pont (including records of the St. Mary Society of Christ Church, Christiana Hundred, Delaware), 1891–1898. DuPont Family Archives, Hagley Museum and Library, Wilmington, Delaware.

Pratt, Marietta. Misc. papers. Manuscript Division, SL.

Ross, Marjorie Drake. "A Brief History of the Fragment Society, 1812–1962." Typescript, Forbes Library Collection, Northampton, Massachusetts.

Secretary's Record Book, Ladies Benevolent Society, Grace Episcopal Church, Madison, SHSW.

Semi-Centennial History, Pleasant Valley Homemaker's Club, 1933–1983, SHSW.

Treasurer's Account Book. Woman's Alliance, First Unitarian Society, Madison, Wisconsin, 1925–1936, SHSW.

Univ. of Wisconsin YWCA Miscellaneous papers, Univ. of Wisconsin-Madison Archives.

Woman's Suffrage Bazaar Association. Records, early Oct. to Dec. 27, 1871, SL.

Women's City Relief Association Annual Report. Boston, 1897, SSC.

Bazaar Programs and Souvenirs

Book of the Bazaar of All Nations. Milwaukee, May 6–14, 1896.

Book of the Boardwalk. Atlantic City Boardwalk, Boston, Dec. 1–9, 1922.

Official Souvenir Program of the Independent Order of Odd Fellows Oriental Bazaar. Worcester, Mass., 1906.

Program, Elk's Street Fair and Trade Carnival. Chillicote, Ohio, May 29–June 3, 1899.

Program, Odd Fellows Home Fair. New York City, Apr. 18–27, 1895.

Program Souvenir, Communist Party District 8 Three-Day Red Election Bazaar. Chicago, Oct. 21–23, 1932.

Program, 10th Annual American Business Women's Association Craft Sale/Bazaar. DeForest, Wisconsin, Oct. 15, 1994.

Program, Wohltatigteits Bazar (Charity Bazaar Association), Fruhlingsfest der Nachstenliebe Zum Besten der notleidendem Jugend in Deutschland und Oesterreich (Spring Festival for the Benefit of German and Austrian Children). Apr. 16–24, 1921.

Programme, Grand Rainbow Bazaar. Holy Redeemer Church, Madison, Jan. 21–26, 1895.

Souvenir, Centennial Year, Mayne Island Fall Fair. Aug. 14, 1971.

Souvenir of Teachers' Mutual Benefit Association Bazaar. New York, Dec. 10–20, 1890.

Souvenir, Fair at the Hotel Vendome for the Benefit of the New England Hospital for Women and Children. Dec. 4–9, 1899.

Souvenir, German Hospital Fair. New York City, Feb. 1889.

Souvenir of Kirmess. Richmond, Virginia, 1896. Valentine Museum Collection, 30.39.

Souvenir: Official Program, Madison's Grand Carnival and Street Fair. Oct. 16–19, 1900.

Souvenir Program, Charity Bazaar for the Widows, Orphans and Red Cross of the Central Powers of Europe. Wilmington, Delaware, June 12–17, 1916.

Souvenir Program, St. Barnabas Hospital Fair. Essex County, New Jersey, Dec. 1908.

Souvenir Program, International Labor Defense Bazaar, Chicago. Dec. 13–15, 1935.

Woman's Journal Souvenir, National Suffrage Bazaar. Boston, Dec. 1900.

Books, Articles, and Scholarly Presentations

Agnew, Jean-Christophe. "The House of Fiction: The American Interior and the Rise of a Commodity Aesthetic." Paper presented at the symposium, "Accumulation and Display: The Development of American Consumerism, 1880–1920," Henry Francis du Pont Winterthur Museum, Wilmington, Delaware, Nov. 7, 1986.

Ames, Kenneth L. "Anonymous Heroes: Background History and Social Responsibility." *Museum News* (Sept./Oct. 1994): 34–35.

An Account of the Labors of the Ladies' Charitable Association of Boston. Boston: Wright and Potter, 1876.

Apostol, Jane. "They Said it With Flowers: The Los Angeles Flower Festival Society." *Southern California Quarterly* 62 (1980): 67–76.

Ardman, Perri, and Harvey Ardman. *The Woman's Day Book of Fundraising.* New York: St. Martin's, 1981.

Association for Befriending Children and Young Girls. Annual Report. New York: Catholic Publication Society, 1874.

The Attic Angels Association, 1889–1949. Madison: Democrat Printing, 1948.

Augur, Helen. *The Book of Fairs.* New York: Harcourt, Brace, 1939.

Bachelard, Gaston. *The Poetics of Space.* Trans. Maria Jolas. New York: Orion Press, 1964.

Barrie, James M. "Bazaars." In *Potpourri: Gifts Literary and Artistic, Contributed as a Souvenir of the Grand Masonic Bazaar in Aid of the Annuity Fund of Scottish Masonic Benevolence,* ed. by W. Grant Stevenson. Edinburgh, 1890.

Beard, Lina, and Adelia B. Beard. *The American Girls' Handy Book: How to Amuse Yourself and Others.* New York: Charles Scribner's Sons, 1893.

Beddoe, Deirdre. *Back to Home and Duty: Women Between the Wars 1918–1939.* London: Pandora, 1989.

Beeker, Jane S. and Barbara Franco, eds. *Folk Roots, New Roots: Folklore in American Life.* Lexington: Museum of Our National Heritage, 1988.

Belenky, Mary Field, et al. *Women's Way of Knowing.* New York: Basic Books, 1986.

Benton, Caroline French. *Fairs and Fetes.* Boston: Dana Estes, 1912.

Berg, Barbara. *The Remembered Gate: Origins of American Feminism: The Woman and the City, 1800–1860.* New York: Oxford Univ. Press, 1978.

Better Homes and Gardens Blue Ribbon Bazaar Crafts. Des Moines: Meredith, 1987.

Better Homes and Gardens. *Country Bazaar Crafts.* Des Moines: Meredith, 1986.

Better Homes and Gardens. *Easy Bazaar Crafts.* Des Moines: Meredith, 1981.

Billington, Ray Allen, ed. *Journal of Charlotte L. Forten.* New York: Dryden Press, 1953.

Blackwell, Elizabeth. *Pioneer Work in Opening the Medical Profession to Women: Autobiographical Sketches.* New York and London: Longmans, Green & Co., 1896.

Blair, Karen J. *The Clubwoman as Feminist: True Womanhood Redefined, 1868–1914.* New York: Holmes and Meier, 1980.

———. *The Torchbearers: Women and Their Amateur Arts Associations in America, 1890–1930.* Bloomington: Indiana Univ. Press, 1994.

Blair, Lawrence. *English Church Ales With a Note on Church Fairs.* Ann Arbor, Mich.: Edwards Brothers, 1940.

Board of Lady Managers of the Louisiana Purchase Exposition. *Report to the Louisiana Purchase Exposition Committee.* Louisiana, 1905.

Bordin, Ruth. "'A Baptism of Power and Liberty': The Woman's Crusade of 1873–1874." In *Woman's Being, Woman's Place: Female Identity and Vocation in American History,* ed. by Mary Kelley. Boston: G. K. Hall, 1979.

Boynton, Charles Brandon, ed. *History of the Great Western Sanitary Fair.* Cincinnati: C. F. Vent, 1864.

Braddon, Mary Elizabeth Maxwell. *Like and Unlike.* London: Simpkin, Marshall, 1887.

Brayton, Mary Clark. *Our Acre and its Harvest: Historical Sketches of the Soldiers' Aid Society of Northern Ohio.* 2 vols. Cleveland: Fairbanks, Benedict, 1869.

Breckenridge, Sophonisba P. *Women in the Twentieth Century: A Study of Their Political, Social and Economic Activities.* 1933. Reprint, New York: Arno Press, 1972.

Bremner, Robert H. *The Public Good: Philanthropy and Welfare in the Civil War Era.* New York: Alfred A. Knopf, 1980.

Britton, Dorothea S. *The Complete Book of Bazaars.* New York: Coward, McCann and Geoghan, 1973.

———. "Peeking Through the Holly—or Thirty Tears of Christmas Nonsense." Booklet distributed to author's bazaar workshop participants. N.d., ca. 1973.

Brockett, L. P., and Mary C. Vaughn. *Women's Work in the Civil War: A Record of Heroism, Patriotism and Patience.* Philadelphia and Chicago: Zeigler, McCurdy, 1867.

Brody, Ralph, and Marcie Goodman. *Fundraising Events: Strategies and Programs for Success.* New York: Human Services Press, 1988.

Bronner, Simon J. *American Folklore Studies: An Intellectual History.* Lawrence: Univ. Press of Kansas, 1986.

Brown, Jane Converse. "Fine Arts and Fine People: The Japanese Taste in the American Home, 1876–

1976." In *Making the American Home: Middle Class Women and Domestic Material Culture, 1840–1940*, ed. by Marilyn Ferris Motz and Pat Browne. Bowling Green, Ohio: Bowling Green State Univ. Popular Press, 1988.

Brumberg, Joan Jacobs. "Zenanas and Girlless Villages: The Ethnology of American Evangelical Women, 1870–1910." Paper presented at the Berkshire Women's History Conference, Vassar College, Poughkeepsie, New York, June 1981.

Burt, Emily Rose. *Make Your Bazaar Pay*. New York: Harper & Bros., 1925.

Campbell, D'ann. *Women at War With America: Private Lives in a Patriotic Era*. Cambridge: Harvard Univ. Press, 1984.

Chambers-Schiller, Lee. "'A Good Work Among the People': The Political Culture of the Boston Antislavery Fair." In *The Abolitionist Sisterhood: Women's Political Culture in Antebellum America*, ed. by Jean Fagin Yellin and John C. Van Horne. Ithaca: Cornell Univ. Press, 1994.

Chesley, Albert M. *Social Activities for Men and Boys*. New York: Associated Press [with the YMCA], 1921.

Chester, Marjorie Fatt. *McCall's Book of Fundraising Ideas*. New York: Prentice-Hall, 1963.

Clarke, Ida Clyde. *American Women and the World War*. New York: D. Appleton, 1918.

Cleveland Branch, U.S. Sanitary Commission. *Our Acre and its Harvest: Historical Sketch of the Soldier's Aid Society of Northern Ohio*. Cleveland: Fairbanks, Benedict and Co., 1869.

Coates, James Roland, Jr. "Recreation and Sport in the African-American Community of Baltimore, 1880–1920." Ph.D. diss., Univ. of Maryland, 1991.

Cogan, Frances B. *All American Girl: The Idea of Real Womanhood in Mid-Nineteenth Century America*. Athens: Univ. of Georgia Press, 1981.

Cott, Nancy. *Bonds of Womanhood: "Woman's Sphere" in New England 1780–1835*. New Haven: Yale Univ. Press, 1977.

The Craft and Bazaar Book. RIT Dyes, n.d., ca. 1965.

Cromwell, Otelia. *Lucretia Mott*. Cambridge: Harvard Univ. Press, 1958.

Csikzentmihalyi, Mihaly, and Eugene Rochberg-Halton. *The Meaning of Things: Domestic Symbols and the Self*. Cambridge: Cambridge Univ. Press, 1981.

Cutlip, Scott M. *Fundraising in the United States: Its Role in America's Philanthropy*. New Brunswick, N.J.: Rutgers Univ. Press, 1965.

Darney, Virginia Grant. "Women and World's Fairs: American International Expositions, 1876–1904." Ph.D. diss., Emory Univ., 1982.

Davidhoff, Leonore. *The Best Circles: Society, Etiquette and the Season*. Totowa, New Jersey: Rowman and Littlefield, 1973.

Davis, Susan G. *Parades and Power: Street Theatre In Nineteenth Century Philadelphia*. Philadelphia: Temple Univ. Press, 1986.

Dawson, Mary. *Money-Making Entertainments: For Church and Charity*. Philadelphia: D. McKay, 1911.

Dayton, Helena Smith, and Louise Bascom Barratt. *The Book of Entertainments and Theatricals*. New York: Robert M. McBride, 1924.

De Soto, Carole. *For Fund and Finds: Creative Fundraising Ideas for Your Organization*. West Nyack, N.Y.: Parker, 1983.

Dee, Anne Patterson. *How to Have a Successful Craft Show in Your Home*. Deerfield, Ill.: Daedalus Publications, 1981, 1983.

Dew, Louise E. *Entertainment for All Seasons*. New York: S. H. Moore & Co., 1904.

Dissanayake, Ellen. *Homo Aestheticus: Where Art Comes From and Why*. New York: Free Press [Macmillan], 1992.

———. *What Is Art For?* Seattle: Univ. of Washington Press, 1988.

Dohr, Joy H. "A Framework for Examining Aesthetic Meaning in Women's Lives." Paper presented at Univ. of Wisconsin System Women's Studies Conference, Oshkosh, Wisconsin, Sept. 1986.

Douglas, Ann. *The Feminization of American Culture*. New York: Avon Books, 1977.

Duran, Dorothy B., and Clement A. Duran. *The New Encyclopedia of Successful Program Ideas*. New York: Associated Press, 1967.

Dyer, Gary R. "The 'Vanity Fair' of Nineteenth Century England: Commerce, Women, and the East in the Ladies' Bazaar." *Nineteenth Century Literature* 46, no. 2 (Sept. 1991): 196–222.

Elliot, Maude Ward. *Memories of the Civil War, 1861–1864.* Boston: privately printed for the Red Cross, 1945. Mss. in the Massachusetts Historical Society Archives.

Elmore, Grace. "The Last Bazar." In *South Carolina Women of the Confederacy: Experiences During the Civil War,* ed. by Mrs. T. Taylor, Mrs. Smythe, Mrs. Kohn, et al. Columbia: The State Co., 1903.

Epstein, Barbara Leslie. *The Politics of Domesticity: Women, Evangelism and Temperance in Nineteenth Century America.* Middletown, Conn.: Wesleyan Univ. Press, 1981.

Ethridge, F. Maurice, and Jerome L. Neopolitan. "Amateur Craft-Artists: Marginal Leisure Roles in a Marginal Art World." *Sociological Spectrum* 5 (1985): 53–76.

Eureka Entertainments. Philadelphia: Pennsylvania Publishing, 1894, 1895, 1927.

Falassi, Alessandro. *Time Out of Time: Essays on the Festival.* Albuquerque: Univ. of New Mexico Press, 1987.

Featherstone, Mike. *Consumer Culture and Postmodernism.* London: Sage Publications, 1991.

Few, Marian Lariviere. *The Bazaar Handbook.* New York: Van Nostrand Reinhold, 1980.

Fox, Richard Wightman, and T. J. Jackson Lears, eds. *The Culture of Consumption: Critical Essays in American History 1880–1980.* New York: Pantheon, 1983.

Foy, Jessica H., and Thomas J. Schlereth, eds. *American Homelife 1880–1930: A Social History of Spaces and Services.* Knoxville: Univ. of Tennessee Press, 1992.

From the Slavery of 1776 to the Freedom of 1876: An Account of the Labors of the Ladies Charitable Association of Boston. Boston, 1876.

Gilligan, Carol. *In a Different Voice: Psychological Theory and Women's Development.* Cambridge: Harvard Univ. Press, 1982.

Glassberg, David. *American Historical Pageantry: The Uses of Tradition in the Early Twentieth Century.* Chapel Hill: Univ. of North Carolina Press, 1990.

Glover, Ellye Howell. *Dame Curtsey's Book of Party Pastimes for the Up-to-Date Hostess.* Chicago: A. C. McClurg, 1912. Reprint, 1921.

Gold, Doris. "Women and Voluntarism." In *Woman in Sexist Society: Studies in Power and Powerlessness,* ed. by Vivian Gornick and Barbara K. Moran. New York: Basic Books, 1971.

Goodrich, Frank. *The Tribute Book: A Record of the Munificence, Self-Sacrifice and Patriotism of the American People During the War for the Union.* New York: Derby and Miller, 1865.

Gordon, Beverly. "Aesthetic Meanings in Women's Turn-of-the-Century Fundraising Fairs." *Turn-of-the-Century Women* 3, no. 1 (Summer 1986): 15–28.

———. "Dress and Dress-up at the Fundraising Fair." *Dress* 12 (1986): 61–72.

———. "Dressing the Colonial Past: Nineteenth Century New Englanders Look Back." In *Dress in American Culture,* ed. by Patricia A. Cunningham and Susan Voso Lab, 109–39. Bowling Green, Ohio: Bowling Green State Univ. Popular Press, 1993.

———. "The Souvenir: Messenger of the Extraordinary." *Journal of Popular Culture* 20 (Winter 1986): 135–46.

———. "Victorian Fancygoods in the American Home: Fantasy and Accommodation." In *Making the American Home: Middle Class Women and Domestic Material Culture,* ed. by Marilyn Motz and Pat B. Browne. Bowling Green, Ohio: Bowling Green State Univ. Popular Press, 1988.

———. "Woman's Domestic Body: The Conceptual Conflation of Women and Interiors in the Industrial Age." *Winterthur Portfolio* 31, no. 4 (Winter 1996): 281–301.

Gordon, Janet, and Diana Reische. *The Volunteer Powerhouse: The Junior League.* New York: Rutledge Press, 1982.

Gordon, Jean, and Jan McArthur. "American Women and Domestic Consumption, 1800–1920: Four Interpretive Themes." *Journal of American Culture* 8, no. 3 (Fall 1985): 27–47. Reprinted in *Making the American Home: Middle Class Women and Domestic Material Culture,* ed. by Marilyn Motz and Pat B. Browne. Bowling Green, Ohio: Bowling Green State Univ. Popular Press, 1988.

Graydon, Nell S. *Tales of Columbia.* Columbia, S.C.: Nell Graydon [R. L. Bryan], 1964.

Greenhowe, Jean. *Jean Greenhowe's Bazaar Bestsellers.* Devon: David and Charles, 1987.

Grier, Katherine C. *Culture and Comfort: People, Parlors and Upholstery 1850–1930.* Rochester, New York: Strong Museum, 1988.

Gunn, Virginia. "Western Reserve Women and the U.S. Sanitary Commission, 1861–1865." *Western Reserve Studies* 3 (1988): 75–85.

Hale, Lucretia, and Margaret E. White. *300 Decorative and Fancy Articles for Presents, Fairs, etc.* Boston: S. W. Tilton, 1885.

Halttunen, Karen. *Confidence Men and Painted Women: A Study of Middle Class Culture in America 1830–1870.* New Haven: Yale Univ. Press, 1982.

Hammond, Harold Earl, ed. *Diary of a Union Lady 1861–1865.* New York: Funk & Wagnalls, 1962.

Hansen, Debra Gold. *Strained Sisterhood: Gender and Class in the Boston Female Anti-Slavery Society.* Amherst: Univ. of Massachusetts Press, 1993.

Harris, Neil. "Museums, Merchandising and Popular Taste: The Struggle for Influence." In *Material Culture and the Study of American Life,* ed. by Ian M. G. Quimby. New York: W. W. Norton for Winterthur Museum, 1978.

Hawes, Harriet, and Eleanor Edelman. *McCall's Complete Book of Bazaars.* New York: Simon and Schuster, 1955.

Hayes, Florence. *Daughters of Dorcas: The Story of the Work of Women for Home Missions Since 1802.* New York: Board of National Missions, Presbyterian Church, 1952.

Heath, Lillian M. *Enjoyable Entertainment.* Boston: United Society of Christian Endeavors, 1913.

Hendrickson, Robert. *The Grand Emporiums: The Illustrated History of America's Great Department Stores.* New York: Stein and Day, 1979.

Henrotin, Ellen. *The Attitude of Women's Clubs and Associations Toward Social Economics.* Washington: Bulletin of the Department of Labor, no. 23, July 1899.

Henshaw, Sarah Edwards. *Our Branch and its Tributaries: The History of the Work of the Northwest Sanitary Commission.* Chicago: Alfred L. Sewell, 1868.

Hersh, Blanche Glassman. *The Slavery of Sex: Feminist Abolitionists in America.* Urbana: Univ. of Illinois Press, 1978.

Hewitt, Emma C. *Queen of the Home—Her Reign From Infancy to Age, From Attic to Cellar.* Oakland, et al: H. J. Smith, 1889.

Hewitt, Nancy. *Women's Activism and Social Change: Rochester, New York, 1822–1872.* Ithaca: Cornell Univ. Press, 1984.

Hill, Patricia R. *The World Their Household: The American Woman's Foreign Mission Movement and Cultural Transformation, 1870–1920.* Ann Arbor: Univ. of Michigan Press, 1985.

Hine, Thomas. *Populuxe.* New York: Alfred Knopf, 1986.

History of the Brooklyn and Long Island Fair. Brooklyn: The Union, 1864.

History of the North-Western Soldiers' Fair. Chicago: Dunlop, Sewell and Spalding, 1864.

Holloway, Laura C. *The Hearthstone; or, Life at Home: A Household Manual.* Chicago and Philadelphia: L. P. Miller, 1888.

The House and Home: A Practical Book. New York: Scribner's Sons, 1894.

Houston, Jule, ed. *Woman's Day Bazaar Best Sellers.* New York: Sedgewood Press, 1983.

How to Decorate Halls, Booths and Automobiles. Framingham, Mass.: Dennison Manufacturing Co., 1923.

How to Make Paper Costumes and *How To Make Crepe Paper Flowers.* Framingham, Mass.: Dennison Co., n.d.

Huizinga, J. *Homo Ludens: A Study of the Play-Element in Culture.* Trans. by R. F. C. Hall. London: Routledge and Kegan Paul, 1949. orig. German edition, 1944.

Hurn, Ethel Alice. *Wisconsin Women in the War Between the States.* Wisconsin Historical Commission, May 1911.

James, Bessie. *For God, For Country, For Home: The National League for Woman's Service.* New York: G. P. Putnam's Sons [Knickerbocker Press], 1920.

Johnson, Rossiter, ed. *A History of the Worlds' Columbian Exposition.* New York: D. Appleton, 1898.

Jones, Michael Owen. *Exploring Folk Art: Twenty Years of Thought on Craft, Work and Aesthetics.* Ann Arbor, Mich.: UMI Research Press, 1987.

Kantor, Alvin Robert, and Marjorie Sered Kantor. *Sanitary Fairs: A Philatelic and Historical Study of Civil War Benevolence*. Glencoe, Ill.: SF Publishers, 1992.

Keith, Alice B. "White Relief in North Carolina, 1865–1867." *Social Forces* 17, no. 3 (Mar. 1939): 337–55.

Kerber, Linda. "Separate Spheres, Female Worlds, Woman's Place: The Rhetoric of Women's History." *Journal of American History* 75 (June 1988): 9–39.

Kirshenblatt-Gimblett, Barbara. "The Moral Sublime: The Temple Emanuel Fair and Its Cookbook, Denver, 1888." *Rocky Mountain Jewish Historical Notes* 13, nos. 1–2 (Spring–Summer 1995): 1–7.

Knowles, Helen K. *How Groups Raise Funds*. Freeport, Maine: Bond, Wheelwright, 1955, 1961.

The Ladies Fair: A Poem in Aid of the Funds of the Ladies' Scrap Society of Christ Church, North Hempstead. Brooklyn: By the Author, 1836.

Lancaster, Clay. *The Japanese Influence in America*. New York: Walton H. Rawls, 1963.

Lasser, Carol, and Marlene Deahl Merrill, eds. *Friends and Sisters: Letters Between Lucy Stone and Antoinette Brown Blackwell, 1846–1893*. Urbana: Univ. of Illinois Press.

Leach, William. *Land of Desire: Merchants, Power and the Rise of a New American Culture*. New York: Pantheon, 1993.

———. "Transformations in a Culture of Consumption: Women and Department Stores, 1890–1925." *Journal of American History* 71, no. 2 (Sept. 1984): 319–42.

———. "Strategists of Display and the Production of Desire." In *Consuming Visions: Accumulation and Display of Goods in America, 1880–1920*, ed. by Simon J. Bronner. New York: W. W. Norton for Winterthur Museum, 1989.

Lears, T. J. Jackson. "Beyond Veblen: Rethinking Consumer Culture." In *Consuming Visions: Accumulation and Display of Goods in America 1880–1920*, ed. by Simon J. Bronner. New York: W. W. Norton for Winterthur Museum, 1989.

———. *No Place of Grace: Anti-Modernism and the Transformation of American Culture 1880–1920*. New York: Pantheon, 1981.

Levine, Lawrence W. *Highbrow/Lowbrow: The Emergence of Cultural Hierarchy in America*. Cambridge, Mass.: Harvard Univ. Press, 1988.

Lewis, Russell. "Everything Under One Roof: World's Fairs and Department Stores in Paris and Chicago." *Chicago History* 12, no. 3 (Fall 1983): 28–47.

The Liberty Bell. Boston: Massachusetts Anti-Slavery Fair, misc. volumes, 1833–58.

Linsley, Lesley. *The Great Bazaar*. New York: Delacorte Press, 1981.

Livermore, Mary A. *My Story of the War: A Woman's Narrative of Four Years Personal Experience*. Harford, Conn.: A. D. Worthington, 1889.

Lubove, Roy. *The Professional Altruist: The Emergence of Social Work as a Career 1880–1930*. Cambridge, Mass.: Harvard Univ. Press, 1965.

Luckhurst, Kenneth. *The Story of Exhibitions*. London and New York: Studio Publications, 1951.

Lynd, Robert S., and Helen Merrill Lynd. *Middletown: A Study in Modern American Culture*. New York: Harcourt, Brace & World, 1929.

———. *Middletown in Transition*. New York: Harcourt, Brace, 1937.

Marling, Karal Ann. *Blue Ribbon: A Social and Pictorial History of the Minnesota State Fair*. St. Paul: Minnesota Historical Society Press, 1990.

Marling, Karal Ann, and Jessica H. Foy, eds. *The Arts and the American Home, 1890–1930*. Knoxville: Univ. of Tennessee Press, 1994.

Massey, Mary Elizabeth. *Bonnet Brigades*. New York: Alfred A. Knopf, 1965.

Mayer, John. "Private Charities of Chicago, 1871–1915." Ph.D. diss., Univ. of Minnesota, 1978.

McCall's Big Book of Bazaar Crafts. Radnor, Pa.: Chilton Books, 1984.

McCarthy, Kathleen D., ed. *Lady Bountiful Revisited: Women, Philanthropy and Power*. New Brunswick, N.J.: Rutgers Univ. Press, 1990.

McCarthy, Kathleen D. *Women's Culture: American Philanthropy and Art, 1830–1930*. Chicago: Univ. of Chicago Press, 1991.

McCullough, Edo. *World's Fairs Midways*. Carnivaland Enterprises, 1966. Reprint, Arno, 1976.

McCullough, Jack. *Living Pictures on the New York Stage.* Ann Arbor, Mich.: UMI Research Press, 1981.

McKechnie, Samuel. *Popular Entertainment Through the Ages.* London: Sampson, Low, Marstone, 1932.

McLaurin, Melton A. "The Nineteenth Century North Carolina State Fair as a Social Institution." *North Carolina History Review* 59 (July 1982): 213–29.

McTeer, Frances, and Minnie Dubbs Millbrook. *Michigan Women in the Civil War.* Lansing: Michigan Civil War Centennial Observance Commission, 1963.

Meyer, Pauline. *Keep Your Face to the Sunshine: A Lost Chapter in the History of Woman's Suffrage.* Edwardsville, Ill.: Alcott Press, 1980.

Miers, Earl Schenck, ed. *When the World Ended: The Diary of Emma Le Conte.* New York: Oxford Univ. Press, 1957.

Miller, Jean Baker. *Toward a New Psychology of Women.* Boston: Beacon Press, 1976.

Mitchell, Margaret. *Gone With the Wind.* New York: Macmillan, 1936.

Mollenhoff, David Vincent. *Madison: A History of the Formative Years.* Dubuque: Kendall/Hunt, 1982.

Moore, William D. "Funding the Temples of Masculinity: Women's Roles in Masonic Fairs in New York State, 1870–1930." *Nineteenth Century* 14, no. 1 (1994): 19–25.

Musselman, Virginia W. *Money-Raising Activities for Community Groups.* New York: Associated Press, 1969.

Myers, Alfred E. *The Sociable, the Entertainment and the Bazaar: A Discussion of Church Customs.* Philadelphia: Presbyterian Board of Publications, 1882.

Neely, Wayne Caldwell. *The Agricultural Fair.* New York: Columbia Univ. Press, 1935.

Nenno, Faustina. *Placentia Round Table Club: The First Thirty-five Years, January 1902–December 1937.* Placentia, Calif.: Placentia Courier Publishing, 1938.

Neubauer, John. *The Fin-de-siecle Culture of Adolescence.* New Haven, Conn.: Yale Univ. Press, 1992.

Nightingale, Joseph. *The Bazaar: Its Origin, nature and objects explained, and recommended as an important branch of political economy* (reprint of letter to Hon. George Rose, M. P., May 4, 1816). London: Davies, Michael & Hudson, 1816.

Orvell, Miles. *The Real Thing: Imitation and Authenticity in American Culture 1880–1940.* Chapel Hill: Univ. of North Carolina Press, 1989.

Parker, Roszika, and Griselda Pollock. *Old Mistresses: Women, Art and Ideology.* New York: Pantheon Books, 1981.

Peiss, Kathy. *Cheap Amusements: Working Women and Leisure in Turn-of-the-Century New York.* Philadelphia: Temple Univ. Press, 1986.

Philipson, David, ed. *Letters of Rebecca Gratz.* New York: Jewish Publication Society, 1929. Reprint, Arno Press, 1975.

Prevots, Naina. *American Pageantry: A Movement for Art and Democracy.* Ann Arbor, Mich.: UMI Research Press, 1990.

Prochaska, Frank. *Women and Philanthropy in Nineteenth Century England.* New York: Oxford Univ. Press, 1980.

Prosterman, Leslie Mina. "The Aspect of the Fair: Aesthetics and Festival in Illinois County Fairs." Ph.D. diss., Univ. of Pennsylvania, 1982.

Prentice, Archibald. *History of the Anti-Corn Law League.* 2 vols. London: W. and F. G. Cash, 1853. Reprint, London: Frank Cass, 1968.

Prown, Jules David. "Mind in Matter: An Introduction to Material Culture Theory and Method." *Winterthur Portfolio* 17, no. 1 (1982): 1–19.

Przybysz, Jane. "Quilts, Old Kitchens and the Social Geography of Gender." Paper presented at the H. F. DuPont Winterthur Museum conference entitled "The Material Culture of Gender/The Gender of Material Culture," Wilmington, Delaware, Nov. 1989.

Record of the Metropolitan Fair in Aid of the U.S. Sanitary Commission, Held at New York, April 1864. New York: Hurd & Houghton, 1867.

Report of the Boston Female Anti-Slavery Society. Boston, 1836.

Report of the Christmas Bazaar, December 14–22. Rochester: Benton & Andrews, 1864.

Report of the Executive Committee of the Fair for the Relief of Suffering in France. Boston: Rand, Avery & Co., 1872.

Review of "An Address to the Citizens of Philadelphia on the Subject of Fancy Fairs." Philadelphia: M. Fithian, 1834.

Reynolds, Robert Lester. "Benevolence on the Home Front in Massachusetts During the Civil War." Ph.D. diss., Boston Univ., 1970.

Robertson, Michael. "Cultural Hegemony Goes to the Fair: The Case of E. L. Doctorow's *World's Fair.*" *American Studies* 93 (Spring 1992): 31–44.

Rook, Patricia, and R. L. Schnell. "The Rise and Decline of British and North American Protestant Orphan's Homes as Woman's Domain 1850–1930." *Atlantis* 7, no. 3 (1982): 22–35.

Roth, Rodris. "The New England, or 'Olde Tyme' Kitchen Exhibit at Nineteenth Century Fairs." In *The Colonial Revival in America,* ed. by Alan Axelrod. New York: W. W. Norton, 1985.

Rousmaniere, John P. "Cultural Hybrid in the Slums: The College Woman and the Settlement House, 1889–1894." *American Quarterly* 22 (Spring 1980): 45–66.

Rowley, Nancy J. "Red Cross Quilts for the Great War." *Uncoverings* [American Quilt Study Group] 3 (1982): 43–44.

Ruckman, Jo Ann. "Knit Knit and Then Knit—The Women of Pocatello and the War Effort of 1917–1918." *Idaho Yesterdays* 26, no. 1 (1982): 26–36.

Rush, N. Orwin. "Lucretia Mott and the Philadelphia Antislavery Fairs." *Friends Historical Association Bulletin* 35 (Autumn 1946): 69–75.

Ruutz-Rees, Janet E. *Home Decoration: Art Needlework and Embroidery, etc.* New York: Appleton, 1881.

Ryan, Mary P. *Womanhood in America: French Colonial Times to the Present.* New York: Franklin Watts, 1983.

———. *Women in Public: Between Banners and Ballots, 1825–1880.* Baltimore: Johns Hopkins Univ. Press, 1990.

Rydell, Robert W. *All the World's a Fair: Visions of Empire at American International Expositions, 1876–1916.* Chicago: Univ. of Chicago Press, 1984.

Santmeyer, Helen Hoover. *Ohio Town.* 1956. Reprint, New York: Berkley Books, 1985.

Saum, Lewis O. "The Broom Brigade, Colonel Donan and Clementine." *Missouri Historical Society Bulletin* 25, no. 3 (1969): 192–200.

Saxton, Sadie Boyd, and Elizabeth Bowman. "Stages and Highlights of Ossoli Circle's History." *Chronological History, 1885–1960.* Knoxville: Ossoli Circle, 1960.

Schnell, J. Christopher. "Mary Livermore and the Great Northwestern Fair." *Chicago History* n.s. 4 (Spring 1975): 36.

Scott, Anne Firor. "Women's Voluntary Associations: From Charity to Reform." In *Lady Bountiful Revisited: Women, Philanthropy and Power,* ed. by Kathleen McCarthy. New Brunswick, N.J.: Rutgers Univ. Press, 1990.

Shoop, Michael I. "A History of the Museum of the Confederacy, Richmond, Virginia, and its Library, 1896–1946." Master's thesis, Univ. of North Carolina, Chapel Hill, 1983.

Sills, Ruth C. *Sweet Bitter Charity: A Cheerful Guide to Society Fundraising.* New York: John Day, 1970.

Simkin, Colin. *Fairs Past and Present.* Hartford: The Travelers, 1939.

Sklar, Kathryn Kish. *Florence Kelley and the Nation's Work.* New Haven, Conn.: Yale Univ. Press, 1995.

Soldiers' Relief Association. *To The Friends of the Southern Cause at Home.* Columbia, 1864.

Stallybrass, Peter, and Allon White. *The Politics and Poetics of Transgression.* Ithaca: Cornell Univ. Press, 1986.

Stein, Roger B. "Artifact as Ideology: The Aesthetic Movement in its American Cultural Context." In *John Ruskin and Aesthetic Thought in America, 1840–1900.* Cambridge: Harvard Univ. Press, 1967.

Sterling, Dorothy, ed. *We Are Your Sisters: Black Women in the Nineteenth Century.* New York: W. W. Norton, 1984.

Stevenson, Robert Louis. "The Charity Bazaar: An Allegorical Dialogue." In *Letters and Miscellanies of Robert Louis Stevenson: Sketches, Criticisms, etc.* New York: Charles Scribners, 1898.

Stewart, Susan. *On Longing: Narratives of the Miniature, the Gigantic, the Souvenir, the Collection.* Durham, N.C.: Duke Univ. Press, 1993.

Stille, Charles J. *History of the United States Sanitary Commission.* Philadelphia: J. B. Lippincott, 1866. Reprint, New York: Hurd and Houghton, 1868.

Stubbs, Ansel Hartley, ed. *Financial and Social Success in Welfare Plans.* Kansas City: Inter-Collegiate Press, 1932.

Susman, Warren I. *Culture as History: The Transformation of American Society in the Twentieth Century.* New York: Pantheon, 1984.

Taylor, Clarence. "Black Churches of Brooklyn from the Early Nineteenth Century to the Civil Rights Movement." Ph.D. diss., City Univ. of New York, 1992.

Tuan, Yi-Fu. *Passing Strange and Wonderful: Aesthetics, Nature and Culture.* Washington, D.C.: Island Press, 1993.

Underwood, J. L. *The Women of the Confederacy.* New York: Neal Publishing, 1906.

Vermeer, Jackie, and Marian Lariviere Frew. *The Bazaar Handbook.* New York: Van Nostrand Reinhold, 1980.

A Visit to the Bazaar. London: J. Harris, 1818. Facsimile edition published as part of the Osborne Collection of Early Children's Books. Toronto, London, and Sydney: The Bodley Head, 1981.

Walters, Ronald G. *The Antislavery Appeal: American Abolitionism After 1830.* Baltimore: Johns Hopkins Univ. Press, 1976.

Weimann, Jeanne Madeline. *The Fair Women: The Story of the Woman's Building, World's Columbian Exposition, Chicago 1893.* Chicago: Chicago Academy, 1981.

Weiner, Lynn. *From Working Girl to Working Mother: The Female Labor Force in the United States 1820–1980.* Chapel Hill: Univ. of North Carolina Press, 1985.

Weisenburger, Francis Phelps. *Columbus During the Civil War* [Ohio Civil War Centennial Commission Series 12]. Columbus: State Univ. Press for Ohio Historical Society, 1963.

Wells, Emmeline. *Charities and Philanthropies: Woman's Work in Utah.* Salt Lake City: George Q. Cannon and Sons, 1893.

Whites, Lee Ann. "The Charitable and the Poor: The Emergence of Domestic Politics in Augusta, Georgia, 1860–1880." *Journal of Social History* 17 (Summer 1984): 601–16.

Williams, Susan Reynolds. "In the Garden of New England: Alice Morse Earle and the History of Domestic Life." Ph.D. diss., Univ. of Delaware, 1992.

Witherspoon, Edna J. *Fancy Drills for Evening and Other Entertainments.* London and New York: Butterick, 1894.

Woolson, Abba Gould. *Woman in American Society.* Boston: Roberts Brothers, 1873.

Yonge, Charlotte M. *The Long Vacation.* New York: Macmillan, 1895.

Newspapers

Anne Arbor News.

Atlanta Constitution.

Baltimore Morning Sun.

Boston Globe.

Boston Herald.

Boston Transcript.

Boston Traveller.

Brooklyn Chronicle.

Charleston Daily Courier.

Chicago Tribune.

Daily Worker.

Frank Leslie's Illustrated Newspaper.

Los Angeles Examiner.

Madison Capital Times.

Milwaukee Journal.

New York Herald.

New York Times.

North Shore Breeze.

Northampton Courier.

Northampton Democrat .

Northampton Free Press.

Northampton (Hampshire Co.) Gazette.

Philadelphia Enquirer.

Philadelphia Public Ledger.

Richmond Compiler.

Richmond Dispatcher.

Springfield (Mass.) Republican.

Warrenton (Va.) Sentinel.

Wisconsin State Journal.

Special Fair Newspapers

The Bazaar Gazette. Anti-Corn Law League [Free Trade] Bazaar. London, Dec. 1845.
The Weal-Reaf. The Essex Institute Fair. Salem, Mass., Sept. 1860.
The Canteen. The Albany Army Relief Bazaar. Albany, Mar. 1864.
The Spirit of the Fair. The Metropolitan [Sanitary] Fair. New York, Apr. 1864.
Our Daily Fare. Great Central [Sanitary] Fair. Philadelphia, June 1864.
The Drumbeat. The Brooklyn and Long Island [Sanitary] Fair. Brooklyn, Feb. 1864.
Voice of the Fair. Chicago Soldiers' Fair. Chicago, May 1865.
The Home Fair Journal. Milwaukee Soldiers' Home Fair. Milwaukee, June 1865.
The Balloon Post. Fair to End the Suffering in France. Boston, Apr. 1871.
Bazaar Gazette. Equal Woman Suffrage Fair. Boston, Dec. 1871.
The Mayflower. Congregational House Fair. Boston, Oct.–Nov. 1872.
The Knapsack. Seventh Regiment Armory Fair. New York, Nov.–Dec. 1879.
The Sword and the Pen. Soldiers' Home Bazaar. New York, Dec. 1881.

Popular Magazines

America.
American Home.
American Magazine.
American Mercury.
Arthur's Home Magazine.
Atlantic Monthly.
The Bellman.
Better Homes and Gardens.
Business Week.
Canadian Magazine.
Century Magazine.
Changing Times.
Chatauquan.
Christian Century.
Collier's Weekly.
Coronet.
The Craftsman.
The Delineator.
Dennison's Party Magazine (also called *Parties*).
The Farmer's Advocate.
The Forum.
Godey's Lady's Book.
Good Housekeeping.
Good Words.
Harper's.
Harper's Bazar.
Hobbies: The Magazine of Collectors.
Homiletic Review.
Horticulturist and Journal of Rural Art and Recreational Taste.
House and Garden.
Industrial-Arts Magazine.

The Ladies Floral Cabinet and Pictorial Home Companion.
Ladies' Home Journal.
Ladies Magazine.
The Ladies World.
The Liberator.
Look.
Modern Priscilla.
Murray's Magazine.
Needlecraft.
New England Galaxy.
New York.
New Yorker.
Opera News.
Outlook.
Parent's.
Peterson's.
Publisher's Weekly.
Recreation.
Recreational Digest.
Retirement Living.
Scribner's.
Seventeen.
Survey.
Teen.
Time.
Vogue.
Woman's Day.
Woman's Home Companion.
Woman's Journal.
Women's Cycle.

Index

Bazaars and Fair Ladies was designed and typeset on a Macintosh computer system using PageMaker software. The text and titles are set in Caslon. This book was designed and composed by Kay Jursik and was printed and bound by Thomson-Shore, Inc. The recycled paper used in this book is designed for an effective life of at least three hundred years.